FOUNDATIONS OF COMMERCIAL LAW

D0922456

FOUNDATIONS OF COMMERCIAL LAW

Robert E. Scott

George G. Triantis

LexisNexis™
Matthew Bender®

ISBN: 9781422498897

NOTE TO USERS

To ensure that you are using the latest materials available in this area, please be sure to periodically check the LexisNexis Law School web site for downloadable updates and supplements at www.lexisnexis.com/lawschool.

Editorial Offices
121 Chanlon Rd., New Providence, NJ 07974 (908) 464-6800
201 Mission St., San Francisco, CA 94105-1831 (415) 908-3200
www.lexisnexis.com

(Pub.3340)

PREFACE

When we were invited to prepare this reader on commercial law, we thought about its appropriate scope, and its place among other readers in this series. The most straightforward approach is to follow the definition of commercial law that is adopted in most law school curricula, which reflects the Articles of the Uniform Commercial Code. This scope, however, falls somewhat short of being coherent in functional terms. It is underinclusive because commercial enterprises enter into a much wider range of contracts. It also seems overly broad because parts of the UCC (particularly, secured transactions and guaranties) address core features of business finance and the capital structure of corporations.

We chose nevertheless to stick with the conventional understanding of commercial law and embraced the opportunity to present this field as an informative arena for applying and testing scholarly theories of contract and of contract law. We have used this approach on several occasions in the past, teaching upper-year, law school seminars in the theory and practice of commercial transactions. Our goal in these seminars, and now in this reader, is to examine a selection of foundational contributions to commercial law scholarship and invite readers to consider whether these articles offer insights into the contracting patterns and issues of the real world. We prepared this book as a text for an advanced contracts or commercial law seminar, or a companion to a course in commercial law. In light of the book's application of contract theory, it may also be assigned in an undergraduate or graduate law-and-economics course.

We examine four bodies of law in the UCC: sale of goods, payments, letters of credit and suretyship, and secured transactions. Sale of goods law is the most similar to mainstream contract law and should be familiar to students who are taking or have taken the basic contracts course. Indeed, a comparison of the legislative provisions governing sales and the common law governing service contracts can offer insights into institutional competence and biases in law making.

Transactions involving security interests and/or guaranties (or sureties) are more closely allied with finance. Although consumer finance is an important topic, we focus on the core question of how to employ these transactions to minimize the cost of financing a business enterprise. This has been a very active area for investigation by both financial economists and lawyers, and we have reproduced many of the important insights. Payments law, in contrast, attracts very little attention in law school curricula and scholarship. Yet, we are in a period of rapid technological change, toward paperless payment instruments such as debit and stored value cards, and forms of e-cash. This raises the question of whether the framework in Articles 3 and 4 continue to be useful in designing the regulation of the newer mechanisms.

Our perspective in this book might be characterized as predominantly economic, but we emphasize its applied approach. An important feature of this approach is to appreciate the interconnectedness of contracts and of contract law. Clients ask lawyers to draft their contracts at least partly because lawyers know the governing law: particularly, the terms that courts are not willing to enforce and the terms that the courts will add to an incomplete contract. Lawmakers, in turn, are guided by the needs of transacting parties and they should be informed as to contracting patterns. Although this reader focuses on commercial law, it repeatedly asks whether the law, and the scholarly commentary, fully appreciates the realities of commercial practice. In our seminars, we ask students to look at actual commercial contracts, now available in electronic databases such as *cori.missouri.edu* and *onecle.com*.

Throughout this reader, we urge the student also to consider the institutional structure of commercial law making, beginning with an introduction to these factors in Chapter 2.3. In our legal system, law is made by courts, legislatures and regulators. Given the significant differences in their information and biases, readers might speculate about the different rules that would emerge from each of these institutions to address any given legal issue. This analysis becomes even more interesting and complicated when one allows for a choice of processes within each institution: such as the legislative drafting process of the NCCUSL and the ALI.

We thank our series editor, Roberta Romano, for her helpful comments on an earlier draft. We also benefitted from the reactions and comments of students in a number of seminars in commercial transactions that we have taught at Columbia, Harvard, Miami and Virginia. We thank George Pence for his research assistance. We have made every effort to keep the excerpts from selected articles brief, while distilling in a comprehensible form the important insights from each. We indicate deletions from the original texts by ellipses, but have deleted footnotes and subheadings without indication.

Robert E. Scott

George G. Triantis

October 2009

FOUNDATIONS OF LAW SERIES

ROBERTA ROMANO, General Editor

Foundations of Administrative Law
Edited by Peter H. Schuck, Yale Law School

Foundations of Commercial Law
Edited by Robert E. Scott, Columbia Law School and George G. Triantis, Harvard Law School

Foundations of Contract Law
Edited by Richard Craswell, Stanford Law School and Alan Schwartz, Yale Law School

Foundation of Corporate Law
Edited by Roberta Romano, Yale Law School

Foundations of Criminal Law
Edited by Leo Katz, Michael S. Moore and Stephen J. Morse, all of the University of Pennsylvania Law School

Foundations of The Economic Approach to Law
Edited by Avery Wiener Katz, Columbia Law School

Foundations of Employment Discrimination Law
Edited by John Donohue III, Stanford Law School

Foundations of Environmental Law and Policy
Edited by Richard L. Revesz, New York University Law School

Foundations of Intellectual Property
Edited by Robert P. Merges, University of California Berkeley and Davis School of Law and Jane C. Ginsburg, Columbia University School of Law

Foundations of International Income Taxation
Edited by Michael J. Graetz, Yale Law School

Foundations of Labor and Employment Law
Edited by Samuel Estreicher, New York University Law School and Stewart J. Schwab, Cornell Law School

Foundations of The Law and Ethics of Lawyering
Edited by George M. Cohen, University of Virginia School of Law and Susan P. Koniak, Boston University School of Law

Foundations of Tort Law
Edited by Saul Levmore, University of Chicago Law School and Catherine M. Sharkey, New York University School of Law

CONTENTS

Chapter 1
The Normative Foundations of Commercial Law

1.1 What is Commercial Law?

Most commonly, the term "commercial law" is understood as a reference to the various statutory rules that are embodied in the Uniform Commercial Code (UCC). But this informal definition is seriously under and over inclusive. First, the "commercial" law of the UCC is under-inclusive. Major areas of business contracting, particularly commercial real estate, construction contracting, information transactions and contracts for professional services between firms are outside the scope of the UCC and thus are governed by the common law of contracts as well as other specific statutory rules. Article 2 (Sales) applies only to transactions in "goods" (§ 2–102) which is limited, by definition, to sales of tangible personal property (§ 2–105). And, under the new Amendments to Article 2, the term "goods" specifically excludes transactions in "information" (Amended § 2–105). Yet these activities clearly fall within the concept of commercial activities in ordinary understanding (and in the understanding of practicing lawyers). Second, the linkage between "commercial law" and the UCC is also over-inclusive: the UCC governs all transactions within its jurisdiction whether the parties are individual consumers or business firms. In other words, under the UCC the term "commercial" refers to the activity being regulated rather than the nature of the parties to that activity. Thus, Article 2 (Sales) governs contracts for the sale of goods between merchants, between merchants and their consumers, and between non-merchant individuals. Similarly,

1

Article 3 (Commercial Paper), Article 4 (Bank Collections), 4A (Electronic Transfers) and Article 5 (Letters of Credit) govern promissory notes, drafts and letters of credit when used as a means of payment and/or credit in transactions between commercial banks and their customers, between individuals, and in pure business to business transactions. Continuing the same theme, Article 9 (Secured Transactions) provides rules governing the creation and enforcement of all personal property security interests even where one (or both) parties are individuals seeking (or providing) financing for non business purposes.

One result of the heterogeneity of the UCC is that the normative foundations of the Code are complex and remain unclear. Because the Code regulates commercial activity between unsophisticated parties as well as between business firms, it is highly problematic to assume that the parties to any UCC transaction are rational, informed parties who understand how to make business contracts. Freedom of contract is thus a much more contestable norm in those contexts. Moreover, in addition to party sovereignty, plausible arguments can be made that the commercial law should respond to societal concerns such as distributional fairness or to the likelihood that the parties to the transaction are susceptible to cognitive error. These considerations argue for mandatory rules that constrain party choice in certain contexts. The questions then become which norm(s) should govern the choice of a legal rule and in what circumstances does any particular norm apply?

One way to begin to answer these questions is to initially define commercial law narrowly in terms of parties and broadly in terms of transactions. Thus, one can start by first examining the normative foundations of the law regulating commercial transactions between business firms. Here the primary focus is the commercial transaction (as just defined). Many times these transactions are governed by the rules embodied in the UCC, but equally often the relevant transactions will be subject to the rules of common law contract and/or other statutory provisions. By beginning with a more limited definition of "commercial law" one can more confidently rely on freedom of contract norms such as efficiency or joint welfare maximization to evaluate the legal rules.

But even this narrower perspective does not eliminate the problem of overlapping or incompatible norms. To do so, one needs to further partition commercial transactions between business firms into two subcategories. Some parties obviously are sophisticated economic actors (i.e., the General Electric Corporation). Other parties function in commercial contexts but have many of the characteristics of ordinary persons (i.e., a gift shop owned and run by a retired teacher). Any effort to analyze commercial transactions between "firms" thus confronts an initial boundary problem. How should one define a firm for purposes of the analysis? For example, some have suggested defining a commercial firm as (a) an entity that is organized in the corporate form and that has five or more employees; (b) a limited partnership; and (c) a professional partnership such as a law or accounting firm. The underlying principle is that these economic entities are typically peopled by sophisticated parties who apparently understand how to make business contracts. Even in these contexts, freedom of contract is constrained. Sophisticated parties might well be permitted great latitude in devising their own rules (i.e., contract terms) but only so long as their contract does not impose negative external consequences on third parties. Determining when such externalities exist, and when decision-makers are justified in promulgating mandatory rules regulating particular contracting practices, is thus a crucial part of any normative framework for evaluating commercial law.

Finally, modern commercial law has been significantly affected by new technology. In particular, a number of the major changes in the law of payment systems are a product of electronic data processing. We will study these developments specifically in Chapter 4 (Payment Systems) and there our focus will turn more broadly to consumer transactions. Consumer interests are relevant in other contexts as well—such as mass-market sales transactions, secured financing and bankruptcy. We will touch on these questions in Chapter 3 (Sales Law) and Chapter 6 (Secured Credit). In all of these contexts, there is more tension between the goals of efficiency and other societal values. Thus, in these contexts decision makers might plausibly choose to adopt a more pluralistic normative framework, one that would include other societal considerations such as distributional equity, fairness or the capacity of the relevant actors to make informed, rational market choices.

1.2   Why Do Commercial Parties Contract?

Both the efficiency norm as well as notions of autonomy imply that a principal role of the state in regulating commercial transactions is to develop legal rules that reduce commercial parties' costs of solving contracting problems (subject only to the constraint that their contracts do not impose external costs on third parties or otherwise undermine the public interest). A commitment to facilitating commercial parties efforts to maximize the value that results from their contractual relationship necessarily requires us to begin with the question: What motivates parties to contract in the first place; that is, what deleterious consequences, if any, would follow if the law *did not* enforce the promises exchanged between commercial parties?

1. *Self–Enforcing Agreements.* A contract has an intertemporal aspect: Parties agree today to do something tomorrow. It is a separate question whether (or when) the state should enforce the promises in these agreements. In the first place, state enforcement is unnecessary when contracts are self-enforcing. Agreements are self-enforcing whenever the parties contemplating noncompliance face effective sanctions that do not depend on the actions of third-party enforcers. The traditional analysis of self-enforcement points to two key factors—repeated interactions and reputation. Consider first a long-term relationship between a supplier and a producer in which both firms make investments in the contract and face significant costs in switching to different partners. Both parties appreciate their own and their counterparty's vulnerability to opportunism. As we discuss in more detail below, the risk of opportunism is a function of the extent to which either party (or both) have made investments that are specific to the relationship. Both parties have a credible capacity to retaliate against opportunism in any particular transaction. Such an agreement is self enforcing, therefore, when the threat by either party to no longer deal with the other is sufficient to induce performance. A significant constraint on the efficacy of such retaliatory threats, however, is the extent of the parties' expectation of future benefits. A party will act opportunistically when the returns from doing so outweigh the loss of future benefits from the relationship. As the term of an agreement draws to a close, the parties anticipate fewer future benefits and thus the threat of retaliation may lose its potency. This end-game problem plagues all relationships that have definite concluding points. End games aside, exogenous changes that lead one or more parties to devalue what it would gain from the agreement also diminish the effectiveness of retaliatory threats.

As an alternative to the discipline to repeated dealings, commercial agreements may invoke community-based sanctions based on reputational losses. Reputation deters breach when third parties can readily learn the reasons why a deal broke down. Thus, a number of scholars have shown that reputation works well in small trading communities, especially those with ethnically homogenous members, where everything that happens soon becomes common knowledge to all the members of the community. Reputation also can work in industries with trade associations; in that setting the associations become a form of collective memory regarding the contracting behavior of their members. But this review of the contexts in which mutual promise are credible despite the absence of legal enforcement mechanisms also underscores the limits of reputation as a self-enforcement mechanism. For example, reputation cannot operate very effectively if the parties are strangers to each other, or when one party intends to withdraw from the community (and thus is unconcerned about a loss of reputation within the community), or when the anticipated benefits from behaving opportunistically exceed any reputational costs. In short, the range of contexts in which reputation works as an effective means of self-enforcement is inherently limited.

Contract scholars have recently focused attention on an additional mechanism for self-enforcement by considering the tendency of people to value reciprocal fairness. Experimental evidence from a number of studies suggests that the instinct to reciprocate is a potent force that expands the contexts in which informal agreements may be self-enforcing. These studies have produced three key findings: (1) Many people deviate from purely self-interested behavior in a reciprocal manner. Reciprocity means that in response to friendly actions, many people are much more cooperative than predicted by the axioms of rational choice. Conversely, in response to hostile actions many people are also more nasty and vengeful; (2) People repay gifts and take revenge even in one shot interactions with complete strangers and even if such action is costly for them and yields neither present nor future material rewards; and (3) This is a heterogeneous world. Some people exhibit this quality of reciprocal fairness and others are appear selfish. Taking all the experiments together from countries as diverse as Austria, Indonesia, Russia and the U.S., the evidence supports the claim that the fraction of fair subjects ranges from 40 to 60% as does the fraction of subjects who are selfish.

The experimental evidence thus suggests that coercive legal enforcement may be unnecessary to enforce promises even in circumstances where retaliatory threats and reputational sanctions might not work. As long as the fraction of reciprocally fair individuals in the relevant population is consistent with the experimental evidence, even strangers and one-time transactors predictably will rely on the promise of the other party. Note, however, that these experiments have yet to be rigorously tested in real-world contexts. After all, individuals in laboratory experiments may respond differently than commercial parties, perhaps because experimental subjects do not face the same pressures to make maximizing decisions as do commercial actors.

Notwithstanding the fact that some (or even many) agreements may be self-enforcing, no one claims that *all* agreements are self-enforcing. Thus, it is important to understand just what benefits flow from the *legal enforcement* of promises. To begin, note that commercial transactions are often conducted without promises. Commercial parties often choose to make simultaneous exchanges of cash for goods or services. A law of contracts is unnecessary to protect these transactions. Instead, the state need only protect each party's property rights, since, in such a world, a party will only part with property or money if she values more highly what is offered in exchange. In contrast to simultaneous exchanges, a contract is a set of promises regarding future behavior. Such promises are costly to make and to memorialize. To understand how the state can best facilitate commercial contracting, we must first establish why parties would incur the costs of making contracts in the first place.

There are two paradigmatic cases where parties rely on legal enforcement to accomplish their contracting purposes: (1) When parties want to make an investment whose value to one of them is greater than its value to any other prospective contracting partner; and (2) When the parties seek to lock in particular prices, quantities or other terms in order to avoid the disruptive effects of future market movements. To the extent that these cases occupy most of the universe of cases where commercial parties choose to write contracts, they justify a general presumption favoring state enforcement of private agreements against reluctant promisors.

2.   Protecting   Relation–Specific   Investment.[1] Legal enforcement increases social welfare whenever a commercial contract requires
an investment (by one or both parties) that is specialized to the particular transaction. Specialized investments can be of any sort. They might
require the production of customized goods, or perhaps an investment in
human capital to perform a particular service, or even investments by
the parties in information, say about future price fluctuations. As an
example, suppose you represent a seller of software systems who operates in two different markets. The seller produces off-the-shelf software
that is suitable for many business needs. This business is highly competitive. The seller also accepts special orders for individual customers,
creating specialized software systems that are designed for a single
buyer's needs. Buyer is interested in purchasing one of these systems.
The specialized software system configured to fit Buyer's particular
business needs would cost $70,000 to produce and would be worth
$100,000 to Buyer. Assume the parties agree on a price of $85,000 for
the specialized system. Seller could also provide Buyer its off-the-shelf
system at a cost of $40,000. Since the market for off-the-shelf business
software is competitive, Seller sells that system for $40,000 (recall that
price equals cost in a competitive market). The off-the-shelf system is
worth $50,000 to Buyer. If the parties did contract for the specialized
system and Buyer subsequently breached, Seller could only resell the
system on the market for $20,000 (the specialized system is tailored to
the needs of Buyer and, thus, is not as valuable to another buyer). There
are two key questions: Which kind of contract would it be socially
desirable for these parties to make? Second, which kind of contract
would they make were contracts not legally enforceable?

The answer to the first question is easy. Recall that social welfare is
the sum of the parties' gains from contracting. Thus, the total surplus is
the difference between buyer's valuation and seller's cost. The off-the-
shelf contract would produce a surplus of $10,000 ($50,000 buyer's
valuation less $40,000 seller's cost). On the other hand, a contract for
the specialized machine would create a surplus of $30,000 ($100,000
buyer's valuation less $70,000 seller's cost). Therefore, joint welfare
would be maximized if the parties contract to produce the specialized
system.

But in the absence of legal enforcement, the seller would never
agree to produce the specialized system. To see why, suppose that the
parties did contract for the specialized system. Now consider the parties'
positions *after* Seller has already incurred the $70,000 production cost.
Buyer now knows that if he refuses to pay the contract price, he can still
purchase an off-the-shelf system on the market for $40,000 and earn a
profit of $10,000. Seller knows that if Buyer breaches her only recourse
is to sell the specialized machine on the market for $20,000 and incur a

---

1. The following discussion is drawn from Alan Schwartz & Robert E. Scott, *Contract
Theory and The Limits of Contract Law*, 113 Yale L. J. 541, 559–65 (2003).

$50,000 loss. On these facts, unless Buyer is concerned about his reputation or the loss of future dealings with Seller (such as post-sale service support) he will propose to renegotiate the price (perhaps offering some pretext such as unanticipated hardship).

To understand what will occur in this renegotiation, we need to be precise about the concept of bargaining power. The outside options that either party has if they fail to reach agreement are an important determinant of power in their bargaining relationship. A deal between the parties thus is impossible unless the deal would create enough surplus so that each party will receive at least the payoff it would receive under its next best alternative. These minimum payoffs are called the parties' "disagreement points" or "threat points." Parties therefore bargain only over the portion of the expected surplus that remains after each of them is assured its disagreement point unless the surplus is sufficiently large that an equal division would be larger than *both* of the parties' disagreement points. Under these latter conditions, a common solution to this bargaining problem predicts that the parties will simply split the difference since neither party's threat to take the next best option is credible. This solution is known as "deal me out" bargaining. The intuition is that so long as each party's disagreement point is less than one half of the surplus, either party's threat to exit unless they receive more than one-half of the surplus is simply not credible since they would do better by splitting the difference.

We now can be precise about the renegotiation bargain that the parties in our example will reach (again using the same bargaining solution). Buyer's disagreement point is $10,000 which is the value he would receive if he purchased the off-the-shelf system from another seller. Seller's disagreement point is $-50,000$ which is the net amount she would lose if she had to resell the specialized system to another buyer ($70,000 production cost − $20,000 resale price = − $50,000). The potential surplus from a renegotiation is $80,000 (the difference between the value of the system to Buyer ($100,000) and its value to Seller ($20,000)). Since one-half of this surplus ($40,000) is greater than both the buyer and the seller's next best alternative, the parties will agree to split the surplus equally. A renegotiation price of $60,000 achieves this division.

This bargaining outcome illustrates why, absent legal enforcement, the parties would not contract for the specialized system in the first place. A seller who is not myopic would realize that the buyer will renegotiate the price after the seller invests. Thus, her ultimate payoff under the specialized contract will be a loss of $10,000 rather than the anticipated gain of $15,000 the contract promises initially. Seller knows that she is assured of at least breaking even if instead she produces and sells the off-the-shelf system. Therefore, the "equilibrium contract" will have the seller produce and sell the off-the-shelf system for a price of $40,000. However, this contract is inefficient because it generates a social surplus of only $10,000 rather than the $30,000 that could be realized under the contract for a specialized system. The difficulty here is that Buyer's initial promise to pay $85,000 for the specialized system is not credible: Both parties realize at the time of contracting that Buyer will later have an incentive to renege. Since Seller cannot resell the specialized software system for a price above cost—this is the definition of a relation specific investment—the specialized contract would yield an expected negative payoff for Seller. This unhappy result illustrates the need for the state to enforce Buyer's initial promise to pay $85,000 for the specialized system. Legal enforcement of the resulting "contract" entirely forecloses Buyer's temptation to renegotiate. Now Seller can face Buyer with a credible threat to sue for breach of contract if the buyer repudiates the agreement, thus eliminating any incentive for Buyer to act strategically.

    3. *Allocating Risks In Volatile Markets.* Assume now that the seller and buyer both operate their business in a thick market. A market is thick when a seller can sell her output to many buyers and a buyer can purchase from many sellers. It is difficult to explain why parties in these markets would make enforceable contracts: A seller could sell goods as she produces them and a buyer could purchase goods when he needs them.

    One explanation is that one or both of the contracting parties may wish to reduce the risk of potentially disastrous outcomes. For example, assume that a seller has incurred significant debt. If a subsequent market fluctuation led to prices falling below costs and to substantial losses, the seller might be unable to repay her debt obligations and thus could be forced into bankruptcy. In other words, a market price below seller's costs could actually impose collateral losses on the seller over and above the losses from fluctuating prices. To be sure, the seller has numerous alternative means for addressing this risk. It could, for example, reduce its leverage by trading equity interests for outstanding debt claims. Alternatively, it could purchase third-party insurance or hedge at least some of the risk by trading in options or futures markets. In many cases, however, an executory commercial contract is the most cost-effective means of insuring against the risk of business disruption.

    This objective of "smoothing the bumps" in volatile markets is essentially a question of how best to minimize the transactions costs of reducing uncertain future risks. There are other transaction cost justifications for legal enforcement of commercial contracts even in thick markets. Thus, for example, a buyer may need frequent deliveries of particular goods over a period of months or years. In this event, it can be efficient to have one reliable supplier rather than have to make a series of purchases, some from unfamiliar sellers. To be sure, parties could always make sequential contracts with a single supplier. But that solution also has difficulties, including the problem of opportunism by the supplier and the drafting cost of multiple contracts with essentially the same terms. In any event, when the gain to contracting parties from reducing the risk of high variance outcomes (such as avoiding business disasters) or from reducing the transaction costs of multiple market sales exceed the costs of contracting, even parties in thick markets will contract to freeze prices if the law permits them to do so. Thus, it is efficient for the state to enforce sales contracts for future delivery of market goods.

1.3 Why Do Commercial Parties Write Incomplete Contracts?

Most commercial contracts negotiated between sophisticated parties are drafted with the assistance of legal counsel. Unsurprisingly, therefore, most of these contracts are in writing with detailed terms and specifications, addressing many elements of uncertainty that might affect performance. Yet, whenever a dispute subsequently arises, it turns out that the contract was seriously incomplete, in the sense that the rights and obligations of each party are not specified for each possible future contingency. The parties will have failed to reach an express understanding about who should bear a particular risk that has materialized in the interim, or the contract term that purports to allocate the risk in question will be framed in terms of a broad standard that requires subsequent interpretation by a court. Why would parties in such a position ever leave such important questions unresolved in their contract? And, how should the law react in cases where these unresolved questions become relevant?

One possible answer is that contracting parties systematically will fail to write complete contracts (that is to specify the consequences of all possible contingencies that may affect their performance) because the *transactions costs* of writing complete contracts are simply too onerous. Let's think about those costs. One cost of writing complete contracts is the resource costs of negotiating and reducing to a written form the agreed upon allocations of risk. Those resource costs, in turn, include not only the time and effort to negotiate and draft the clauses in question, but also include the possibility that in doing so the parties might make a mistake in their written contract. A clause that they regard as perfectly clear may, upon subsequent examination, appear ambiguous or vague. This "formulation error" may then lead to costly litigation over the appropriate meaning that should be given to the clause in question.

Another significant transaction cost is the burden of adequately identifying in advance all the possible contingencies that might occur and then specifying the appropriate outcome for each one. Given the limits of human cognition, some (or all) parties may simply be unable to identify and foresee all of the uncertain future conditions or may be incapable of characterizing adequately the complex adaptations required to accommodate all the possibilities that *might* materialize. One way to visualize these two problems of *uncertainty* and *complexity* is to imagine that a homeowner asks his attorney to write a contract providing for the care of his fine home garden during a summer when he is out of town. The drafting lawyer's first task is to deal with an uncertain future; that is, to specify in advance all the relevant risks that the gardener must account for: climatic conditions, possible incursions of the gypsy moth, wind-borne powdery mildew, etc. Assuming the drafting lawyer can overcome the uncertainty problem, she must then resolve the complexity problem; that is, she must specify to the gardener exactly what responses should be made in each case: how much to spend on sprays, whether and when to water, when a diseased plant should be cut down to prevent infection of adjacent ones, and so on.

There is a second reason why commercial parties may choose to write incomplete contracts. Assume, for example, that the homeowner in our hypothetical is unable to monitor and observe the amount of care the gardener provides in nurturing young plants in the garden. Under those conditions, it would be foolish for the drafting attorney to specify a compensation scheme that provided a bonus of $5,000 for extra care and attention to the plants over the summer. Rather, she might voluntarily choose to leave the question of a bonus unresolved; that is, the lawyer might choose to write an incomplete contract even where the transactions costs were quite low. This is an example of the effects of *asymmetric information* on the contracting process. When conditions of private or hidden information exist—one party cannot observe or readily prove to a court the actions of the other party or the conditions necessary to trigger a contractual contingency—commercial parties will voluntarily choose to leave their contracts incomplete even when transactions costs are very low. To do otherwise would require that the parties either disclose information that they wish to keep private or have enforcement turn on facts that one or both could not observe or establish in court. Writing an incomplete contract may be preferable to these unpalatable alternatives.

The realization that parties may have good reasons to leave contracts incomplete leads to the next logical question: How can or should the state assist the parties to incomplete contracts when they subsequently dispute the nature of their respective obligations? Should the law leave the parties as they find them or should the state seek to complete the contract for the parties? And, if it is appropriate to choose this second option, should the missing contract terms be supplied from an ex ante perspective (as of the time of contracting) or from an ex post perspective (as of the time of the dispute)? These important questions are the subject of our inquiry in Chapter 2, Section 2.1 infra.

1.4 The Nature of Commercial Law Rules

Fortunately, commercial parties do not have to write their contracts on a blank slate. Rather, in many situations the law will provide the parties with a set of implied terms or *default rules*. Putting aside for the moment the separate question of how the law chooses the right default terms, when should the drafting attorney elect to "opt out" of the state-provided defaults and write an explicitly more complete contract for her client? A plausible answer is that a good attorney would compare the resource costs of negotiating, drafting (and perhaps subsequently enforcing) an expressly dickered clause against the possible benefits of a tailor-made contract term that was a better fit for the client's particular situation. The benefits of a designer term derive from the capacity of particular parties to define their respective obligations more precisely than would any state-supplied default. The costs of a customized arrangement (in addition to the up front transactions costs) are a function of the risk that courts, being unfamiliar with the new term, may misinterpret its meaning.

If high transactions costs are the primary reasons why commercial parties write incomplete contracts, then the law properly should fill the gaps with default terms that solve those problems, assuming that the state's contracting costs are lower than the sum of the costs to contracting parties. But this argument rests on the crucial assumption that courts (and/or legislatures) are capable of devising useful default rules that would be suitable for many parties. Any rule maker, whether a statutory drafter or court adjudicating a disputed contract, lacks an infinite set of resources, and so faces many of the constraints that private parties face. This fact makes relevant a distinction between the (relatively small) set of default rules that have evolved at common law and the many more default standards that have been proposed in Article 2 of the Uniform Commercial Code and the Restatement (Second) of Contracts.

Consider the difference between two possible contractual gaps. In the first, a fire destroys the seller's plant prior to the manufacture of custom-made contract goods required by a contract with the buyer. In the second example, the parties agree to agree subsequently upon a price in a volatile market, but fail to do so. In the fire example, there are two relevant future states: A fire could occur or not. In the price uncertainty example, there are a very large number of relevant future states, many of which are likely. A legal rule-maker with limited resources can attack problems such as the risk of a fire because they often can be solved with a simple rule: The seller is (or is not) excused when the goods are destroyed without fault while in her possession. The rule maker, however, could not easily create an optimal contract term to solve price volatility problems because it would be too costly to regulate all of the states that could arise in all of the existing markets. Instead of creating a rule, therefore, law makers faced with such a challenge typically create a standard: "The price is a reasonable price at the time of delivery."

Thus, commercial law generally provides broad standards when the conditions for specifying more precise rules are not met. There are many examples of such standards. For instance, when the question is whether the seller has properly complied with its default obligation to supply goods of a certain quality, the UCC provides that the product must be "fit for the ordinary purposes for which it is to be used" or "fit for the buyer's particular purpose" *if* the seller has "reason to know" that purpose. UCC §§ 2–314 & 2–315. To be sure, as the tax laws illustrate, state-created rules can be precise and complex. But contract law rules often are created by courts who lack expertise and staffs or by private law reform groups (for recommendation to courts or legislatures), who suffer from similar deficiencies. Contract law drafters thus are different from administrative agencies that commonly write complex rules.

The possibility that contracts are incomplete because of hidden information or other related factors further complicates the task for courts seeking to create useful default rules for contracting parties. If the parties themselves will decline to base key contractual contingencies on information that they cannot observe or easily verify, they would elect to opt out of a legally-supplied default rule that is similarly conditioned on that information. But even if the state's task of supplying useful default rules is daunting, there remains the question of what better alternative is open to a court that is asked to resolve a dispute over the terms of an incomplete contract. One alternative is to do nothing, declare the contract unenforceable because of indefiniteness, and leave the parties where they are. Courts following this approach will decline to fill gaps except in clear cases of linguistic ambiguity or where the law has already provided relatively clear, simple default rules.

1.5   The Normative Principles of Commercial Law

What normative principles are embodied in our commercial law, and particularly in the Uniform Commercial Code? As we will see in the materials that follow, this is not an easy question to answer. When a court confronts a gap in an incomplete contract, its duty in interpreting the Uniform Commercial Code is to use the processes of analogy and extrapolation to find a solution consistent with the purposes and policy of the codifying law. In the UCC, this methodology is specified in § 1–103 (2001 revision) which directs courts to liberally construe and apply the specific provisions of the act "to promote its underlying purposes and policies." One effect of this language is that the Code not only has the force of law, but is itself a source of law. For example, Comment 1 to § 1–103 states:

> The Uniform Commercial Code is drawn to provide flexibility so that . . .
> *it will provide its own machinery* for expansion of commercial prac-
> tices. . . . to make it possible for the law embodied in the Code to be
> developed by the courts in the light of unforseen and new circumstances
> and practices.

Section 1–103 contains three fundamental statements of purpose: a) to simplify, clarify and modernize the law governing commercial transactions; b) to permit the continued expansion of commercial practices through custom, usage and agreement of the parties; and c) to make uniform the law among the various jurisdictions. Executing these purposes consistently is a difficult task. For one thing, the principle of uniformity (expressed in § 1–103(3)) has not been clearly understood. Since most commercial law rules are default rules, they function as implied contract terms in commercial contracts that are otherwise incomplete. A uniform commercial law rule thus must be one that is interpreted uniformly by courts resolving contractual disputes; such a rule is "uniform" when it is transparent to the litigating parties and predictable to other parties. Uniform interpretation, therefore, has both a jurisdictional and a temporal dimension. One uniformity value is for parties to know at the time they write contracts that their obligations will be interpreted in the same manner by courts in different jurisdictions. In addition, uniformity values are enhanced if parties are certain that courts in any given jurisdiction will interpret the same obligations uniformly over time. If the courts perform this function inconsistently, the costs of contracting will rise.

Moreover, a second objective of § 1–103—to expand the law by incorporating custom and usage—may itself be in conflict with the goal of making the law truly uniform. For example, an impediment to uniformity is the contextualist interpretive methodology adopted by the Code to implement this incorporation principle. Sometimes, parties may wish to have their contracts interpreted according to the plain meaning of the written terms of the agreement. These parties will frequently include merger clauses in their contract and wish to have the courts adhere to a "textualist" interpretive approach rather than the contextualist approach that the Code seems to endorse. Courts that seek to obey the injunction of § 1–103(2) and admit evidence of a custom or usage, even though the usage appears to conflict with the written terms of the contract, may thus be undermining the efforts of parties to have their contractual language interpreted "uniformly" over time.

To be sure, sometimes there are significant benefits from permitting parties to rely on contextual understandings rather than requiring them to specify all of these background conditions in the written contract itself. The resolution that best serves the goals of the Code, therefore, might be to permit parties to choose whether to have their contracts interpreted according to the Code's contextualist approach or according to a textualist "plain meaning" approach (similar to that of the common law of contracts). It is an open question, however, whether the interpretive rules of a particular common law court or the Code are mandatory rules or default rules. In form, the parol evidence and the plain meaning rules are background norms that apply to all contract disputes, and, in that sense, are mandatory. Functionally, however, parties can, by appropriate specification, signal how they wish their agreement to be interpreted. Thus, the question reduces to the ease with which individual parties can opt out of the prevailing interpretation norm. In any case, the question of whether the Code rules on interpretation are mandatory or whether parties can choose the interpretive approach that best suits their needs looms large in Code methodology.

One unambiguous norm that undergirds the UCC is its general commitment to freedom of contract. Section 1–302(a) states that the "effect" of specific provisions of the Code may be varied by agreement, except in limited and prescribed circumstances. The obligations of good faith, diligence, and reasonableness may not be disclaimed by agreement, but the parties may by agreement determine the "standards" by which performance of those obligations is to be measured unless those standards are "manifestly unreasonable" (§ 1–302(b)). In one respect, this broad commitment to freedom of contract has been well understood by courts interpreting contracts under the Code. Thus, courts have endorsed explicit contractual provisions that purport to opt out of the Code's default rules governing remedies, warranties, rejection and cure, commercial impracticability and many others. As a common example, in the place of Code warranties and the rules for rejection, revocation and cure, parties who trade in hard goods, most especially in sales of equipment, frequently substitute standardized "repair and replacement" clauses. Such clauses purport to divide quality risks between buyer and seller and to displace the binary default rules governing rejection, revocation of acceptance and cure.

What has not been as well recognized, however, is that this commitment to freedom of contract has broader normative implications than simply a willingness to protect the right of individual parties to opt out of the Code's defaults. Not only does an expansive domain of free contract have implications for the kind of default rules that courts might add to the Code's existing menu (in the sense that the freedom to opt out of most Code rules raises the question of what value the rules themselves provide), but as we will see in the succeeding Chapters of this book, it also implicates the way in which commercial contracts are (or ought to be) enforced and interpreted.

1.6 The Political Economy of the Uniform Commercial Code (in a nutshell)[2]

1. Karl Llewellyn and Article 2. The story of the Uniform Commercial Code project and Karl Llewellyn's unique role in the drafting and process of initial enactment has been told many times. The rise of the modern industrial state in the late nineteenth century exposed the significant diversity that existed in the commercial law of various states. The resulting uncertainty led to proposals for the enactment of a federal commercial code to govern interstate commercial transactions. These

---

2. The following discussion draws on Robert E. Scott, *The Rise and Fall of Article 2*, 62 La. L. Rev. 1009, 1029–32 (2002).

proposals, in turn, stimulated the formation of the National Conference of Commissioners on Uniform State Laws (NCCUSL) in 1892. Rather than accept federal intrusions on traditional state authority, the National Commissioners proposed to formulate and seek adoption of various uniform laws governing different aspects of commercial law. One of those uniform statutes was the Uniform Sales Act, drafted by Samuel Williston and adopted by NCCUSL in 1906. The Sales Act, in turn, was modeled on the English Sale of Goods Act of 1893.

As the years went by, many scholars noted problems with the Sales Act and, in fact, a number of states declined to enact the statute. One of those critics was Karl Llewellyn, then teaching at the Columbia Law School. Llewellyn had two principal objections to the Sales Act. First, he objected to those default rules that were based on artificial doctrinal conceptions, such as the location of "title" in the goods. These defaults were "inefficient" in the sense that they did not reflect the terms of agreement that most parties in the relevant trade would have made for themselves. Second, the Sales Act default rules applied in the main to all transactions equally and thus were insufficiently tailored to the circumstances of particular trades and industries. The deficiencies of the Sales Act led to reform initiatives. In 1940, the Federal Sales Act was introduced in Congress. The National Commissioners reacted to the threat of federalization by lobbying against federal enactment and beginning to draft a revised Uniform Sales Act. Perhaps most significantly, they recruited Karl Llewellyn, one of the strongest advocates for the federalization of sales law, to their project.

Llewellyn was committed to the idea of filling contractual gaps with default terms that reduced expected contracting costs by mimicking the arrangement most (or at least many) commercial parties would have made for themselves. The solution to the dilemma of the poor fit between broad standards and complex relationships seemed straightforward. Rather than impose abstract and general standards to regulate ongoing relationships, the law should simply identify and incorporate the "working rules" already being used successfully by the parties themselves. These working rules needed the imprimatur of the state because their "jurisdiction" was uncertain since they arose from custom and practice. Legal incorporation was necessary, therefore, in order to tailor the general default rules to particular practices and trade usages. This notion of incorporation of custom and practice was deeply imbedded in the Code. For example, UCC § 1–303, Comment 3 provides that "[Usages and customs] furnish the background and give particular meaning to the language used [in the contract] and are the framework of common understanding controlling any general rules of law which hold only when there is no such understanding." In this way, Llewellyn's draft of Article 2 explicitly invited incorporation. In addition, the new parol evidence rule under the Code admitted inferences from trade usage even where the express terms of the contract seemed perfectly clear and were apparently "integrated." The invitation to contextualize the contract in this manner was explicitly embodied in the Code's definition of agreement, which is defined as "the bargain of the parties in fact as found in their language or by implication from other circumstances including course of dealing or usage of trade or course of performance ..." (§ 1–201(3)).

Since Llewellyn's purpose was to incorporate flexible and tailored defaults, he needed a mechanism by which these local norms could be identified by courts. In his mind, that mechanism was the merchant tribunal. The merchant jury was to be a panel of experts that would find specific facts—such as whether the behavior of a contracting party was "commercially reasonable." Unfortunately, the idea of the merchant tribunal was too radical for the commercial lawyers who dominated the drafting process. By 1944, Llewellyn had abandoned this key device for discovering the relevant social norms, while still retaining the architecture of incorporation. As we suggest below, eliminating the merchant jury while retaining the pervasive notion of incorporation of commercial norms was a serious drafting mistake.

By 1945, the NCCUSL had formed a collaboration with the American Law Institute (ALI) and, working in tandem, they expanded the revised sales act project to include the drafting of a comprehensive Uniform Commercial Code. Llewellyn and the other proponents of the project sought to avoid previous difficulties in achieving uniformity by creating a "code" in the true sense—a systematic, preemptive and comprehensive enactment of a whole field of law. Many observers have noted, however, the striking differences in the rule form between Article 2 and the other substantive articles of the Code. Article 2 contains a large number of broad standards, vague admonitions and "muddy" rules. Many sections are little more than statements of principle that delegate broad discretion to courts to apply them to specific circumstances.

There are several explanations for the many vague standards of Article 2. First, Llewellyn believed that codes differed from ordinary statutes in their resistance to amendment. Second, the rule form of Article 2 is a product of the political economy of its enactment. Several scholars have predicted that, in the absence of influence from outside interest groups, private legislative bodies such as the ALI and NCCUSL will tend to promulgate many vague rules that delegate substantial discretion to courts (See e.g., Alan Schwartz & Robert E. Scott, *The Political Economy of Private Legislatures,* 143 U. Pa. L. Rev. 595 (1995)). The argument is that these rules result not solely because of their intrinsic merits but because law reform projects of this sort are dominated by academic reformers with preferences that are typically far different from those of the median member of the legislative body. The reformers propose vague rules (so the argument goes) when they are unable to get clear, bright-line rules adopted. And, in fact, the original Article 2 project was dominated by Llewellyn and his cohort of fellow reformers, and their political preferences were far from those of the ALI and NCCUSL members who were considering the UCC during the 1940's and '50's. We will evaluate more critically the various theories that seek to explain the uniform law making process and to contrast it with the products of private legislatures in Chapter 2, section 2.3, infra.

But beyond this, there are vague standards in Article 2 because sales law applies to a wide range of contexts and parties. As we suggested above, standards are common because the conditions for creating good default rules are difficult to meet. Parties are heterogenous in modern economies; good rules sometimes have to be complex; and parties often must take into account many relevant future states of the world. The greater the heterogeneity of the parties and the greater the variety of contexts to which a particular rule applies, the more convenient (and less costly) it is for a lawmaker to draft rules that are more open-ended and abstract. In short, it is less costly for the drafter of a broadly applicable statute to instruct parties to behave "reasonably" than to draft clear, sensible rules for a large number of contexts.

Perhaps because of the open-ended standards of Article 2, the "incorporation mechanism" introduced by Llewellyn has not functioned as he intended. Llewellyn intended the key instruction to courts—focus on commercially reasonable merchant practices—as a direction for courts to admit expert evidence of the contracting customs of particular trades and then announce default rules that would apply to those particular populations of commercial parties. But the abandonment of the merchant tribunal doomed this effort from the start. Courts have subsequently interpreted these statutory instructions not as directions to incorporate specific commercial norms and customs but rather as invitations to use context as a source of subjective meaning—a determination of what the parties to the particular dispute "must have meant" by their agreement. This exercise sometimes results in reformation of the apparently clear express terms of the contract; other times it leads courts to decline to enforce commercial contracts in the face of apparently clear contractual language to the contrary.

2. *Karl Llewellyn and the Drafting of Articles 3, 4, and 9.*
While Llewellyn worked on the Code project for more than ten years, responsibility for drafting key provisions dealing with credit instruments, bank collections and secured transactions—Articles 3, 4, and 9— was assigned to others. William Prosser was the principal reporter for Article 3, Fairfax Leary followed by Walter Malcolm were the reporters for Article 4, and Allison Dunham and Grant Gilmore were the reporters for Article 9. In short order, the drafting process of these articles came to be dominated by representatives of banking and commercial financing interests. Articles 3, 4, and 9 were, in the main, characterized by detailed, precise rules that allocated commercial risks in ways favorable to the commercial interests that participated so actively in the drafting

process. No doubt the clarity of the new rules governing secured financing, credit instruments and payment systems reduced transactions costs in the relevant credit markets. But, equally clearly, the rules favored the interests of sophisticated repeat players in those markets over those of occasional participants in financing transactions.

The promulgation of Article 9 illustrates these two themes most vividly. Secured financing has undergone an enormous transformation since the enactment of Article 9. Perhaps the most vivid illustration of this is the dramatic increase in the number and size of firms that rely on secured credit as their principal means of financing both ongoing operations and growth opportunities. Previously, with a few exceptions (such as factoring and trust receipts), secured financing principally had served second-class markets as the "poor man's" means of obtaining credit. Small businesses show a particularly keen preference for secured credit. One survey of about 500,000 small firms showed that 62% of the respondents' debt was secured for the years in question. With the rise of securitization, secured credit has become the linchpin of private financing, prompting even large firms to employ leveraged buyouts as a means of fleeing public equity markets for the safe harbors of Article 9. When viewed in these terms, most practitioners and commentators regard Article 9 as a blazing success. The question, however, which we consider in detail in Chapter 6, section 6.6, infra, is whether the precise rules that make it easier for creditors to secure their debts are bad for debtors. For the moment, you might begin by asking what evidence might be brought to bear on evaluating the impact of Article 9 besides the evidence of the increased usage of secured debt?

In any case, financial institutions, and those sympathetic to their needs, played a significant role in the drafting and ratification of Article 9. For example, when the UCC project had just gotten underway after World War II, Homer Kripke, then associated with C.I.T. Financial Corp., served as a key advisor to the reporter, Grant Gilmore, and to the other drafters of what eventually became Article 9. In addition, Kripke served as one of the two principal drafters for what became the 1972 revision of Article 9. All this is not to impugn the motives of the managers of these financial institutions, nor the business lawyers who represented their interests. It is quite clear that Homer Kripke sincerely believed that "the legal structure of secured credit developed to make possible mass production and the distribution of goods" and "that these developments have increased human welfare" (Homer Kripke, *Law and Economics: Measuring the Economic Efficiency of Commercial Law in a Vacuum of Fact*, 133 U. Pa. L. Rev. 929, 931 n.14 (1985)). Nonetheless, the enthusiasm that secured lenders showed for Article 9 begs the question of why they found it so attractive.

Two partial explanations emerge. First, Article 9 imposed certainty and uniformity onto a field previously characterized by quirky, indeterminate, and widely varying rules. As Grant Gilmore wrote, "[p]re-Code personal property security law may be described as closely resembling that obscure wood in which Dante discovered the gates of hell" (Grant Gilmore, *The Good Faith Purchase Idea and The Uniform Commercial Code: Confessions of a Draftsman*, 15 Ga. L. Rev. 605, 606 (1981)). The emergence of Article 9's scheme of bright-line rules to regulate asset-based financing permitted both prospective creditors and debtors to feel secure that the new system provided laws superior not only to the quagmire of regulations that previously governed the field, but to other entirely different methods of financing as well. The second explanation, also undoubtedly true in part, is that Article 9 unabashedly promotes the institutionalization of secured credit; it not only regularized what was there but vastly expanded it, both in explicit coverage and in a dramatic lowering of costs. The "floating lien," and, to a lesser extent, the purchase money security interest (PMSI) serve as key evidence for this point. Both essentially exempt certain secured creditors from important features of Article 9's general "first-in-time" priority rule, thus giving such creditors a favored status compared to other secured and unsecured creditors. Moreover, both classes of creditors are afforded relatively lenient filing requirements for preserving their priority claims to the debtor's assets.

When one views Article 9's dual characteristics of certainty and partiality towards certain classes of secured creditors in tandem, the reason for the enthusiasm of financial institutions becomes clear. The new scheme provided secured lenders a regulatory system that not only reduced uncertainty in general, but settled many of the longstanding doubts in their favor.

3.   *The Contemporary Revisions to the Code.* In recent years, there have been efforts to substantially revise all the Articles in the Code. The principal impetus for the reform project has been the need to adapt the statute to technological change. This process resulted initially in the revisions of Articles 3 (Commercial Paper) and 4 (Bank Collections) (as well as the promulgation of Article 4A on Electronic Transfers), the recommended repeal of Article 6 (Bulk Sales), and the addition of Article 2A (Leases). Subsequently, revisions to Articles 5 (Letters of Credit) and 8 (Investment Securities) were completed. The two substantive revisions that then remained were especially important events in commercial law: Article 9, regulating secured lending, was last rethought in 1972 and Article 2, regulating sales, had never been revised. Both revisions have generated substantial controversy and much of the scholarly literature of the past decade concerns the question whether the revisions promote the normative purposes of the Code or whether they reflect the political economy of the revision process itself.

The outcome in each instance was quite different, however. Some scholars have argued that these different outcomes were predictable. Where the legal regime regulates the interests of relatively cohesive industries, the UCC law-making process is likely to function much differently than where the regulatory effects are diffused. Thus, the normative implications of a revision of Article 9 are likely to differ substantially from the implications of a revision to Article 2. Since Article 9 regulates asset-based financers, a paradigmatic example of well-organized and cohesive interests, the process is susceptible to dispropor-tionate influence by a single, active interest group representing particu-lar financing interests. In such a case, the argument is that the law revision process will tend to propose precise, bright-line rules that are both transactionally efficient and distributionally favorable to the domi-nating interests. These rules confine the discretion of courts who subse-quently interpret the statute and thus preserve the "victory" of the interest group in the legislative process.

To be sure, one can argue that securing favorable distributional effects can be difficult to achieve without some price regulation. After all, many scholars believe that the non-price terms are the ones that drive efficiency and that the price term distributes the (maximized) surplus. If that's true, what does it mean to say that the non-price terms favor the dominating interests? One response is to suggest that the market will price inefficiently because of market imperfections such as monopoly power or asymmetric information. Any such distributional effects are likely to redistribute wealth from the relatively poor and uniformed to the rich and sophisticated. A slightly different argument is that, even if the political deals are *on average* fully priced out in the resulting contracts, the costs are too high because the losers do not adjust prices in individual transactions that favor the winners (See Lucian Arye Bebchuk & Jesse M. Fried, *The Uneasy Case for the Priority of Secured Claims in Bankruptcy,* 105 Yale L. J. 857 (1996)). In any case, even though the revision to Article 9 was subject to much academic criticism, the new statute was promptly approved by both the ALI and NCCUSL and subsequently adopted in all 50 states, effective December, 2001.

The story with the Article 2 revision process has been markedly different. In August 2001, NCCUSL members voted overwhelmingly to reject the Amendments to Article 2 that had just been approved the preceding May by the ALI. The vote followed a last minute effort by the Article 2 drafting committee to amend the scope provisions of Article 2 in response to continuing criticism from representatives of the software and information industries. In the months that followed, the Article 2 drafting committee approved a new version that did not amend the basic scope section of Article 2, but did amend the definition of "goods" to exclude "information." The Amendments, as revised, were then ap-proved by NCCUSL in August 2002 and subsequently by the ALI in May 2003. To date, however, the Article 2 Amendments have not been introduced for adoption in a single state legislature.

These events followed a concerted effort by the ALI and NCCUSL during the late 1990's to remove controversial proposals from the Article 2 revision process so as to ensure approval by both bodies and ultimate adoption by the states. In the process of downsizing the "revisions" to "amendments," the reporter and associate reporter of the original Article 2 drafting committee, who had worked on the project for over a decade, resigned in protest. The effort to sanitize the Article 2 revisions developed because industry and consumer interests squared off against one another to produce deadlock on key substantive recommendations. Thus, even though the ALI and NCCUSL were eventually able to overcome their differences, this public split between the two bodies that together shepherded the UCC project for over fifty years seemed to represent the end of a fifteen year effort to revise substantially the law of sales as embodied in Article 2.

The unhappy outcome of the Article 2 revision process may be predictable. Unlike the reformer-dominated processes that characterized the initial drafting and enactment of Article 2, the recent revision process saw the emergence of cohesive and competing interest groups. When interest groups compete, some scholars have predicted that the strong institutional bias of these private legislatures to behave conservatively will be reinforced. Cohesive interest groups (the argument goes) are able successfully to block the proposals of the groups they oppose but are unable to get their own proposals enacted. The noise resulting from their competition leads the private legislature to reject any significant reform in favor of the status quo. Indeed, as the unsuccessful efforts to strip Article 2 of controversy over the past decade may have shown, a strong enough status quo bias can induce rejection of even apparently innocuous proposals. We will return to these issues and consider them in depth in Chapter 2.

1.7 Conclusion

Unraveling the story of modern commercial law requires a student to focus on two somewhat divergent themes. The first is to evaluate commercial law rules in terms of a handful of widely-accepted normative criteria, such as efficiency, autonomy and distributional fairness. This exercise is particularly important in assessing the default rules designed to fill contractual gaps and the interpretation rules used to ascertain the meaning of parties obligations. Given the express normative purposes embodied in the UCC, a primary criterion of Code analysis is to assess particular outcomes against the Code's commitment to freedom of contract. This implies that the commercial law should respect party sovereignty so long as the deals that sophisticated and informed parties reach are not infected by fraud or duress, are not unconscionable and do not create externalities. We then might ask: what kind of commercial law rules would such parties prefer? This question is the principal focus of Chapter 2, section 2.2. A plausible response is that the best approximation of the preferences of commercial actors is adopt legal rules that maximize the size of the contractual surplus that the contract divides between them. To the extent, therefore, that commercial law rules are efficient, there are good reasons to believe that they promote the ex ante preferences of sophisticated parties. To be sure, the interests of unsophisticated or otherwise disadvantaged parties—the paradigmatic individual consumer—are not so easily characterized. In these instances, autonomy values or distributional concerns may call for mandatory rules that limit contracting freedom. We consider these questions in Chapter 2, section 2.5. To the extent that commercial law rules cannot be justified on any of these criteria, however, a second theme runs through contemporary commercial law. These rules are produced by a unique political process which may influence the content of the rules themselves. Given the peculiar mechanisms by which private legislative bodies produce the relevant statutory rules, we therefore must also ask: To what extent are the rules influenced by their political economy rather than by a motivation to advance any neutral normative goals? We turn to this question in Chapter 2, section 2.3.

Chapter 2
The Value of Commercial Law: The Design of Defaults

2.1 Introduction: Contract Incompleteness, Gap–Filling and Defaults

As noted in Chapter 1, many commercial relationships proceed and even thrive without commercial law. Others are supported by contract—that is, by legal enforcement of their bargains. The courts play an important role in enforcing those bargains, and the law serves an equally significant function in reducing the transaction costs of the parties, particularly those that arise from the fact that information is costly, sometimes prohibitively so. In drafting their agreement, parties incur the costs of anticipating future contingencies and specifying the obligations that arise in each contingency ("front-end" costs). When the obligations come due, the parties incur the costs of monitoring and enforcing performance of these obligations in court ("back-end" costs). These transaction costs prevent parties from writing complete contracts whose performance can be simply coerced, as written, by the courts.

Transaction costs can lead to two types of incompleteness. In the first, the contract fails to describe the obligations of the parties in all possible future states of the world because of the cost of contemplating and providing for each contingency. Should a state of the world materialize that falls within the gap, the enforcing court must choose either to decline to enforce the contract or to fill the gap with a default obligation. However, transaction costs do not necessarily lead to this type of incompleteness. The cost of making contracts complete in this sense is trivial: the parties can simply provide for an obligation that applies to a broadly defined set of contingencies. For example, a contract term that states, "the seller shall deliver a blue widget on September 1, 2009 for a price of $10,000" may be interpreted to require delivery in all possible states, even if delivery is not efficient. The second type of incompleteness occurs when the contract fails to provide for the *efficient* (or optimal in any other sense) set of obligations in each possible state of the world. Even if the widget contract is obligationally complete, because it has no gaps, it may be "informationally incomplete" because it fails to cancel the exchange if circumstances arise such that the cost of the delivery exceeds the benefit to the buyer.

By creating default terms, commercial law can reduce the front-end costs of contracting and enhance the completeness and efficiency of contracts. The most common type of default is the term that most parties would choose if there were no front-end costs. By establishing this default provision, the law reduces the contracting cost of those parties in the majority who would have chosen it. It also increases the completeness of those contracts whose parties would have found it too costly to design this provision by themselves. Where contracting costs vary across different relationships, a default term might reflect the preferences of the minority if they face much higher transaction costs than the majority. Yet another type, sometimes called penalty defaults or information-forcing default terms, may improve the efficiency of the contract by inducing one party to reveal private information to the other. The common law cap on foreseeable damages is a frequent example: it induces the exceptionally vulnerable promisee to disclose its unusual circumstances. Some doubts have been raised as to whether many other default terms fall in this category. See, e.g., Eric A. Posner, *There Are No Penalty Default Rules in Contract Law*, 33 Fla. St. U. L. Rev. 563 (2006). In response, a cynic may argue that commercial law contains a number of defaults that are confusing or otherwise unattractive in order to induce the parties to address certain aspects of their agreement explicitly: the implied warranty in sales of goods might be an example (§ 2–314).

Commercial law provides a number of defaults. Some go to the core of the parties' agreement: for example, if the parties omit the price of goods being sold, the court will enforce a price that is reasonable in the circumstances. There are limits, however, to the extent to which commercial parties can rely on default provisions provided by law. For example, the courts will not enforce a sales contract that does not specify a quantity. More generally, if a contract is too indefinite, the courts will decline to enforce it. Indefiniteness may raise doubts about the intent of the parties to make a legally enforceable contract. In other cases, the law requires that the parties observe formalities in order to send a definite signal of their intent to incorporate a set of default terms.

The role of default provisions in enhancing efficiency by reducing contracting costs and completing contracts has occupied much of the agenda of the law-and-economic branch of contract law scholarship. *See e.g.*, Robert E. Scott & Charles J. Goetz, *The Mitigation Principle: Toward a General Theory of Contractual Obligation*, 69 Va. L. Rev. 967 (1983); Ian Ayres & Robert Gertner, *Filling Gaps in Incomplete Contracts: An Economic Theory of Default Rules*, 99 Yale L. J. 87 (1989); Ian Ayres and Robert Gertner, *Strategical Contractual Inefficiency and the Optimal Choice of Legal Rules*, 101 Yale L. J. 729 (1992); Jason Johnston, *Strategic Bargaining and the Economic Theory of Contract Default Rules*, 100 Yale L. J. 615 (1990); Alan Schwartz, *The Default Rule Paradigm and the Limits of Contract Law*, 3 S. Cal. Interdisciplinary L. J. 389 (1994). Default provisions are explored in considerable detail in Chapters 1.2 and 1.3 of Richard Craswell and Alan Schwartz, *Foundations of Contract Law* (1994).

Objectives other than efficiency might also guide law makers in completing contracts. Some scholars argue that courts might fill contractual gaps with terms that are fair from an ex post perspective. Under this approach, the courts can impose an equitable adjustment to the contract based on information that was unknown or unforeseeable to the parties at the time of contract. See, e.g., Ian R. Macneil, *Contracts: Adjustment of Long–Term Economic Relations Under Classical, Neoclassical, and Relational Contract Law*, 72 Nw. U. L. Rev. 854 (1978); Ian R. Macneil, *The Many Faces of Contracts*, 47 S. Cal. L. Rev. 691 (1974); Robert Hillman, *Court Adjustment of Long–Term Contracts: An Analysis Under Modern Contract Law*, 1987 Duke L. J. 1; Richard E. Speidel, *Court–Imposed Price Adjustments Under Long–Term Supply Contacts*, 76 Nw. U. L. Rev. 369 (1981); Richard E. Speidel, *The New Spirit of Contract*, 2 J. Law & Comm. 193 (1983).

The material in sections 2.2, 2.3 and 2.4 of this chapter address three sets of features of default provisions in commercial law. First, the default provision may be a rule or a standard. The distinction between a rule and a standard in this context hinges on whether the content of the provision is determined before or after the state of the world is revealed. More accurately, a rule and standard define opposite ends of a range. For example, the Code provides that, in general, the risk of loss passes from the seller to the buyer at the time of delivery (§ 2–509(1)). Although the time of delivery may need to be determined after the fact, this term is more of a rule than, for example, the provision that imposes a reasonable price on contracts in which the price has not been specified or has failed (§ 2–305(1)). Section 2.2 identifies some of the basic factors that inform the choice between rules and standards.

Second, default provisions can be chosen by one of the three legal institutions: the legislature, the courts or administrative bodies. (Default standards would typically be applied by the courts). The material in section 2.3 encourages the reader to examine the relative strengths and weaknesses of the courts and legislatures, and their inclination to produce rules or standards, respectively. These law-making institutions differ significantly in their access to information and their incentives to produce the optimal defaults. As described in Chapter 1, the UCC was the product of an idiosyncratic legislative process: it was created by private, not-for-profit groups of lawyers and academics (the American Law Institute and the National Conference of Commissioners of Uniform State Laws) and was then introduced to and passed by state legislatures. The excerpt by Professor Schwartz and Scott analyzes the expertise and incentives of these bodies.

Third, law makers might simply incorporate the practices they observe in the industry. The excerpts in section 2.4 reflect the scholarly debate over whether industry practices provide superior default contract terms to those which legislatures or courts might design.

Part 2.5 provides an opportunity to consider mandatory terms. In contrast to default provisions, mandatory terms cannot be waived or varied by the parties. Mandatory terms come in various forms across areas of commercial law, and they have various justifications. In many cases, they are meant to protect weaker parties, especially those that are vulnerable to cognitive error. For example, a debtor may not waive its procedural protections against the secured creditor's repossession of the collateral, until after the debtor has defaulted. This may be justified by the debtor's tendency to underestimate its likelihood of default or its inability to fully contemplate its circumstances at that time. Other mandatory terms address contract terms that, while beneficial to both parties, inflict external costs on third parties. For example, § 2–718 prevents parties from stipulating breach of contract damages that exceed the promisee's actual damages from breach or a reasonable estimate of its damages at the time of contracting. Among the possible justifications for this restriction is the anticompetitive effect it has on the ability of the promisor to pursue business with other parties. See Note 2 in section 2.5.

2.2   Default Rules Versus Default Standards

Rules Versus Standards: An Economic Analysis*
LOUIS KAPLOW

This Article offers an economic analysis of the extent to which legal commands should be promulgated as rules or standards, a question that has received substantial attention from legal commentators. Arguments about and definitions of rules and standards commonly emphasize the distinction between whether the law is given content ex ante or ex post. For example, a rule may entail an advance determination of what

* 42 DUKE L. J. 557, 559–67 (1993).

conduct is permissible, leaving only factual issues for the adjudicator. (A rule might prohibit "driving in excess of 55 miles per hour on expressways.") A standard may entail leaving both specification of what conduct is permissible and factual issues for the adjudicator. (A standard might prohibit "driving at an excessive speed on expressways.") This Article will adopt such a definition, in which the only distinction between rules and standards is the extent to which efforts to give content to the law are undertaken before or after individuals act. [. . .]

The analysis in Part I [of this Article] examines the relative desirability of ex ante versus ex post creation of the law in terms of legal costs and the extent to which individuals' behavior conforms to the law. It focuses on an intentionally simple example—made more complex later—that is used to identify fundamental differences between rules and standards. The example has three stages: (1) A law is promulgated, either as a rule or as a standard. (2) Individuals decide how to act. Being imperfectly informed of the law's commands, they either act based on their best guess of the law, or they acquire legal advice, which allows them to act with knowledge of a rule or a prediction of the application of a standard. (3) After individuals act, an adjudicator determines how the governing law applies. Rules are more costly to promulgate than standards because rules involve advance determinations of the law's content, whereas standards are more costly for legal advisors to predict or enforcement authorities to apply because they require later determinations of the law's content.

To illustrate the analysis, consider the problem of regulating the disposal of hazardous substances. For chemicals used frequently in settings with common characteristics—such as dry cleaning and automotive fluids—a rule will tend to be desirable. If there will be many enforcement actions, the added cost from having resolved the issue on a wholesale basis at the promulgation stage will be outweighed by the benefit of having avoided additional costs repeatedly incurred in giving content to a standard on a retail basis. Moreover, with regard to the countless acts of individuals subject to these laws, a rule will tend to be better as well. Because learning about a rule is cheaper, individuals may spend less in learning about the law, and may be better guided by a rule since the law's content can be more readily ascertained.

Contrast this result to that in the case of chemicals used rarely, and in settings that vary substantially. Designing a rule that accounts for every relevant contingency would be wasteful, as most would never arise. Although it might be more difficult and costly for an individual and an enforcement authority to apply a standard in a particular instance, such an application need be made only if its unique set of circumstances actually arises. Thus when frequency is low, a standard tends to be preferable.

Two features of this example are worth highlighting. First, the frequency of individual behavior and of adjudication is of central importance. Note in this regard that a law may still govern much behavior even though adjudications—which receive more emphasis in legal commentary—are rare, whether because most acts do not give rise to a lawsuit or because most cases are settled. Laws in which the frequency of application in recurring fact scenarios is high include many traffic laws, aspects of the law of damages (how to value disability, loss of life, or lost profits), regulations governing health and safety, and provisions of the federal income tax (some of which apply to millions of individuals and billions of transactions). In contrast, some laws govern more heterogeneous behavior, in which each relevant type of act may be rare. For example, the law of negligence applies to a wide array of complex accident scenarios, many of which are materially different from each other and, when considered in isolation, are unlikely to occur.

Second, the advantage of rules at the stage involving individuals' behavior depends on whether individuals choose to acquire legal advice before they act. If the benefits of learning the law's content are substantial and the cost (whether of hiring legal experts or learning more on one's own) is not too great, individuals' behavior under both rules and standards will tend to conform to the law's commands. The advantage of rules in this case would be that the cost of learning the law is reduced. If, however, the cost of predicting standards is high, individuals will not choose to become as well informed about how standards would apply to their behavior. The advantage of rules in this case would be improved legal compliance. Thus, even if an enforcement authority were to give the same content (or "better") to a standard as might have been included in a rule, the rule might induce behavior that is more in accord with underlying norms.

After developing these ideas, the framework is extended in two ways. First, the analysis is reconsidered in light of the possibility that a standard might be converted into a rule through the creation of a precedent. Second, an inquiry is made into how much effort should and would be invested in promulgating and applying laws. It is noted, for example, that more should be spent on determining the appropriate resolution of issues when a rule is designed once for many cases than when applying a standard (adjudication) or predicting the application of a standard (legal advice) in a single case. Finally, Part I concludes by observing that the problem of choosing between rules and standards can be viewed as one concerning how the government should acquire and disseminate information about the appropriate content of the law.

Part II seeks to illuminate the intersection between the debate over rules and standards (ex ante versus ex post creation of the law) and the debate over the appropriate degree of detail in legal commands. The focus is on the familiar suggestion that rules tend to be over-and underinclusive relative to standards. This Part indicates that the suggestion is misleading because typically it implicitly compares a complex standard and a relatively simple rule, whereas both rules and standards can in fact be quite simple or highly detailed in their operation.

For rules, the potential variation in complexity is familiar, even if often ignored. A motor vehicle code could specify a single speed limit, a handful (one each for expressways, city streets, and alleys), or a plethora (identifying different types of roads, vehicles, weather conditions, traffic densities, and driver characteristics). For standards, this point has two important dimensions. Standards may admit few or many considerations in determining their application. A standard that one not drive at an excessive speed may allow only time and safety considerations or may also permit energy conservation considerations; it may deem relevant only road conditions or may also take into account vehicle types. There is, however, another important dimension that is commonly overlooked when analyzing standards: the level of detail actually employed by the adjudicator. A standard that one not drive at excessive speed might well permit consideration of dozens of factors. But if ninety-nine out of a hundred juries make their decisions based on the same two or three factors, although the other factors are relevant in principle, the de facto standard might usefully be described as a rather simple one.

Thus, there are simple and complex rules as well as simple and complex standards. Moreover, as a matter of legal practice, it is not always the case that rule systems are simple compared to the standards that could be adopted in their place. Consider the federal income tax. It hardly seems plausible that a standard requiring individuals to pay "their appropriate share of the federal government's revenue needs," applied case by case, would generate a more detailed law—one that took into account more factors, in more intricate ways—than the one embodied in the Internal Revenue Code and its accompanying regulations.

The conceptual distinction between the questions of how complex a law should be and whether any aspect of its detail is best determined ex ante or ex post has practical importance. For example, a complex standard might be preferred to a simple rule because of its complexity or because of the advantages of ex post formulation, or both. As a result, in some instances in which the complex standard is superior, it may be that complexity is better than simplicity, but a rule—a complex rule—would be preferable to a standard; or, it may be that a standard is better than a rule, but a simple standard would be preferable to a complex one. For example, a standard (implicitly complex) that one dispose of toxic substances "appropriately" may be preferable to a rule that simply prohibits the dumping of petroleum byproducts into bodies of water. But, at least for substances frequently used in common settings—such as dry cleaning and automotive fluids—a complex rule detailing the appropriate manner of disposal for different substances may be even better.

Preliminary Thoughts on Optimal Tailoring of Contractual Rules*

IAN AYRES

The rather minimal thesis of this paper is that the ability of private parties to contract around rules or standards affects their optimal level of precision. It is not appropriate to simply import the tort, administrative law and immutable rule theories to the contract context where parties have the private option to exit. It may be exceedingly hard, however, to provide a general theory. While the works of Ehrlich and Posner, Diver and Kaplow contain compelling insights, none succeeds in providing a truly general or complete analysis—in part because the topic is so amorphous. The normative choice between rules and standards becomes even more difficult when parties can contract around the law. [. . .]

Before proceeding, I will try to define some terminology. It is difficult to be precise in this area (indeed, one might argue that the definitions are more standard-like than rule-like). Ehrlich and Posner distinguish between rules and standards in the following way: "A rule withdraws from the decision maker's consideration one or more of the circumstances that would be relevant to decision according to a standard. . . . The difference between a rule and a standard is a matter of degree—the degree of precision." Louis Kaplow, however, distinguishes between the two terms on different grounds: "[T]he only distinction between rules and standards is the extent to which efforts to give content to the law are undertaken before or after individuals act." Kaplow distinguishes between the degree of complexity and when that complexity becomes known—only the latter determines whether the law is a rule or a standard. Thus, Kaplow envisions four permutations: Simple Rules, Simple Standards, Complex Rules, and Complex Standards. Kaplow's notion of complexity captures Ehrlich and Posner's concern with whether the decision turns on many or few facts—but Kaplow emphasizes that, independent of its complexity, the content of a rule may or may not be known until after individuals act.

Kaplow argues that legal consideration of rules vs. standards often confuses these independent dimensions—wrongly comparing complex standards with simple rules. Instead, he suggests that we would do better to compare rules and standards of equal complexity. While Kaplow's distinction between complexity and timing is powerful, in this paper I cleave to Ehrlich and Posner's initial distinction between rules and standards which focuses on the number of facts upon which decisions turn (what Kaplow calls complexity). [. . .]

---

* 2 S. Cal. Interdis. L. J. 1, 2–18 (1993).

[I]ndividuals have an additional option when the legal rule or standard is merely a default or gap-filler: they can contract not only for different substantive provisions, but also for a different degree of precision. Indeed, although default analysis is often couched in terms of substituting one rule for another, parties could contract around a default standard for a more precise rule (or contract around a precise default rule for a less precise standard). We see both types of movements along the precision spectrum in actual practice. Parties sometimes will draft "reasonableness" clauses and at other times specify more specific rule-like clauses (such as for liquidated damages).

Kaplow has recognized the importance of this option of contractual exit: "Sometimes ... it might be cheapest simply to include such provisions in the contract without incurring the cost to determine whether they are necessary. Thus, many contracts contain extensive boilerplate providing for the result an adjudicator would likely reach in any event." Contracting parties may avoid the costs of becoming informed about a default standard or rule by instead bearing the costs of explicitly contracting around the rule.

An efficiency analysis of rules vs. standards will often turn on whether contractual parties decide to explicitly contract instead of bearing the costs of becoming informed. For this reason, Kaplow argues that the costs of becoming informed will often drop out of the standard vs. rule analysis: "[T]he calculus determining whether [default] rules or [default] standards are preferable would emphasize ex ante promulgation costs and ex post enforcement costs, giving less attention to costs of advice by contracting parties because they often would not choose to acquire advice about such matters." Kaplow's frequency analysis, however, plays out much differently when the parties have the option of contracting around the rule or the standard. It may no longer be efficient to expend the high promulgation costs of a rule if private parties nonetheless intend to contract for an express private provision. The higher costs of promulgating a rule are only likely to be efficient if the rule deters private parties from contracting to substitute their own provisions.

Alan Schwartz and Bob Scott have recently argued that many U.C.C. provisions are inefficient for the very reason that parties often contract around them. Schwartz and Scott focus on the incentives of the parties to contract around default standards, but either default rules or default standards may induce explicit contracting.

Indeed, any of Kaplow's four permutations of complexity/simplicity and ex ante/ex post content may induce the majority of contracting parties to contract for alternative treatment. Simple (untailored) default rules can act as penalty defaults because of the well-known properties of over- and underinclusiveness. Complex default rules might induce more complete contracting because it is comparatively less costly to write

comprehensive provisions than it is to become informed of the complex
rule. And, either simple or complex standards could induce more complete contracting if the parties expect that judicial application of the
standard will be expensive and/or inaccurate.

There are certain provisions such as price and quantity where
private contracts are likely to contract around any default regardless of
either its complexity or the precision of its ex ante or ex post implementation. Price and quantity defaults represent a striking counterexample
to Kaplow's frequency hypothesis. Regardless of the extremely high
frequency of transactions, it would be inefficient for lawmakers to
expend resources promulgating more complex and tailored rules, because
the expenses in creating this default would be wasted as private parties
could be expected to almost universally contract around.

Instead, where parties are likely to explicitly contract, contract law
has responded in two ways that entail very low promulgation costs. The
default price term is a "reasonableness" standard, while the default
quantity term is non-enforcement or a zero-quantity rule. While the
zero-quantity default is more explicitly a penalty (because no parties
would contract to sell zero), the reasonableness standard acts as a
penalty default because almost all parties prefer to incur the costs of
explicit contracting rather than leave the matter to ex post court
determination.

When contracting parties are going to contract around the defaults,
rule-like defaults are least likely to be efficient. The examples of price
and quantity terms can help us see that such explicit contracting is most
likely to occur when:

(1) the parties have heterogeneous preferences about what the term
should be; and

(2) the term relates to a high probability contingency. Price and quantity terms fulfill both of these conditions.

The U.C.C. default rule that the sales price is due at the time of
delivery is probably better than a "reasonableness" default because a
majority of contracting parties may homogeneously prefer such a term.
But there is no clear plurality of contracts that have any particular
quantity—because there is an extreme heterogeneity of preferences. This
heterogeneity makes any particular quantity default rule act like a
penalty default for the vast majority of contracting parties.

Parties are also much more likely, ceteris paribus, to contract over
contingencies that have a higher probability of occurrence. Thus, we see
more explicit and detailed provisions about terms of performance for the
normal course of events than we do for low probability contingencies.
Since parties are likely to contract about high probability contingencies
anyway, it makes less sense to expend resources on a particularized rule.

Even when most people are likely to explicitly contract, different
defaults may produce different gains from trade for those who fail, for

one reason or another, to contract around the default. The appropriate default choice should grow out of one's theories for why there are contractual gaps. One of the great difficulties of thinking about the appropriate gap filler for price and quantity is that it is hard to model why parties would leave these terms out of their express agreements.

As a general matter, policy makers should explicitly compare the contractual equilibria resulting from various defaults and choose the type of tailoring that produces the best equilibrium. Efficiency minded lawmakers, for example, would choose the type of tailoring that minimizes a host of costs associated with contracting: these include the costs of contracting around the defaults (successfully or unsuccessfully) as well as promulgation, application and information costs.

Kaplow cogently argues that many authors conflate issues of complexity together with the timing issue of when the law is given its content. But simple rules will often dominate both complex rules and simple standards, so that policy makers' operative default choices may often devolve to a choice between simple rules and complex standards. Simple rule defaults are likely to dominate simple standard defaults because they are more accessible for the parties and the courts to see and therefore likely to economize on the costs of explicit contracting. Simple standards needlessly interject ambiguity into the law. [. . .]

Simple rule defaults are also likely to dominate complex rule defaults. When contracting parties have homogeneous preferences, complex, tailored rules will be unnecessary. And when contracting parties have heterogeneous preferences, it will be extremely costly for courts to provide tailored defaults that succeed at minimizing transaction costs. As I have said with regard to corporate contracting: "[L]egislatures are effectively limited to choosing among the class of untailored and unconditional entitlements and obligations. To put the point most simply, any contractual provision that a legislature could write ex ante, corporations could write better." In the non-corporate context, the only "rule-like" defaults that are likely to reduce transaction costs are simple, transparent rules that may allow parties to avoid the costs of contracting over homogeneously preferred provisions.

It should be stressed that in a world without transaction costs, parties may want more fully contingent contractual provisions, but the same costs that prevent private parties from writing fully state-contingent contracts may all the more prevent lawmakers from providing these default provisions. Viewed in this sense, it is unlikely that legislative provision of defaults will make contracts less "incomplete" as the term is used by economists.

It is possible, however, that complex standards may be more efficient defaults than simple rules. In a recent review of Easterbrook and Fischel, I argued that complex standards might make presumptively better defaults for publicly traded corporations, because it would be trivially easy for parties to contract around reasonableness standards for more rule-like provisions in their articles of incorporation (but parties might have much harder time contracting around rules for muddy treatment).

[In the cited earlier article, Ayres explains:

> "Contracting around an unconditional default rule by adopting some variant of a 'reasonableness' provision would accordingly be attended by much more uncertainty than failing to contract around a muddy 'reasonableness' default. In the former instance, the multiplicity of possible contractual provisions is likely to splinter the precedents and deter mud-seeking corporations from contracting for their preferred rule. By contrast, few firms should be deterred from contracting around a muddy default. Firms that want unconditional contractual duties can contract at a trivial cost-for provisions that unconditionally allow or prohibit particular types of management behavior.
>
> Moreover, muddy defaults may lead to less judicial nullification than defaults that carve out unconditional managerial obligations. While courts may have a tendency ultimately to nullify any private attempts to modify the default obligations of contracts, it may be that courts are less likely to nullify explicit unconditional provisions than attempts to contract for muddy ex post determinations." Ian Ayres, Making a Difference: The Contractual Contributions of Easterbrook and Fischel, 59 U. Chi. L. Rev. 1391, 1405–6 (1992).]

The greater cost in affirmatively specifying complex contractual provisions also makes it more difficult to draw inferences from private contractual behavior. If contracting parties fail to contract around a complex standard default in favor of a simple rule, then one might infer that the complex standard is the superior default. Failure to contract out of a complex standard implies that there is no simple (and therefore cheap to specify) provision that would do better.

In contrast, the failure to contract around a simple rule default for a complex standard does not indicate that the simple rule default is superior: "Because of the substantial difficulties that [contracting parties] will have in affirmatively contracting for fully contingent obligations or entitlements, the failure of firms to try should not persuade policy makers that [contracting parties] do not want muddy default rules."

As promised, this section does not provide anything like a general theory as to when contractual defaults should be rules or standards. But hopefully it shows that frequency need not lead toward the adoption of rules. Simple rule defaults are likely to be efficient when contracting parties have homogeneous preferences for a particular rule and when the rule addresses high probability events. Unless lawmakers intentionally want to induce contracting (as with information-forcing strategies), evidence that parties generally contract around the simple rule suggests that a standard-like default might be more efficient. [. . .]

The choice between rules or standards is extremely complex and becomes all the more complex when one introduces the possibility that parties can contractually alter the law. In many circumstances the dichotomous choice between rules or standards may be a false one, because lawmakers may prefer to enact a complementary set of rules and standards. Thus, in most jurisdictions, highway speed is regulated by supplementing a rule with a standard. As Ehrlich and Posner observed: "It can be made unlawful to drive more than 60 miles per hour or to drive at any lower speed that is unreasonably fast in the particular circumstances." In areas of contract performance, contract law might specify per se rules of performance and non-performance, but specify a "reasonableness" standard to govern conduct falling outside the rule-governed conduct.

This method of combining rules and standards is clearly the sensible way of governing the conditions for contracting around rules. Rules should establish clear "magic words" that are sufficient to contract for particular kinds of treatment; however, the common law should back up these rules with a general standard of following the commonly under-stood meaning of the parties' explicit language—even when that language fails to employ the "magic words" for contracting around particular defaults.

NOTES

1.   The scholarly debate. The rules versus standards debate has been the subject of a considerable body of legal scholarship, often focusing on public law, including constitutional law and regulation. As illustrated by the foregoing excerpts, the concern of most authors is the cost and imperfections of information. See Ehrlich and Posner, *Economic Analysis of Legal Rule-making*, 3 J. Legal Stud. 257 (1974); Colin S. Diver, *The Optimal Precision of Administrative Rules*, 93 Yale L. J. 65 (1983). The difficulties that individuals have in processing information drives the concerns in Russell Korobkin, *Behavioral Analysis and Legal Form: Rules vs. Standards Revisited*, 79 Or. L. Rev. 23 (2000). For other perspectives, see Duncan Kennedy, *Form and Substance in Private Law Adjudication*, 89 Harv. L. Rev. 1685 (1976); Pierre Schlag, *Rules and Standards*, 33 UCLA L. Rev. 379 (1985); Kathleen M. Sullivan, *The Justices of Rules and Standards*, 106 Harv. L. Rev. 22 (1992).

2.   Are default *rules* even possible in sales law? The drafters of Article 2 of the UCC created default provisions that would cover a wide range of sales contracts. Is there too much variation across different goods, and does technology evolve too quickly, to allow for effective default *rules* for sales contracts? An alternative to general standards (or rules) in sales law would be specific rules that are tailored to narrower subsets of goods.

In light of the heterogeneity of goods, standards may overwhelm the court's expertise so that neither default rules nor default standards are desirable. Professor Scott writes:

> [T]he more heterogeneous the contracting parties are, the less the economies of scale for any default and the greater the likelihood that the state is less capable than the parties themselves in solving their contracting problems. Unless the contracting solution is immanent in the commercial practice and relationship of the parties (as Llewellyn, for example, believed it was), and a court can identify and standardize the practice or experience as a default, a court is likely to create ill-fitting defaults in complex commercial environments.

Robert E. Scott, *The Case for Formalism in Relational Contract*, 94 Nw. U. L. Rev. 847, 863 (2000).

3. What law-making institution chooses between rules and standards? The Code drafters of the Code had a choice between using default rules and standards. According to Kaplow's definition, a standard delegates lawmaking to the court that adjudicates disputes ex post. The drafters also delegate rule-making to the courts by permitting them to create precedent that is binding on later litigation. Therefore, the decision to use standards instead of rules in the Code is also a choice among lawmaking institutions: whether default rules should be provided by the Code drafters and legislatures, or by the courts. We examine this choice in the next section of this chapter.

4. Are rules and standards stable? Neither rules nor standards in the Code are stable in the face of judicial application. As Professor Schauer suggests in the following excerpt, courts can manipulate rules when their faithful application yields undesirable outcomes. And, as we have observed, courts can turn standards into rules by creating precedent.

> [T]he choice between rules and standards, between specific and vague directives, may not make nearly as much of a difference as is ordinarily assumed. And this is *not* because there is no difference between rules and standards. There is a difference, but there is also reason to believe that the adaptive behaviour of rule-interpreters and rule-enforcers will push rules towards standards, and push standards towards rules. [. . .]
>
> Rules will tend towards standards ... One way for this to occur is for the rule-enforcer or rule-interpreter to engraft an exception to the rule at the moment of its application ... Even more common is to understand all rules as being subject to an implicit "reasonableness qualification" ... A third strategy of rule-avoidance is to take even the most specific rule to be subject to override by considerations external to the rule itself ... Fourth, rule-enforcers and rule-interpreters will often depart from the specificity of a rule in order to rely on its less specific purpose. [. . .]

[R]ule enforcers, rule-interpreters and rule-appliers ... [may] supplement the standards with more specific "guidelines" or "rules of thumb" that in practice have all of the characteristics or rules.... Standards may come to resemble rules in less direct ways as well. When a court holds that a vague standard incorporates the common law on its subject, or incorporates a statute dealing with similar subject matter, it is in effect importing a specific rule from outside of the non-specific standard in order to make the non-specific standard more specific. [...]

Frederick Schauer, *The Convergence of Rules and Standards,* 2003 New Zealand L. Rev. 303, 305–18.

Carol Rose offers a different hypothesis that rules and standards oscillate between the two extremes rather than converging in a single point. Carol M. Rose, *Crystals and Mud in Property Law,* 40 Stan. L. Rev. 577 (1988). Can you think of standard-to-rule conversions under the UCC? Of rule-to-standard conversion? If Professors Schauer and Rose are correct in their observation of the courts, how much control do the legislatures have over the optimal flexibility of the law to address specific contexts?

5. Contract design and litigation uncertainty. As Kaplow suggests, standards lead parties to invest in information helping them predict how the courts will rule in any given set of circumstances. Some uncertainty is likely to remain, and the relationship between uncertainty in litigation on the one hand, and contract performance and design on the other, is complex. See Gillian K. Hadfield, *Judicial Competence and the Interpretation of Incomplete Contracts,* 21 J. Legal Stud. 271 (1992); George G. Triantis, *The Efficiency of Vague Contract Terms: A Response to the Schwartz–Scott Theory of U.C.C. Article 2,* 62 La. L. Rev. 1065, 1071–72 (2002); Robert E. Scott & George G. Triantis, *Anticipating Litigation in Contract Design,* 115 Yale L. J. 814 (2006). It is further complicated by the fact that litigation is also costly and error prone. See Albert Choi and George Triantis, *Completing Contracts in the Shadow of Costly Verification,* 37 J. Legal Stud. 503 (2008); Chris William Sanchirico and George Triantis, *Evidentiary Arbitrage: The Fabrication of Evidence and the Verifiability of Contract Performance,* 24 J. Law, Econ. & Organ. 72 (2008).

6. The effect of contracting out on the choice between rules and standards. The rules and standards of commercial law, unlike public law and regulation, are predominantly defaults. As Ayres indicates in the excerpted section above, contracting parties can choose for themselves by contracting out of the rule or standard, as the case may be. If parties to some contracts would prefer a rule and others would prefer a standard, what form should the optimal default take? According to the conventional theories, the law should provide the default that minimizes the contracting costs of all parties. Ayres suggests that it is more costly to contract away from rules to standards than from standards to rules (it is easier for parties to contract around muddy standards than crystalline rules). For other arguments in favor of default standards in contract, see Jason Scott Johnston, *Bargaining Under Rules versus Standards,* 11 J. L. Econ. & Org. 256 (1995); Albert Choi and George Triantis, *Strategic Vagueness in Contract Design: The Case of Corporate Acquisitions*, 119 Yale L.J. ___ (2009).

2.3 Institutional Competence in Commercial Law–Making

The first major codification of contract and commercial law came in 1893 when England passed the Sale of Goods Act. In the United States, sales law was first codified in the Uniform Sales Act, drafted by Professor Samuel Williston and promulgated for adoption by the states in 1906. A parallel development occurred in the codification of the law governing negotiable instruments. The Negotiable Instruments Law (NIL), the most successful pre-Code uniform statute, was drafted in the late 19th century and was based on the English Bills of Exchange Act of 1882. Ultimately, the NIL was adopted in 48 states. Each of these efforts were designed to reproduce the existing law of sales and negotiable instruments in a systematic fashion rather than to effect major changes in the law.

The UCC, on the other hand, was an ambitious (and largely successful) effort to simplify, modernize and standardize the various state laws governing the sale of goods, commercial paper, bank collections, and secured financing. As we discussed in Chapter 1, the UCC was drafted in the 1940s by a group of scholars and practitioners headed by Professor Karl Llewellyn and working under the auspices of the ALI and the National Conference of Commissioners on Uniform State Laws (NCCUSL). By 1967, every state, with the partial exception of the civil-law jurisdiction of Louisiana, had adopted the Code, and it has significantly influenced the developments in contract and related areas of law.

Subsequently, the ALI and NCCUSL have worked together to improve and update the Code, seeking to adapt it to new conditions and new needs. As noted in Chapter 1, the attempt to revise Article 2 has been more controversial than the revision to other Articles of the Code. Revisions of Articles 3, 4 and 9, for examples, have been adopted without significant controversy in almost all jurisdictions. In the case of Article 2, however, the controversial revision process led ultimately to proposed "Amendments" that were finally approved by NCCUSL and the ALI in 2003. But as yet the Article 2 Amendments have not been introduced in a single state and the prospects for adoption appear remote.

The continuing debates over amendments to Article 2 raise the issue of whether the ALI and NCCUSL—the unique combination of private law reform organizations that together produce the provisions of the UCC that are then offered to the states on a "take it or leave it" basis—do a good job in formulating commercial law rules. The specific questions that underlie this issue include the following: what does this process do relatively well and what does it do relatively badly in comparison to an appropriate baseline such as the ordinary legislative process? And further, are there structural factors that bias the products of the uniform laws process notwithstanding the good will and effort of those who have worked hard in the law reform process?

Several scholars have argued that the uniform laws process works well when it focuses on projects that require technical legal expertise but does a poor job when it tackles the task of harmonizing value conflict and regulating those commercial and economic endeavors about which there are strong and competing views. This is because (the argument goes) the outcome of the uniform laws process is the product of powerful structural forces: the pressure to formulate rules that will be uniformly adopted together with the pressure from competing interest groups can distort the rules themselves in ways that may, quite perversely, undermine the very objective of a uniform law in the first instance. Why might the uniform laws process perform badly relative to the ordinary legislative process? One possibility is that there are inherent limitations in the uniform laws process that are not found in the ordinary legislative process. Consider that possibility as you evaluate the following articles.

An Economic Analysis of Uniform State Laws*
LARRY E. RIBSTEIN and BRUCE H. KOBAYASHI

Interest Groups

Interest groups can influence uniform law drafters even if these drafters are appointed on a nonpolitical basis rather than elected. The NCCUSL [National Conference of Commissioners on Uniform State Laws] maximizes widespread adoption of its proposals by heeding groups that may influence enactment. First, the NCCUSL invites "advisers" representing the groups to attend and participate in drafting and annual meetings. Advisers can most influence those commissioners who lack independent knowledge that would enable them to take positions that are not advocated at the meetings. Second, the NCCUSL's Constitution requires uniform law drafters to consult with the appropriate American Bar Association (ABA) committee. Third, the NCCUSL Constitution maximizes the influence of interest groups that are strong only in some states by requiring approval of uniform acts by at least 20 state delegations and a majority of states voting rather than simply by a majority of the Commissioners. In short, rather than ignoring interest groups, the NCCUSL helps coordinate their activities.

Although the NCCUSL listens to and invites representatives of all groups, the drafting process may be biased toward business rather than consumer groups. Business groups such as banks may have scope economies of representation in the NCCUSL process: a narrow segment of the industry can contribute enough business to the practice of a fairly large law firm that it would incur the costs of participating in drafting

* 25 J. Legal Stud. 131, 142–148, 186–187 (1996).

meetings and keeping up with developments in uniform laws over a multiyear drafting period. By contrast, bank customers, although they may be represented by consumer groups who can exert pressure directly on legislators, may lag in influence on the uniform law drafting process [...]

Lawyers

Uniform laws also reflect the interests of lawyers, who are influential as both advisers and commissioners. Lawyers can benefit from rules that are complex and vague enough to discourage settlement but not so complex as to discourage litigation. Nonlitigators may prefer vague or complex rules that increase the need for legal advice, drafting, and planning. Although commercial planners may favor simple default rules that make planning more valuable, litigators' gains from litigation-maximizing rules may outweigh planners' relatively modest additional drafting or planning fees from enforceable contracts. Even if uniform laws reduce litigation over choice of law, lawyers can use the uniform lawmaking process to ensure the widespread use of mandatory vague "good faith" and fiduciary standards. In other words, lawyers might prefer uniform complex laws to nonuniform simple laws, particularly if the uniform regime does not significantly reduce the costs of determining the applicable law.

Commissioners

The commissioners draft, approve, and lobby for enactment of uniform laws. NCCUSL emphasizes that the commissioners have long tenure and receive no compensation beyond reimbursement for expenses. This purportedly ensures that the commissioners will work for the "public good," free from "partisan political considerations." But the commissioners do have private interests that affect the content of uniform laws. First, they contribute their time for which they receive a return in the form of reputational benefits from having participated in drafting uniform laws. Commissioners can sell their expertise through law practice and as expert witnesses on the background of uniform laws.

Second, the commissioners benefit from expense-paid trips to pleasant places for drafting meetings. To the extent that this reward exceeds the value of the commissioners' time in other uses, it can motivate the commissioners to work on as many uniform laws, in as many legal areas, as possible. Commissioners therefore have an interest in maximizing the number of proposed uniform laws rather than the number of adoptions per law. In other words, although commissioners may try to maximize the number of adoptions of each law they decide to promulgate, they have an incentive to promulgate laws that are not likely to be widely adopted. This means that they are particularly susceptible to interest group requests that laws be proposed even in situations in which there is little public interest reason for uniformity.

Third, commissioners may attempt to promulgate provisions that serve the business interests of their clients. Even if these provisions are not adopted widely, they may be able to have the laws adopted in their home states.

This analysis of commissioners' incentives leads to the important prediction that the commissioners will craft proposals in ways they believe will maximize the number of adoptions. Although commissioners can earn reputational benefits from having worked on the uniform law in a particular area even if this law is not widely adopted, these benefits increase the more widely the law is adopted.

Commissioners' incentive to maximize the number of proposals they issue affects only the process of selecting areas in which to issue uniform laws and not the content of the resulting proposals.

The commissioners' enactment-maximization motive has important implications. First, it means that the commissioners have little incentive to institute radical reforms that the states are unlikely to accept. At most, the commissioners may seek to "modernize" the law if they think state legislators want to move in this direction. To the extent the commissioners have reforming instincts, these are satisfied by being able to work toward what the NCCUSL believes is the worthy goal of uniformity. The enactment-maximization goal also relates significantly to the above discussion concerning the influence of interest groups. The NCCUSL's goal causes it to be open to compromise and accommodate groups that could help or hinder adoptions [. . .]

The NCCUSL'S Enactment Potential

The NCCUSL cannot create uniformity by edict. Proposals by the NCCUSL might be widely adopted if the groups that are influential in promulgating uniform laws also are strong enough at the state level to cause their enactment. But it is not clear why such groups would bother with the intermediate stage of pressing their interests before a group of uniform lawmakers. Although influencing a single uniform lawmaking body may be less costly than lobbying 50 state legislatures, the advantages of lobbying the NCCUSL depend on whether the NCCUSL's endorsement is likely to result in adoptions of state laws.

There are at least three ways in which the uniform lawmaking process may help interest groups. First, the NCCUSL provides camouflage for interest group legislation. The NCCUSL is the officially accredited group that produced the widely adopted Uniform Commercial Code and that promotes the seemingly beneficial and disinterested goal of uniformity. This may help legislators sell NCCUSL-sponsored proposals to constituents.

Second, the NCCUSL can facilitate wide adoption of interest-group-oriented legislation by serving as a focal point for coordinating interest group activity. Uniformity depends on the states' being able to agree on a particular proposal, and the existence of an official organization significantly increases the possibility of such an agreement. Because of NCCUSL's quasi-official status, interest groups may conclude that a NCCUSL proposal is their best chance of achieving widespread passage of a particular law. Also, the NCCUSL can obtain the concurrence of competing interest groups by inviting advisors to participate in drafting and by clearing proposals with the relevant ABA committee. Because of the NCCUSL's ability to promote particular proposals, an influential group may decide to take less of a benefit from a uniform law than it could win in a few states in order to secure a law that is likely to be widely adopted. Wide adoption may more fully achieve the group's objectives by making it harder for those who lose under the law to escape it by moving or by contracting to apply the law of a nonenacting state.

Third, the NCCUSL can reduce the costs of interest group activity by undertaking some of the functions that interest groups otherwise would have to bear. Commissioners personally lobby state legislators for enactment of uniform laws and do legislative drafting and bargaining. Commissioners also pressure legislators to adopt their proposals in toto in order to ensure uniformity. This can provide lobbying support for even the most blatantly pro-interest-group provisions.

The NCCUSL's effect on state lawmaking is, of course, limited. In many situations interest groups may have more to gain from local adoption of a law that favors their interests than from adoption of a NCCUSL proposal. Conversely, states may have incentives to defect from inefficient uniformity in order to attract residents or industry from neighboring or other states that have adopted inefficient NCCUSL proposals.

Concluding Remarks

The theory and evidence discussed in this article support several conclusions. To begin, there is a public interest case for uniform laws, based largely on the costs created by inefficient and parochial state laws. But the case is more limited than many have supposed, and uniform lawmaking carries significant risks of facilitating the enactment of inefficient laws.

Our data do show that the states have done an effective job of sorting out which uniform law proposals should be enacted. However, our data also show that the NCCUSL affects which laws are adopted. Laws that the NCCUSL identifies as "model" receive fewer enactments than laws supported by the full weight of a NCCUSL uniformity recommendation. Moreover, NCCUSL proposals have a higher probability of enactment in states with part-time legislatures, indicating that NCCUSL recommendations have particular power in states that would be expected to rely on outside expertise. Because the NCCUSL does have some effect on which laws are enacted, and because its adoption process facilitates the promulgation of inefficient laws, it is desirable to find some alternative means of addressing the problems caused by inconsistent and inefficient state laws.

Wider enforcement of contractual choice of law is one possible solution. However, it is not always feasible to settle choice of law by contract. Even so, there is little reason to suppose that mandating uniformity through federal law is preferable to NCCUSL proposals. A resort to federal law would frustrate the desirable sorting that occurs through state selection among NCCUSL proposals. At best, federal law would not create more efficient laws, but simply a different set of winners and losers.

Reform of the NCCUSL process also is, at best, a partial solution. Many of the problems with the NCCUSL discussed in this article, including the influence of interest groups and the NCCUSL's reliance on ill-informed generalists, may be inherent in the concept of an official organization dedicated to maximizing uniformity of state laws. One feasible improvement that is consistent with the NCCUSL's goals is to focus its work along the lines suggested in this article—that is, on procedural, commercial, and probate statutes—instead of attempting to promote uniformity wherever there is inconsistency.

In the long run, the best solution to the problem of inefficient and inconsistent state laws may be more competition among the states rather than more uniform laws. Indeed, the NCCUSL's continued survival may impede the efficient evolution of statutory law by crowding out superior "unofficial" promulgators of proposed model and uniform laws, including private groups and entrepreneurial states, such as Delaware. In short, this article's most important lesson is that one should be skeptical about the production of law by any rulemaking elite.

The Political Economy of Private Legislatures*
ALAN SCHWARTZ and **ROBERT E. SCOTT**

The ALI [American Law Institute] and NCCUSL [National Conference of Commissioners on Uniform State Laws] have created large portions of American contract and commercial law and have made major contributions in other areas as well, such as tort and property law. Despite these groups' significance, they have never been seriously studied. Rather, uniform laws and restatements have been evaluated as if they were produced by rule-generating "black boxes." Lawyers know that these boxes can produce bad laws as well as good ones, so serious critical attention is devoted to ALI and NCCUSL products. In contrast, the relation between the institutional structures of these organizations and the rules they adopt has been entirely neglected. This lack of attention apparently is because ALI and NCCUSL members are thought

---

* 143 U. Pa. L. Rev. 595, 596–598, 604–607, 651–652 (1995).

to be disinterested legal experts who pursue only the public good: the task is not to study this ideal but rather to extend it to other areas.

The legal community's inattention to the consequences of ALI and NCCUSL procedures, however, is unjustified. Positive political theory teaches us that the form and substance of a law are significantly endogenous to the law-creating institution. Put more simply, a legislature's output is a function both of the preferences of the legislators, whether selfish or altruistic, and of the institutional structure in which the legislators perform. Thus, ALI and NCCUSL outputs also should be endogenous to their organizational forms.

A Typology of Rules Produced by the ALI and NCCUSL

In order to evaluate the products of private law-making groups such as the ALI and NCCUSL, we begin with a taxonomy of the types of legal rules such groups produce. Legal rules commonly take one of three forms. These forms are conveniently illustrated by considering the task of creating a traffic rule regulating the speed of automobiles. A Model 1 traffic rule would recite that driving more than X miles per hour is prohibited. Such a rule is binary, in that it purports to distinguish between compliance and noncompliance with a single criterion. The rule also is "bright-line" because it restricts the set of information on which application turns to objective facts—X miles per hour—and thus is relatively easy to apply.

Model 1 rules have the virtue, from the viewpoint of the legislature, of confining the rule applier's discretion (assuming that the rule applier actually enforces rules as written; the discretionary enforcement by police of the fifty-five-mile-per-hour speed limit illustrates the difficulty of constraining discretion even when a rule is clear on its face). The vice of Model 1 rules is their crudeness: such rules are invariably both under- and over-inclusive. Thus, a Model 1 rule can influence behavior only imperfectly.

Model 2 rules are written on a higher level of abstraction. For example, a Model 2 rule would require persons to drive in a "reasonable manner." Such abstract statements vest more discretion in the rule applier than Model 1 rules permit. A possible consequence of not articulating the specific criteria for application of the rule in the rule itself is an increased risk of "misapplication" (the rule may be applied in a manner inconsistent with the intent of the rule maker). On the other hand, some believe, stating the underlying norm (in this case "reasonable driving") in the rule itself can increase the likelihood that the rule will be enforced in accordance with its animating purpose.

A Model 3 rule attempts to find a middle ground between the first two. Such a rule both includes and then purports to illuminate the underlying norm that is set out in a Model 2 rule. As an example: Persons must drive in a manner reasonable under the circumstances.

The factors relevant to assessing reasonableness include (1) pavement conditions, (2) number of cars on the highway, (3) the speed of other cars on the highway, (4) visibility conditions, (5) eyesight and reflexes of this driver generally, and (6) the condition of the driver at the time.

Models of Private Legislatures

In this section, we develop a theory of private law-making groups such as the ALI and NCCUSL. These groups function similarly to legislatures. Rules are first proposed in committees that are dominated by members with technical expertise. The initial committee process results in a blueprint for reform that is delivered to a second committee which casts the blueprint into statutory form. The final product is then put to the larger body for a vote. The models developed below incorporate the salient features of such a private legislature (or "PL").

Three types of participants act in PLs: (1) interest groups, such as banks; (2) reformers, such as law professors; and (3) PL members who attend annual meetings but do not participate in creating proposals. We model the interaction of these participants as a single-shot stage game. First, a reformer or interest group member requests that a PL draft a proposed law. Second, the PL leadership decides whether the PL should create a study group to consider the matter. The probability that a PL will go forward increases with the likelihood of widespread enactment because creating laws is costly. We consider here the set of legal subjects that satisfies this "enactment constraint"—that is, the set of subjects the uniform laws of which are likely enough to be adopted to justify PL action. Third, the study group creates a uniform law and reports its proposal to the PL under a closed rule. A closed rule is assumed because the size of PLs and the limited time they can devote to particular proposals precludes significant floor amendments. Fourth, the PL decides whether to adopt the proposal or reject it. Fifth and finally, a proposal that passes is introduced as a bill in state legislature.

The enactment constraint that purportedly operates at the second stage is seldom binding on PLs for three reasons. First, PLs exist to do law reform. This generates pressure to create uniform laws and model rules. Second, the probability of widespread adoption is difficult to assess when a law-reform subject is proposed, because it would entail predicting the behavior of a large number of state legislatures and courts. Moreover, there is an extensive time lag between the decision to consider a subject and the promulgation of a law. For example, the UCC took twenty years to create. Such long delays make prediction difficult. As a consequence, the pressure to generate proposals is hard to defuse even with a plausible claim that a particular proposal has a low enactment probability. Third, reformers, we will argue, view participation in PLs as a gain and do not view the probability of ultimate enactment of a PL proposal as a constraint. Hence, PLs have a large supply of free labor to consider subjects and this inclines them to resolve doubts in favor of creating proposals.

The low enactment rate of NCCUSL uniform laws is consistent with this analysis. Because the enactment constraint is weak, we do not analyze the legislative role; that is, we suppose that the decision of a PL whether to accept or reject a proposal is not importantly influenced by the likelihood that the proposal will be widely enacted.

Our models of this game, developed and analyzed in the remainder of this Article, yield the following results:

(1) When all of the participants in the PL process are symmetrically informed about the consequences of reform proposals, (a) a PL will produce many vague rules; (b) the ALI will produce more vague rules than NCCUSL; and (c) an interest group will attempt to participate on PL study groups and advisory boards and seek to generate Model 1 rules when its preferences over reform are similar to those of the PL itself, but interest groups will not lobby PL legislators.

(2) When information is asymmetric (the typical PL member/legislator is poorly informed about the consequences of proposals while other participants know these consequences), the following can be expected: (a) the penchant of a PL to produce vague rules is either unaffected or may increase; (b) when only one interest group would be affected by a PL reform proposal, the group will attempt to participate in study groups and may also lobby, thereby having a greater effect on PL outcomes than on ordinary legislative outcomes; (c) an interest group may have less power in PLs than in ordinary legislatures when interest groups compete over a reform proposal; (d) as a consequence of (c), the presence of competing interest groups before a PL should be less common than the presence of a single group or no group at all, but a reasonable equilibrium exists in which interest groups will compete; and (e) the institutional bias of PLs to behave conservatively, eschewing significant reform, is reinforced.

The Participants' Utility Functions and the Information Structure

This section first describes the preferences of PL participants informally and then gives a formal representation. An interest group can only lobby an ordinary legislature; the group cannot officially participate in the process of creating legislation. In contrast, an interest group can participate in the process of creating PL legislation by having its members, supporters, or lawyers participate in PL study groups and on advisory boards. An interest group has substantial incentives to participate in these ways. Legislatures may be more likely to pass a reform if it comes with the approval of the PL. Moreover, participation in the PL may reduce the group's total lobbying costs. Finally, the payoff from successfully lobbying a PL can exceed the payoff from lobbying Congress or federal agencies because uniform laws are hard to alter. For example, suppose that the Federal Reserve Board can be persuaded to adopt a regulation favoring banking interests and that NCCUSL can be persuaded to propose a similar uniform law that would be widely adopted. The banks would prefer the uniform law because an administrative regulation can be repealed with a change of agency membership, while the approval of numerous states would be required to repeal the uniform law.

Reformers differ from interest group members in two relevant ways. First, a reformer derives utility from a PL's passage of a reform proposal independently of whether the proposal ultimately becomes law. The reformer is commonly a law professor who can write about and teach PL proposals because the proposals are plausible candidates for becoming law. Moreover, status in academia attaches to one who causes a PL to adopt a proposal. In contrast, an interest group member derives utility from PL adoption of a proposal only when adoption increases the likelihood or reduces the costs of securing ultimate, stable legislative enactment. Second, participation in a PL is consumption to a reformer; she gets utility from being part of a law-reform movement. In contrast, participation in a PL and before a legislature is production to an interest group member. Because reformers benefit from PL participation and from PL adoption of a law, they seldom are constrained by legislative preferences. Reformers may not work for proposals that have no chance of becoming law, but almost any probability above zero will induce a reformer to participate in a PL.

The third participant is the PL member/legislator. Ordinary legislators are interested in reelection prospects and in policy. PL legislators are not elected and so may be thought to have an interest only in policy, but this assumption is too strong. Law-reform proposals generate both economic and political consequences. An economic consequence is either the substantive effect a proposal would have "in the world" or the direct effect the proposal would have on a PL participant's income. As an example of economic consequences, a proposal to cap tort damage awards may reduce deterrence, shift wealth from the seriously injured to injurers, and reduce the income of the plaintiffs' lawyers who are PL participants. Commonly, only a small minority of PL participants have a direct economic stake in the fate of any proposal.

A political consequence refers to the effect that a proposal could have on a PL participant's reputation. Support for a proposal that is regarded as utopian or foolish could damage a participant's reputation for good judgment. A lawyer's income is a function of his reputation, but reputational effects are sufficiently influential to distinguish them from direct economic effects. Both the economic and political effects of a proposal will influence how PL legislators vote.

PL participants also derive utility from having a PL adopt a law-reform proposal, independently of the merits of the proposal in question. This is because participation in law-reform organizations implies the desire to do at least some law reform. Consequently, PL participants are inclined to reject the status quo. A participant nevertheless may prefer the status quo to any particular reform proposal that is presented to her, all things considered [. . .]

The median voter's ideal point in an ordinary legislature can be affected by logrolling, but there is no cross-subject logrolling in the ALI and NCCUSL. Consequently, debate in a PL can only illuminate the relation between proposals and their consequences; it cannot change the preferences that typical (that is, disinterested, non-reformer) participants have over those consequences. Logrolling does not occur initially because reporters and drafting committees are recruited for particular projects and principally concentrate on them: an ALI Article 9 reporter usually is unaware of what the Article 2 reporters are doing, and never consults with them officially. Reporter and drafting committee projects thus are presented to the relevant PL as independent entities.

In order to logroll, therefore, the membership itself would have to condition passage of one project on the passage of another. The structure of the ALI and NCCUSL, however, makes logrolling on the floor impractical. The ALI membership is three times the size of Congress, heterogeneous, not organized in political parties, and meets annually for one week. NCCUSL also is large, heterogeneous, lacks internal structure, and meets annually for a short time. Hence, it is difficult to make numerous, significant deals on the floor.

Logrolling also is risky because trades are hard to enforce. In an ordinary legislature, committees enforce trades. For example, consider a trade among legislators that would reduce corporate taxes in return for increasing environmental protection. In a later session, legislators who favor high taxes may wish to renege on the trade and repeal the tax reduction. The committee that initiates tax proposals can enforce the original deal, however, because amendments to statutes in its jurisdiction cannot be considered by the larger body without its consent—it is the gatekeeper for tax matters. The parties that appoint committees have reputations to protect, and so will choose committees that act as gatekeepers. Because deals are enforceable, pro-business legislators may be willing to trade with pro-environmental legislators. PLs such as the ALI and NCCUSL lack enforcement power because they have no gate-keeping committees. Reporters and drafting committees are instructed to create single projects and are dismissed when projects are completed. Without gatekeepers, a promise by one NCCUSL or ALI faction to another not to change a proposed uniform law seldom will be credible. Hence, trading on important issues is risky. In sum, if a PL cannot logroll, the assumption that PL participants have exogenous ideal points in policy space is realistic.

Voting in the ALI and NCCUSL is by majority rule. This and the assumption of single peakedness imply that the equilibrium outcome of a PL vote will correspond to the preferences of the median PL participant. Thus, we follow standard political science practice in modeling a unicameral legislature in which only the preferences of the median legislator are considered. We also assume that study groups vote by majority rule. Hence, the preferences of the median study group member determine study group outcomes. When the median member is a reformer, we describe the group as a "reformer-dominated study group"; similarly, when the median member belongs to an interest group, the group is referred to as an "interest-group-dominated study group." The assumption that study groups (in the usual case, committees) can be modeled in this way is standard and does not affect the results.

Finally, obtaining information about a proposal's consequences is costly. This implies the possibility of information asymmetries: some players will find it worthwhile to become informed about the consequences of proposals while others will not. An informed player is said to have "expertise." We assume that study group members have expertise owing to their roles. An interest group that lobbies a PL is also assumed to have expertise (that is, to have incurred the cost of evaluating a proposal). In the following discussion, PL performance is analyzed first under the assumption that the typical PL legislator/participant has expertise, and second, under the assumption that she lacks it.

PLs Under Symmetric Information

We begin with the assumption that all PL participants are equally (that is, "symmetrically") informed about the consequences of any proposal. We do so in order to explore PL performance under a variety of conditions. It is more plausible to suppose, however, that the typical PL participant knows less than reformers and interest group members do. Moreover, such an asymmetric information model, which is set out below, explains more of the data than the symmetric information model. Nevertheless, the two models share many of the same predictions, a reassuring coherence on the theoretical level.

First, assume that a study group proposes a related set of rules to a PL and that all of the participants are symmetrically informed as to the consequences of adopting those rules. Then, (i) a large number of the rules that pass will be Model 2 rules; (ii) many of the Model 1 rules that pass will advance the interests of industry groups; and (iii) interest groups will not lobby PL legislator/members.

Four reasons support result (i). First, the description of the participants' utility functions above implied that a vague rule that leaves the status quo relatively intact is preferred, cet. par., to doing nothing. Second, Model 2 rules are less likely to create reputational losses for participants and may actually create reputational gains. Reputational losses are unlikely because these rules delegate much of the legislative power to courts; thus, a PL participant cannot be embarrassed by the adoption of a Model 2 rule in the way she can be embarrassed by the adoption of a clearly directive Model 1 rule that actually accomplishes something. Reputational gains derive from the fact that Model 2 rules commonly are couched in phrases with positive affect (such as "good faith" or "reasonable") or appear to consider all relevant factors; hence, a participant may be thought to be well-motivated or sage when her PL adopts such a rule. Third, vague rules can create direct economic gains for PL participants. These rules increase or maintain uncertainty, and thus increase, or do not reduce, the occasions on which lawyers will have to give advice or be involved in litigation. Thus, these three reasons imply a PL preference for Model 2 rules, but this preference can be outweighed by a participant's preference for the consequences that a particular Model 1 rule would create.

A study group's best alternative to proposing a losing Model 1 rule often is to propose a Model 2 rule rather than none. To see why this is so, consider the decision of an interest group to participate in the process. In a symmetric-information world, a study group will get its Model 1 rules adopted only if its preferences are close to the preferences of the median PL voter. Interest group members will not incur a participation cost unless the expected gain is greater, that is, unless participation will sufficiently increase the probability that the study group will propose a winning rule. Hence, interest groups participate on study groups if (a) they will have influence and (b) their preferred policies are in or, in this illustration, to the right of the win set. When these groups do participate, a study group probably will propose Model 1 rules. This rule-type best constrains courts to follow the industry's policy rather than their own.

Reformers also want to influence study groups when their preferences are near the preferences of the median PL participant. Reformers, however, prefer anything that can plausibly be called a reform to the status quo. Thus, a reformer will participate on a study group although the most likely consequence of participation is that the PL will adopt Model 2 rules. This consequence actually is likely because, as we argue below, reformers often have ideal points that lie far from those of median PL participants. Hence, reformers are reluctant to propose Model 1 rules in a PL's win set. Because reformer-dominated study groups are common, and because these study groups are preference outliers but want "reform," study groups often will propose Model 2 rules. This, then, is the fourth factor inclining PLs to the production of Model 2 rules.

The preceding analysis also explains why, in a symmetric-information world, the Model 1 rules that PLs pass often will advance the goals of interest groups. Industry groups will play only when they can pass Model 1 rules (otherwise, their participation is not cost-justified). Hence, given the incentive of reformers not to propose Model 1 rules, the presence of Model 1 rules in a world of symmetric information is a strong signal of industry influence [. . .]

PLs Under Asymmetric Information

We generate three principal results in an asymmetric-information world. First, the incentive of study groups to propose vague rules in lieu of unpassable precise rules remains, and may even be stronger. Second, interest groups may have more power or less power in PLs than in ordinary legislatures, depending on whether one interest group is interested in a proposal or whether interest group preferences conflict. Third, when interest groups lack power or there are no interest groups involved (only reformers are active), the existence of asymmetric information reinforces the tendency of PLs to behave conservatively.

An institution behaves conservatively if it commonly prefers the status quo to reform. The status quo is not a PL participant's ideal point, however. We thus call a PL conservative if it commonly prefers the status quo to Model–1–style reform proposals. In order to see whether such a status quo preference exists, and to understand the median PL participant's response to the efforts of reformers and interest groups to exert influence, we begin by assuming that the participant is substantially uninformed. To be precise, suppose (a) the median PL participant knows the location of the status quo (that is, she can evaluate the consequences of doing nothing); (b) she knows, in an approximate way, the proposal space (the set of possible proposals that could be made on a subject); (c) she has no independent knowledge of the consequences of any proposal that is made to her; and (d) she can infer nothing about a proposal's consequences from the composition or actions of study group members.

The median PL participant's optimal decision rule for voting on proposals in these circumstances is derived formally below, but the rule has a simple intuitive version: if the median PL participant likes the status quo, she should reject every Model 1 rule proposal that is made to her; if she dislikes the status quo, she should accept every such proposal that is made to her. The logic of this conclusion follows from the fact that the median PL participant knows her ideal point and the location of the status quo. Because she also knows the proposal space, she can make a (rough) estimate of the likelihood that she will prefer any particular proposal to the status quo. In particular, if the participant likes the status quo, then there is a fairly high probability that every meaningful reform proposal (that is, Model 1 rule) will make matters worse for her; hence, she should vote no. On the other hand, if the participant dislikes the status quo, then there is a fairly high probability that every meaningful reform proposal will make matters better for her; hence, she should vote yes. The strategy of voting no if one likes the status quo and yes otherwise we call the "uninformed decision rule." A PL that uses this rule thus will have a conservative bias if the median PL participant likes the status quo [. . .]

This degree of dissatisfaction does not seem to exist for the PLs we study. Observers often remark that the senior lawyers and judges who constitute such PLs as NCCUSL, the ALI, and the American Bar Association are unsympathetic to radical reform. This preference is as much institutional as personal. Significant reform requires a change in the underlying normative framework that supports the legal regime. The ALI's founding documents and NCCUSL's constitution, however, commit these PLs to reject controversial reform and to restrict themselves to "technical" improvements in the law. That commitment to incremental change implies that the median PL participant's ideal point lies near in policy space to the status quo. And this in turn makes the condition for voting yes hard to satisfy. As a consequence, these PLs tend to behave conservatively.

Finally, study groups anticipate this voting behavior. Hence, when a study group cannot credibly inform a PL about a proposal's location, its decision rule is as follows: (a) when the median PL participant's condition for voting yes is satisfied, propose the Model 1 rule that is the study group's ideal point; (b) when the condition is not satisfied, propose a Model 2 rule or no rule at all [. . .]

The Proposed Revisions to Article 2

[W]e predict that the original Article 2, as well as the current revisions, will contain many Model 2 rules. The effects of sales law do not fall systematically on any interest group-businesses and consumers are both buyers and sellers. Also, business parties conveniently can contract out of sales law rules that they dislike. Thus, sales law revisions will initially be proposed by reformer-dominated study groups; reformers are the only people interested enough to put in the time to alter the status quo.

Moreover, the ideal points of the reformers such as Karl Llewellyn, who drafted Article 2, were far from the ideal points of the ALI and NCCUSL members considering the UCC project, especially concerning such key issues as the appropriate scope of freedom of contract. Indeed, in the campaign to pass the UCC in the 1960s, William Schnader, a strong proponent of the Code, was hesitant to incorporate amendments suggested by the academic reformers because they represented views so far from the rank and file of the ALI and NCCUSL membership. When reformers dominate a study group and have ideal points that lie far from the ideal point of the median PL participant, we predict that the PL will adopt a large number of Model 2 rules whether information is symmetric or not.

There is an additional reason why Article 2 will have more vague rules than Articles 3, 4, and 9. Model 2 rules sometimes impose high compliance costs relative to Model 1 rules because it is difficult to know what a Model 2 rule requires. Interest groups sometimes can block the enactment of rules that would impose high compliance costs. The tack is to persuade uninvolved PL participants that passage of such a vague rule would adversely affect their reputation. A large majority of these participants will not derive direct economic benefits from the passage of any one proposal, nor do Model 2 rules produce results specific enough to advance a participant's policy preferences. Under these circumstances, an interest group sometimes can argue credibly that a particular Model 2 rule will create excessive uncertainty, so that support for the rule would be perceived as inconsistent with having good judgment. Such an argument is likely to be advanced in deliberations over Articles 3, 4, and 9, where cohesive interest groups dominate, but it is unlikely to be advanced in connection with Article 2 because the costs and benefits of sales law Model 2 rules are spread widely and shallowly. Hence, no group has an incentive to lobby in order to block them. Article 2, therefore, is more likely than Articles 3, 4, and 9 to have Model 2 rules.

The study group to revise Article 2 seems reformer-dominated. So far as it appears, no commercial interest group has lobbied to change the statute. Because academics were and are in charge, we predict that both the original Article 2 and the revisions will contain many vague rules. The former prediction is confirmed on the face of the statute. Almost everyone who has studied the subject agrees that the original Article 2 has many Model 2 rules.

A salient example of the continuing predominance of Model 2 rules in sales law can be found in the Article 2 Drafting Committee's approach to the issues of contract formation and enforceability. According to the Reporter of the Drafting Committee, the Committee "has preserved the original approach to contract formation and modification attributable to Karl N. Llewellyn.... This approach minimizes formality, but when necessary, expands rather than limits the opportunity to contract. The emphasis is upon flexible standards, mutual conduct, and the intention of the parties." Specific examples of the Model 2 rules that follow from this "emphasis" include proposals to repeal the Statute of Frauds requirement of section 2-201, to revise section 2-204(3) so as to link contractual obligation primarily to the existence of "a reasonably certain basis for giving an appropriate remedy," and the following proposed revision to section 2-207:

> Varying terms contained in the writings and other records of the parties do not become part of a contract unless the party claiming inclusion proves that the party against whom they operate (i) expressly agreed to such terms, or (ii) assented to such terms and had notice of them from trade usage, prior course of dealing or course of performance. Except between merchants, the burden of proof under this subsection is satisfied by clear and convincing evidence.

We also predict that reformer-dominated study groups will attempt to enlist interest group support and diffuse interest group opposition. The only groups that were possibly cohesive enough for the reformers to consider in connection with the Article 2 revisions were those that represented consumers. Representatives of consumer groups have been included in the drafting process.

Conclusion

Private law-making groups such as the ALI and NCCUSL have not received serious scrutiny. This is because their members are widely believed to be disinterested experts when they act on behalf of the group. This conventional view has led to a disjunction in academic commentary: ALI and NCCUSL products sometimes receive severe criticism while ALI and NCCUSL procedures are ignored. This disjunction is unfortunate because the procedures largely determine the products. In particular, theory suggests that a private legislature with a membership similar to that of the ALI and NCCUSL and procedures similar to theirs will have a strong status quo bias and sometimes will be captured by powerful interests.

In addition, the products of these private legislative processes will sometimes be characterized by vague and imprecise rules and other times by crude but precise bright-line rules. On its face this choice-of-rule form does not seem normatively objectionable. Precise (Model 1) rules are useful in some contexts, while vague (Model 2) rules delegating broad discretion to courts are useful in others. Our analysis shows, however, that groups such as the ALI and NCCUSL produce these rules in consequence of a particular institutional dynamic and not because of their intrinsic virtues as instruments for social control. We suggest that Model 1 rules result from the desire of a dominant interest group to preserve its victory in the legislative process (by confining the discretion of the rule applier) and not because they are socially desirable. On the other hand, Model 2 rules result, we believe, because reformers propose them when they are unable to get Model 1 rules enacted. The impressionistic data that we marshal is consistent with this theory.

Our analysis does not establish conclusively that the rules produced by the ordinary legislative process would be less driven by these institutional factors. We suspect, however, that typical legislatures perform well relative to PLs for two reasons. First, legislatures have mechanisms for agreement that permit normative debate to reach a resolution—a resolution that will be more clearly reflected in the resulting statutory product. Second, ordinary legislatures have mechanisms for finding facts that are unavailable to PLs, and are exposed to many more sources of information concerning the effects of the proposals that they consider. Truth is a likely corrective to outputs that are skewed by the process itself. In any event, our purpose in this Article is to advance a much more modest claim: whatever the relative merits of private and public legislative bodies, the complacency that has heretofore marked the academic attitude toward the private law-making groups is not warranted.

There are two lessons to draw from this. The first is that academic attention should focus on inputs as well as outputs: there should be more theory and more evidence relating to how private law-making groups function. It may be possible (we are dubious but far from certain) that PLs such as the ALI can be reformed. The second lesson is that the ALI and NCCUSL, at least provisionally, should no longer be immune from critical investigation. A concrete implication of this view is that debates about whether a subject is best regulated by a uniform law or a federal act should be influenced by a perception of how uniform laws are actually made. Because this Article makes strong claims about PLs, we close by noting our sympathy with the views of the founders of the ALI and NCCUSL. The founders intended their proposed organizations only to deal with issues that satisfied two "jurisdictional" requirements: first, that society had reached a consensus concerning the relevant values; and, second, that those values could be translated into laws solely with the use of traditional legal expertise. The organizations would perform poorly, the founders believed, were they instead to attempt the typically legislative tasks of harmonizing value conflict and regulating complex economic activity. This Article is evidence of the founders' wisdom.

Does Interest Group Theory Justify More Intrusive Judicial Review?*

EINER R. ELHAUGE

Those advocating more intrusive judicial review rarely address this comparative question. Instead the tendency is to emphasize the flaws of the political process and then assume without analysis that the litigation process will operate better. The litigation process plays the role of a deus ex machina that can correct the flaws that grip the other lawmaking branches but is apparently without flaw itself.

But the litigation process cannot be treated as exogenous to interest group theory: it too is susceptible to interest group influences. Under the analysis developed in Section I.A, individual members of groups that would benefit from favorable legal precedent have free rider incentives not to contribute toward the costs of establishing that precedent because they must share the benefits with other group members. Large diffuse groups unable to organize effective efforts to influence the political branches, where they at least have the advantage of more votes, are also likely to be unable to organize effective efforts to influence the litigation process. Accordingly, the same interest groups that have an organizational advantage in collecting resources to influence legislators and agencies generally also have an organizational advantage in collecting

* 101 YALE L. J. 31, 67–86 (1992).

resources to influence the courts. Increasing the lawmaking power of the courts may only exacerbate the influence of interest groups.

We thus need to examine whether there is any reason to believe that the litigation process is less susceptible to interest group influence than the political process, and whether any factors that make it less susceptible are likely to make it better at lawmaking. Although rarely delving directly into these comparative assessments, the literature taken as a whole suggests four reasons for having greater faith in the litigation process. First, some argue that the common law process of lawmaking allows the law to evolve toward efficiency. Second, class actions help groups overcome the free rider problem in litigation. Third, the adversarial structure of litigation guarantees that at least two viewpoints are represented. Finally, the litigation process is more insulated from political influence and thus from interest groups. I address each of those arguments in turn in the following sections. [. . .]

First articulated by Paul Rubin, the basic thrust of this evolutionary theory is that litigation challenges to inefficient precedents will be more frequent and skillful than challenges to efficient precedents. Assuming efficiency is defined as wealth maximization, those aggrieved by an inefficient rule suffer costs that, by definition, exceed the benefits to those who profit from the rule, and an inefficient rule imposes greater net costs than would a more efficient rule. Further, the theory notes, litigation is costly and will only be pursued to the extent that the benefits parties derive from litigation exceed its costs. Because the benefits from overturning a precedent are greater if the precedent is inefficient, parties are more likely to pursue litigation (to trial or on appeal) when it challenges inefficient precedents than when it challenges efficient precedents. For similar reasons, parties challenging inefficient precedents (or defending efficient ones) will tend to expend more resources than their opponents on making skillful legal arguments.

This difference in the frequency and skill of litigation will, evolutionary theory concludes, create a tendency for the law to evolve toward efficiency regardless of whether judges generally have the ability or the desire to make the law more efficient. Even if judges randomly decide which side wins in litigation, the increased frequency of litigated challenges to inefficient rules will make those rules more likely to be reexamined, and overruled, than efficient rules. And assuming judges respond favorably to skillful legal arguments, the generally greater skill of legal arguments for efficient rules will, on balance, give challenges to inefficient rules a higher probability of success than challenges to efficient rules. Thus, over time, and without any conscious design, the common law process of making law through litigation will tend to displace inefficient rules in favor of efficient ones.

However, as may already be evident, this analysis faces serious problems under interest group theory. Namely, as Paul Rubin himself has come to acknowledge, the collective action problems described by interest group theory undermine evolutionary theory's premise that those with the greater economic interest will invest in more frequent and skillful litigation. Just as with laws enacted by statute or regulation, so too laws (or precedents) adopted through adjudication tend to confer benefits on a class of persons, whether or not they contribute to efforts to get that law adopted. This creates the same free rider problems that face groups in petitioning political actors; the groups that enjoy organizational advantages in collecting resources to petition the political branches should also enjoy the same advantages in collecting resources to petition the courts. Groups that are less susceptible to free rider problems, or better able to curb them, should fund more frequent and more skillful litigation than their counterparts.

Thus, far from explaining why the litigation process should be less susceptible to interest group influence than the political process, evolutionary theory explains the very mechanisms by which interest groups are likely to exert their "disproportionate" influence over the litigation process. This suggests not only that the litigation process is susceptible to interest group influence, but that increasing the lawmaking power of courts will simply encourage interest groups to invest more resources in litigation and thus exacerbate their influence over the litigation process.

Moreover, to the extent it has force, evolutionary analysis could just as well be applied to the political process. Inefficient statutory and regulatory rules, like inefficient common law rules, confer fewer benefits and impose greater costs than do efficient rules. Parties aggrieved by an inefficient statute or regulation thus gain more from its repeal or nonenactment than their opponents gain from its retention or enactment. Parties who profit from an efficient statute or regulation gain more from its retention or enactment than their opponents gain from its repeal or nonenactment. Applying the same analysis, one might thus expect that efforts to repeal or block inefficient statutes or regulations (and efforts to retain or enact efficient statutes or regulations) will be more frequent and successful than counterefforts. If so, statutes and regulations will also tend to evolve toward efficiency. And, in fact, the literature arguing that the common law tends to evolve toward efficiency has a parallel in the statutory and regulatory world: Gary Becker's work arguing that, in the political arena, competition among interest groups will tend to lead to efficient laws.

In both the judicial and political processes, a mixed picture is more accurate. Where efficient rules benefit organized groups at the expense of less organized groups, those rules are likely to become law in either forum. Where inefficient laws benefit organized groups at the expense of disorganized groups, the result is more uncertain. Sometimes the increased frequency and intensity of petitioning associated with better organization will exceed the increased frequency and intensity associated with opposition to inefficient laws. Sometimes the opposite will hold true. In any event, evolutionary theory provides no reason to believe that any disproportionate influence associated with better organization will be more pronounced in the political process than in the litigation process. [. . .]

Adversarial Structure

Another argument for why the litigation process is less susceptible to interest group influence relies on the adversarial structure of litigation. Because of this structure, at least two opposing views are represented in every litigated case. Thus, unlike legislators and agencies, judges generally do not make law having only heard the arguments supporting the resulting law.

This is an important advantage of the litigation process. Unfortunately, it does not offset an interest group's ability to exercise any disproportionate influence it has. Small intensely interested groups are still likely to spend more on their litigation efforts than any large diffuse groups opposing them. They will on balance be able to hire more skilled lawyers and thus have more influence on the information presented to the court about the social desirability of the parties' conduct and any legal rule under consideration. And, as Section III.A suggests, the very fact that they can fund more frequent litigation will ultimately tend to lead to more decisions favoring small intensely interested groups.

Moreover, the adversarial structure has offsetting disadvantages. First, courts generally only hear (or pay attention to) the arguments of the actual litigants. Other persons interested in the precedential implications of the case, but not in the judgment itself, generally lack standing and receive inadequate consideration. Nor, assuming there are more possible policy positions or legal rules than there are litigants, will the courts necessarily be presented with the full array of policy arguments and regulatory options. Each party may argue only for the policy or rule that is best for it; none may argue for the policy or rule that is best for society. [. . .]

A second, and related, problem is that courts tend to underweigh, or be underinformed about, the systemic and prospective consequences of their decisions because they focus on the particular parties and adjudicated historical facts before them. A trial record usually reveals less about the social and economic consequences of the court's possible decision than does the information presented to legislatures or administrative agencies. Even if a court is informed about the systemic effects on unnamed persons, those effects are unlikely to carry an emotional impact proportional to the plight of the identified human beings who will be bound by the court's judgment. Legislators and regulatory rulemakers, on the other hand, deal in systemic effects, and are less likely to be distracted by the idiosyncratic situations of particular persons.

The adversarial structure of litigation also creates a third serious problem: it permits parties to settle strategically in cases where the type of judge or set of facts seems likely to lead to unfavorable precedent. A trade association seeking a favorable regulatory ruling may, for example, choose to settle a case if it gets assigned to a judge hostile to regulation. Or the trade association may be willing to refrain from appealing contrary judgments until it has a good "test case" where the facts seem particularly sympathetic. More recently, some courts have even allowed parties to vacate unfavorable precedent through post-judgment settlements.

Small intensely interested groups will be better positioned to pursue a policy of molding precedent through strategic settlement. Such groups are repeat players with a relatively large stake in the value of setting precedent and a relatively low stake in how an individual case comes out. Large diffusely interested groups will be harder pressed to collect the funds necessary to pay off litigants bringing worrisome cases. And isolated individuals, even if intensely interested in their case, have little interest in precedent and thus a strong incentive to accept any settlement favorable in the case at hand.

In the political process, a policy of strategic settlement is, on the whole, harder to implement. An interest group cannot usually expect that settling with opposing petitioners will vacate unfavorable legislation or regulation; nor can a group normally hope that, by settling today, an issue will get assigned to a different legislature or agency next time. Moreover, action taken by a legislature or agency is typically not targeted at specific individuals. This makes it both less likely that selective settlement will focus lawmakers on a more favorable set of facts and more difficult to pay off all the persons who might object to the lawmakers' actions. One can think of exceptions to these general tendencies, but for our purposes it is not necessary to show that the political process is immune from strategic settlement, just that it is less susceptible than the litigation process.

In sum, the adversarial structure of litigation has offsetting advantages and disadvantages. Litigation guarantees that any decision takes into account at least two views and a particular factual situation, and that parties control the settlement of their own disputes. But litigation also means that decisions fail to consider the full range of views and societal facts, and that settlements do not reflect the entire spectrum of considerations. Litigation is thus likely to be more desirable where it is highly important to focus on the views, factual situations, and interests of a limited number of persons, and less important to have other views, facts, and interests fully represented. Or, to put the matter in more familiar terms, the adversarial structure of litigation generally makes it better suited for the adjudication of fact-specific disputes than for general rulemaking.

Political Insulation

Perhaps the most seriously pressed interest group argument for why judges make superior lawmakers is that they are insulated from political influence. Richard Posner, for example, stresses that judges have life tenure, that their salaries cannot be reduced, and that procedural rules limit the standing and ex parte contact of interest groups. Because this general political insulation also shields judges from interest group pressure, judges are better able than legislators to fashion wise policy.

The political insulation of judges, however, does not insure the insulation of the litigation process from interest group influence. Under the mechanisms already discussed, organized interest groups will still be able to litigate more frequently, to influence better the information tribunals receive, and to settle strategically cases that may produce unfavorable precedents. These methods do not require that the judge sympathize with any particular view; they depend solely on parties' (differential) decisions about when to litigate, what resources to devote to litigation, and when to settle.

In fact, these methods seem more effective for influencing courts than other lawmakers. Unlike courts, legislators and regulators do not have their lawmaking power triggered by party action: they can initiate lawmaking on their own and are not forced to make a decision when a party petitions. Legislators and agencies also usually have far more resources to conduct their own investigations, whereas courts must generally rely on the information the parties present to them. Further, whereas in the political process the organizational advantages of small groups are somewhat offset by the greater votes of large groups, no such offset exists in the litigation process.

Nonetheless, one might conclude that these disadvantages of litigation are not only reduced, but outweighed, by the greater political insulation of judges. This conclusion, however, faces two main difficulties, which the following sections discuss in turn. First, interest groups can influence judicial appointments and are more likely to do so if we convert judges into more general regulators by expanding judicial review. Second, interest group theory does nothing to demonstrate that greater political insulation is desirable. [. . .]

Interest Group Theory Does Not Show Political Insulation Is Desirable

This is not the place for an extended discussion of the benefits and dangers of politically insulated judicial review. Fortunately, an extended discussion is unnecessary because the issue here is whether interest group theory provides any affirmative reason to regard political insulation as desirable, not whether political insulation is desirable for other reasons.

In answering this more limited question, we must remember that the critical bite of interest group theory comes from its claim that the political process inaccurately reflects the will of the polity. The theory demonstrates that groups' structures affect their political influence in a way that can, under some normative baselines, distort how the political process aggregates the affected social interests or otherwise defines the public interest. In particular, the theory demonstrates that the political process can produce outcomes harmful to the majority, a result that is undesirable under a (crude) majoritarian baseline.

But this critique provides no reason to prefer lawmaking insulated from political pressure, for such insulation shields lawmakers not only from interest groups but from the rest of the polity as well. This insulated lawmaking can produce even worse distortions and results that even more antimajoritarian. While the political process may disproportionately reflect the views of minority groups, an insulated judicial process can disproportionately reflect the views of single individuals- namely the views of judges who may make no effort to represent the views or interests of the polity. Even if judges do try to represent the polity, the very unresponsiveness to, and unfamiliarity with, the affected interests that creates political insulation also makes judges more likely to err in assessing, canvassing, weighing, or maximizing the affected interests. As inaccurate as the political process may be in reflecting the will of the polity, there is no reason to believe it is less accurate than judicial lawmaking. [. . .]

If politically insulated lawmaking does not represent the polity, and we put aside its potential for developing fundamental principles, what sort of predictions does interest group theory suggest about insulated lawmaking? Within the paradigm of interest group theory, it seems that consistency requires ascribing some sort of self-centered motivation to judges. This is not, of course, to deny that judges have more altruistic motivations, but interest group theory cannot consistently assume that all legislators act solely out of self-interest but that judges do not. The theory must employ the same behavioral assumption across the board.

Some suggest that judges seek to expand their own power. It is hard to see why this should be expected to improve decisionmaking. In specific cases, the motive to expand judicial power would often lead to undesirable results. More generally, the judicial power expansion likely to result from such a motive appears unlikely to be desirable unless we have some independent reason for believing judicial lawmaking is better than political lawmaking.

Other possible public choice theories are that judges seek to maximize their salaries, their budgets, or their jurisdiction by pleasing legislators. A Congress displeased with judicial decisions might effectively reduce judicial salaries by refusing to adjust for inflation, might make insufficient appropriations for judicial support staff, or might dilute judicial power by expanding the number of judgeships or shrinking a court's jurisdiction. But such methods of legislative retaliation are unlikely to be effective because they are not selective: they cannot punish the judges or judicial activity that the legislature dislikes without also punishing the judges and judicial activity that the legislature likes. And individually, each judge will conclude that the likelihood of her decision provoking a favorable or unfavorable legislative response is low. It is thus not surprising that historically there is little connection between judicial decisions and legislative action on judicial pay and jurisdiction. In any event, to the extent these motives do operate, they suggest judges are unlikely to be better decisionmakers than the legislatures they seek to please.

Another hypothesis is that courts seek the approval of lawyers and legal academics. To the extent this is true, courts are accountable, but to a rather narrow segment of society. This creates its own distortion because lawyers and legal academics hardly represent a cross section of the polity. Moreover, interest groups who realize where the real power lies can exert influence on the bar or the academy through hiring and foundation grants. In any event, judges are unlikely to care about the approval of lawyers and academics unless they already share the judge's political leanings: a conservative judge will not be swayed (and will probably be relieved) if her decision has been critiqued by a leftist law professor, and a radical judge will not lose much sleep if his decision garners the disapproval of the corporate bar.

NOTES

1. The costs and benefits of uniform laws. The objective of the NCCUSL is to promote uniform state laws. Ribstein and Kobayashi assert that there is a public interest case for such laws arising from the inefficiencies that obtain where contracting parties in different states are subject to different laws. These include inconsistency costs (e.g. exposing a manufacturer that sells its product nationally to many different product liability design standards), information costs (e.g. determining which law applies between parties from different states), and litigation costs (e.g. trivializing otherwise difficult choice-of-law issues). However, they also identify certain costs to uniformity, such as exit costs (the ability of people of firms to exit jurisdictions whose laws they do not prefer), reducing innovation and experimentation (a decentralized lawmaking process may produce at least some laws that are better than what a single uniform lawmaker could write), and reducing local variation (some laws might be "better" in a particular locality.) See Larry E. Ribstein and Bruce H. Kobayashi, *An Economic Analysis of Uniform State Laws*, 25 J. Legal Studies 131, 138–141 (1996).

The alternative to uniform, or harmonized, laws is a regime in which each jurisdiction chooses its laws separately, or noncooperatively. The choice between the two approaches is well known to corporate law academics, who have debated the substantive benefits of jurisdictional competition for corporate charters. One camp argues that states attract corporations by offering the most efficient set of rules (the "race to the top"). See, e.g., Roberta Romano, *Law as a Product: Some Pieces of the Incorporation Puzzle*, 1 J. Law, Econ. & Org. 21 (1985); William J. Carney, *The Production of Corporate Law*, 71 S. Cal. L. Rev. 715 (1998); Roberta Romano, *The Genius of American Corporate Law* (1993); Ronald J. Daniels, *Should Provinces Compete?: The Case for a Competitive Corporate Law Market*, 36 McGill L. J. 130 (1993). Another camp argues that jurisdictional diversity stimulates a rent-seeking "race to the bottom" by corporate managers searching for corporate law rules that permit managerial entrenchment. See, e.g., Lucian Bebchuk, *Federalism and the Corporation: The Desirable Limits on State Competition in Corporate Law*, 105 Harv. L. Rev. 1435 (1992); Lucian Bebchuk and Allen Farrell, *Federalism and Takeover Law: The Race to Protect Managers from Takeovers*, NBER Working Paper 7232 (July 1999). The debate is discussed in Robert Romano, ed., *Foundations of Corporate Law* ch. 3A (1993).

2.   Schwartz–Scott's predictions for UCC terms. In another part of their article, Schwartz and Scott apply their theory to the different kinds of provisions found in the various articles of the UCC. (See Schwartz & Scott, *Political Economy* at 637–650.) This analysis leads them to advance three predictions. The first prediction is that, in the absence of influence from outside interest groups, these private legislative bodies will tend to promulgate many standards that delegate substantial discretion to courts. Such rules result not solely because of their intrinsic merits but because law reform projects of this sort are dominated by academic reformers with preferences that are typically far different from those of the median member of the legislative body. The reformers propose standards when they are unable to get clear, bright-line rules adopted. Is there any evidence to support this first prediction? The original Article 2 project was, in fact, dominated by Karl Llewellyn and a cohort of fellow reformers, and their political preferences were far from those of the ALI and NCCUSL members who were considering the U.C.C. during the 1940s and 1950s. Moreover, the original Article 2 is famous for its many open-ended, undefined terms. The use of generalized guides to decision such as custom and usage as well as open-ended standards (such as reasonableness, good faith, and unconscionability) necessarily requires subsequent adjudication to give content to the parties obligations in particular cases.

Their second prediction is that, when interest groups compete, the strong institutional bias of these private legislatures to behave conservatively will be reinforced. Cohesive interest groups are able successfully to block the proposals of the groups they oppose but are unable to get their own proposals enacted. The noise resulting from their competition leads the private legislature to reject any significant reform in favor of the status quo. Can this prediction be supported? The current attempts to revise Article 2 might be seen as some support for this second claim. Indeed, as the unsuccessful efforts to strip Article 2 of controversy over the past two years have shown, a strong enough status quo bias can induce rejection of even apparently innocuous proposals.

Their third prediction may be relevant to understanding Articles 3, 4 and 9. The third claim is that where there is only one interest group that is dominant in the law reform process, the private legislature will generate proposals with many bright-line, clear rules. These rules will result not solely from their inherent merits but because they confine the discretion of courts and thus preserve the victory of the interest group in the legislative process. You should keep this prediction in mind and assess its validity as you analyze the materials in Chapters 4, 5 and 6 infra.

3.   Alternative explanations for the rule form in Article 2. As noted above, Schwartz and Scott argue that the standards in Article 2 of the UCC can be explained by the absence of the strong influence from interest groups. Might there be other reasons for the rule form in the UCC other than the influence of interest groups? Section 2.2, above, discussed the relative merits of rules and standards under different circumstances, suggesting reasons why standards in Article 2 may be efficient. Article 2 covers a wide range of contexts and parties and, as noted in the previous section, default standards may be sensible in light of the heterogeneity. Moreover, many parties contract explicitly for standards: see, for example, the common use of "best efforts" or "reasonable efforts" clauses. If there are good reasons for parties to agree to such terms in their contracts, then perhaps the use of vague terms as defaults reflects efforts to mirror party preferences rather than a response to interest group activity. For discussion see George G. Triantis, *The Efficiency of Vague Contract Terms: A Response to the Schwartz–Scott Theory of U.C.C. Article 2*, 62 La. L. Rev. 1065, 1071–72 (2002); Albert Choi and George G. Triantis, *Completing Contracts in the Shadow of Costly Verification*, 37 J. Legal Stud. 503 (2008).

The Notes in Chapter 6.6 address the Schwartz–Scott claim that the bright line rules in Article 9, which appear to favor financial institutions, are the product of that industry's lobbying group pressure within the private legislature.

4.   Who should make the rules? In light of Scott and Schwartz' concerns about the lawmaking of private bodies such as the ALI and NCCUSL, should commercial law defaults be designed by the courts, by administrative bodies or the legislatures themselves (without the help of academics!). Which institution would be superior? In the excerpt above, Professor Elhauge points out that the court system has its own problems. Avery Katz argues that PL outcomes are more likely to be efficient than public legislatures. Avery Wiener Katz, *The Economics of Form and Substance in Contract Interpretation*, 104 Colum. L. Rev. 496 (2004). And, administrative agencies are susceptible to well known regulatory capture.

A related, narrower question is the degree to which each institution (private legislature, legislature, court or regulatory agency) may be biased toward enacting standards rather than rules, or vice versa. In the context of corporate law, Professors Kahan and Kamar argue that Delaware courts use standards more frequently than the Model Business Corporations Act, despite the fact that corporate lawyers provide the driving lawmaking force behind each. Marcel Kahan and Ehud Kamar, *The Myth of State Competition in Corporate Law*, 55 Stan. L. Rev. 679 (2002); Marcel Kahan and Ehud Kamar, *Price Discrimination in the Market for Corporate Law*, 86 Cornell L. Rev. 1205 (2001).

5. The political economy of the choice between generally applicable and specific rules. The various concerns about the lawmaking process also bear on the choice between standards and rules, as noted in the previous section. It also has implications for the choice between general and specific rules governing transactions. Consider the following comment by Professors Mahoney and Sanchirico:

> Because decision makers are typically less informed about the social and private costs and benefits of a legal rule than are the agents subject to the rule, they inevitably rely on information provided by the regulated entities and others whose welfare is affected by the regulated activity to determine how best to regulate. Individuals affected by the decision maker's choice of rule, then, have an incentive to influence that choice ... Those who have the most at stake—the individuals who engage in an activity and bear the cost of care—may influence the decision to the exclusion of other parties who are affected, but not as much. This tendency can be overcome, however, by the decision maker's announcement that he intends to adopt a single rule to govern all activities. This induces all regulated actors to moderate their influence, recognizing that in aggregate they may lose as much from a reduction in care levels for all activities as they gain from the reduction in care level from their own activity.
>
> When an individual produces some product or service and consumes others, he would prefer not to internalize the social costs of his activity, but for all other producers to do so. When his activity is governed by its own unique rule, the producer may lobby for a rule that imposes minimal cost on the activity. However, when rules are applied to all activities, the would-be lobbyist must consider both the costs of regulating his own activity and the benefits of regulating others'. ... [N]arrowly-tailored rules will tend to be biased in favor of the interests of the party with the largest stake. A broadly-applicable rule, by contrast, does not suffer from bias but can diverge substantially from the social optimum for any particular activity.

Paul G. Mahoney and Chris William Sanchirico, *General and Specific Legal Rules,* 161 J. Inst. & Theor. Econ. 329, 330–1 (2005).

2.4   Incorporation of Industry Practice

Courts under the UCC, consistent with its institutional design, have interpreted the meaning of express terms in a contract by looking to the commercial and legal context to determine whether to incorporate custom and usage as default rules. The Code reverses the common law presumption that the parties' writing and the official law of contracts are the definitive elements of the agreement. Evidence derived from context, including commercial experience and practice, will, under the Code scheme, trigger the incorporation of additional, implied terms. Indeed, the parol evidence rule under the Code admits inferences from

trade usage, prior dealings and course of performance even if the express
terms of the contract seem perfectly clear and are apparently "integrated" (§ 2–202). This result follows from the liberalization of the parol
evidence rule under the Code, the abandonment of the plain meaning
rule, and the further direction to courts to construe express terms and
the commercial context as consistent with each other (§ 1–303(4)). While
this last presumption is limited by the corollary that inconsistent usages
and experiences should give way to express contractual language, courts
have frequently abandoned this principle on the grounds that there is
almost always some contextual argument upon which seemingly inconsistent terms can be rationalized. In practice, therefore, the presumption
of consistency in the Code, coupled with the expansive definition of
"agreement", has placed a considerable additional burden on parties
seeking to opt out of either the legally-supplied defaults or of the
commercial context. The verifiable express terms of a relational contract
are frequently construed as conditioned on the broader contractual
context. Whatever benefits this practice may provide in incorporating
commercial context as tailored default terms, it clearly results in less
predictable interpretation of express contractual language.

But has activist, contextual interpretation under the Code at least
promoted the useful incorporation the immanent norms of industry
practice? Robert Scott's study of the litigated cases under Article 2
reveals that, while the Code was explicitly designed to incorporate
evolving norms and customs into an ever growing set of trade-specific
default rules, incorporation as such has not occurred. Robert Scott, *The
Uniformity Norm in Commercial Law*, in THE JURISPRUDENTIAL FOUNDA-
TIONS OF COMMERCIAL LAW at 165–7 (2000). To be sure, courts have
interpreted many disputed contracts where context evidence has been
evaluated along side the written terms of the contract. But while these
decisions affirm the institutional bias toward contextualizing the contract, the fact-specific nature of the contract dispute leaves, in virtually
every case, little opportunity for subsequent incorporation as default
terms suitable for other contracting parties.

It is not surprising that litigation over the meaning of the contract
does not provide occasions for incorporating commercial context. These
cases typically arise as disputes over the meaning of particular express
terms and particular usages and provide little opportunity for announc-
ing generalizable rules whether from an ex ante or an ex post perspective. The vehicle for this latter aspect of the incorporation project, in
Llewellyn's mind, was the pervasive direction to courts (a direction
found in a majority of the specific provisions of Article 2) to apply the
Code provision in question according to the norm of commercial reasonableness. Commercial reasonableness is perhaps the most significant and
innovative of the admonitory concepts in the Code. Commercial reasonableness is not defined in the Code, but appears prominently in numerous contexts. For example, the Code requires that all "contracts made by

a merchant have incorporated in them the explicit standard not only of honesty in fact but also of observance by the merchant of reasonable commercial standards of fair dealing in the trade" (§ 1–203 comment). The notion of commercial reasonableness reflects the legal realists' belief that the law can be (and is) revealed by the behavior and practices of commercial parties. Thus, the admonition to act in a commercially reasonable manner functions for courts as an empirical directive: to decide if the parties have acted in a commercially reasonable manner, the decision maker is asked to look to the marketplace and observe relevant commercial behavior to determine the legal norm.

But this exercise, too, appears to have failed in implementation. An examination of the litigated cases interpreting the Code's "reasonableness" standards shows that courts have consistently interpreted these statutory instructions not as directions to incorporate actual commercial practices and customs but rather as invitations to create broad standards based on "Code policy" or other non-contextual criteria. For whatever reason, courts charged with the responsibility of implementing the Code's activist policy towards incorporation have declined to enhance the supply of useful defaults for appropriate subsets of commercial contractors.

The experience of judicial enforcement of commercial services contracts under the common law over the same thirty year period differs from the litigation under the Code. The interpretive methodology of the common law has stubbornly resisted the contextual modes of interpretation adopted by the Code. A strong majority of jurisdictions continue to adhere to a textualist interpretation of commercial service contracts, primarily through rigorous adherence to the plain meaning rule. Thus, most courts called upon to interpret commercial services contracts under the common law rules have been unwilling to engage in contextualization. But the past thirty years has nonetheless seen the development of a menu of legally recognized, standardized terms and conventions that are useful to parties in specific service industries. Standardization of express terms has been stimulated in construction contracting, for example, through the offices of key intermediaries such as the American Institute of Architects and the Associated General Contractors. These two trade organizations have each produced model contractual terms that define the contractual obligations and risks associated with construction contracts. Subsequently, courts have interpreted key provisions of the newly proposed standard form terms, and, through the process of common law adjudication, these industry-wide prototypes have received legal recognition.

One might argue, therefore, that the common law interpretive process has led to a greater degree of predictability in the interpretation of trade-specific contractual language and an increase in the supply of appropriately tailored default terms that can be used by members of the commercial sub-group. In the case of common law commercial contract adjudication, the incorporation process does not rely on a one-step, self-conscious incorporation of the commercial context by a court. Rather, the common law incorporation mechanism involves two steps. First, the relevant industry or commercial sub-group promulgates standard forms to respond to contracting problems peculiar to the industry. Thereafter, those forms are incorporated into the legal vocabulary as additions to the menu of contractual prototypes among which parties within that industry are then free to choose. These model or standard forms thus provide an effective mechanism for internalizing at least some of the benefits from contractual innovation and standardization that private parties may otherwise be unable to capture. By contrast, a similar set of standardized options have been slower to develop under Article 2 of the UCC. In sum, while much of the evidence is anecdotal, it points to a contrast in outcomes between Code and common law regimes. The following excerpts consider in more detail the question of whether the costs of a contextualized approach to interpretation are offset by corresponding gains in the efficient incorporation of industry-specific default terms.

Merchant Law in a Merchant Court: Rethinking the Code's Search for Immanent Business Norms*
LISA BERNSTEIN

This Article challenges the idea that courts should seek to discover and apply immanent business norms in deciding cases. It demonstrates that while the drafters of the Code sought to incorporate these norms into the law in an effort to make commercial law more responsive to and reflective of commercial reality, they failed to recognize that this approach would fundamentally alter the very reality they sought to reflect, and would do so in ways that would have undesirable effects on commercial relationships and would undermine the Code's own stated goals of promoting flexibility in commercial transactions and "permit[ting] the continued expansion of commercial practices through custom, usage and agreement of the parties."

In the spirit of the Code and Karl Llewellyn, this Article begins by looking at merchant practice. It presents a case study of the private legal system created by the National Grain and Feed Association ("NGFA") to resolve contract disputes among its members [. . .]

The study pays especially close attention to the willingness of NGFA's industry-expert adjudicators to take trade usage, course of dealing, and course of performance into account in deciding cases. It finds that despite their industry expertise, NGFA arbitrators are reluctant to look to these indicia of immanent business norms. Unlike courts, which often permit course of dealing, course of performance, and usage

---

* 144 U. Pa. L. Rev. 1765 (1996).

of trade to trump express written terms, NGFA arbitrators take a formalistic approach to adjudication. They do not permit these considerations to vary either trade rules or written contractual provisions. This Article develops a theory to explain why sophisticated merchant-transactors might find NGFA's approach to adjudication preferable to the Code's approach, and then draws on it to analyze the effects of the Code's adjudicative approach on commercial relationships.

The NGFA System

The NGFA is a trade association of firms and individuals who are active in the cash-markets for grain and feed. It began arbitrating disputes in 1896 and has been publishing written arbitration opinions since 1902. As a condition of membership in the Association, members must agree to submit all disputes with other members to the Association's arbitration system. A member who refuses to submit to arbitration or fails to comply with an arbitration award rendered against him may, in addition to having his actions reported in the NGFA newsletter, be suspended or expelled from the Association.

The NGFA has adopted four sets of substantive trade rules that are designed to "reflect trade practice and facilitate trade between NGFA members." The Grain Rules and the Feed Rules each cover the basics of contract formation, performance, repudiation, breach, damages, and excuse. The Barge Rules supplement these rules whenever "shipments are designated by contract to be transported by barge," and the Barge Freight Trading Rules "govern all disputes [involving] ... the purchase and/or sale of barge transportation." Unless they have been explicitly altered or excluded by a specific contractual provision, these rules govern all contracts between NGFA members. Together, they provide a comprehensive set of default rules governing the most important aspects of cash-market transactions in grain or feed.

The trade rules are supplemented by a highly detailed set of arbitration rules, whose applicability to disputes between NGFA members cannot be altered by contract. These rules set out the required filing fee, the guidelines for the selection of arbitrators, the types of information each party must provide to the tribunal, the procedures for requesting an oral hearing, the type of information the arbitrators should include in their written opinions, and the procedures for filing and conducting an intra-association appeal. They include a one-year statute of limitations. Under the trade rules, the time from filing to judgment is supposed to be less than six months.

The typical cash-market transaction in grain or feed that is governed by these rules is negotiated on the telephone, sometimes with the assistance of a broker, and is promptly confirmed through the exchange of written, largely standard-form, confirmatory memoranda. The most common issues arbitrated are those that NGFA classifies as dealing with confirmations, custom of the trade, grades, failure to deliver, and weight. Arbitrated disputes over unforeseen contingencies are rare. Claims of commercial impracticability are infrequently raised and almost never successful.

In deciding cases, the NGFA arbitrators take a formalistic approach to adjudication; they consistently refuse to look behind the letter of a trade rule to discern and take into account the type of behavior that the rule is intended to encourage or discourage. The trade rules do not contain an explicit equivalent of the Code's broad duty of good faith. Although the term "good faith" occasionally appears in NGFA opinions and is sometimes used to signal the arbitrators' view of the propriety of a party's commercial behavior, or to provide additional support for a result reached on other grounds, violation of a general duty of good faith is never the explicit basis of the arbitrators' decision. In a recent case, NGFA held that acting in accordance with the trade rules and the terms of the written contract is per se acting in "good faith."

NGFA arbitrators follow a strict hierarchy of authority, derived from both the trade rules and prior arbitration decisions. As one opinion explained, the arbitrators' first responsibility was to enforce the terms of the contract. When the contract terms are insufficient on their own to decide the case, arbitrators are to rely next upon the Trade Rules, and thirdly, trade practice. Reliance upon the Uniform Commercial Code or any other statutory basis usually comes only after the first three sources have proved insufficient.

In practice NGFA arbitrators rarely look to the Code or other legal sources in deciding cases [...]

Usage of Trade

A review of all the NGFA opinions in which custom or usage of trade was at issue between 1975 and 1995 suggests that NGFA arbitrators adhere strictly to the Association's stated hierarchy of authority. The NGFA tribunal does not permit unwritten customs and usages of trade to vary or qualify the meaning of either trade rules or explicit contractual provisions. Arbitrators use custom to decide cases only when both the trade rules and the contract are silent. Yet even when looking to custom to fill a true contractual gap, the arbitrators often signal their distaste for this type of adjudication by admonishing the parties that the dispute might well have been avoided had they written a sufficiently specific contract. When custom conflicts with a trade rule or an explicit contractual provision, the arbitrators decide the case on the basis of the trade rule or the contractual provision even when they are convinced that the custom both exists and was known by the parties [...]

The Code's Adjudicative Approach

On a formal level, the Code's hierarchy of authority is similar to NGFA's. The Code accords the greatest weight to "express terms of an agreement," followed by course of performance, course of dealing, usage of trade, and, finally, the Code's own gap-fillers. In practice, however, unlike NGFA arbitrators, courts, in a variety of doctrinal guises that are either explicitly or implicitly authorized by the Code, often allow these considerations to vary or trump the express terms of a written contract. In some instances these considerations are permitted to take precedence over express terms on the grounds that they do not contradict, but rather clarify, qualify, or supplement, the express terms of the written agreement. In other instances, such as where the contract's express provisions are silent on an issue or the agreement itself was formed through a course of performance, these considerations are sometimes found to supply additional contractual provisions. In addition, they are frequently introduced to establish an industry-specific meaning of a word or phrase that may or may not have a clear lay meaning. The industry-specific meaning is then given precedence over the lay meaning. Finally, because the Code provides that "course of performance shall be relevant to show a waiver or modification of any term inconsistent with such course of performance," course of performance may have the effect of removing an express written term from an agreement [. . .]

The Theory of Legally Unenforceable Agreements

In order to understand why sophisticated merchant-transactors might find a NGFA-type adjudicative philosophy desirable, it is useful to focus on an observation that has been documented in the law and society literature, namely that the contours of transactors' contracting relationship may not be the same as the scope of the rights and duties memorialized in their written, legally enforceable contract. In many contexts, transactors accept late payment, vary quantity terms, assume new obligations, waive covenants, and adjust prices in ways that their written contracts do not require. They may be moved to do so by social norms, commercial custom, a "concern for relationships, trust, honor and decency," or fear of nonlegal sanctions such as reputational damage or termination of a beneficial relationship. In some instances, these actions may be responses to new circumstances, while in others they may reflect transactors' decisions to abide by the extralegal commitments that supplement their written contracts [. . .]

Transactors may [. . .] fail to include written provisions dealing with a particular contingency because each may fear that the other will interpret a suggestion that they do so as a signal that the transactor proposing the provisions is unusually litigious or likely to resist flexible adjustment of the relationship if circumstances change. These potential relational costs of proposing additional explicit provisions may result in aspects of a contracting relationship being allocated to the extralegal realm, particularly in contexts where the post-contract-formation relationship between the transactors is highly relational in nature so that transactors' perceptions of the value of the transaction will be strongly affected by the attitudinal signals sent during pre-contractual negotiation.

Another reason that transactors may allocate aspects of their relationship to the extralegal realm is that the legal system costs of including a provision in their contract are too high. Legal system costs are those costs that arise from the fact that litigation is costly, prone to delay, and subject to judicial error. In computer software markets, for example, legal system costs are an important reason that both manufacturers and consumers may be better off if shrink-wrap agreements disclaim all warranties and state that no licenses will be granted, but manufacturers promise, in some legally unenforceable way, to fix defective products and grant licenses where appropriate [. . .] As a consequence, both manufacturers and consumers may prefer lower-priced software with broad disclaimers and the manufacturer's extralegal, reputation-bond-backed promise to grant licenses and repair products in appropriate circumstances to higher-priced software with detailed, legally enforceable warranty and license provisions [. . .]

At the outset of a contracting relationship, a transactor may not know if the person with whom he is dealing is trustworthy. Although he would find it ideal to include two sets of written provisions, one that would apply if the transactor turned out to be trustworthy and another if he turned out to be untrustworthy, trustworthiness is not something the contract can condition on because it is unverifiable. As a consequence, the transactor may find it desirable to include terms in the contract that are the best terms if the other transactor turns out to be untrustworthy, while making extralegal commitments, many of which will, over time, ripen into self-enforcing agreements that will govern the relationship if the other party turns out to be trustworthy. In these transactional contexts, the written contract functions as a "bond," while the extralegal relational agreement provides the terms of the contract-governance structure.

Thus, while the Code's adjudicative approach is based on the idea that "the course of actual performance by the parties is considered the best indication of what they intended the[ir] writing to mean," there are a number of reasons that rational transactors may prefer to act or agree to act in ways that they know are different from the rights and obligations memorialized in their written legally enforceable contract. It is therefore important to reconsider the desirability of the Code's definition of agreement by exploring its effects on commercial relationships under the more realistic assumption that there is no necessary relationship between transactors' actions and the intended meaning of the terms of their written contract.

The Code's definition of agreement may impose an efficiency loss on transactors relative to a NGFA-type system that systematically refuses to enforce extralegal agreements. By elevating usage of trade, course of dealing, and course of performance to the status of legally enforceable contract provisions, and commercial context to the status of an over-arching interpretive framework, the Code brings a substantial portion of the extralegal realm of contractual relationships within the purview of legal enforceability. This makes it difficult, if not impossible, for trans-actors to enter into purely extralegal agreements. If transactors rational-ly prefer to structure their transaction to include a combination of legal and extralegal obligations, but the Code prevents them from entering into purely extralegal agreements, transactors will be unable to select their preferred mix of legal and extralegal terms. They may therefore be worse off than they would be in a NGFA-type system [. . .]

Trade Usage, Course of Performance, and Course of Dealing

When courts apply the Code's trade usage provision and look at how a majority of market transactors deal with an issue, or apply the course of dealing or course of performance provisions and look at how particular transactors have dealt with an issue, they will, in many instances, be observing the norms that transactors choose to follow when they cooper-atively resolve disputes among themselves and want to preserve their relationship ("relationship-preserving norms," or "RPNs"). Some RPNs are "performance norms," which reflect the implicit extralegal terms transactors have agreed to abide by as long as they continue to trust one another and/or value potential future dealings. Other RPNs are "dis-pute-resolution norms," norms that transactors follow in attempting to cooperatively resolve disputes in a manner that will not jeopardize future dealings. Even when these RPNs are clear and well-developed, they may be quite different from the terms of transactors' written contracts, which contain the norms that transactors would want a third-party neutral to apply in a situation where they were unable to cooperatively resolve a dispute and viewed their relationship as being at an end-game stage ("end-game norms," or "EGNs") [. . .]

There are a number of reasons that RPNs are likely to diverge from the EGNs contained in written contracts. First, RPNs may reflect adherence to an aspect of the transactors' agreement that they deliber-ately allocated to the extralegal realm, perhaps because the obligation that they sought to create conditioned on information that was observa-ble but not verifiable, or because the legal system costs associated with memorializing the obligation in a legally enforceable provision would have been prohibitively high. Second, RPNs may reflect patterns of adjustments that transactors are willing to make at some stages of their contracting relationship but that they are nonetheless unwilling to promise to make. Third, RPNs and EGNs may also diverge because RPNs whose effectiveness depends on social or reputational sanctions imposed by members of a particular market or social group tend to be simpler than the explicit contractual provisions that cover the same aspects of the transaction. In addition, these RPNs often have special

features that are designed to enable members of the relevant group to
determine whether the norms have been violated. These features may be
both unnecessary and excessively costly if mechanisms for third-party
fact finding, dispute resolution, and enforcement of judgments are available. Fourth, because the best norm to govern a particular situation
often depends on transactors' perception of the likelihood of opportunism, transactors who are in the midst of a cooperative relationship will
often find it desirable to follow norms that would be highly undesirable if
they thought the likelihood of opportunism was high. Finally, RPNs may
diverge from EGNs because there are many adjustments that transactors
would be willing to make to preserve a profitable relationship that they
would be unwilling to make in the absence of the prospect of future gain
[. . .]

Once a contract has been entered into and transactors are considering an action that either conflicts with the terms of their contract or
relates to something the contract does not cover, the Code effectively
gives them three options. First, transactors can take the action while
explicitly disclaiming its prospective applicability. This may damage their
relationship and may not completely eliminate the action's effect on the
court's interpretation of their agreement. Second, they can decide not to
take the action, thereby losing whatever benefits the adjustment would
have created. Third, they can take the action and bear the expected costs
associated with the action's effect on the way a court would interpret
their contract. Regardless of the option they select, however, the transactors are worse off than they would be in a NGFA-type system. The
Code creates barriers, not only to transactors choosing the value-maxim-
izing combination of legally enforceable contractual provisions and extralegal provisions, but also to their flexibly adjusting aspects of their
contracting relationship in ways that might increase the value of their
contracting relationship [. . .]

In contexts where transactors anticipate that they will often have to
renegotiate particular aspects of their agreement, they may select the
written contractual provisions that will set the most desirable parameters for renegotiation. These provisions may differ from the provisions
that particular transactors, or transactors in the market as a whole,
typically agree to when successful renegotiation takes place. In such
contexts, if transactors anticipate that courts will permit course of
performance to alter the meaning of their written contract, it may be
difficult for them to draft provisions that will set a desirable and stable
framework for renegotiation. As their contracting relationship develops
and repeated adjustments are made, the fact that in the event that
renegotiation fails, courts will look to course of performance in defining
and interpreting the terms of the contract or deciding whether a waiver
or modification of its terms has been made means that each transactor's
threat point in the renegotiation, the point which defines the position
that she will be in if renegotiation is unsuccessful, will constantly

change, making nearly any framework for renegotiation established at the time of contracting inherently unstable.

The Code's effects on flexibility and renegotiation may also make it more difficult for transactors to maintain cooperative contracting relationships, particularly in repeat-dealing contexts or long-term relational contracts. In these situations, contractual obligations are often less precisely defined. As a consequence, transactors will sometimes inadvertently behave in ways that appear opportunistic or will mistakenly classify the other transactors' actions as opportunistic. Under such conditions, cooperation is more likely to be maintained when both transactors follow a norm of not responding to every action that appears opportunistic with a suit for breach of contract or termination of a mutually beneficial extralegal agreement. Transactors may, for example, adopt a policy of attempting to negotiate adjustments in response to such actions until either a particularly harmful breach occurs or a pattern of smaller breaches leads one transactor to conclude that he is better off terminating the relationship because he is dealing with an untrustworthy transactor who will continue to behave opportunistically.

The Code's course of performance provision, however, increases the cost of agreeing to forgiving adjustments. It creates a significant risk that a series of such adjustments will be found to constitute a course of performance that will operate as a waiver or modification of the contract's EGNs and will limit the circumstances in which they can be invoked. Thus, by discouraging the emergence of transactional norms that include the most desirable combinations of forgiving adjustments and threats to invoke EGNs in appropriate circumstances, the Code may reduce the likelihood that long-term cooperative relationships will arise and endure.

In Defense of the Incorporation Strategy*

JODY KRAUS and **STEPHEN D. WALT**

Contract law must provide rules for interpreting the meaning of express terms and default rules for filling contractual gaps. Article 2 of the Uniform Commercial Code provides the same response to both demands: It incorporates the norms of commercial practice. This "incorporation strategy" has recently come under attack. Although some question the incorporation strategy for gap-filling, recent scholarship criticizes the incorporation strategy for interpretation as well. Critics charge that the expected rate of interpretive error under an incorporationist interpretive regime is so excessive that almost any plain-meaning regime would be preferable.

---

* in The Jurisprudential Foundations of Corporate and Commercial Law (J.S. Kraus & S.D. Walt eds. 2000), at 193, 195, 198–200, 207–208, 209, 217–218, 224–226.

The attack on the incorporation strategy for interpretation is fundamentally flawed. The best interpretive regime is one that, all else equal, minimizes the sum of interpretive error costs and the costs of specifying contract terms. Critics of the incorporation strategy have focused exclusively on the former and completely ignored the latter. Yet the chief virtue of the incorporation strategy for interpretation is its promise to yield specification costs well below that of plain-meaning regimes. Even if plain-meaning regimes have lower interpretive error costs, the incorporation strategy is superior if its lower specification costs outweigh its higher interpretive error costs. Moreover, most critics treat their objections to Article 2 as objections to the incorporation strategy generally. But Article 2 is just one possible institutional variant of the incorporation strategy. All of the sources of interpretive error critics identify can be substantially reduced, if not avoided, by making feasible alterations to Article 2 that nonetheless preserve its incorporationist character [...]

The Existence Critique

The existence critique argues, on both an empirical and a priori basis, that commercial practices might be less extensive and less clear than proponents of the incorporation strategy have supposed. The extreme form of this critique suggest that commercial practices suitable for incorporation might not even exist. Were this the case, the incorporation strategy at best would be a useless interpretive strategy. Attempts to employ the strategy would end in a vain attempt to identify relevant commercial practices. At worst, fact finders might wrongly believe that a commercial practice exists and thus mistakenly interpret a contract term in light of the nonexistent commercial norm. But the extreme critique must overcome an extremely strong pretheoretical empirical presumption that widespread, identifiable, and effective commercial practices do exist. The near-universal insistence by merchants of all kinds that their conduct is governed, in large measure and important respects, by relatively clear commercial norms justifies a demand that evidence be presented for their nonexistence [...]

The informal norms critique points out that not all commercial practices provide good evidence of the intended meaning of contractual terms. Some commercial practices are indicative of "formal" norms, which parties intend to be given legal effect, while others indicate, "informal" norms, which parties intend not to be given legal effect. The paradigm evidence of a formal norm is provided by trade-wide contractual practices. For example, suppose that 90% of a representative sample of contracts for the sale of horses disclaimed the warranties of merchantability and fitness for a particular purpose. There is little question that this evidence establishes the existence of a commercial norm of warranty disclaimer in sales of horses and that this norm is intended by contractors to be given legal effect.

In contrast, informal norms are common commercial practices that are intended by their practitioners not to be given legal effect. The paradigm evidence of an informal norm is provided by trade-wide testimony that a practice is not intended to be given legal effect. For example, suppose that horse sellers routinely exchange or return the price for lame horses that were accepted by their buyers. But every horse seller will testify that this practice constitutes a legally optional accommodation rather than a legally binding obligation. In fact, sellers might well claim that the desirability of the accommodation practice turns crucially on the availability of the legally enforceable right to enforce the original trade. Such an informal practice might arise in order to preserve an ongoing relationship with a set of repeat buyers. But the same transactors who follow these norms might do so only because they take themselves to have preserved the option of enforcing their more stringent contractual rights—in this case, refusing to exchange or refund the price of the horse. Contractors might invoke their stricter, contractual rights whenever they consider their contracting partner to be behaving opportunistically. Such behavior is more likely at the end of a contractual relationship, when further contractual interaction between the parties is unlikely, rather than in the middle of an ongoing relationship. In specifying the terms of their contract, parties attempt to create an optimal mix of formal and informal norms to mediate their relationship. The informal norms critique argues that the incorporation strategy, as implemented in Article 2, undermines this optimal mix by formalizing informal norms [. . .]

Article 2 does not explicitly direct courts to distinguish between formal and informal norms. However, Article 2 clearly does not contemplate or condone the incorporation of informal norms. No court applying Article 2 would intentionally incorporate informal norms. This is because an informal norm cannot be evidence that the term is intended to be enforced. In other words, the evidence goes to something that is not a term of the contract. Indeed, the informality of a norm entails that no term in the contract at issue can be interpreted as having a meaning governed by the norm. It is simply no part of the parties' enforceable set of obligation. Thus, any court that identified a norm as informal must already have concluded that the norm cannot be used as a basis for interpreting the meaning of the contract. The court's prior determination of the norm's informality would constitute its finding that the norm does not inform the meaning of any of the contract's terms.

Accordingly, the incorporation strategy is not embarrassed by commercial practices reflecting both formal and informal norms. Instead, these practices simply raise another potential source of interpretive error. Under Article 2, for example, judges might mistakenly incorporate an informal norm in the process of interpretation. The possibility is unexceptional. Judges can make mistakes in passing on any aspect of the sale contract, from formation questions to remedies. So the question is whether this kind of interpretive error will be so extensive and costly that Article 2 and other incorporation regimes will be less efficient than available nonincorporation interpretive regimes. The answer depends on the precise design of the incorporation process and on the base rate of observable contractual activity that is inconsistent with the legal duties contractors intentionally undertake in their contracts. When both variables are taken into account, the probability of erroneous incorporation of informal norms is unlikely to be as extensive as the current literature suggests [. . .]

The final critique of the incorporation strategy focuses on the mechanics of the incorporation process of Article 2. Article 2 requires judges to interpret contractual terms in light of commercial practice. But once courts have made an initial determination of the meaning of a term, based at least in theory on an inquiry into relevant commercial practices, they appear reluctant to engage in that inquiry again. Instead, they appear to treat such determinations as canonical. Thus, although courts might initially employ the incorporation strategy, their initial interpretations become "encrusted" as virtual precedents. Courts subsequently disfavor any interpretations inconsistent with these encrusted interpretations. One suggestion is that courts are predisposed to treat statutory interpretation in a static, precedent-bound fashion, rather than the dynamic fashion contemplated by the incorporation strategy. Thus, incorporation implemented by Article 2, rather than through a common law system, might account for this judicial interpretive intransigence.

The judicial practice of one-time incorporation is inconsistent with the goal of interpreting contractual terms in light of their evolving meanings. If parties understand their contractual terms in light of evolving commercial practices, encrustation will lead to interpretive error. If parties recognize and respond rationally to the judicial practice of one-time incorporation, costs of specifying their most preferred terms will increase. If courts will not interpret contractual terms in light of current commercial practices, parties will have to incur the costs of making explicit any of their understandings at variance with outdated practice, or settle for the suboptimal interpretation of their contractual terms according to the outdated practice. The costs of "opting out" of the encrusted interpretations of their terms are exacerbated by the tendency of courts to disfavor such opt-outs. If courts refuse to interpret terms in light of evolving commercial practice, the value of attempting to "opt out" of encrusted interpretations is reduced. Even if parties incur the costs to provide an otherwise clear opt-out, courts might nonetheless refuse to enforce the parties' interpretation. This practice thus reduces the expected joint value of all contracts by depriving parties of the ability to specify their most preferred terms.

Encrustation is a potentially serious problem for incorporationists. The tendency of courts to make one-time interpretations of terms instead of continually updating their interpretations in light of evolving practice is inconstant with the implementation of the dynamic incorporation process contemplated by Article 2's incorporation strategy. The tendency to disfavor even clear efforts to opt out of encrusted interpretations constitutes simple interpretive error. How serious a problem encrustation presents depends on the relative frequency of interpretive error resulting from a failure to recognize changes in commercial practice or a bias against clear opt-outs. These in turn depend on how the incorporation strategy is implemented.

But plain-meaning regimes are likely to suffer from shortcomings similar to those caused by encrustation. First, encrustation undermines the incorporation strategy because it prevents parties from easily invoking the current customary meanings attached to their contract terms. It thus raises the parties' specification costs. But plain-meaning regimes do not even attempt to enable parties to invoke customary meanings at minimal cost. They instead require parties to communicate their customary understandings according to the plain meaning of the terms they use. Thus, although encrustation erodes some of the expected savings in specification costs under the incorporation strategy, the expected specification costs under plain-meaning regimes will be even higher. Second, encrustation undermines the incorporation strategy because judges refuse to honor parties' attempts to opt out of the customary meanings assigned to their contract terms. Again, this judicial practice raises expected specification costs under the incorporation strategy. But if judges favor the customary meaning of contract terms when they interpret under an incorporation regime, we would expect them to favor the plain meaning of terms under a plain-meaning regime. For example, if contractors state that their quantity terms are estimates, judges might nonetheless hold the parties to the plain meaning of their quantity term. It is difficult to understand why judges would be biased in favor of the customary meaning of terms under an interpretive regime that accords primacy to customary meaning while not exhibiting a similar bias in favor of the plain meaning of terms under a regime that accords primacy to plain meaning [. . .]

Incorporation of commercial practice in contract interpretation is best suited to generalist commercial statutes or rules. Generalist commercial laws cover a wide variety of transactions among contracting parties having heterogeneous, transaction-specific preferences. In these circumstances, interpretative approaches must take into account both interpretive error costs as well as specification costs. The case here for incorporation in interpretation argues that an incorporation strategy optimally minimizes the sum of interpretive error and specification costs associated with contract interpretation. The argument rests principally on four sensible empirical assumptions.

First, where party preference is heterogeneous, contracting parties face high costs in signaling to third parties their understanding of contract terms. Thus, specification costs are a variable that interpretive approaches cannot ignore. By interpreting contract terms according to commercial practice, the incorporation strategy saves parties most of the cost of having to signal the aspects of that practice they want applicable to their contract. Second, despite the arguable lack of uniformity of trade custom at the turn of the century, contemporary local and national trade customs are likely to be quite extensive. Third, where norms exist governing heterogeneous transactions covered by a generalist law, they are more likely to be formal norms, intended by the parties to be enforceable, than informal norms, not intended for enforcement. On the whole, formal norms are likely to outnumber informal norms because transactions cover both discrete and relational contracts, informal norms are unlikely to govern discrete contracts, relational contracts are unlikely to predominate discrete contracts, and even within relational contracts, formal norms are likely to predominate informal norms. Thus, the rate of interpretive error in mistaking informal for formal norms probably is low. . . .

Fourth, error costs associated with interpreting terms in light of commercial practice can be reduced by adjusting the way in which incorporation is implemented. This means that mistakes due to bias against op-outs of trade usage, misidentification of informal for formal norms, or identification of trade usage where there is none can be reduced by altering burdens of proof, evidentiary bases and standards of proof, and the like. Adjustment of these elements to affect legal error rates therefore can be made, taking into account their effect on specification costs. In this way, marginal interpretive error and specification costs can be gauged so as to obtain optimal levels of both. The case for the incorporation strategy claims that, given these four sensible assumptions, aggregate interpretive error and specification costs are lower than under plain-meaning interpretive approaches.

The a priori case against the existence of custom raises fair questions about the kinds of judgment necessary to implement the incorporation strategy, but does not undermine the prospect of incorporation itself. However, empirical studies concerning the existence of trade usage or the rates of informal and formal norms in particular industries are important for incorporationists. In fact, they are essential to the incorporation strategy because they affect the way in which it is implemented. For example, the adjustment of standards of proof and evidentiary bases depends on the likely rates of interpretive error. Thus, if trade usage is most local or "thin," or if most norms in a particular industry are informal, as Bernstein's data might suggest, then raising a standard of proof or restricting evidentiary bases might be appropriate. Far from being incompatible with the incorporation strategy, empirical data about the rate of informal norms or the limitations of trade usage are necessary for an intelligent implementation of the incorporation strategy. At the very least, the data require that incorporationists be sensitive to interpretive error and specification costs. Our objection to the critiques of incorporation is not that they fail to identify possible sources of interpretive error associated with consulting commercial custom. It is that the critiques either ignore specification costs, which favor incorporation, or ignore the resources available to incorporation strategies to reduce the interpretive errors they identify.

NOTES

1. Why do members of the NGFA opt out of the Code? Bernstein argues that merchant-transactors have multiple reasons for not aligning the scope of rights and duties memorialized in their written contracts with the scope of the extralegal "immanent business norms" that exist between merchant-transactors. The UCC, with its pervasive "commercially reasonable" provision, invites courts to construe these extralegal usages of trade, courses of dealing, and courses of performance in ways that not only fail to coincide with the merchant-transactors' contractual intent, but also limit the usefulness of these norms in achieving bargaining agreements in the first place. The result is an "efficiency loss" akin to the ones catalogued in the first two sections of this chapter. How might a court limit these efficiency losses without rejecting the UCC's norm of commercial reasonableness? Is the merchant-transactor relationship governed by the NGFA unique in a way that limits the extent to which Bernstein's conclusions might apply generally? Does it matter that Bernstein's study is limited to transactions between parties engaged in the same business? Are her findings particular to certain types of business? Consider that the quality of grain, for example, is relatively easily observable and measurable.

According to Bernstein, the activist interpretive approach embodied in the Code has had several significant effects. One effect is the observed practice of groups of commercial parties opting out of the Code entirely in important classes of cases. Among the principal reasons for the National Grain and Feed Association's decision to abandon the Code was their desire to have written express terms subject to a formalist and objective interpretive methodology and not to be trumped by evidence of course of dealing or usage of trade. Bernstein suggests that the explanation for this practice lies in the parties desire to separate the legal norms that govern their written agreements from the informal social norms that govern their actions. Opting out of the Code permits the grain and feed merchants to substitute a more formal common law approach to interpretation in place of the legal activism of the Code.

2. Do commercial parties "prefer" formalist modes of interpretation? Bernstein's data suggests that the contextualist approach embodied in the Code is premised on a notion of trade custom that, in the words of David Charny, relies on "a nostalgia for an idealized, perhaps mythical premodern age—for the intimate local communities of shared value and custom, enforced by knowledge, reputation, and ties of affectional loyalty." David Charny, *The New Formalism in Contract*, 66 U. Chi. L. Rev. 842, 845 (1999). What we see instead is the evolution of intermediaries and the development of custom by trade association rule making. Moreover, the rules developed by these intermediaries are themselves formalist. The approach to dispute resolution generated by these local "customs" reveals a preference for literal interpretation of express contract terms and a rejection of context specific "situation sense" analysis of particular contractual relationships.

The relative merits of formalist and contextualist contract enforcement continue to be a matter of substantial debate among scholars. For a recent model of the benefits of more active interpretive style, see Steven Shavell, *On the Writing and Interpretation of Contracts*, 22 J. Law, Econ. & Organ. 289 (2006).

3. Should methods of interpretation be default rules rather than mandatory rules? Whether the practice of homogeneous groups of commercial parties opting for formal methods of contractual interpretation reflects an underlying inefficiency in the UCC is a complex question. We would first have to know how widespread is the practice that Bernstein and others have observed. Thereafter, we confront directly the difficult question that Kraus and Walt highlight: Are the benefits of incorporation of context through liberal interpretation rules sufficient to outweigh the costs of the incorporation strategy? At a minimum should commercial parties be free to choose the method of interpretation they prefer? Or is the theory of interpretation properly seen as a mandatory rule designed to serve independent interests of the state? If so, what are those interests? What are the efficiency values that inhere in contractual interpretation? Can courts do what the functionalist strategies ask of them in a complex environment of heterogeneous contractors? Can courts incorporate formal norms, but exclude the informal ones, as suggested by Kraus and Walt?

2.5   The Case for and Against Mandatory Commercial Law Rules

Introduction

As a general matter, contract law enables the creation of legally enforceable commitments and it respects the freedom of the parties to structure those commitments as they see fit. Nevertheless, contract law imposes some constraints on the parties freedom of contract. Courts will not enforce contract terms they find to be unconscionable or the product of duress, fraudulent misrepresentation or concealment. These constraints are justified by concerns of fairness between the parties, but they also enhance efficiency. The principal focus of this book is the default provisions of commercial law. In some cases, they reflect a concern with ensuring the fairness of exchanges between parties. Yet, contracts can avoid these provisions in their agreement, leaving the parties with the possibility of an unfair bargain and the transaction costs of opting out. As a good example of this response, commentators and courts once thought (and may still think) that it is fair for merchant sellers to make implied warranties of quality. Merchant sellers, however, routinely attempt to disclaim the implied warranty of merchantability in UCC § 2–314 and their merchant buyers routinely consent. The effect of

§ 2–314 in business contexts thus often is limited to the increasing of transaction costs.

The UCC also provides mandatory terms: the courts will not enforce terms that deviate or conflict with these provisions. The cost of error in lawmaking is significantly higher in the case of mandatory than default provisions because parties cannot avoid the error by contracting away from mandatory terms. Therefore, the threshold for justifying a mandatory rule is higher than for a default. Scholars have challenged, for example, the common law principle (adopted in the UCC) that caps the enforcement to freely negotiated liquidated damages at the compensatory level, or the principle that denies enforcement to agreements not to renegotiate or modify the initial contract. In an excerpt that follows, Professor Russell Korobkin looks to bounded rationality and the use by individuals of cognitive heuristics, to explain why drafters of contracts might include one-sided and inefficient terms in their agreements, and why the courts need to police contracts accordingly, including through the use of mandatory terms. In the other excerpt, Professors Aghion and Hermalin offer a different explanation based on information asymmetry between the parties.

Bounded Rationality, Standard Form Contracts, and Unconscionability*
RUSSELL KOROBKIN

[. . .] Standard economic reasoning suggests that form contract terms provided by sellers should be socially efficient. Less obviously, economic reasoning also leads to the conclusion that those terms will be beneficial to buyers as a class, in the sense that buyers would prefer the price/term combination offered by sellers to any other economically feasible price/term combination. These conclusions are valid whether all, some, or no buyers shop multiple sellers for the best combination of product attributes and whether the market is competitive or dominated by a monopolist seller. From a consequentialist perspective, then, a policy preference for courts to enforce all terms in form contracts drafted by sellers appears not only plausible, but practically required. Any persuasive argument against the enforcement of form contract terms must begin by challenging the behavioral assumptions that underlie economic theory. Specifically, some form of "market failure" must be identified. [. . .]

[. . .] Efficiency requires not only that buyers be aware of the content of form contracts, but also that they fully incorporate that information into their purchase decisions. Because buyers are boundedly rational rather than fully rational decisionmakers, they will infrequently satisfy this requirement. The consequence is that market pressure will

* 70 U. Chi. L. Rev. 1203, 1216–34 (2003).

not force sellers to provide efficient terms. In addition, under plausible assumptions, market pressure actually will force sellers to provide low-quality form terms, whether or not those terms are either socially efficient or optimal for buyers as a class. [...]

[T]he standard economic model assumes buyers will conduct a thorough cost-benefit analysis of product choices (including the choice of purchasing no product) and select the one that offers the optimal (that is, most desirable) combination of attributes, including price. Such exacting buyer behavior drives out of the market all products with undesirable attributes and all products with attributes that are desirable but cost more to produce than buyers are willing to pay. Products that remain have the optimally efficient combination of attributes, at least for a segment of buyers that is large enough to support the minimum effective scale of production.

For buyers to enforce such effective market discipline on sellers, their comparative analysis of product choices must be both non-selective and compensatory. Non-selective decisionmaking requires that the buyer compare all attributes of each available product before deciding which he prefers. Not only, for example, does the buyer have to compare a red car to one with a stereo; he must compare a red car with a sun roof, a generous financing provision, and a warranty disclaimer, to a blue car with an advanced technology steering system, anti-lock brakes, no financing, and an arbitration clause. In a competitive market for an even moderately complex product, a truly non-selective approach could require the decisionmaker to compare a large number of alternatives on an even larger number of attributes.

Compensatory analysis requires the decisionmaker to trade off the desirable attributes of one product against the desirable attributes of a competing product. If an automobile buyer values a red car and a stereo, and one available car is red but has no stereo while another has a stereo but is not red, he must be able to determine which of the two cars is more desirable. If the buyer values both a low price and the ability to take the manufacturer to court should a dispute arise under the contract, and one car comes with a mandatory arbitration provision while another has no such provision and is $100 more expensive, he must be able to determine whether he prefers the extra $100 in his pocket to keeping the courthouse door open.

Fully non-selective and compensatory decisionmaking, as it turns out, is quite difficult to execute. To make decisions that satisfy these requirements, a decisionmaker must employ something similar to what decision theorists call the "weighted-adding" strategy. To employ this strategy, the decisionmaker assigns an importance weight to each different attribute that defines the product in question: Very important attributes are awarded large weights; less important attributes are given smaller weights. [...]

While most buyers employ decision strategies that require more effort than the random choice approach, they rarely use strategies as accurate as weighted adding. Like other individuals, they usually solve problems using heuristics, or mental short-cuts, that provide solutions with less than maximum effort, as opposed to algorithms, which require patient and often lengthy calculation. Decision theorists have proposed numerous descriptive models of choice that fall between weighted adding and random choice on the accuracy/effort spectrum, all of which are simpler than weighted adding but more complex than random choice. A brief review of a few of these is useful to illustrate how all choice strategies that are less accurate than weighted adding are either selective, non-compensatory, or both.

The lexicographic strategy calls for the decisionmaker to select the product alternative with the highest score on the most important attribute. For example, if "body style" is the most important attribute to a car buyer, the buyer will purchase the car with the most pleasing styling, regardless of how that car ranks on other design attributes, price, or contract terms. [. . .] This approach is both selective, in that it requires the chooser to examine only a single attribute across product alternatives, and non-compensatory, in that different features do not have to be compared to each other. For buyers, the approach requires relatively little effort and promises relatively little accuracy, at least as compared to other plausible strategies. [. . .]

Herbert Simon long ago hypothesized that, rather than optimizing, decisionmakers define a minimum aspiration level and opt for the first alternative that reaches it. A number of decisionmaking models attempt to operationalize Simon's insight. The conjunctive strategy assumes that the decisionmaker will select an alternative that exceeds a minimum acceptable level on all attributes, without regard to whether it exceeds those thresholds by a small or large amount. This approach is non-selective, because all attributes are considered, but non-compensatory, because a high score on one attribute is not compared to a high score on a different attribute. [. . .]

Using an elimination-by-aspects strategy—a variation of the conjunctive strategy—the decisionmaker examines all product alternatives on the attribute most important to him and eliminates from consideration any alternatives for which that attribute does not meet a minimum acceptable level. If multiple alternatives remain under consideration, the decisionmaker goes on to the next most important attribute and eliminates from consideration all alternatives that fail to score satisfactorily on that attribute, and so on. When all products but one have been eliminated by this procedure, the decisionmaker selects the one that remains. Elimination by aspects is non-compensatory, like the conjunctive approach, but also selective because not all of the relevant data will be considered. [. . .]

One of the principal findings of decision research is that decision-making behavior is highly contingent on context, which makes it impossible to identify a single, specific strategy that buyers will use when making purchasing choices in the marketplace or a precise list of which attributes will be salient to them and which will be non-salient. Decision research does provide a basis, however, for predicting that terms found in form contracts frequently will be non-salient to most buyers. This prediction relies on two factual premises. First, purchase decisions involving products with form contracts are sufficiently complex that buyers usually will be selective in their consideration of product attributes. That is, at least some attributes will be non-salient. Second, relative to other product attributes, form terms are particularly likely to be non-salient because their usual content makes them unlikely to attract buyers' voluntary or involuntary attention. This section defends these two premises.

Complexity and selectivity

As the amount of relevant information increases, decisions increase in complexity and demand higher levels of cognitive effort. Because individuals' selection of choice strategies can be viewed as balancing the desire to achieve accuracy with the desire to minimize effort, it follows logically that as decisions become more complex, decisionmakers will tend to adopt simpler choice strategies to cope with that complexity. The research of decision theorists confirms this reasoning, suggesting that increased information load causes increased selectivity in the information processed.

Two obvious sources of complexity that can cause buyers to adopt simpler decision strategies are the number of alternatives available, and the number of relevant attributes for each alternative. Although the evidence is robust that the presence of a large number of alternatives causes decisionmakers to employ relatively simple decisionmaking strategies, this finding will not be emphasized here for two reasons. First, when choosing between product options, buyers might or might not face a large number of alternatives, depending on the particular market and whether they are "shoppers" or "non-shoppers." Second, when buyers face a large number of alternatives initially, they often use one decision-making strategy to pare down the number of alternatives to a more manageable number and then switch strategies when making their choice among the reduced set of options. For both reasons, the evidence of how buyers act in the face of large numbers of options may not have universal application to the context of buyers making a final purchasing decision.

More important for the analysis of form contracts is the empirical research that suggests the number of attributes decisionmakers are likely even to investigate—much less actually price as part of the decisionmaking procedure—when choosing between alternatives is surprisingly modest by contemporary product standards, perhaps as few as five (although this number can certainly vary depending on the individual, the importance of the choice, and the time allotted to make the decision). In one experiment, researchers found that subjects asked to choose among alternative brands of typewriters, each of which with multiple attributes, tended to employ a two-step decision process. First, the subjects used a selective and non-compensatory approach to reduce the number of brands under consideration to a maximum of three or four. Second, they conducted a compensatory analysis of the remaining brands that selectively included only five or fewer attributes, even when information on more attributes was available.

In another experiment, subjects exposed to information about either six or fifteen product attributes of condominium units or stereos were asked to select one of several alternatives, reasoning through their choice process verbally. In the fifteen-attribute condition, the experimenters concluded that "nearly all subjects" ignored certain product attributes in their decisionmaking process. Subjects in another experiment were asked to choose from among two or more alternative apartments, each of which was rated on four, eight, or twelve attributes. Faced with only two alternatives of four attributes each, the subjects consulted all of the available information before making a choice. Even with only two alternatives, some subjects facing eight or twelve attributes did not consult (much less make use of) all of the attribute information prior to choosing. With more alternatives, subjects consulted even less information. Yet another study found that the number of attributes per alternative considered by decisionmakers ranged only from 3.0 to 6.6. Even expert decisionmakers, it seems, are similarly selective in the amount of information consulted when making decisions.

In one particularly revealing study, experimenters first interviewed subjects, collecting information about their preferences concerning a variety of features of houses. They then asked the subjects to select their preferred house from five alternative choices. Subjects' ability to choose the alternative that would maximize their utility (based on the information they provided in the earlier interviews) was constant when descriptions contained between five and ten attributes for each alternative. But when the experimenters increased the number of attributes described to fifteen or more, the subjects made fewer accurate choices, thus suggesting that subjects employed simpler decision strategies when the number of attributes became large. [. . .]

Salience and attention

Psychological research divides the concept of attention into two categories: voluntary and involuntary. In other words, people pay attention to environmental stimuli either because we voluntarily choose to do so, or because aspects of the environment are intrinsically noticeable and capture our attention involuntarily. For a product attribute to be salient to buyers, the attribute must capture the limited attention of those buyers. But the nature of form contract terms suggests that they often will not be the focus of voluntary attention or capable of capturing attention involuntarily.

Individuals devote voluntary attention to information when doing so will help them to obtain their goals. Because buyers usually will wish to maximize the accuracy of their purchase decisions given a fixed amount of effort expended, buyers who focus attention on a limited number of product attributes can be expected to attempt to focus that attention on the attributes that are most important to them. Experience suggests that the terms found in form contracts often, although not always, will be less important to buyers than other attributes such as price, functionality, and physical appearance, and thus will be a less likely focus of attention.

Somewhat more speculatively, the nature of certain types of terms prevalent in form contracts also suggests that buyers might often choose to focus their attention elsewhere, but for a very different reason. Research suggests that individuals experience conflict when forced to compare dissimilar attributes to each other; that is, compensatory decisionmaking is emotionally difficult. This general problem is perhaps most acute, however, when comparing dissimilar attributes would require the decisionmaker to put an implicit price on attributes that she intuitively feels should not be commodified or trade off attributes that she feels should not be sacrificed. For example, a decisionmaker is likely to face more stress when forced to make a tradeoff between lives saved and dollars spent on highway maintenance than between the size of an apartment and the dollars spent on rent. Decision researchers have labeled choices that require particularly uncomfortable tradeoffs as "emotion laden."

A plausible inference drawn from this research is that two typical types of contract terms, usually found buried in the text of standard forms, are likely to cause elevated stress levels for buyers. The first type places limitations on the ability of buyers to recover damages for personal injuries caused by the product, such as liability waivers and exclusions of consequential damages. The second type causes buyers to waive traditional means of legal redress, such as mandatory arbitration provisions and forum selection clauses. If buyers believe that personal safety or the right to seek redress of legal wrongs in a court of law are entitlements that should be inalienable and not subject to commodification, explicitly trading off these types of entitlements against a product's price and physical features might create elevated stress levels.

Research further suggests that decisionmakers often respond to the presence of emotion-laden choices by adopting non-compensatory choice strategies, which alleviate the burden of making explicit tradeoffs between attributes that are stressful to compare. For example, a car buyer might adopt a strategy of purchasing the cheapest car or, alternatively, purchasing only a car with air bags and anti-lock brakes no matter what the cost, in order to avoid the emotionally stressful task of "putting a price on safety." Buyers are likely to respond to the stress caused by sellers' attempts to force them to commodify personal safety or legal rights by employing non-compensatory decisionmaking strategies that allow them to avoid making such tradeoffs—by effectively ignoring these terms during the selection process and thus rendering them non-salient.

Another reason that form terms seem unlikely to garner attention stems from the fact that many such terms govern eventualities that are extremely unlikely to occur. One of the most robust findings of social science research on judgment and decisionmaking is that individuals are quite bad at taking into account probability estimates when making decisions. For low-probability risks, individuals often either overweigh the possibility of harm, taking excessive precaution relative to the actual risk, or ignore the risk altogether. This is a consequence of translating probabalistic risks into judgments that situations are either "safe" or "unsafe". For example, one study shows that people are willing to pay either virtually nothing to insure against a risk or else pay far more than the risk's expected cost.

One explanation for why individuals might treat certain low-probability risks as if they were virtually non-existent is that they are excessively confident in their likelihood of avoiding harm. Such overconfidence cannot be the complete story, however, since there is strong evidence that individuals also exaggerate low-probability risks in some circumstances. A more likely explanation for the phenomenon is that, naturally poor at conducting implicit probability calculations, people often assess risk via the "availability heuristic," judging risk to be high when the type of harm is familiar or easily imagined and low when it is not.

Many of the terms commonly specified in standard form contracts govern what will happen if a low-probability risk comes to pass: if the seller's product does not function; if the buyer does not pay on time; if the parties become embroiled in a dispute that leads to litigation; if the buyer is injured; etc. If these possible but unlikely outcomes are not readily "available" to buyers, they are likely to respond to the risk of these harms by treating them as if they do not exist at all. If buyers are disposed to substantially discount the risks implied by form contract terms, buyers operating in a content-rich environment in which they must consider information only selectively might allocate their attention elsewhere, rendering the form terms that concern low-probability risks non-salient.

If buyers are not likely to focus their limited attention in complex decision environments on form contract terms voluntarily, those terms are also unlikely to capture buyers' attention involuntarily. The way in which sellers display information affects the attention paid to it and thus the likelihood of its being salient in the decision process. Form terms are usually displayed in ways that make them hard to read, hard to understand, and hard to compare to the terms accompanying competing products, thus making them particularly unlikely to be salient product attributes to buyers. [. . .]

The distinction between salient and non-salient product attributes is essential to the analysis of the efficiency of form contracts. Although market forces should ensure that sellers will offer efficient salient contract terms, non-salient attributes are subject to inefficiencies driven by the strategic behavior of sellers attempting to increase their profits at the expense of unknowing buyers. Far from operating as an invisible hand that promotes efficiency, market forces combined with the presence of non-salient product attributes can perversely enforce a regime of inefficiency. Assuming that the price of a product is a salient product attribute for buyers—surely a highly realistic assumption—market pressures will force sellers in competitive markets to offer low-quality non-salient contract terms, whether or not such terms are efficient. Except in the unlikely circumstance in which all efficient terms are low quality, then, there is reason to suspect that form contracts will contain some terms that reduce both the welfare of buyers and social welfare generally. The refusal by courts to enforce such terms would therefore increase social efficiency and buyer welfare. In a competitive market, such action would also increase sellers' welfare.

Legal Restrictions on Private Contracts Can Enhance Efficiency*
PHILIPPE AGHION and **BENJAMIN E. HERMALIN**

A common reaction to legal restrictions on contracts is that they cannot improve efficiency. Either the restrictions are not binding, in which case they have no effect, or they are binding, in which case they prevent the parties from doing as they wish. As we show in this article, however restrictions can in fact enhance efficiency if one party to a contract has better information than the other. Since the terms asked for in the contract can reveal information, the better-informed party can have an incentive to signal information through the terms for which she asks. Inasmuch as this signaling can lead to distortions in the contract, distortions that are undesirable from an ex ante perspective, restrictions on contracts that correct for these distortions can be valuable.

Consider, for example, an entrepreneur who needs to raise capital to fund a project. She knows how likely it is that her project will succeed, but someone who invests in it does not. Because she can get more generous terms from an investor, the more likely he thinks it is that her project will succeed, the entrepreneur has an incentive to signal to the

* 6 J. L. ECON. & ORG. 381, 381–384, 388, 398–401 (1990).

investor that her project is likely to succeed (is a "good" project). Since the expected cost of a large payment to be paid if the project *fails* is greater for an entrepreneur with a "bad" project than it is for an entrepreneur with a good project, on way to signal a good project is to promise a large payment to the investor if the project fails. The cost of signaling in this manner is that the entrepreneur exposes herself to considerable risk (e.g., losing her house if the project fails).

Prohibiting signaling (i.e., prohibiting the entrepreneur from exposing herself to excessive risk) may enhance welfare. To see why, note that because of the additional risk, an entrepreneur with a good project might prefer not to signal, if not signaling only made it seem that her project was "average" (i.e., made the investor believe that the probability of failure was between the probability of a good project failing and a bad project failing). The difficulty is that the investor will interpret "not signaling" as evidence that the project is *bad*; and given the choice between looking good (signaling) and looking bad (not signaling), an entrepreneur with a good project will prefer to look good. If, however, signaling is restricted (e.g., by bankruptcy laws), then not signaling is no longer informative. Consequently, the investor will treat all entrepreneurs as if they have an average project. Both types of entrepreneur are better off: an entrepreneur with a bad project now looks average, while an entrepreneur with a good project avoids the additional risks imposed by costly signaling.

To the extent previous work has explored the desirability of contract restrictions, the perspective has been largely extra-economic. For example, Okun justifies restrictions on equity, moral, and paternalistic grounds. Although these are undoubtedly important grounds, as economists, we would argue that the economic criterion of efficiency is at least as important. Evaluations of contract restrictions based on the efficiency criterion have generally been motivated by a concern for externalities (i.e., without restrictions contract between A and B will adversely affect C). For example, Chung demonstrates that the "penalty doctrine" (the courts' unwillingness to enforce damage clauses that they deem punitive) may be desirable because it eliminates undesirable externalities (Rubin offers another externality-based argument). Concern for externalities is most evident in the antitrust literature; for example, Aghion and Bolton show that restrictions on exclusive-dealing contracts can eliminate the negative externalities suffered by a potential entrant.

What distinguishes our work from previous studies of contract restrictions is that we do not rely on externalities to explain the efficiency of these restrictions. Rather, we rely on informational asymmetries. Because of this, the inefficiencies that exist without contract restrictions are borne by the parties to the contract themselves rather than by a third party [. . .]

Analysis

We define the *symmetric-information contract for the good (bad) type* to be the contract that the good (bad) type entrepreneur would offer if, somehow, the investor was informed that he was dealing with the good (bad) type. That is, the symmetric-information contract is the best (utility-maximizing) contract for the good- (bad)- type entrepreneur to offer, given that the investor is willing to accept the contract when informed that the entrepreneur is the good (bad) type. (Given our assumptions, the symmetric-information contract for each type is unique.) As we are assuming that the investor is not informed about the entrepreneur's type, it will generally be true that the investor will not accept the symmetric-information contract for the good type. The reason for his is that the uninformed investor is worried about being fooled by the bad type; that is, he is worried about unknowingly accepting a contract from the bad type that does not adequately compensate him for the additional risk of investing with the bad type. Furthermore, this is not an idle worry on the part of the investor: as the bad type would like to avoid compensating the investor for that additional risk, the bad type has an incentive to pretend to be the good type by offering the same contract offered by the good type. Loosely, the bad type generally would do better mimicking the good type by offering the symmetric-information contract for the good type than by offering any other contract that the investor would accept in equilibrium. Thus, generally, there is no equilibrium in which the good type can offer her symmetric-information contract and have it accepted.

On the other hand, the investor is always willing to accept the symmetric information contract for the bad type—either the bad type has offered it, in which case the investor is indifferent between accepting and rejecting it, or the good type has offered it, in which case the investor gets the compensation for investing with the bad type, while enjoying the low risk of investing with the good type. A consequence of this insight is that, in equilibrium, the bad type's expected utility must be at least as great as it would be if she offered her symmetric-information contract (since otherwise she could successfully deviate by offering her symmetric-information contract) [. . .]

Limitation on Penalties for Breach of Contract

The issue of which damage measure for breach of contract should be imposed is a well-studied one. Although it is certainly worthwhile to compare the various measures commonly used, as previous work has done, it is also important to ask why it is desirable to use these measures, and not measures that the parties to the contract might choose themselves. As we have shown, an answer is that, without laws fixing or limiting damages, inefficient levels of damages could arise.

In a world of *symmetric* information, the optimal remedy for breach must be *specific performance* (i.e., under the threat of contempt of court, the parties to the contract are forced to carry out its terms). To see this, imagine that the informed party is supposed to do some task (let F be the probability that she fails to do it). In a world of symmetric information (i.e., F is known by both parties), the optimal contract will specify transfers, P_f and P_s, between the two parties contingent on whether the informed party failed or succeeded in doing the task. *Breach* in this model would occur *only if* the amount of transfer was not what the contract had specified for the realization of the task. That is, failure to complete the task does *not* constitute breach (thus, specific performance is not court-ordered task completion). Clearly, the only role for the law (the courts) is to enforce the proper transfers (i.e., the optimal remedy is specific performance with respect to the transfers).

With *asymmetric* information, there exist situations in which the levels of the transfers are set inefficiently because of signaling (e.g., the good type attempts to signal that she is likely to complete the task by promising to make an inefficiently large transfer to the uninformed party if she fails). Now, as we have seen, specific performance may no longer be optimal. Instead, optimality may require that the law *not* enforce contracts calling for inefficiently large transfers (i.e., the law should, and indeed does, adopt a penalty doctrine or otherwise considers "excessively" large transfers as unconscionable—see Friedman). Of course, what constitutes an excessively large transfer is relative, so the law may be compelled to adopt a standard such as *reliance damages, expectation damages,* or *restitution* in order establish what constitutes reasonable transfers. That is, an economic justification for these standards is that they transform inefficient equilibria into more efficient equilibria.

We note that our justification for these standards differs from the one often discussed by legal scholars, specifically that the problem with excessive penalties is that they may cause the party who will receive the penalty to attempt to induce breach (see, e.g., Clarkson, Miller, and Muris). Although this sort of moral hazard is undoubtedly a real concern, it is unclear to us why it should be a concern of the courts and not of the parties to the contract. That is, the parties to the contract should anticipate this moral hazard problem and, thus, should take steps to ameliorate it (including, possibly, not having excessive penalty clauses). Given this, it is unclear to us why the courts should interfere if the parties nonetheless choose to include such clauses. To repeat our earlier point, given that pure moral hazard represents an *(ex ante)* symmetric information problem, we believe in this case that efficiency requires that contracts be enforced as written. Only if excessive penalty clauses are the consequence of *asymmetric* information should the courts interfere.

NOTES

1. Policing bargains where parties fail to maximize. Both Korobkin and Aghion/Hermalin present reasons why parties may not maximize their joint surplus from transacting, unless their bargain is policed by the imposition of mandatory terms. Aghion and Hermalin's analysis applies when parties are asymmetrically informed about critical features of their exchange and the information is difficult to communicate. Korobkin's concerns arise even if the parties are symmetrically informed, but one or both suffer from cognitive limitations (or bounded rationality). As an exercise, construct a list of mandatory terms in U.C.C. Articles 2, 3, 4 and 9, and consider whether either set of justifications might apply.

2. Mandatory rules and externalities. Another class of justifications for mandatory terms address externalities from contracting. Philippe Aghion and Patrick Bolton suggests that parties may agree to high liquidated damages in order to extract more value in bargaining with a future entrant. Consider a hypothetical case in which a buyer of a widget pays the price up front and values the widget at $10. If the seller's liability for breach is the buyer's expectation of $10, then the seller may decide to sell to any third party who values the widget more than $10. The seller and the third party would agree to a price somewhere between $10 and the third party's valuation. If the third party's value is $16 and the parties have equal bargaining power, they would agree to a price of $13. Now, suppose that the initial contract sets liquidated damages of $15 and these are enforceable. Then, the seller will demand at least $15 from a third party entrant; in the case of the entrant identified above, the price would be $15.50. The seller and initial buyer as a group would enjoy an extra $2.50 of the value the third party assigned to the widget. The seller, however, would not find it profitable to switch to any third party who valued the widget less than $15, and this would yield a social loss if the third party nevertheless valued the widget more than the buyer did. Aghion and Bolton's central insight is that the parties themselves might find the gain from the ones who value the widget more than $15 greater than the loss of future partners who valued it between $10 and $15. The former is a distributional gain to the parties and the latter is a social welfare loss. See Philippe Aghion & Patrick Bolton, *Contracts as a Barrier to Entry*, 77 Am. Econ. Rev. 388, 389 (1987).

There are other examples of externalities that are not taken into account by parties to a commercial contract. Article 9 permits the secured creditor to use self-help in repossessing the collateral only if it does not commit a breach of the peace (§ 9–609). The parties may not opt out of this provision (although they can define in reasonable terms what constitutes breach of the peace). The constraint may be justified by the fact that a debtor who might agree to waive this protection probably fails to internalize all the costs of disruptions to the peace.

Chapter 3
Sales Law

3.1 Introduction[1]

Since the focus in recent years has turned to the deficiencies of the UCC and particularly of Article 2, it is easy to neglect the Code's singular contribution to sales law: a series of efficient default terms for salvaging broken contracts that reduce contracting costs for many (if not most) parties to commercial sales transactions. As noted above, in drafting Article 2, Karl Llewellyn was committed to the idea of filling contractual gaps with defaults that reduced expected contracting costs and thus, presumably, mimicked the arrangement most commercial parties would have made for themselves. Under the Sales Act, most risk allocation questions were resolved by determining who had the title to the contract goods. Thus, for example, title governed questions of "risk of loss, action for the price, the applicable law in an interstate transaction, the place and time for measuring damages, and the power to defeat the other party's interest, or to replevy, or to reject." Karl Llewellyn, *Through Title to Contract and a Bit Beyond,* 15 N.Y.U. L. Rev. 159 (1938). The problem was, that while everyone knew that the party who had the title assumed the relevant risk, no one knew who had the title. As Llewellyn observed

> this would be an admirable way to go at it if the Title concept had been tailored to fit the normal course of a going or suspended situation during its flux or suspension. But Title was not thus conceived, nor has its environment of buyers and sellers had material effect upon it. Id.

---

1. The discussion that follows in this section draws on Robert E. Scott, *The Rise and Fall of Article 2,* 62 La. L. Rev. 1009, 1032–1041 (2002).

The resulting uncertainty increased transactions costs and complicated efforts to contract out of the legal default. Llewellyn's risk of loss
rules illustrate his commitment to sales law defaults that reduce transactions costs for contracting parties. Rather than using artificial conceptions of title, Article 2 assigns the risk of loss in general to the party in
control of the goods, on the (generally sound) intuition that the party in
control can best take precautions to reduce endogenous risk and/or
insure against exogenous risks (§ 2–509). A similar approach is reflected
in the "salvage" rules of Article 2—rejection, cure, acceptance, and
revocation of acceptance (§§ 2–601—2–608). These rules were also drafted with the purpose of reducing contracting costs by encouraging ex post
adjustments by the party with the comparative advantage in mitigating
the costs of broken contracts.

Llewellyn was particularly sensitive to the costs of strategic behavior
in the performance of sales contracts. He initially proposed to substitute
a substantial performance standard in place of the traditional perfect
tender rule (requiring that the tender conform to the contract in every
respect). His argument was that substantial performance was the better
default rule for those sales contracts in which the seller's relation-
specific investment in the transaction exposed it to the risk of opportunism by the buyer. Llewellyn understood, however, that a substantial
performance rule operated as a double-edged sword. Requiring a buyer to
accept goods that "substantially conformed" to the contract reduces the
risk of strategic rejections by the buyer, but, in turn, it exposes the
buyer to an opportunistic tender by the seller of substandard goods. His
solution to this dilemma reflects his understanding that legal defaults
that impose flexible adjustment on one party become opportunities for
exploitation by the other. The answer, in his view, lay in the practices
and norms of the particular trade and industry. These norms presumably would have evolved with sufficient fact-specificity to screen legitimate requests for adjustment from strategic ones. As noted above,
Llewellyn proposed to solve this conundrum by establishing a merchant
tribunal—a specialized fact finder that would measure each party's
performance and its responses to the other's performance against established industry norms. The merchant jury proposal was abandoned,
however, in the face of objections from more conservative members of
the ALI establishment. In the end, Llewellyn returned to the perfect
tender rule but, by incorporating a cure provision in § 2–508, he was
able to create a structure for mutual adjustment that accomplishes many
of the same purposes as a substantial performance rule.

Llewellyn's solution for regulating on-going contractual relationships was even more ambitious than his scheme for regulating broken
contracts. But here he had fewer theoretical guideposts on which to rely.
Long term relational contracts are difficult for the law to address. Here
parties use price and quantity flexibility to adjust to an uncertain
furture. But the very flexibility of these contracts opens each party to

the other's opportunism at various times during the life of the contract. Here, Llewellyn relied on an intuitive sense (derived from his years as a commercial lawyer) that ongoing contractual relationships were not well regulated by binary default rules that allocated risks on an "all or nothing" basis. What Llewellyn saw was similar to the findings of Stuart Macaulay a generation later. See Stuart Macaulay, *Non-Contractual Relations in Business,* 28 Am. Soc. Rev. 555 (1963). Parties adjusted voluntarily to changed circumstances during the life of the contract. If an exogenous shock delayed the delivery of goods in a particular industry, the buyer would accept the late delivery and look for a price discount on a subsequent transaction. Not only were these patterns of flexible adjustment ubiquitous, but Llewellyn saw as well that the parties coped with moral hazard problems in much the same way: strong social norms in the form of trade practice or even contract-specific patterns of interaction developed to police opportunism on both sides of the transaction.

Llewellyn believed that custom and usages—the bylaws of commercial practice—were indistinguishable from legal rules. Thus, when a court incorporated a relevant norm as the rule of decision in a contract dispute, this action would not, he assumed, change either the character or the utility of the norm itself. But making a norm of cooperation a legally enforceable duty may have unintended effects. For example, a legal rule that makes the promisee's duty to cooperate a condition of the promisor's duty to perform may invite *both* cooperative responses from the promisee *and* strategic behavior from the promisor. The promisor may be tempted to claim that the promisee's efforts to cooperate are inadequate thus justifying a suspension of her duty of performance. Indeed, there is growing evidence that social norms and legal rules operate in different domains. One might argue, therefore, that rather than building in flexible price and quantity terms that are legally enforceable, many parties might prefer to be governed under separate regimes of bright-line legal default rules and flexible relational norms that are not legally enforceable.

A final illustration of the system of default rules for Sales contracts is the remedial scheme introduced in Article 2. Llewellyn began by focusing on the central question of all disputed contracts: which party should be responsible for salvaging the broken contract? This question, in turn, requires one to answer a deeper one: given a default rule of expectation damages equal to the value of the broken contract to the promisee, why would anyone ever breach (except inadvertently)? And yet, we observe advertent breach. The efficient breach hypothesis— which holds that breach enables the promisor to take advantage of a better market opportunity while guaranteeing the promisee the value of its bargain—fails to explain breach in markets where substitute goods are available. In such a case, the promisor can always "perform" the contract by covering on the market from a third party and tendering the substitute "performance" in satisfaction of the contract, thereby freeing the promisor to purse any alternative market opportunity without having to suffer the reputational consequences of breaching a contract. Thus the question: in a market where goods are available in substitution for the contract, what explains why any party would advertently breach?

There are two possible explanations for a promisor's decision to breach in the face of an expectation damages rule. The first is benign: the decision to breach is a "cry for help"—a request that the contracting partner adjust to the broken contract by covering (or reselling) on the market and submitting a "damages" bill to the promisor. The assumption here is that the promisor recognizes that it will suffer a loss on the contract and wishes to enlist the promisee's assistance in minimizing that loss. The decision to breach, on this view, is made after comparing the promisor's costs of acting on the market with the (presumably lower) salvage costs of the promisee (for example, a breaching seller presumably would incur greater costs in finding a substitute seller from whom to purchase conforming goods to tender to the buyer than would the buyer, who knows better the market for the goods that it requires). The alternative explanation is strategic: breach is motivated by the imperfections in the judicial system that systematically deny the promisee his contractual expectancy. Promisors who breach, under this conception, are able to exploit these imperfections to secure a favorable settlement of the disputed transaction. If the benign story is the more probable explanation for the promisor's breach, an efficient default rule would direct courts to award only a damages remedy to the promisee, thus encouraging the promisee to respond to the cry for help by acting appropriately on the market. On the other hand, if the malign scenario is the more probable in the particular case, the rule should direct the court to grant specific relief to the promisee, thus trumping the (presumptively) strategic request for assistance.

Under the Article 2 scheme, the nature of the market for substitute goods determines which of these explanations is assumed to be more likely in any particular case. Where the market is thin, the implicit assumption is that breach is more likely to be strategic and the promisee can trump the "cry for help" by demanding either specific performance or the contract price (as the case may be) (§§ 2–716, 2–709(1)(b)). The argument is that, in a thin market, a promisee is unlikely to enjoy a comparative advantage over the promisor in covering on the market while, at the same time, the promisee is more vulnerable to strategic claims that the cover contract was unreasonable since market prices are more difficult to prove. The Code's remedial scheme implicitly assumes, however, that sales transactions are conducted in markets. Thus, specific performance (or an action for the price) is an extraordinary remedy (§§ 2–703, 2–711). Where there is an available market for the contract goods, therefore, the promisee is limited to market damages: the promisee is presumed to have the comparative advantage in salvaging the broken contract and must act on the market and subsequently submit a damage claim to the breaching promisor. This motivates the promisee to adjust efficiently to the broken contract by salvaging the broken contract on the market, either by resale or by cover (or, in the alternative, by relying on proof of what such an action on the market would have yielded).

In the excerpts that follow, we consider in depth the issues just raised, each of which continues to concern both scholars and courts. We focus first in section 3.2 on three different perspectives on Llewellyn's jurisprudence and how his notion of law as being embedded in the mores and practices of the parties influenced the rules that ultimately were promulgated in Article 2. In section 3.3 we turn to an analysis of the so-called "salvage" rules of sales law: the doctrines of perfect tender, rejection, revocation and cure. Professors Sebert and Priest offer two different perspectives on the efficacy of these rules based on whether one evaluates them from an ex ante or an ex post perspective. We then turn in section 3.4 to the problems regulating on-going or relational contracts. The excerpt from Professor Joskow focuses on the use of price adjustment mechanisms to cope with future uncertainty; Professor Weistart tackles a related issue: the challenge for sales law in developing effective rules for regulating quantity variations in output and requirements contracts. Section 3.5 turns to the remedial scheme of the Code and the wisdom of relying on a default rule that protects the expectation interest in the event of breach. Professors Scott and Triantis reframe the breach and damages question in terms of the exercise price of an option to terminate; an option that is purchased by the promisor at the time of contract. This perspective illuminates the question considered by Professor Kandel: when can the promisor "return" goods without incurring damages liability for breach. In the final section, 3.6 we turn to the law of good faith purchase and examine two views on the rules that protect the good faith purchaser from the interests of third parties.

3.2   Karl Llewellyn and the Normative Underpinnings of Article 2

The Limits of Vision: Karl Llewellyn and the Merchant Rules*

ZIPPORAH BATSHAW WISEMAN

In the 1930s, lawyers, merchants, and legal scholars reached a consensus that the Uniform Sales Act of 1906 was obsolete. Each of these groups criticized the Act for failing to relate meaningfully to the demands and complexities of modern commercial relations. Karl Llewellyn shared the general view that the Act was obsolete in the sense of

---

* 100 Harv. L. Rev. 465 (1987).

being out of date. As a realist, however, he also believed that it was obsolete in a second, more specific sense. He believed that the 1906 Act embodied an obsolete form of law—consisting of rules derived from a few broad abstractions, removed from practical experience, and expected to answer all questions. The consensus for change provided Llewellyn with the opportunity to rewrite sales law. That consensus also provides the context in which his specific vision of sales law, and his successes and failures in the pursuit of that vision, must be evaluated.

Samuel Williston drafted the Uniform Sales Act of 1906 for the National Conference of Commissioners on Uniform State Laws.... Fifteen years later, however, only twenty-three jurisdictions out of a possible fifty-three had adopted the new Sales Act. The failure of more than half the jurisdictions to adopt the Act resulted in a signal lack of uniformity. A sales transaction involving more than one state might be governed in state courts by either the Uniform Sales Act or by the common law of sales of the non-Uniform Sales Act state.... To provide the missing uniformity, an ABA committee in 1921, working with Professor Williston, proposed a Federal Sales Act based on the Uniform Sales Act. The bill was first introduced in Congress in 1923 and was reintroduced without success ... Although by 1935 the Uniform Sales Act had been adopted in eleven more states, including the most important commercial jurisdictions, complete uniformity remained elusive.

As Williston's Uniform Sales Act approached its goal of uniformity, Llewellyn published his first major work criticizing it as ill-suited to sales transactions.... Llewellyn was correct in calling the Uniform Sales Act a "rebuilt machine." It was based on the English Sales of Goods Act of 1893, which itself was based on nineteenth-century English sales law that reflected the organization of nineteenth and even eighteenth-century commerce. In nineteenth-century commerce, the prototypical sales transaction was the face-to-face sale in which the buyer paid cash and took her goods home. Llewellyn sought, instead, a model that reflected the reality of a twentieth-century "nationwide indirect marketing structure." In the modern world of sales, Llewellyn's and ours, most commercial sellers and buyers of goods do not deal face-to-face and do not immediately take the goods home. Rather, they contract for a sale in the future; their agreement is usually on the buyer's or seller's printed form; their sale is on credit; and their relationship has just begun. In addition, there may be one or more middlemen between the seller-manufacturer and the buyer, who may be buying for resale or for use. Both the commercial structure of a sale and the needs of the parties to it will vary markedly depending on whether it is a sale to a business buyer for resale or for use, or to a consumer. Williston's law of sales, reflecting faithfully the English Act on which it was modeled, took no cognizance of these complexities.

The doctrine of title offers the best example in sales law of the sort of abstract doctrine to which Llewellyn objected. At common law and in the Sales Act of 1906, the answer to the question "who had title" was used to resolve a wide range of issues when a sale of goods went awry. In a modern sales transaction—that is, any transaction more complex than a face-to-face exchange of goods for cash—this question is often difficult, if not impossible, to answer.... By the late 1930s, Llewellyn was not alone in seeing problems of obsolescence in the Uniform Sales Act. Indeed, the merchants were the first to complain, followed by the academic community and the commercial bar. All agreed that the Act was obsolete, but Llewellyn's vision of reform was far more dramatic and comprehensive than that of his political allies.

* * * * *

[In the] spring [of 1940] Llewellyn began planning with [William] Schnader to unveil their much grander idea of reform—the Uniform Commercial Code. This new code was to be drafted by the Conference for adoption by the states.... [F]or the first stage, Llewellyn did it himself. In "five weeks' work by the clock, and uninterrupted," Llewellyn wrote an eighty-eight page draft of a "Uniform Sales Act 1940." .... Llewellyn's vision of sales law, reflected in that 1940 draft and in his earlier writings and subsequent revisions of the draft, was no mere update of Williston's approach. Nor were its revisions limited to the rules for foreign and interstate trade that first motivated Thomas. Obsolescence in general was an important starting point, but modernization was not Llewellyn's only end. Llewellyn's objective was to reformulate sales law in light of his normative vision of both merchant practice and judicial decisionmaking.

The Llewellyn Vision

Llewellyn proposed to bring the law more in line with merchant reality and to encourage Grand Style decisionmaking by judges. In advocating merchant reality as a standard, Llewellyn was arguing for an approach that accepted the marketplace norms of speed and efficiency ... Llewellyn, however, was not entirely uncritical in his acceptance of mercantile reality. His vision also encompassed a normative belief that the law should encourage the better practices and control the worst abuses of the market. In addition, he recognized the potential unfairness of applying merchant standards to individuals who lacked knowledge of these standards and experience with them. On at least one occasion, he proposed extra protection for the private purchaser and the ultimate user—introducing the idea of strict liability for dangerous product defects decades before consumerism was born as a movement.

In addition to proposals seeking to promote the better merchant practices, Llewellyn offered a new vision of judging. Llewellyn believed that judging in the "Grand Style" was the surest route to law that was certain, predictable, and true to its underlying purposes. This belief may appear either unexceptionable or naive to the modern reader, but in

1940 Llewellyn was seeking to replace verbally simple unitary rules of sales law, removed from the actual facts of commercial transactions, with purposive reasoning in the Grand Manner. Whether his Grand Style of judging could ever attain the goals Llewellyn ascribed to it is a difficult question; but in its time, it was a radical change from the abstract formalisms of the contemporary law of sales.

Llewellyn's vision of sales law was, in many respects, a clear example of his realist method applied to commercial law. As a realist, Llewellyn viewed law as a means to social ends and recognized the need to reexamine the law constantly to ensure that it fit the society it claimed to serve. As a scholar and draftsman of sales law, he advocated that the law conform to a normative vision of merchant reality; that it focus not on abstractions such as "title" but on fair allocation of risk in the particular type of case or circumstance; and that it distinguish the burdens imposed on merchants from those imposed on consumers. As a realist, he understood the manipulation of argument and result. He sought, therefore, to make clear through both the statutory provisions and the Comments of his new Sales Act the principles and reasons that should guide judicial decisionmaking in the Grand Style.

As his 1930 casebook demonstrates, Llewellyn recognized early on the gap between the Uniform Sales Act's approach to sales and the commercial realities of his day. It was not simply that the Act failed to take account of growing complexities but that its approach had little to do with the facts of the transactions it governed. The problem with title, for example, in Llewellyn's realist vision, was not simply locating "title", [but that title] bore no necessary relationship to the issue the concept was used to solve. Llewellyn pointed out, for example, that the question of who bears the risk of loss or damage to goods sold but not yet delivered should be answered by determining who was in the best position to prevent the loss or damage and who had an insurable interest at the time. For Llewellyn, the issue was fair allocation of risk, not determination of who has title. He believed that such commercial realities, rather than general abstract concepts, should form the basis for the law.

Yet if merchant reality was a cornerstone of Llewellyn's vision and approach, it was at least partially a prescriptive conception of merchant reality that he sought in his drafts of the Code. Llewellyn's willingness to incorporate the realities of the market in the law did not extend to a total abdication of judicial control to the expediencies of the market. . . . In 1940, although Llewellyn described commercial law as "largely non-political in character," he made clear that he did not believe "merchant reality" was a justification for legalizing practices that he considered oppressive or sharp-dealing. The forms used by merchants, he maintained, need as much "firm court control as . . . firm court understanding." Courts and lawmakers must not close their eyes to "differential knowledge, power and bargaining skill" among parties to contracts, "lest old rules based on Adam Smithian postulates be made tools of outrage." Thus, in drafting article 2, Llewellyn sought simultaneously to incorporate merchant reality, to insist on the "better rules" of merchant practice, and to impose his own "better" rules in the interest of fostering a better reality.

Llewellyn's vision of laws that would take into consideration merchant reality and permit Grand Style judging found expression in his proposals for merchant rules. He had long advocated the separation of the law of nonmerchant sales, which he called the law of "horse" and "haystacks," from law governing merchant sales. In his 1940 and 1941 drafts of a new sales act, he made specific proposals for rules designed to apply to merchant transactions. The 1940 draft included merchant provisions relating to many aspects of contracts for the sales of goods, their formation, the risk of loss of the goods, performance, warranties, and the remedies for breach. In 1941, Llewellyn expanded these proposals and also include new merchant provisions relating to trade usage, warranties, and expert merchant tribunals for the resolution of issues of mercantile fact.

Merchant provisions, Llewellyn maintained, would make the law better suited to merchant transactions in three ways. First, the law would reflect to a degree, if not explicitly incorporate, the better standards and practices, as well as the understandings and needs, of merchants. Second, separate provisions would generate a separate body of precedent that merchants and their lawyers could consult without the confusion caused by trying to predict whether approaches adopted in a nonmerchant context would be followed in cases involving merchants. Finally, under the merchant tribunal provision discussed below, issues of mercantile fact arising under the merchant provisions could be submitted by merchants to an expert panel of their peers, eliminating the perceived risks of submitting such questions to lay jurors....

The notion of merchant rules might be seen by some as an example of Llewellyn's commitment to a vision of merchant reality devoid of any normative component—or at least devoid of any normative component other than speed and efficiency in the marketplace.... Some of Llewellyn's rules did seek only to codify the common practices and understandings of the marketplace. The rule relating to trade usage is one example: it simply provided that the usage of trade, or of a particular trade, is "presumed to be the background which the parties have presupposed in their bargaining and have intended to read into the particular contract." ... In advocating these changes, Llewellyn was not imposing standards on the marketplace but calling on courts to incorporate the existing standards honestly and explicitly.

However, Llewellyn proposed other significant merchant rules that did not simply try to make sales law more realistic or closer to the patterns of actual merchant transactions. Some of his rules sought to establish at least some outer bounds of unfairness between merchants in their dealings. The substantial performance rule, the merchant exception to the Statute of Frauds, and the provision binding merchants to additional terms in contracts in which they receive notice and fail to object, are clear examples of Llewellyn's concern for establishing new legal norms of fairness among merchants. In offering these provisions, Llewellyn's target was the worst of the "sharpers," and his goal was to impose his vision of the fair rule for merchants.

   1. Substantial Performance.—The common law had long distinguished between contracts for the sale of goods, where goods could be rejected for any deviation from the contract terms (described as the absence of a "perfect tender"), and nonsales contracts, for which failure of perfect tender, termed "substantial performance," gave rise at most to damages but not to a right to rescission. The Uniform Sales Act followed the common law in enforcing the "perfect tender" rule in sales contracts against both merchants and nonmerchants. Llewellyn proposed the substitution of a "substantial performance" rule to govern sales of goods between merchants....

   In theory, his definition reflects an effort to focus on the realities of the marketplace; in practice, its application invites a battle of experts, with the jury ultimately required to choose among them in determining the substantiality of the seller's performance, the materiality of any increase in the buyer's risks, and the extent to which the buyer's operating requirements had been met. The only answer to these practices offered by Llewellyn in his 1940 draft was to allow the parties the option by agreement to submit the issue of the substantiality of the breach to conclusive arbitration. "Substantiality of the breach" was one of a number of "narrow points of fact" for which responsibility for decision could be placed on expert arbitrators whose "competence makes possible speedy and accurate judgment." Thus, where the parties opted for binding arbitration, the problem of a lay jury unfamiliar with commercial realities choosing among conflicting expert testimony would not arise.

   2. The Merchant Tribunal.—Llewellyn's merchant tribunal proposal called for merchant experts to sit with a court "not as party representatives, but as a special sworn expert tribunal to find the true facts." Either party could request a merchant jury; the consent of the other side was not required. The issues that could be submitted to the merchant jury included not only the substantiality of any breach but also the effect of mercantile usage or the usage of a particular trade on the terms of the contract: "the mercantile reasonableness of any action by either party," and "any other issue which requires for its competent determination special merchants' knowledge rather than general knowledge." The merchant experts were to render a written, unanimous verdict, which, in order to meet constitutional objections based on the right to trial by lay jury, would then be received in evidence at the trial. The trial jury would be instructed what the merchant panel was and how its members were selected, and would be told "that the finding can be disregarded by the jury if they can in conscience disregard it." Presumably, such exercises of conscience would be rare.

The Fate of the Exemplary Provisions

1. Substantial Performance.—The substantial performance rule was an effort by Llewellyn to impose the better practice of the market-place as a rule of law ... In this instance, the visions of Llewellyn and the merchants diverged completely. When Llewellyn looked to merchant reality, he saw the perfect tender rule as a tool of those who would abuse its right of rejection. He had confidence that the legal system, with juries instructed and reviewed by Grand Style judges, could remedy those abuses. By contrast, the merchants had confidence in their own ability to remedy abuses in the market. When they looked to the legal system, they saw the substantial performance rule as a tool for abuse in the hands of courts and juries. Thomas argued that a standard of substantial perform-ance was unthinkable with a lay jury. Yet even if the notion of merchant juries could be worked out—which he doubted and ultimately opposed—Thomas asserted that there would be no need for a substantial perform-ance standard, because in a case of abuse of the right of rejection "your merchant's jury will be very apt to set it right."

2. Merchant Tribunals.—Llewellyn's detailed proposal for a panel of merchant experts to sit with the court "to find the true facts" within the scope of their expertise was received with a mixture of admiration and skepticism at the 1942 Conference.' Even its admirers raised doubts about the constitutionality of the procedure under state constitutions and the serious obstacles it might therefore pose to consideration and passage of the Act in the states.... The merchant jury proposal died with the 1942 meeting.

Conclusion

Article 2 of the Uniform Commercial Code of 1962 is a patchwork. The frame and basic design are Llewellyn's, but many of the pieces discussed in this Article are missing. The scars of the twenty-year drafting process are manifest. How would he have evaluated that results in terms of his own goals as a commercial lawyer and legal realist? Llewellyn's single most important change in sales law, the elimination of the traditional "lump-concept" of title as the touchstone to answer questions in sales law ranging from remedies to risk of loss, is now universally acknowledged as a great success. The idea of having the rights between sellers and buyers turn on the "step by step action taken by the parties in relation to the contract" instead of on the passing of title was a brilliant contribution to the law of sales. Despite Professor Williston's dire warning, the "seamless web" of the law has not been rent asunder. Instead, courts, lawyers, and commercial actors all benefit from the realist commitment to resolving legal problems by reference to their factual circumstances rather than to abstract legal categories. The realist goal of grouping legal situations into "narrower categories" that fit, that are based on the actual commercial circumstances, has indeed been achieved in this respect.

But in other areas article 2 did not secure this realist vision. Llewellyn's original conception of the merchant rules has essentially disappeared. The rules have been drastically reduced in number and effect. And when a conflict arises, courts frequently apply the remaining rules in a manner that Llewellyn would describe as the essence of Formal Style judging.

Commercial Law and the American Volk: a Note on Llewellyn's German Sources for the Uniform Commercial Code*

JAMES WHITMAN

American commercial law is largely the creation of America's most eccentric legal philosopher. Karl Llewellyn was the principal author of the Uniform Commercial Code (U.C.C.). He gave the Code an often baffling jurisprudential framework: The U.C.C. regularly refuses to supply substantive rules. Instead, with startling frequency, the Code directs courts to determine whether the parties in a given commercial dispute have acted "reasonably" or in accordance with "customs" and "usages of trade" that are nowhere specified or described in the Code itself. The Code's routine use of these vague directives has irritated some commentators and thrilled many others. Almost as soon as it appeared, a body of scholarly commentary began to grow up around Llewellyn's strangely indefinite Code, and scholars continue to search for the intellectual sources of the Code in the peculiarities of Llewellyn's personality and in the history of his contribution to the decade-long drafting process of the U.C.C.

Despite these many scholarly efforts, no consensus about the meaning of Llewellyn's work has emerged. Some commentators have seen the Code as the product of a carefully conceived philosophical program, as part of a campaign to "liberalize" commercial law, or to put some form of philosophical realism into practice. Others have seen the Code less as a calculated philosophical effort than as a piece of historical revivalism in commercial law, an attempt, through the ratification of trade usage, to bring back to life the medieval law merchant, which was based on commercial customs and practices. As Homer Kripke, one of Llewellyn's collaborators, put it, Llewellyn's Code was intended "to correct some false starts, to point the law in the indicated directions, and to restore

* 97 YALE L. J. 156 (1987).

the law merchant as an institution for growth only lightly kept in bounds by statute." These divergent explanations coexist unreconciled in the Llewellyn literature; no scholar has been able to explain what relation Llewellyn's commitment to liberalization might bear to his love of the historic law merchant. Llewellyn's biographer has simply concluded that no "clearcut answer" can be given to the question of what part Llewellyn's jurisprudential ideas played in the shaping of the Code. Forty years of debate have thus left us with the picture of a Code created by an inexplicable original genius.

When Llewellyn accepted William Schnader's 1940 invitation to become Chief Reporter of the new Uniform Commercial Code, he brought with him the . . . idea that law made by the sound instincts of merchant jurors, freed of constricting formalism, was true law of the people. As Llewellyn took up his duties, he declared his dissatisfaction with an American legal order that did not permit the establishment of special commercial courts. The task of commercial codification, he declared, was to find some way to integrate mercantile arbitration into American law. A year later Llewellyn had designed the elaborate legal machinery of Section 59 of the Second Draft of the new Sales Act, which provided for the submission of a wide range of questions to merchant jurors on the motion of either party. Section 59 put into legal form the German model Llewellyn had proposed for America in 1932. To be sure, Llewellyn insisted he was reviving a Common Law tradition, not importing a German one: Possibly because German institutions had an ugly association with Hitler, Llewellyn declared repeatedly that the scheme of Section 59 was intended, not as a Germanization of American law, but as a revival of the practices of Lord Mansfield.

Llewellyn's proposed code was intended to do more than just restore the law merchant. Llewellyn intimated throughout his comments and memoranda that his Code was intended somehow to promote a rule of the American people through an altered form of the rule of law. . . . Commercial courts could give the American small-town Volk a chance to exercise pressure for "reasonableness and decency"; commercial law would be "known to be friendly, even neighborly."

To be sure, Llewellyn's 1940–41 conception of the "friendly . . . neighborly" Volk was not a German one. The Llewellyn of 1941 was guided as much by the social vision of Frank Capra as by the legal, historical vision of Levin Goldschmidt; behind Llewellyn's theorizing lay a Depression-era longing for small-town cooperation and social normalcy, in which the power of the community would stand by the "little man" in his conflict with the "big man." . . . . [H]e was motivated, not only by a sober intellectual distrust of formalism, but by an intoxicated faith that courts could somehow speak for the spirit of the nation. Llewellyn's scheme represented, to be sure, realism of a kind. But it was realism with a democratist tinge. Rule of merchant jurors, premised on staunch anti-formalism, would be rule of the people. Commercial "reasonableness" would be a subset of the American people's "reasonableness and decency." The draft that Llewellyn laid before the Conference of Commissioners on Uniform State Laws in September of 1941 would be a code for the American Volk.

Conclusion

But the commissioners did not accept Llewellyn's draft—or rather they accepted it only in a partial, indeed in a mangled, form. Discussion of Section 59 was adverse to Llewellyn's scheme. By 1942, the institution of merchant juries had vanished from the working draft of the Uniform Commercial Code. The loss of Section 59 was, perhaps, no great loss. One may doubt whether Llewellyn's vision of a people's commercial law cultivated by special merchant juries could ever have been realized in practice. But when the commissioners abandoned Section 59, they did not abandon a host of provisions that assumed the institutional framework of Section 59. Llewellyn's Code retained its deference to "custom," the "law merchant," "good faith" and "reasonableness." In Llewellyn's Romantic vocabulary, however, "custom," the "law merchant," "good faith" and "reasonableness" were not terms of substantive law, but procedural directives, indications to a court that it should refer its decision to lay specialists with a feel for commercial law. Without a body of laymen whose intuitions—or whose feel for business—made it possible to navigate the waters of custom, none of the . . . theorizing had much meaning.

And indeed, faced with a code studded with reference-less procedural directives, courts flounder. The many provisions of the U.C.C. that call upon courts to decide "reasonableness" have proven a source of constant confusion. These provisions were composed on the assumption that Section 59 merchant juries would be available to develop a case-law of "reasonableness." In the absence of such juries, courts have been wholly unable to agree whether questions of "reasonableness" are to be decided by judge or by trier of fact; "reasonableness" has shown itself to be a major source of non-uniformity in the jurisprudence of the Uniform Code. Determining "custom" and "usage" has proven problematic as well: Without Llewellyn's merchant jurors, courts have had to cope with complex hearsay and burden of proof problems. As for the "law merchant," the phrase has become little more than a dead letter. Courts almost never refer to the "law merchant," and when they do, they treat the words as synonymous with "Common Law" or "Equity"; the idea of the ancient customary lex mercatoria, which Llewellyn hoped to see his Code revivify, has been quite forgotten.

Karl Llewellyn and the Origins of Contract Theory*
ALAN SCHWARTZ

Karl Llewellyn was America's leading legal realist, academic law reformer and Contract Law theorist. There are extensive analyses of Llewellyn's performance as a realist and reformer but his contracts scholarship, written between 1925 and 1940, has not been seriously analyzed.... There are marked differences between the Llewellyn to whom modern scholars commonly refer and the Llewellyn who created the theory (or perhaps differences between the earlier and later Llewellyns).

Llewellyn's contract theory was meant to tell decisionmakers how to regulate sales transactions. The decisionmakers in the theory were courts and law reform organizations such as the National Conference of Commissioners on Uniform State Laws; legislatures played a minor role. The theory had a substantive aspect (what the legal rules should be) and an institutional aspect (which legal institutions should make the rules and what form should the rules take). Both aspects of the theory implied views that would be regarded as conventional in today's law and economics world.

A theory directed to decisionmakers should identify and motivate its norms. Law reformers then were concerned with efficiency and redistribution. Llewellyn believed that distributional goals had no place in a contract theory because the commercial actors in the theory commonly occupied the two relevant roles of buyer and seller. This multiplicity of roles would vitiate the pursuit of distributional ends, for what a party would gain when wearing her seller hat she would lose when wearing her buyer hat. The regnant norm in Llewellyn's contract theory thus was efficiency, as then understood. Llewellyn never explicitly justified the pursuit of efficiency. Rather, he believed that American society had accepted the efficiency norm and he did as well.

The Substantive Aspect

The substantive aspect of Llewellyn's contract theory followed from four premises: (1) Courts should interpret contracts in light of the parties' commercial objectives and the context in which they dealt; (2) Decision makers should complete incomplete contracts with rules that reflect the deal typical parties would make in the circumstances; (3) A court should not enforce a contract without an independent inquiry into its substantive fairness if one party's consent to the contract was unconscionably procured; (4) Decisionmakers should reduce the transaction costs of doing deals.

* THE JURISPRUDENTIAL FOUNDATIONS OF CORPORATE AND COMMERCIAL LAW 12–53 (J.S. Kraus & S.D. Walt eds. 2000).

Versions of these premises (except perhaps the fourth) were held when Llewellyn wrote. Llewellyn took the first two premises more seriously than his contemporaries did, however. He believed that the typical court or law reformer viewed the commercial world through the distorting lens of taught legal doctrine. This produced the incorrect interpretations and flawed rules that much of his work sought to correct. Llewellyn also was more concerned than other scholars of his time with the question when the state should restrict private contract. The most original aspect of Llewellyn's work, however, lay not in his recognition of the relevance of these four premises, but rather in the many provocative substantive and institutional implications he drew from them.

Law and economics scholars today commonly attempt to develop contract rules by identifying the cost minimizing solution to a contracting problem. Thus, an analyst will develop a model to show what contract term respecting damages would be efficient for a particular transaction type. The scholar then will recommend that the law adopt this term as the default solution when the parties' contract is silent concerning damages. Llewellyn seldom worked in this way because the economics of his time was too primitive. Continuing with the example, optimal contract terms respecting damages today are derived as the equilibria of asymmetric information contracting games. Game theory had not been developed when Llewellyn wrote, so he could not identify game theoretic solutions to the particular contracting problems his theory had to solve.

Llewellyn thus worked "indirectly": he used commercial practice as the best evidence of the efficient transaction. Parties, he believed, pursued their self interest when contracting (maximized their expected utility). Hence, the parties' consent to a deal was good evidence that the deal was efficient. It was this method of analysis that made Llewellyn sensitive to freedom of contract issues. When one party dictated the contract terms, an analyst could infer only that those terms maximized the utility of the powerful party, not that the deal was globally efficient. Dictation would occur, in Llewellyn's view, if one party had structural market power or was more knowledgeable or sophisticated than the other. Such "fiat contracts" lacked the epistemological relevance of "bargained for" contracts. Consequently, courts must make an independent inquiry into a contract's normative suitability when a party's consent to the contract was not conscionably procured. To use practice as evidence of efficiency, that is, requires a theory of unconscionability.i

Llewellyn also interestingly pursued several implications of his epistemological view that common practice commonly is efficient. The typical judge, he thought, seldom could discern the parties' commercial goals, but a judge could become sophisticated by repeated acquaintance with the facts. Thus Llewellyn was ambivalent regarding the ability of courts to develop good commercial law rules. Judges of unusual ability with an interest in commerce could do well, as could judges on courts that saw many commercial cases. But the ordinary judge needed help. He could find it from three sources: arbitrators; custom; and trade association rules. Arbitrators were helpful, in Llewellyn's view, because they had the expertise to identify the deal the parties actually made.

Llewellyn had a nuanced view of custom and trade associations. He believed that trade custom could be good evidence of the efficient arrangement, but also that the existence of a custom often was irrelevant to adjudication. Custom commonly is challenged in law suits: the party against whom the custom is asserted claims that the custom does not exist or does not apply to the case at bar. Llewellyn was sympathetic to these challenges. Customs, he thought, reflected the solutions to normal business problems, but the disputes that came to court often were caused by exogenous economic shocks. A custom meant to govern in normal times could shed no light on the efficient resolution of unusual—"trouble"—cases. Rather, the court or law reformer must solve directly for the best solution.

Llewellyn was similarly cautious regarding the epistemological relevance of trade association rules. If all parties whom a rule affects are represented in the trade association, the rule is a contract between parties of equal bargaining power, and as such is good evidence of the efficient arrangement. Trade associations, however, often imposed rules on outsiders such as unorganized consumers, and these rules were like contracts between parties of unequal bargaining power; one could not conclude that such a rule was efficient just because the sophisticated side of the market liked it.

To summarize the substantive aspect of Llewellyn's thought, Llewellyn believed that decisionmakers should enforce, facilitate and enact efficient commercial arrangements. The decisionmaker could infer the efficient solution from what parties commonly did. Llewellyn's frequent references to the parties' goals, their deals, custom and rules of the trade thus were epistemological in intention. What is out there is evidence, but not always reliable evidence, of what maximizes social welfare. Contrary to Llewellyn's reputation among some modern scholars, he did not believe that decisionmakers could infer values from facts, nor did he think that the state should delegate lawmaking power to private groups.

When practice did not supply reliable evidence of efficiency, Llewellyn sometimes would derive the transaction cost minimizing solution directly. As one example, he argued that sellers should be permitted to sue for the price when buyers rejected in distant markets. After rejection, either the buyer or the seller could mitigate damages by reselling the goods. A successful price action would force the buyer to resell because the buyer would become the owner. It is efficient to make distant rejecting buyers resell because these buyers have a comparative advantage at maximizing resale revenue: the goods are in the buyer's market and he commonly knows that market well.

The Institutional Aspect

Contract Law rules performed three functions in Llewellyn's theory: to fill gaps in incomplete contracts; to develop and apply appropriate constraints on the parties' freedom to contract; and to direct or "channel" the adjudicator's fact finding function. Creating rules to perform these functions requires expertise, and the rules themselves must be clear. The need for expertise underlay Llewellyn's view that commercial law rules are best created by administrative agencies or specialized law reform organizations. Llewellyn's stress on rule clarity presupposed the ability of rules to guide parties and constrain courts, and Llewellyn accepted this presupposition. Rule scepticism played no role in his theory. Legal rules, he thought, also should ask courts to find facts—which party had possession of the goods when the fire struck?—rather than require conceptual analysis—which party had title when the fire struck? Llewellyn, however, rejected conceptual analysis only at the level of rule application. Otherwise, he admired this form of analysis and sometimes did it.

Llewellyn's thought about rules written for commercial codes was a major exception to these views. Llewellyn believed that codes were difficult to amend, and so would have to be applied in quite varied commercial circumstances. As a consequence, code rules should not reflect solutions to specific contracting problems, but rather should constitute normative premises for reasoning or channel the courts' fact finding function. Llewellyn's position concerning the appropriate level of abstraction for UCC rules thus did not reflect his thought on rules generally.

Critique

Llewellyn's general substantive and institutional approaches to Sales and Contract Law rules remain relevant. Modern law and economics scholars believe, with Llewellyn, that the state should pursue efficiency in the contract area because efficiency is the only implementable goal. And efficiency should be pursued, by and large, in the ways that Llewellyn advocated: courts should enforce the deals that parties make, which requires courts to understand the economics of commercial transactions; and doctrine or statute should attempt to reduce the costs to parties of making deals by choosing as the default solution the efficient contract term. Llewellyn's major achievement was to develop this general approach to the legal analysis of contract.

Many of Llewellyn's specific analyses, however, rest on errors and it is therefore a mistake to rely on his recommendations for what should be done in concrete cases. Without the concepts and tools of modern economic analysis, Llewellyn could not understand how market power is acquired and exercised, and so his unconscionability theories are too primitive. He also had perceptive insights respecting when rules should be mandatory or defaults and which transaction costs the state likely could reduce. But because Llewellyn could not understand these concepts as moderns do, his work often is unhelpful. Llewellyn, however, sometimes did not satisfy the standards of his time. Other realists recognized that more can be learned about the world by studying it directly than can be learned from Llewellyn's method of reading appellate opinions with particular attention to the facts. And consistency in thought has always been a virtue. A perhaps illuminating way to summarize this critique is to remark that Newton's theory remains true over much of the domain it was created to explain but a fair amount of Llewellyn's work is not true in this sense because it never was true.

Conclusion

Karl Llewellyn's contract theory can be analyzed on two levels of abstraction. On the high level, Llewellyn's general approach to the legal regulation of contracting behavior is powerful and current. Llewellyn understood that the law had three tasks, to enforce the parties' deal when the deal was discernable, to create default rules to complete incomplete contracts and to mark the limits of freedom of contract. Llewellyn justified the law's performance of the first task on efficiency grounds and used the efficiency norm to help the law perform the second task. Llewellyn's commitment to efficiency also informed his analysis of freedom of contract, for he thought that efficiency was unlikely when the bargaining process was conducted under much less than ideal conditions, and the results of such flawed processes therefore were not entitled to the law's deference. On the lower level of application of the approach, Llewellyn seldom is relevant to us. Llewellyn could only work with the tools he had, and those tools were too primitive for the task he set himself. No analyst could make much progress on the creation of good default rules or on developing criteria for efficient interventions in markets without a knowledge of game theory, transaction cost economics and the economics of information. Because these bodies of knowledge were created after Llewellyn worked, many of his particular applications were mistaken. In addition, Llewellyn was a poor empiricist (at least in economic areas), and he was not always consistent in his thinking. Nevertheless, Llewellyn's general approach easily accommodated itself to the use of new economic tools and indeed facilitated their introduction. In this significant sense, he was the major founder.

NOTES

1. What do courts do in interpreting Article 2? Wiseman and Whitman both agree that the idea of the merchant jury was too radical for the lawyers who made up the private legislative groups (the ALI and NCCUSL) who were responsible for drafting the Code and securing its adoption by the states. They also concur that the abolition of the merchant jury together with the retention of vague terms such as commercial reasonableness has produced a less than satisfactory codification of sales law. But they differ as to what courts are doing. Wiseman suggests that courts retreat to "formal reasoning" while Whitman suggests that the result has been inconsistent outcomes and confusion. Since formal reasoning implies adherence to abstract principle while confusion implies the absence of discernable principle, can they both be right? Do you agree with the proposition that the elimination of the concept of title and the introduction of realist notions that the law should track actual practice is a contribution that outweigh's the reliance by Article 2 on unmoored concepts of "reasonableness"? Does your answer depend on your view of the likelihood of judicial error in applying these concepts?

2. Where did Llewellyn's ideas come from? Wiseman attributes Llewellyn's normative framework to legal realism, while Whitman suggests that it's an evocation of an "American style" sense of reasonableness and decency. Schwartz on that other hand, argues that by focusing on Llewellyn's contract law writings themselves, one find the normative foundations of modern law and economics. Are there any unifying principles that tie these apparently diverse methodologies together or is this simply a further reflection of Llewellyn, the "inexplicable genius"?

3. Yet another view of Llewellyn. Professor Robert Scott offers another view of Llewellyn's normative commitments in *The Rise and Fall of Article 2*, 62 La. L. Rev. 1009 (2002):

> At first blush, Llewellyn's views on the normative concerns of contract law seem to be hopelessly inconsistent. On the one hand, he held a strong view that parties, not courts, should determine the terms of their contracts. Parties should be permitted to make "any contract they please" because the "animals probably know their own business better than their keeper does—a theory that has not only charm but virtue most of the time." On the other hand, he advocated a theory of regulation that empowered courts to strike down and/or rewrite contract terms whenever the contract was "unbalanced.".... For Llewellyn, however, the tension was only a technical and not a normative problem. He did not view the regulatory function as representing a clash of interests—as between retail sellers and consumer buyers—but rather as an exercise in policing outlier sellers, the "contract-dodger" or "sharper." Viewed through this lens, the regulatory task could be appropriately confined to policing aberrant transactions without hindering the facilitation of efficient contracting for the vast majority of contracting parties. In short, for Llewellyn, the distributional question was derivative of the efficiency question. Thus, he was willing to privilege the freedom of parties to contract out of default rules over the regulatory role of courts in policing unbalanced bargains because he viewed the former as the norm and the latter as atypical. The regulatory role could be properly confined because, in Llewellyn's view, the key unit of analysis was the group—merchants in a particular trade or practice—and the group can and would engage in self-policing.

Llewellyn was particularly influenced by the work of John Commons and the other members of the Institutional school of economics. Commons' principal contribution was to replace the individual with the transaction as the basic unit of analysis. The larger unit in Commons framework was the "going concern." According to Commons, "a going concern is a joint expectation of beneficial bargaining, managerial and rationing transactions, kept together by *working rules* ... and by control of the changeable strategic or limiting factors which are expected to control others."

Llewellyn adopted Common's notion of working rules (social norms in contemporary terminology) and incorporated them as a "common law" applying not only within an economic unit but between economic units as well. Since these rules were produced by the strategic interactions between economic units in society, those units had an ongoing motivation to police those members of the group who attempted to chisel or otherwise violate the norms. Hence his commitment to group-policing of contractual chiselers was based on a theory of the group's self-interest in protecting its place in the economic order.... The best option for regulating lopsided bargains, therefore, lay with the groups themselves.... In sum, the principle that evolved into Llewellyn's doctrine of unconscionability was specifically designed to permit courts to regulate lopsided contracts by finding and then simply applying group outrage at the excesses of the "chiseler."

3.3   Rejection, Revocation, and Cure

Rejection, Revocation, and Cure Under Article 2 of the Uniform Commercial Code: Some Modest Proposals*

JOHN A. SEBERT, Jr.

When drafted in the 1940s and 1950s, Article 2 of the Uniform Commercial Code contained several innovations including the creation of a new concept of "revocation of acceptance" (section 2–608), which for the first time imposed more stringent substantive standards on the buyer's right to return goods for latent defects, and the grant to sellers of a broad, but not unlimited, right to "cure" defects in the goods they have tendered (section 2–508). Over the past thirty-five years, a substantial body of case law has developed around those provisions, as well as in connection with the much less innovative section 2–601, which purports to preserve the traditional perfect tender rule by permitting the buyer to reject "if the goods or the tender of delivery fail in any respect to conform to the contract...." While the buyer's right to reject and revoke, and the seller's right to cure, have also been treated extensively

---

* 84 Nw. U. L. Rev. 375 (1990).

in the academic literature, the primary focus of almost all of those discussions has been upon decisions under and possible interpretations of the existing provisions of Article 2. There has been little consideration of potential revisions to the Code's rejection, revocation, and cure provisions.

The Basic Statutory Scheme

During the initial drafting stages of Article 2, there was considerable debate about whether to retain the perfect tender rule that had traditionally applied to contracts for goods. Many argued for jettisoning the perfect tender rule in favor of the substantial performance standard that had long been the constructive condition precedent to a performing party's right to recover under most other contracts, particularly construction contracts. Karl Llewellyn, the principal drafter of Article 2, was among the leaders of this movement, urging the adoption of a substantial performance standard at least for contracts among merchants. Tradition won out, however, apparently buoyed by arguments concerning the need for certainty and concerns that lay juries would not be able to apply a substantial performance standard satisfactorily. Thus, section 2–601, the Code's provision governing the buyer's right to reject, incorporates the perfect tender rule: a buyer may reject "if the goods or the tender of delivery fail in any respect to conform to the contract...."

Article 2 does contain, however, significant express statutory exceptions to the perfect tender rule.... [One] explicit exception to the perfect tender rule involves revocation of acceptance. After a buyer has accepted goods, she may no longer reject them. After acceptance, the only way to return goods to the seller and obtain a refund of past payments (and avoid liability for any remaining portions of the price is for a buyer to revoke acceptance). In a change from prior law, section 2–608 overtly adopts a substantial performance standard by permitting a buyer to revoke acceptance of a lot or commercial unit only if the "nonconformity substantially impairs its value to him...." The right to revoke is also restricted in other significant ways. First, the buyer must demonstrate an "excuse" for having accepted the defective goods, and therefore may revoke only if the goods were accepted on the reasonable assumption that the defects would be cured or if the buyer reasonably failed to discover the defects before acceptance because of the seller's assurances or the difficulty of discovering the defects. Second, the seller's interest in timely notice and in not having to take back deteriorated goods is protected by a requirement that revocation occur within a reasonable time after the buyer discovers or should have discovered the defect, and before any substantial change in condition of the goods that is not caused by their own defects. Third, and often very significantly, after acceptance the buyer bears the burden of persuasion to establish any defect in the goods.

The most important new device relevant to rejection and revocation found in the Code is the seller's right to cure, established by section 2–508. Unable to prevail in his advocacy of an overt substantial performance standard, Karl Llewellyn at least moved the law of sales to a new middle ground between the perfect tender rule and the substantial performance standard. While some may argue that the right to cure is not actually an "exception" to the perfect tender rule because cure still requires that the seller substitute goods that fully conform to contract specifications, this distinction strikes me as a little too fine. The fact remains that the right to cure, when it exists, establishes a major new barrier between the buyer and the object for which one employs the perfect tender rule, which is to gain the right to return the goods, cancel the contract, and obtain a refund of the price paid plus the right to recover damages based upon rejection or revocation....

Evaluation of the Present Standards

The law that has evolved concerning rejection, revocation, and cure is deficient in some significant respects. First, there is substantial uncertainty concerning the effective substantive standard for rejection. While the Code purports to continue the perfect tender rule, a buyer's freedom to reject for immaterial defects (and often also for substantial nonconformities) is explicitly circumscribed, even in a one-shot contract, by the seller's right to cure and further limited by the lurking presence of the duty of good faith.... The problem caused by the uncertainty of the standard for rejection is compounded because the scope of a seller's right to cure remains open to substantial debate, both as to whether the preconditions to the right to cure have been met and as to whether there is a right to cure after acceptance, when the buyer is attempting to revoke. Accurate prediction is further complicated by the necessarily flexible standard for determining acceptance, which results in considerable variation from case to case in determining whether the buyer has accepted and thus must satisfy the more rigorous standards for revocation of acceptance.... Some of the sources of uncertainty, however, could be eliminated. To the extent that they are not, it seems clear that the rejection, revocation, and cure standards of the Code unnecessarily increase post-breach costs of negotiation and create incentives for strategic behavior.

Second, a buyer's rejection (or revocation) and attempt to cover by obtaining substitute goods on the market often may be the most costly and least efficient remedy available. In particular, rejection (or revocation) and cover involve two separate types of transaction costs that would not normally be incurred if the seller cured the defects: (1) the buyer's costs of seeking and arranging cover and (2) the seller's costs of reselling the goods that have been returned. In addition, it may frequently take the buyer as much time to obtain substitute goods as it would take the seller to repair or replace the goods initially tendered.

Consequently, rejection or revocation often will neither assure the buyer of the most prompt delivery of conforming goods nor minimize consequential loss. Some support for the efficiency of a remedial scheme that emphasizes the seller's curing defects rather than the buyer's rejecting and covering may be found in the increasing prevalence of contract provisions that give the seller an unfettered right to cure (such as provisions limiting the buyer's remedies to repair and replacement), and in the fact that those provisions not only have survived judicial scrutiny but also have not elicited strong objections from buyers.

Finally, [t]he seller may be substantially prejudiced if the buyer is permitted to reject or revoke rather than compelled to retain the goods and recover only damages for breach of warranty. Rejection and revocation force the seller both to retake goods that may have depreciated considerably from use and to assume any risk of falling market prices. Moreover, rejection and revocation may permit a buyer to avoid a bad bargain, since he is entitled to a refund of all his payments to the seller even if the value of fully conforming goods would have been less than the contract price. Surely there are circumstances in which the seller appropriately must bear this type of loss and the buyer should be able to avoid a bad bargain, but those circumstances primarily are when the buyer must be given the right to cancel the contract and obtain substitute performance in order to preserve his bargain or to avoid consequential loss. At minimum, the perfect tender rule of section 2–601 and some of the limitations on the seller's right to cure under section 2–508 divert the courts' attention from those questions, and the result may be to permit rejection when that remedy is not at all necessary to preserve valid interests of the buyer. Even if a buyer does not use the perfect tender rule to reject for a minor defect, the rule and the risk of an effective rejection may significantly enhance the buyer's negotiating position and enable the buyer to obtain a substantial price reduction or other concession from the seller even though the defect is quite minor.

Recommendations for Revising Article 2

My review of the decisions implementing the Code's provisions on rejection, revocation, and cure leads me to suggest that fundamental changes be made to some of those provisions as Article 2 is revised over the next few years. The first and most important recommendation is that all pretense of the perfect tender rule finally be abandoned, and that a substantial impairment standard be adopted across the board as the test for when a buyer may force the seller to retake the goods.... The adoption of a clear substantial performance standard would help ensure that a buyer would obtain the very significant advantages of rejection or revocation, including the ability to avoid an otherwise bad bargain, only when the defects are major and there is good reason for giving the buyer the right to cancel the contract and obtain substitute performance on the market. Second, the seller should be given an unconditional right to cure, thus eliminating the unnecessary inquiries into whether the seller had reason to believe his tender would be acceptable and abandoning the silly and counterproductive refusal to permit cure when the buyer is attempting to revoke acceptance. The only precondition to the seller's right to cure should be giving the buyer timely and sufficient notice of the seller's intent to cure. Such a right to cure is similar to that granted sellers under typical agreed remedy provisions. Third, various changes should be made to increase the chances that a buyer will obtain a timely and effective cure, including giving the buyer a right to "adequate assurances" of cure as a condition to the seller's exercising her right to cure. [W]hen a seller notifies a buyer that he intends to cure, revised Article 2 should explicitly give the buyer the right to demand adequate assurances that the cure will be effective and timely. If those assurances are not forthcoming in a reasonable period of time, the seller's right to cure should terminate and the buyer should be permitted to reject or revoke (as appropriate) for uncured material defects.

Breach and Remedy for the Tender of Nonconforming Goods Under the Uniform Commercial Code: An Economic Approach*

GEORGE L. PRIEST

The basic structure and fundamental distinctions of the tender provisions of the Code derive from Llewellyn's proposals, which, as we have seen, were often responsive to costs. While it is overstatement to describe the underlying policy of the Code's tender provisions as the minimization of costs, many of the distinctions incorporated into the Code can be explained, in hindsight, as rational responses to the desire to choose the cheaper remedy. Yet because Llewellyn's perception of the relative costs of the remedies was intuitive and imprecise, and because his objectives were compromised in the course of drafting, specific provisions of the Code depart from cost minimization. As a result, a literal interpretation of the Code will increase the costs of sales transactions in certain common situations involving defective tenders.

The seller's cure of a defective tender provides an initial example. Llewellyn perceived correctly that the joint costs of breach can be reduced if the seller can cure at a cost less than the diminution in the value of the goods because of the defect. Yet he failed to appreciate that the discrepancy between the costs imposed on the seller where the buyer recovers damages and where the buyer successfully rejects will tempt the seller to invest in cure whether or not the value of the goods is enhanced. Where the buyer recovers damages, the seller who fails to cure loses an amount equal to the diminution in the value of the goods

* 91 HARV. L. REV. 960 (1978).

because of the defect. This amount establishes an upward constraint on his investment consistent with the joint maximization of value. Where the buyer successfully rejects, however, the seller loses the same amount, as well as the costs of retrieval and resale and the depreciation of the goods while in the buyer's hands. His incentive to invest in cure therefore is increased by the total of these other costs. A decline in the market price of the goods before rejection increases the seller's incentive to invest in cure still further. In either case, the amount invested may be significantly greater than the value of the investment in cure, and the difference will increase the joint costs to the parties from the breach.

The difference in practice between the standards for rejection and revocation of acceptance by merchant buyers and consumer buyers is susceptible to similar criticism. Though this difference has a foundation in efficiency, the rules of the Code implementing it are only crudely related to cost minimization. In general, merchants have lower costs of resale than consumer buyers, so that damages will more often be the cheaper remedy. But not every merchant buyer is able to resell defective goods as cheaply as the seller. Rather, the cost of reselling defective goods is a function of the nature of the particular defect and of the specialization in the buyer's resale trade. The appropriate question for cost minimization is the relative resale costs of the buyer and seller. There will be a continuum of merchants' and consumers' resale costs overlapping a similar continuum of those of sellers, so that any broad distinction between merchants and consumers, while efficient in general, will fail in particular cases.

Furthermore, the implementation of the distinction—by a substantial performance standard as opposed to a perfect tender rule—is not directly related to minimization of costs. A defect may be literally "insubstantial," but if the merchant buyer's market is specialized, his costs of reselling defective goods may be higher than the seller's, so that rejection minimizes costs. If the buyer's resale trade is general, it may be less costly for him to sell goods that fail to conform in substantial respects. For example, if a manufacturer sends a sporting goods store baseballs instead of golf balls, the nonconformity is substantial, but there is no reason to presume that rejection will minimize costs.

The same may be said about the standards for rejection and revocation of acceptance. Where the buyer has retained the goods for a period of time before attempting to return them, it is more likely that the market price or the buyer's information about the goods has changed, but the concept of the "substantiality" of the defect does not precisely capture the effect. Moreover, a defect may be sufficiently serious to raise the buyer's costs of resale above the seller's—so that rescission is the cheaper remedy—although it may not satisfy the substantiality criterion of the Code. Finally, the more lenient standard for revocation by consumer buyers, based on the acknowledgment of their personal values, may also increase the costs of breach. There is little reason to believe that consumers, any more than merchants, will fail to see the advantage of revoking where the market price of the goods has declined. Deferring to the personal values of consumer buyers also exposes sellers to the risk of revocation and the incentive to overinvest in cure where the buyer has chosen unwisely and has found the goods to be unsuitable.

These criticisms suggest that there are significant discrepancies between the effect of the Code's provisions and the ideal of cost minimization. As a consequence, the role of the courts in interpreting and applying the provisions of the Code will be extremely important in determining its practical effect on costs. It is the hypothesis of this Article that the courts have interpreted the Code's provisions in ways that minimize costs in nonconforming tender disputes.

There are two principal ways of testing the hypothesis that courts interpret the provisions of the Code so as to achieve efficiency. The first and best test is to compare the judgment rendered in a given case with the efficient result, derived from balancing the costs and benefits as discussed in Part I. This test is limited, however, by the fact that the only available information on costs is that drawn from the opinions themselves, which may not be accurate or complete. A second method for testing the hypotheses is to observe whether the facts that the court views as determinative of its legal holding are similar to those which would be determinative in an economic judgment. If legal rules, regardless of their terminology, give controlling weight to factors bearing on efficiency, it is likely in general that judicial decisions will be consistent with efficiency. In testing the cost minimization hypothesis under these methods, the author reviewed every reported decision from 1954 through 1976 in cases involving the buyer's attempt to return goods to the seller due to their failure to conform to the contract. In all, 183 cases were reviewed....

Rejection and Revocation of Acceptance

   1. *Rejection: Interpreting the Contract.*—Where the buyer in a rejection case claims that the goods are defective with respect to a characteristic not explicitly described in the contract, a court is required to determine whether or not there has been a breach. The cost minimization hypothesis implies that the court will do so by comparing the cost to the seller of avoiding the alleged defect with the loss suffered by the buyer because of it.

Decisions in this area are consistent with efficiency. One, for example, inferred conformity of the tender from behavior of the buyer—reordering identical goods after discovery of the alleged defect. Here the costs of breach might have been avoided if the buyer had acted upon the information in his possession before the disputed order.

In other cases, the tender, although failing to conform to the letter of the contract, conformed to "customary standards" in the trade or conformed to goods tendered earlier, and was held to have been accepted by a past course of dealing between the parties. These decisions were consistent with the Code's explicit adoption of both the "course of dealing" between parties and the "usage of trade" in an industry as criteria of contract interpretation—criteria which themselves promote efficiency by encouraging buyers to take advantage of economies in information achieved through standardization, trade custom, and established routines of trade.

   2. *The Substantive Grounds for Rejection and Revocation of Acceptance.*—This subsection examines the hypothesis of consistency of case law with cost minimization in a new way: it ignores the particular legal issue in the case and compares the judicial resolution of the disputes to the efficient resolution as determined from facts reported in the opinion.

   Grants of rejection should be much less frequent than the broad language of section 2–601 might imply since the conditions under which rejection will minimize costs are quite limited. Of the sixty-two appellate rejection decisions announced between 1954 and 1976, rejection has been affirmed in only seventeen cases, equal to twenty-seven percent. This aggregate figure, of course, confirms the prediction in only a general way, for it conceals the presence or absence of the particular cost-minimizing conditions in individual cases. One refinement is to distinguish suits brought under section 2–601 by consumers from those brought by merchants. As discussed earlier, the cost minimization hypothesis implies that rejection should be awarded more frequently where the buyer is a consumer. Again, the findings are confirming. Rejection was awarded in eight of eighteen suits brought by consumer buyers (forty-four percent), but in only nine of forty-four suits brought by merchant buyers (twenty percent).

   A second way of testing the hypothesis is to examine attempts to reject goods specially designed for the buyer. Since custom-made goods, even if defective in some respect, are likely to be more valuable to the buyer than to anyone else, damages are probably the cheaper remedy in cases involving such goods. Five rejection cases have been decided in which the goods were specially designed for the buyer, and rejection was denied in all but one. In Beco, Inc. v. Minnechaug Golf Course, Inc., a typical example, the seller had begun setting the first portion of specially designed restaurant equipment in position when the buyer refused to allow any further work. The seller voluntarily agreed to make alterations, but before they were completed the buyer rejected all of the equipment as nonconforming. The issue in the case was not whether the contract had been breached, but whether rejection was the appropriate remedy. Although there are no statutory grounds for such a holding, the court denied rejection but awarded the buyer damages for certain nonconformities. The decisions in three other cases denying rejection are similar. Although a court awarded rejection in one case involving custom-made goods, rejection was awarded only because extensive efforts to repair the goods by the seller had been unsuccessful.

A final method of testing the cost minimization hypothesis for rejection cases is to look individually at the seventeen cases in which rejection was awarded. The hypothesis implies that in each, either the costs of reselling the defective goods will be higher to the buyer than to the seller or the costs of calculating the buyer's damages will be high. We have already mentioned that the eight cases in which rejection was awarded to consumer buyers are generally consistent with the prediction. A closer look at these cases provides additional support. Five of the cases involved the purchase of a new automobile from a dealer. In general, it is plausible that a dealer will be able to resell a defective automobile more cheaply than the initial purchaser. These particular decisions, however, are notable for the court's emphasis in each on the relevance of the nature of the defect to the award of rejection. Each of the five cases involved defects of a very complex nature: the fusing of a differential to an axle, transmission failure, emission of smoke and fumes, or multiple defects costing several thousand dollars to repair. Two opinions draw attention to the difficulty to the consumer buyer of discovering the full extent of the defects, because of the likelihood that other parts of the auto had been affected. This difficulty, of course, increases both the cost of calculating the buyer's damages and the cost to the buyer of reselling the goods, especially relative to the cost of resale to an expert in automobile repair. In cases of this nature, rejection is likely to be the cost-minimizing remedy.

Eight of the nine cases in which rejection was awarded to merchant buyers are equally consistent with the hypothesis.

Cure of Defective Tender

[T]he provisions of the Code make it very difficult for courts to devise rules to achieve efficiency where the nonconformity in the goods can be cured. Where the price of the goods or the buyer's information has changed, courts must either permit overinvestment in cure or grant a windfall to the buyer. This dilemma has led to contradictory decisions and to interpretations that are less coherent among the various jurisdictions than interpretations of the Code's rejection and revocation provisions.

Judicial decisions have had some effect in promoting efficiency where the buyer attempts to refuse the seller's cure. The text of the Code, of course, makes no reference to the buyer's right to refuse cure, although it does require that cure be "seasonable." Courts, however, have allowed buyers to reject or revoke acceptance, despite the seller's willingness to continue repair, in situations in which it is plausible that the cost of the seller's investment outweighs the benefits conferred upon the buyer. In Melby v. Hawkins Pontiac, Inc., for example, the court allowed the buyer to revoke his acceptance after the automobile he purchased had been in the seller's shop for repair for 191 of 197 days since purchase.

Courts have not permitted the buyer to refuse cure, however, where the costs to the seller of effecting cure and the costs to the buyer of waiting for the goods to be cured are low. In Wilson v. Scampoli, for example, the buyer was denied rescission because she had refused to allow the seller to remove a defective television to the seller's shop for repair. The court's consideration of costs was explicit: it found that the defect could be cured in a short period of time at a cost of "no great inconvenience" to the buyer. In other decisions courts have prohibited the buyer from refusing the seller's cure in situations where it is plausible that the buyer's refusal to allow cure was motivated by a change in the market price or in his information about the goods....

Certainly the criterion of economic efficiency is nowhere expressed as a basis of the Code in law or policy. Yet the narrow legal doctrines embodied in the Code's provisions are often responsive to an underlying concern for efficiency and are usually applied so as to minimize the costs of sales. Analysis of the costs of a given transaction thus may permit parties to predict the outcome of a judicial decision. And whenever case law diverges from the literal interpretation of the text of a statute, some method of prediction becomes essential.

NOTES

1. The tension between "ex ante" and "ex post" efficiency. As the preceding excerpts make clear, there are a series of rules in Article 2 governing the process by which the parties perform their obligations under a sales contract. These rules travel under various labels—inspection, rejection, acceptance, revocation of acceptance and cure. It is frequently said that a central purpose of these rules is to identify the cost-minimizing solution to the particular commercial problem at issue. Yet both of the scholars whose work we have just read seem to agree that the Code's rules fail to achieve their goals. An initial question, therefore, is why the rules don't work as well as they might (or should). One reason these rules will not reliably lead to the cost minimizing outcome is that there is an inevitable tension that exists in rules governing the performance of sales contracts.

In the usual case, where markets exist, the parties will have alternatives to the contract under negotiation. Thus, the "deal" that is reached is generally the best deal that the parties can achieve. This is another way of saying that each negotiated sales contract is ex ante efficient; it generates more expected surplus (over cost) for the parties to divide up in some fashion than other alternatives. After a deal is made, however, parties may receive new information about the state of the world in which performance is to occur. In light of that information, the parties may realize that their contract will not maximize the surplus to be shared. Thus, the contract was ex ante efficient (it maximized expected surplus) but it was not ex post efficient (it did not maximize actual surplus). If so, the parties have an incentive to bargain to a new arrangement. The tension mentioned above exists because the effort to achieve ex post efficiency may sacrifice ex ante efficiency. Assume for example, that sellers anticipate that the law will permit them to render a substantial performance whenever their costs increase. If so, sellers would have less incentive to confine cost increases or to perform just as they said they would. In addition, a vague substantial performance standard itself may create a disincentive to perform (it is more difficult for the buyer to prove deviations from substantiality than from perfection). For these reasons, buyers may prefer ex ante a contract that requires a perfect tender. But a perfect tender rule may generate ex post inefficiencies when the seller's costs actually have increased and the loss to the seller from having to satisfy the perfect tender rule is greater than the loss to the buyer if the seller delivered a modified good that is almost as good as the original contract good.

There is no easy resolution of this tension between ex post and ex ante efficiency in the default rules governing performance of a sales contract. Thus, the Code reflects this tension but fails to eliminate it. For example, § 2–601 contains a perfect tender rule, but §§ 2–508 (cure) and 2–608 (revocation of acceptance) significantly limit the buyer's ability to insist on perfect tender.

2.   Comparing the "solutions" to the tension inherent in the Code's rules. Each of the authors excerpted above have grappled with the inherent tension in the Code's rules governing performance of the sales contract. Note, however, that each treats the problem in a significantly different way. Sebert believes that the tension can be ameliorated by changing the perfect tender rule to substantial performance, and by giving the seller an unqualified right to cure any defect. He argues that buyers would be protected from exploitation by sellers by a rule that permits buyers to demand "adequate assurances" of any promised cure. Are you confident that this solution overcomes the risk of buyer undercompensation noted above? Priest believes that the answer to that question is "yes." Indeed, he argues that despite the literal language of the various rules governing rejection, revocation and cure, courts interpret the Code rules in ways that assign liability to the party with the comparative advantage in minimizing the costs of a transactional breakdown. If Professor Priest is correct, and courts actually impose liability ex post based on which party could best minimize costs ex ante, would there then be any need to reform the Code rules to more explicitly reflect this policy goal?

3.   Another view of the rules governing rejection, revocation and cure. Professor Jody Kraus believes that these rules fail because they seek to do too much. Not only do they indicate which party must work to "salvage" a broken contract, but they also assign burdens of proof of nonconformity and provide a compensation standard for buyers when sellers breach by tendering nonconforming goods. Consider the following argument of Professor Kraus:

[T]he Code's burden-of-proof, salvage, and undercompensation rules should be decoupled from one another and from the acceptance-rejection fulcrum. I reject the acceptance-rejection fulcrum not only because it inefficiently lumps together the distinct policy goals underlying these rules, but also because it would be inefficient even if it governed only one of these policy goals ... [T]he acceptance and rejection doctrines serve three distinct purposes. The first is to allocate the burden of proving that a tender of goods was noncon- forming. The second is to regulate the salvage of goods in a failed transaction. The third is to accomplish the second without unduly exacerbating the nonbreacher's risk of undercompensation by re- quiring the nonbreacher to incur additional expenses that are subject to systematic undercompensation.

[T]he Code's express salvage requirements for the rightfully reject- ing buyer could reasonably be expected to result in the most efficient resale of rejected goods in most cases. But because the rules presuppose the buyer's right to reject nonconforming goods, the rules do not require her to adjust to and use nonconforming goods even when doing so is the most efficient salvage of rejected goods. This feature of the Code's salvage rules might be justified under standard majoritarian default analysis if, in most cases, maximum net resale value will exceed maximum net use value in salvaging goods in a failed transaction. Moreover, the likelihood of ex post bargains that will lead to the efficient salvage of the goods will ameliorate, to some extent, the inefficient allocation of the salvage duty in this minority of cases. It is difficult, however, to determine whether resale or adjustment will be the most efficient salvage option in most failed transactions. More important, even if resale more frequently provides the most efficient salvage of the goods, it would be ideal if a more refined default rule could effective- ly allocate the duty to adjust to and use rejected goods to the buyer when that option maximizes the value of the goods. Yet, because such a default rule would likely exacerbate the buyer's exposure to undercompensation, the Code's default rules might represent an acceptable balance between the competing goals of efficiently sal- vaging the goods and reducing the nonbreacher's exposure to under- compensation.

Jody S. Kraus, *Decoupling Sales Law from the Acceptance–Rejection Ful- crum*, 104 Yale L.J. 129 (1994).

Kraus' decoupling substitutes more standard-like approach for the rough rules generated by the acceptance-rejection dichotomy. This raises the questions introduced in Chapter 2 concerning the desirability of standards and the competence of the courts in making the required determinations. Among Professor Kraus' proposals is a requirement that the parties share information at the time goods are tendered and that one party or the other must adjust to a nonconforming tender depending on which of them had the comparative advantage in minimizing salvage costs. Consider the ability of the courts to determine which party was in the better position to adjust in cases where the parties subsequently dispute each others' actions under the contract.

4.   The consequences of acceptance. The consequences of acceptance of the goods by the buyer are elaborated in § 2–607. It provides in relevant part:

> (1) The buyer must pay at the contract rate for any goods accepted.

> (2) Acceptance of goods by the buyer precludes rejection of the goods accepted and if make with knowledge of a non-conformity cannot be revoked because of it unless the acceptance was on the reasonable assumption that he non-conformity would be seasonably cured. . . .

> (3) Where a tender has been accepted (a) the buyer must within a reasonable time after he discovers or should have discovered any breach notify the seller of breach or be barred from any remedy. . . .

> (4) The burden is on the buyer to establish any breach with respect to the goods accepted.

> . . . .

Read that section carefully and note that significant changes in the relationship between the parties result from "acceptance." Why should a buyer be denied the right to reject the goods for any non-conformity (as provided in § 2–601) merely because his possession or use of the goods continued long enough to be called an acceptance before he notifies the seller of his dissatisfaction? If a buyer has accepted non-conforming goods, why should the law require him to pay at the contract rate instead of reopening negotiations? Are buyers in effect penalized for acceptance by being allocated the burden of proving breach? If the buyer is not seeking to return the goods, why should he be denied a damage remedy for failure to give notice of breach?

5.   Does Section 2–508 permit a seller to cure by repair? Nothing in the text or comments to § 2–508 suggests that repair is a permissible means of cure. (But see Comment 2 to § 2–510). In any case, no court has yet held that repair is per se insufficient to effect a cure of a defective tender. Why do you suppose that is so? One answer is that courts may believe that limiting sellers to replacement would effectively negate the right to cure. On the other hand, surely it is the case that repaired goods are not as valued on the market as goods that are conforming at the initial time of performance under the contract. Professor Alan Schwartz notes that

> If the Code is read to permit sellers to cure without discounting the price to reflect the . . . decrease in value that cure by repair can cause, its effect is to shift those costs to buyers. . . . Requiring the buyer to accept a repaired good if the seller determined that repair "corrected" the defects would impose an unwarranted cost on the buyer and may produce economic waste. . . . No principle distinguishes these costs from others which sellers cause and which sales law does not require buyers to bear.

Alan Schwartz, *Cure and Revocation for Quality Defects: The Utility of Bargains,* 16 B.C. Indus. & Com. L. Rev. 543, 547, 550, 551–55 (1975).

3.4   Contract Flexibility: Price and Quantity

A seller and buyer may complete an exchange without any significant contract (that is, legally enforceable promise). They may, for example, simply make a contemporaneous exchange of goods and money. Alternatively, they may trust each other or have extralegal reasons to believe that each side will honor its bargain in a consensual future exchange. If the parties wish to enter into a legally enforceable contract, it is usually because they seek to (1) allocate risks or protect the reliance investment of one or both parties and (2) invoke legal commitments to serve these objectives, because the parties deem the extralegal forces to be insufficient.

In Chapter 2, we discussed the costs of contracting and the resulting incompleteness of commercial contracts. When contracts are incomplete, a tension exists between the legal commitment that protects reliance investments and risk allocation, on the one hand, and the flexibility to adjust the terms of exchange to changed circumstances. A rigid contract with fixed terms, for example, protects reliance and risk allocation, but may lead to inefficient exchange when circumstances change (unless the parties agree to modify their agreement). In contrast, an incomplete contract with an open price or a flexible quantity permits flexibility in the parties' relationship but it might also discourage reliance investment or undermine the integrity of the desired risk allocation.

In the first excerpt of this section, Professor Joskow discusses the pricing option facing parties to long-term gas contracts, and in the second excerpt, Professor Weistart explores the merits of flexible quantity terms in requirements or output contracts.

Price Adjustments in Long–Term Contracts: The Case of Coal*

PAUL L. JOSKOW

For several reasons, coal supply arrangements are helpful for examining how long-term contracts provide for, and actually work in, adapting to changing market conditions. Electric utilities routinely enter into very long-term coal supply relationships via contract. Contracts with specified durations of twenty years or more are frequently utilized. Creating appropriate price-adjustment provisions in such contracts while simultaneously preserving the other benefits of long-term contracts would appear to be a formidable task. Yet coal supply relationships are rarely terminated prematurely, and utilities have continued to rely on long-term contracts as market conditions have changed. It is reasonable

* 31 J. Law & Econ. 47 (1988).

to hypothesize that some way has been found to keep the costs of long-term contracts low relative to their benefits [. . .]

Let us focus on a long-term coal supply contract that involves deliveries of pre-specified quantities of coal over a period of several years. In order for a supplier to agree to provide supplies, the present discounted value of expected future revenues must be greater than or equal to the present discounted value of expected future costs, including the opportunity costs of any future sales forgone by the seller in committing to a long-term supply agreement. If coal markets are competitive, as they appear to be, buyers, on average, will pay no more than the present discounted value of expected future production costs (including rents and opportunity costs) [. . .]

We can narrow down the likely structure of mutually satisfactory price-adjustment provisions in long-term contracts by recognizing that the parties are likely to want to structure price-adjustment provisions so that they achieve certain objectives [. . .] These include *(a)* a desire to guard against "opportunism," "hold-up," or haggling problems associated with the presence of relationship-specific investments; *(b)* a desire to minimize the incentives that the contractual provisions themselves give the parties to breach their contractual promises; *(c)* a desire to provide enough flexibility to facilitate efficient adaptations to changing market conditions; and *(d)* because the price the buyer (a regulated electric utility) can charge customers for the final product is in this case regulated by state and federal regulatory agencies, there would be a desire to avoid pricing provisions that might lead a regulatory agency to consider a fraction of the coal costs "imprudent."

Fixed-Price Contracts

In a world in which nominal production costs are expected to increase over time, a fixed-price contract that reflects ex ante expectations of future costs increases is likely to have bad properties from all of these perspectives. A long-term, fixed price contract necessarily "front loads" the revenues as well as the expected profits of the seller relative to the flow of costs when nominal costs are expected to increase over time. A fixed price that satisfies [condition] (1) [i.e. the price accurately reflects the expected present value price per unit supplied of a good] will involve an initial price that is high relative to current spot prices, high relative to prices in older fixed-price contracts, and high relative to current production costs. If actual cost changes equal the ex ante expected changes in costs, at some point later in the term of the contract the price will be below the then-current spot market prices and below the prices in new fixed-price contracts. If the expected rate of cost increase is fast enough and the contract long enough, the fixed price could fall below the then-current costs of providing incremental supplies at some future date. In either case, the seller will have strong incentives to breach on quantity or quality promises, both because he can sell his supplies elsewhere at a higher price, and possibly because the additional direct costs of meeting his commitments may be greater than the revenues he will receive. If production costs and market prices rise more quickly than anticipated, the seller will face even stronger incentives to breach. While the buyer can always appeal to the courts to enforce the contract or to award damages, this route is costly and the results uncertain. While almost any price-adjustment provision could lead to large disparities between contract prices and "market prices" if certain contingencies arise, and thereby provide incentives for either the buyer or the seller to breach, a fixed-price contract almost guarantees that these problems will arise, even if there is no uncertainly about how costs and market values will change over time [...]

Market Price Contracts

A potentially attractive alternative to a fixed-price contract would be a "market price" contract. Such a contract would involve the parties simply agreeing that prices will be adjusted to reflect changes in the "market price" of coal with identical quality attributes that is available from (approximately) the same location as the coal that has been contracted for. If coal markets are competitive, we would expect that the expected present discounted value of future market prices would satisfy [condition] (1) [defined above]. A market price provision eliminates any incentives the buyer or seller may have to breach the agreement as a result of better alternative opportunities during the term of the agreement. The pricing provision is, in theory, easy to state and easy to enforce by the courts and, therefore, is potentially attractive to guard against ex post opportunistic behavior. If the supplier produces efficiently, it is unlikely that the price will fall below his incremental cost of meeting his contractual commitments, and if it does he could meet them by buying rather than by producing (and this would be efficient). This price-adjustment mechanism would be potentially very attractive for electric utilities concerned about prudence reviews that are based on comparisons between contract price and some measure of the "market price."

The primary problem with a "market price" contract is defining an appropriate market price norm to use for this purpose. Coal is not a homogeneous commodity. There are wide variations in heat content, sulfur content, ash content, moisture content, and chemical composition, all of which affect the value of the coal to buyers, as well as its market price. Because transportation costs are an important component of the delivered price of coal, prices at the mine also vary from area to area in such a way that they reflect proximity to coal consumers and the costs of transportation. While the government reports the average FOB mine price per ton by producing district (with a considerable lag), there is no breakdown between spot and contract prices FOB the mine, and only limited information that would make it possible to adjust accurately for differences in coal quality or variations in the "quality" of the coal supply relationship. Even within producing districts that have reasonably homogeneous coal deposits, a very wide variation in FOB mine prices can be observed at any point in time. In short, there does not appear to be a single simple number that a contract can rely on as a good indicator of the relevant market price of coal [. . .]

Escalating Price Contracts

Over the long term we expect that coal prices will change as the costs of production (including rents and opportunity costs) rise and fall, other things being equal. It is natural, therefore, to think of starting with a base price that reflects current supply and demand conditions and then allowing it to vary with changes in the costs of producing coal. This might be accomplished by structuring a contract that establishes an initial or base price equal to the seller's current productions costs, plus an economic rent component, and then provides for prices to change in accordance with the seller's actual costs of production (for example, some type of cost-plus contract). There are at least three potential problems with a cost-plus contract, however. First, pure cost-plus contracts may not provide adequate incentives for the supplier to produce efficiently. Second, even if a particular supplier makes his best effort to supply efficiently, a specific mine may turn out to have significantly higher or lower costs than the typical mine, and contract prices may consistently be above or below the market value of the coal. Third, it will not be sensitive to unanticipated changes in market supply and demand conditions that would affect market values more or less than changes in the supplier's costs of production. In each case, costly haggling and renegotiation problems resulting from large differences between contract prices and prevailing market values may make this kind of contract unattractive.

An alternative to a cost-plus contract is a contract that specifies a base price reflecting supply and demand conditions when the contract is signed, and which then provides for adjustments in the base price using a formula that incorporates a weighted average of exogenous input-price indexes reflecting the anticipated input/output mix of the supplier, combined with exogenous indexes of changes in labor and capital productivity that reflect "general" changes in production opportunities. Instead of using the actual costs incurred by a specific seller to adjust prices, exogenous indexes that reflect general market opportunities are used at least in part. These contracts are generally called "base price plus escalation" (BPE) contracts.

As long as the market value of the coal moves along with changes in input prices, general productivity changes affecting comparable mines, and so on, this approach seems superior to a cost-plus contract. It helps to solve the first incentive problem associated with pure cost-plus contracts since prices are at least partially decoupled from the actual costs incurred by a specific supplier. Similarly, it solves the second problem associated with a mine that is unusually costly or unusually efficient. It does not solve the third problem, however. Indeed, there is no obvious way to solve the third problem without tying contract prices directly to market values in some way. With either a cost-plus contract or a BPE contract it is impossible to tract large short-run changes in the market value of coal associated with demand-side shocks. Short-run, supply-side shocks would be more easily captured, but certainly not perfectly. If one of these adjustment mechanisms is chosen, the parties would have to recognize that serious haggling problems may emerge if markets are subject to unanticipated demand or to supply-side shocks that lead to large increases or decreases in the expected market value of coal over the term of the contract.

Clearly, none of the price-adjustment alternatives is ideal. Long-term (nominal) fixed-price contracts are simply not credible in a market like this, and I would not expect them to be used extensively. Market price contracts are attractive, but both the difficulty of defining an appropriate market price norm and the problem of providing for damage penalties that appropriately reflect the quasi rents associated with the difference in value of relationship-specific investments between the intended use and alternative uses implies that they will not be relied on very much in coal markets, except in special circumstances. Both BPE and cost-plus contracts have attractive features in that both could do a reasonably good job of tracking market values in the long run, as long as changes in market values move closely with changes in the average cost of production. Large unanticipated demand or supply-side shocks could lead to problems, however.

Requirements and Output Contracts: Quantity Variations Under the UCC*

JOHN C. WEISTART

Production Flexibility

A true requirements contract allows the buyer to adjust his intake of materials and supplies to fluctuations in markets in which he sells his products or in the markets from which he secures supplies. As demand for his product decreases, for example, the requirements buyer is both able to reduce his production and to avoid the economic burden of committing capital to unneeded supplies. Similarly, if demand for his product increases, he is able to adjust his production immediately to the extent his supplies are furnished on a requirements basis. Also, if costs for labor and equipment increase to the point of seriously impairing profitability, the buyer can respond by reducing production.

* 1973 DUKE L. J. 599, 600–602, 605–607, 609–616, 642–646 (1973).

The buyer under a fixed-quantity contract, of course, does not necessarily lack a capacity to respond to changes in his markets. The point can be made, however, that the fixed-quantity purchaser is more restricted in his production options. If he secures his supplies through a series of fixed-quantity contracts, he runs the risk, on the one hand that he will over-purchase. A subsequent contraction in his product market or a price increase in his market for other supplies may leave him in a position in which he is legally obligated to accept goods which he does not need immediately. The resources which are necessary to meet that commitment might have more profitably been applied to other aspects of his business. On the other hand, the fixed-quantity purchaser at other times may find that his fixed-quantity arrangements have resulted in his purchasing insufficient quantities. When demand for his product increases, he can, of course, enter additional contracts to satisfy his needs. But in doing so, he faces the risk of a price increase, a risk which could be avoided, or at least controlled within manageable limits, by an appropriately drafted requirements contract.

In short, a requirements contract can serve as a risk-shifting device. By his utilization of this form of agreement, the buyer can shift to the requirements seller some of the risks of the buyer's business. Among the most important of these is the risk that the market in which the buyer sells his product will contract. And the seller who agrees to a fixed-price requirements arrangement also accepts the risk that the market price for his commodity will increase and thus he must forego potential opportunities for more profitable sales to other buyers.

The extent to which a buyer will seek a requirements contract for the purpose of preserving production flexibility may ultimately depend upon the predictability of his future needs. For the buyer who has a highly stable demand for a particular commodity, the requirements contract offers little in terms of risk-spreading that could not be secured from a series of fixed-quantity arrangements. As discussed below, a buyer in this situation may select the open-quantity contract for other reasons. But the buyer who faces variable supply needs may find a substantial advantage in avoiding the more rigid commitment of a fixed-quantity contractual arrangement.

While the flexibility in production which is assured by a requirements contract may offer a substantial advantage to the buyer, such arrangements must offer some inducement to the seller to accept the risks which the buyer avoids. The nature of the incentive for the seller will ultimately depend upon his perception of the extent of the risk which he confronts. In the situation in which there is considerable uncertainty as to the buyer's requirements, the means which the seller will most likely use is a price adjustment; he can use the fact of his risk assumption as a basis for bargaining for a selling price above that of the then established market price. While this would seem to be the most typically applicable means for compensating the seller, there are other features of the arrangement which may be attractive. As the rate of the requirements buyer's consumption becomes more predictable, price adjustments are less likely and these other considerations presumably will play a greater role. The seller may anticipate, for example, that the buyer will buy the contract goods in sufficiently large quantities that he is compensated for the risk of a quantity fluctuation. The guaranteed market of the requirements contract will relieve the seller of the burden of pursuing other markets and may yield a substantial reduction in selling expenses. Similarly, a predictable demand will assist the seller in planning for his business and permit the more efficient allocation of resources.

From the seller's perspective, the requirements contract also has the effect of excluding other competitors from the outlet which he has secured. Where the seller already holds a dominant market position, this attribute may have serious antitrust implications. In. other situations, the effect of the open-quantity contract in restricting competition may be quite desirable, for a seller who is a new entrant into an established product market may be attracted by the protection which the requirements contract provides. If the market is already occupied by established sellers, a prospective competitor may be unwilling to enter it unless he secures a protected market, such as that provided by a requirements buyer with a stable demand. When the seller has secured such a contract, the decision to commit resources to the development of a market position can be made with an assurance that a demand will exist for the seller's product. In this situation, the seller exchanges the risk of his own lack of competitiveness during the start-up period for what he may perceive as a lesser risk that his prediction of the buyer's demands will prove to be inaccurate.

Much of the analysis concerning the importance of production flexibility to the requirements buyer can also be applied to the seller under an output contract. Such a contract, from the perspective of the seller, has the attraction of insuring a constant demand for his product. it is true, as accepted by traditional analysis, that the advantage of such a contract likely to be given highest priority by the seller is the savings of marketing costs which flows from the assured demand. Indeed, the articulated expectations of the seller are likely to emphasize this cost-saving feature. If the arrangement is a true output contract, however, it will afford the seller greater freedom to control the production levels of his operation than might be available if his sales were limited to fixed-quantity orders. If the seller's only obligation is to sell his output, production volume can be adjusted to insure that the goods are produced at a level which achieves maximum profitability in his plant. If the cost of supplies increases and it is necessary to increase the volume of production to further spread these costs, the seller is assured that a market will exist for the commodities produced. Were the seller's product marketed only through fixed-quantity contracts, the desired result could be achieved only if the seller could locate or stimulate demand from other buyers. If production of the commodity becomes unprofitable due to material shortages or increased costs, the seller will reduce his output, assuming that he is permitted to do so by applicable legal constraints. If he were bound under a series of fixed-quantity contracts, he would not have this option and would be forced to continue production to the extent necessary to meet pre-existing commitments. Because of this and other advantages to the seller, the buyer is likely to be able to secure a more favorable price for the commodity sold than would be available in the open market at the time of the contract. A basic assumption of this arrangement is, however, that the potential for profit will prompt the seller to maintain production whenever feasible. Hence, the buyer's assessment of the risk he assumes—and, thus, his desire for a price advantage—reflect the weight of this consideration as well as such factors as the seller's prior output levels, the capacity of his plant, and the availability of his supplies.

Thus, a central feature of both output and requirements contracts in their pristine forms is the flexibility which is afforded the quantity-determining party in the operation of his business. When business reversals arise, the party is in a position to adjust his production to minimize the risk of financial loss. Similarly, the open-quantity arrangement allows the quantity-determining party to respond when there is an opportunity for greater profits. Thus, in addition to other advantages, the requirements buyer or output seller retains a capacity to respond to changes in the profitability of his business, and thereby achieves an objective which is central to any commercial operation. While the quantity-determining party in these capacities will often trade off other advantages—usually price—to maintain the desired flexibility, resort to the open-quantity contract offers greater flexibility of business operation than would exist under fixed-quantity arrangements in which obligation to accept some goods—or right to demand additional quantities—is predetermined.

Other Functions

Open-quantity contracts serve commercial functions other than assuring the quantity-determining party flexibility in establishing the production level of his business. These include minimization of supply risks other than those identified above, achievement of greater operational efficiency, and reduction of direct operational costs. In particular cases, these other functions may be the feature which ultimately attracts a party to the arrangement, although it is often the case that this contractual form is used to satisfy a mixture of motives which encompasses both the flexibility function and one or more of those discussed herein. There is likely to be considerable variation in the degree to which each of these functions is represented in the articulated expectations of particular buyers and sellers. And, in many cases, a function may be assumed but not expressly identified by the quantity-determining party. In other situations, the circumstances of the contractual setting will suggest that a function is not operative.

Minimization of supply risks. For a particular manufacturer, there may be a substantial risk that the availability of material will be restricted. The cause may be supply limitations which exist irrespective of price, as in the case of scarce natural resources, or which are related to the presence of unpredictably fluctuating cost. By resort to a requirements contract, the purchaser can surmount these supply risks. The buyer is locked into a source of supply and assured that the seller will not market a product of limited availability to other buyers. Where the buyer's concern is with future fluctuations in market price, a fixed-price requirements contract will provide protection from that uncertainty.

It should be apparent that a fixed-quantity contract could also be used to preserve a source of supply. The utility of such an arrangement, however, would approximate that of the open-quantity contract only in the situation in which the buyer could predict his needs with precision. Where the buyer is attempting to meet short-term supply needs, he may very well find that the requirements contract offers no particular advantage in securing his supply source. If the buyer's concern for the quality or availability of his supplies extends over a longer term, however, the element of predictability is less certain. In this situation the choice of a requirements arrangement can serve both to secure the needed supplies and permit flexibility in the rate of consumption. The buyer could, of course, attempt to satisfy his long-term requirements by a series of fixed-quantity contracts in which a new contract was negotiated as his supply needs became susceptible to a reasonably accurate projection. Such an approach would, however, offer a number of disadvantages. In addition to the possibility of an over- or under-purchase of goods, the buyer would not only incur transactions costs—which, as explained below, include the cost of seeking out and negotiating with sellers—but would also expose himself to price increases. A requirements contract could he used to avoid these difficulties.

The seller under an output contract also gains advantages in the market from which he secures supplies. The output contract assures a constant demand, a feature which is not present where the seller relies on fixed-quantity sales to dispose of his production. To meet that demand, the seller can produce his product at an even rate and his supply needs will have greater stability than would exist were he not competing in a guaranteed market. He can use this feature of a constant and predictable consumption level as a basis for bargaining for an advantageous price arrangement with his suppliers. The supplier shares in the advantage of the output contract by receiving some protection against his own over-production.

Increased operational efficiency. The ability of the output seller to operate his plant more efficiently is apparent: the seller's rate of production can be stabilized, thus insuring efficient use of his labor force, equipment, and physical facilities. Unlike the seller who must respond to a varying demand, the output seller can make extensive use of short-and long-term planning for the most productive operation of his business. The buyer under a requirements contract can also increase his operational efficiency and may commit himself to such an arrangement with that objective. He is assured that his supply of materials will be constant, which in turn allows him greater control of his production schedule than would exist if he were forced to secure his supplies through periodic negotiations with suppliers. Variations in the availability of the material, which might otherwise affect the buyer's ability to arrive at an even production schedule, are avoided. In addition, the buyer may substantially enhance the predictability of his cost if he can secure his requirements on a fixed-price basis. By isolating some of his costs in advance of production, he can plan for more efficient allocation of his other resources. Consistent with a theme developed above, similar results could be achieved under fixed-quantity contracts only where supply needs could be accurately projected, a condition not likely to be found over a long term.

Decreased direct operational cost. While increased operational efficiency will produce cost savings, cost reduction of a more direct sort can be identified as flowing from an open-quantity arrangement. Once a source of supply is secured under an open-quantity contract, the requirements buyer no longer needs to devote time or personnel to searching out suppliers and negotiating materials contracts. Moreover, a buyer who attempts to satisfy uncertain supply needs by fixed-quantity contracts is likely to make purchases in quantities greater than those needed for immediate consumption in order to minimize both transactions costs and the risk of price variations. The resulting expenditures for storage and maintenance of inventory could be more closely controlled by a requirements arrangement in which the level of periodic orders reflects short-term needs.

The cost reduction which the output seller experiences is more certain. Indeed, it is this function which is often regarded as that which attracts the seller to an output contract. Assured of a steady demand for his production, he need not incur the costs which are usually necessary to stimulate and respond to demand. Thus, he need not advertise or otherwise promote his product and he need not employ personnel to negotiate and administer sales contracts [. . .]

Policy Support for Limiting Quantity Increases

1. *Potential for undue advantage.* An obvious objection to permitting drastic and relatively sudden increases in quantity is that such a change is not likely to be anticipated by the party required to supply

requirements or purchase output. This element of surprise, in itself, perhaps suggests the desirability of imposing a quantity limitation, for development of complex economies is, to a significant degree, dependent upon the stability of commercial relationships. But ultimately there must be inquiry into the risks which each party has assumed to determine whether the unanticipated detriment is one against which generalized protection should be afforded.' [. . .]

2. *Absence of a natural limitation on fluctuations.* As discussed above, the risk of decreases in quantity is limited by the presence in the quantity-determining party of a desire for profit maximization. This feature provides an impetus to that party not to reduce his level of business. The desire for profitability will often prompt the party to overcome market difficulties rather than pass them on in the form of reduced requirements or output. Thus, the desire for profitability—tempered with the requirement of good faith—serves as a natural limitation upon decreases in quantity and, to the extent it is operative, lessens the need for more artificial limitations such as that which some find in section 2–306.

Increases in requirements are not affected by a similar constraint. Indeed, the desire for profit maximization may have the opposite effect of encouraging constantly larger levels of requirements consumption or output production. Given other favorable conditions, the quantity-determining party will seek to decrease his marginal unit costs, and hence increase his profits, by increasing the number of units which he produces. If, for example, the quantity-determining party has unused production potential at the time of contracting, he would be inclined to maximize the return of capital and other resources to the extent that market conditions would permit. Since these pressures for enlargement are not naturally suppressed, there may be a need for artificial limitations. At a minimum, the absence of a natural limitation on increases makes this form of variation a more appropriate subject of statutory control.

3. *Absence of interference with business judgment.* The thesis has been developed that a capacity to decrease quantities, restrained only by the requirement of good faith, is desirable because it preserves to the quantity-determining party relative freedom to exercise his business judgment in the operation of his facility. It is posited that a party who entered an open-quantity agreement is not likely to have relinquished the right to decrease requirements or output in response to business or market conditions. Because flexibility in effectuating business judgment is likely to be a fundamental concern of the party who has chosen not to accept a fixed-quantity obligation, a statutory interpretation which significantly inhibits it must be suspect.

Alleviation of the harsh consequences of an unexpected, abnormal increase in quantity, however, need not be subverted to an overriding concern for the preservation of business judgment, for a limitation upon disproportionate increases represents a less disruptive intrusion upon that fundamental precept. A requirements buyer, for example, can continue to operate his business so as to maximize profit even if his requirements seller is not required to meet disproportionately increased needs. The buyer is simply forced to look elsewhere for his supplies. While alternative sources may not be as desirable in terms of price or quality, the buyer is left free to attempt to minimize a disparity through negotiation or substitution. He continues in full control of his business and resources, with the means to overcome the consequences of an artificial limitation on variations under his open-quantity contract.

In the final analysis, the relative absence of impact upon business judgment may not stand alone as a reason for imposing a limitation upon quantity increases. It does suggest, however, the rationality of a rule which differentiates between types of quantity variations; and it does influence the decision to impose a limitation, since that conclusion represents a balancing of the relative impact of the result upon buyer and seller. While decreases in quantity have potentially harsh consequences for the requirements seller or output buyer, there can appropriately be a paramount concern for the quantity-determining party's control of his business. Since the concern for intrusions upon business control is not as compelling where quantity increases are involved, the need to alleviate the potential for undue advantage should, in that con text, be given greater weight.

NOTES

1.   Dealing with pricing issues in relational contracts. Chapter 2 introduced the important focus of commercial law scholarship on the problems of contracting costs and incomplete contracts. Where contracts are obligationally incomplete, commercial law provides default rules or standards, thereby enabling the courts to fill many kinds of gaps. Faced with significant contracting costs, the parties have alternative courses of action other than silence. Professor Joskow's article recognizes that there are many different ways of responding to the contracting challenges posed by relational contracts,. Parties might write fixed price, market price, escalating price contracts, and long-term, open price-term contracts. His analysis seeks to show why it is that in the coal industry open price-term contracts are both widespread and infrequently the cause of litigation. Joskow concludes that this category of relational contracts provide for both price flexibility and some potential long-run rigidities. Overall, they did "a fairly good, but far from perfect, job of adapting to changing market conditions." Joskow, *Long-Term Contracts* at 81.

2.   Long-term v. short-term contracts. Uncertainty surrounding future conditions increase contracting costs, particularly in long-term contracts. We might therefore expect parties dealing under very significant uncertainty to enter into shorter-term agreements, or even spot exchanges. Or, we might ask why parties would enter into long-term contracts under such conditions. Fixed prices may insulate one or both parties against future market fluctuations. This is less likely to be the motivation for long-term contracting when parties choose alternative price terms described in Joskow's article. Beyond market risk, however, there might be a risk to the security or stability of supply. Alternatively, the parties may wish to protect the reliance investment of one or both parties.

3. Constraints on discretion. Open terms avoid front-end contracting costs by leaving terms of exchange to the discretion of one party. Under output contracts, the buyer agrees to take everything that is produced by the seller, usually on a per-item basis. The buyer is free to purchase comparable items from other sellers; the seller, however, can only sell the contract output to that particular buyer. Under requirements contracts, the quantity is determined not by the seller's production, but by the buyer's needs. The seller is free to sell to multiple buyers, but the buyer cannot buy any of the contract-specified requirements from other sellers. The granting of discretion to one party injects flexibility in their agreement, but can give rise to opportunism by that party. The parties or the courts often constrain the discretion by requiring that it be exercised in "good faith" or consistent with "best efforts." Nevertheless, these constraints are imperfect and give rise to costs at the back-end of the transaction: such as the cost of litigating whether good faith or best efforts were met.

The UCC default rule for requirements and output contracts is found in § 2–306. Weistart recognizes that, prior to the introduction of the Code, the common law had often imposed a "good faith" limitation on quantity variations in open price-term contracts. The Code adopted this "good faith" limitation. However, ambiguities in the text and in the accompanying comment have fostered divergent interpretations of what constitutes "good faith." The Code language established a limitation for some quantity variations, but, as Weistart recognizes, "it is not clear whether the limitation applies equally to the four varieties of fluctuations—that is, increases in requirements, increases in output, decreases in requirements, and decreases in outputs." Weistart, *Requirements* at 601.

The good faith requirement is the subject of a lively debate in legal scholarship: not merely about what "good faith" means, but whether a "good faith" default best serves the interests of commercial parties. For example, Charles Fried, in *Contract as Promise* (1981), argued that the words "good faith" stand for "a way of dealing with a contractual party: honestly, decently. It is an adverbial notion suggesting the avoidance of chicanery and sharp practice (bad faith) whether in coming to an agreement or in carrying out its terms." *Id.* at 74. On the other hand, Victor Goldberg has criticized the application of the good faith standard in open quantity contracts. Goldberg argues that, rather than limiting a party's discretion, the "good faith" test of 2–306(1) often involves supplanting the party's careful balancing of various concerns in the initial contract with a "wooden, uninformed reading of the agreement." Because courts have no theory of what constitutes good faith, Goldberg claims that they have required producers to behave in most peculiar ways: "for example, running a plant at below full capacity for the life of the contract." Victor Goldberg, *Discretion in Long–Term Open Quantity Contracts: Reigning in Good Faith*, 35 U.C. Davis L. Rev. 319, 320 (2002).

4.   Open terms and homogeneous communities. Open terms might be found in contracts between parties who have ongoing relationships, such as repeat transactions, or who operate within relatively close knit communities. These extralegal contexts (characteristics of what legal scholars call "relational contracts") also help to deter opportunistic exercise of discretion. We might therefore expect that open terms are more likely to appear in relatively close-knit communities, such as those described by Professor Bernstein in Chapter 2, supra.

3.5   Contract Flexibility, Termination Rights and Damages

Embedded Options and the Case Against Compensation in Contract Law*

ROBERT E. SCOTT and **GEORGE G. TRIANTIS**

Compensation is the governing principle in contract law remedies. This principle shapes the key doctrines that specify the consequences of breach. Expectation, the default measure of damages that derives from the compensation principle, aims to put the promisee in the position she would have occupied had the promisor performed. Alternatively, specific performance is available at the option of the promisee only when the court believes money damages are inadequate compensation for her loss. Although parties may agree to liquidated damages, contract doctrine instructs them to abide by the compensation norm. But despite its profound influence on contemporary contract law doctrine, the compensation principle has tenuous historical, economic, and empirical support. Its evolution in the common law resulted primarily from ill-conceived path dependence; compensation is virtually ignored in the theoretical analysis of efficient contract design; and compensation plays little role in the contracts actually negotiated by commercial parties and agreed to by consumers. As a result of an unfortunate turn in history, lawmakers view contract damages as compensation for wrongs. This has impeded both the efficient evolution of default remedies and the efficient regulation of liquidated damages.

Rather than conceiving of damages as compensation, the right to breach and pay damages is better understood as a valuable option sold by the promisee to the promisor. Indeed, the right to breach is only a subset of a broader category of termination rights that gives one party an option to walk away from the contemplated exchange. A firm offer or unilateral promise, for example, grants the promisee such an option.

* 104 COLUM. L. REV. 1428–63 (2004).

Broad warranties, such as satisfaction-or-your-money-back provisions, give buyers similar options. Requirements, output, or installment contracts grant one party substantial discretion to determine the contract quantity. And a contract may provide that one party has the right to terminate, cancel, renew, return, or redeem goods.

Either or both parties to a contract, therefore, commonly enjoy the right to terminate at some cost. For the purposes of analysis and argument, we focus on the option held by a buyer of goods or services. The buyer holding an option has the right to avoid the exchange by paying either a termination fee or damages. The price of an embedded option is determined just as the price of any other product: It is a function of the option's value to the option holder, the cost to the option writer, and the competitiveness of the market in which they transact. Options are essentially insurance contracts that divide risks according to their respective exercise prices. For any given exercise price, the option price divides between the parties the surplus created by the option—namely, the difference between the option's value to the buyer and its cost to the seller. The parties should choose a pairing of option price and exercise price that maximizes this surplus. Sometimes the option price is fixed by the contract (e.g., in the form of a nonrefundable deposit or termination fee), and at other times it is left to be judicially determined as damages for breach of contract. Given the great variety of conditions under which parties contract for this option, it should not be surprising that commercial and consumer contracts contain a wide range of option prices. We explain the heterogeneity in option prices and argue that they are rarely equivalent to the measure of the seller's expectation in a completed sale.

Consider an electronics store that sells television sets for $400 and offers full refunds for any returns made within thirty days. This contract gives the buyer a free thirty-day option to purchase the television set for $400. A buyer who does not know whether her family needs a television set or will like this particular model values the opportunity to return it free of charge. Thus, the option is valuable to her because she is uncertain as to the value of the television set to her family. The retailer in this case bears significant costs in accepting returns, including the cost of receiving, inspecting, and reselling the returned goods, often through a discount outlet or internet sale. Yet, the retailer often does not charge for the option. Such "free" options are particularly interesting for our purposes because these contracts make no attempt to compensate the seller for losses it suffers when the buyer walks away from the contemplated exchange.

Under many other termination provisions, buyers pay positive option prices in the form of fees or damages. These fees sometimes exceed the compensatory amount—for example, the seller's foregone profit. Consumers are familiar with instances of such overcompensation in a variety of transactions. For example, economy fares on airlines are typically conditioned on a penalty of $100 if the passenger chooses to cancel and apply the ticket price against the fare of another flight. The penalty applies even on flights that are overbooked and almost certain to be full. Thus, the penalty is not simply compensation for the airlines' losses.

Indeed, casual observation reveals that termination fees in both commercial and consumer contracts regularly depart from the compensatory amount in both directions. Retailers often have the right to return unsold merchandise to the wholesaler or distributor. Rights of return are common, for example, in the retailing of books, journals, newspapers, musical compact discs, jewelry, and cigarettes. Aircraft manufacturers permit purchasers to cancel orders or to change the type of aircraft at no charge even after the manufacturer has made a significant investment in production.

In this Article, we offer an explanation for these contracting patterns based on the insurance (or risk management) function of embedded options. It is well known that compensatory remedies insure the buyer against the seller's breach and thereby against the risk of fluctuations in the seller's cost of performance that lead it to breach. The buyer, however, still bears the risk of fluctuations in the value of the seller's performance. Options created by termination rights insure buyers against this risk and thereby may promote the risk management objectives of business contractors.

When the buyer's option comes in the form of the right to breach and pay expectation damages, the buyer's liability on termination is a function of the profit that the seller would gain from the exchange. Under an expectation damages rule, therefore, the buyer shrugs off some of the risk of fluctuations in performance value, but assumes some of the risk in fluctuations in the seller's profit. If the buyer contracts for the right to terminate and pay a fixed amount rather than expectation damages, the buyer can also avoid the risk associated with the seller's cost. The buyer may be prepared to pay a premium to be able to shift both the risk in the value of performance and the risk in the seller's costs. In these cases, the parties may agree to pay fixed liquidated damages that are greater than the (ex ante) expected amount of the seller's loss from breach. Under the current penalty rule, however, courts will refuse to enforce this term. Our analysis suggests a benign explanation for this supercompensatory damages term: It is the product of a negotiated sale of insurance from the seller to the buyer in the form of an embedded option.

Given the close link between options and insurance, it should not be surprising that the optimal terms of embedded options are a function of considerations that determine insurance contracts—namely, risk-bearing capacity, adverse selection, and moral hazard. Although we discuss the role of these considerations in the structuring of embedded options, our principal contribution is to show that many contracts contain embedded options and that the optimal terms and prices of these options are heterogeneous. This analysis is consistent with our observation of a wide variety of termination provisions in practice.

Our analysis has important normative implications for the default rules of contract damages and for the freedom of parties to contract away from the defaults. Termination provisions serve valuable risk management objectives when they depart from the compensation principle. The characterization of breach damages as the price of an option that yields value to the buyer reinforces the criticisms of the penalty rule that have been raised by contracts scholars. The recent litigation concerning late fees charged by Blockbuster video stores is illustrative. There, the plaintiffs argued that the fees were unenforceable penalties. But the court recognized that the right to extend the rental period was valuable, that a rational consumer would pay a price for this right that might be higher than the cost to Blockbuster, and that courts should not engage in regulation of this price. We argue that courts similarly should enforce all termination provisions, regardless of their form.

Courts are not well suited to set default contract damages either. It is unlikely that any given damages default will reflect the option price that most parties would adopt in their contracts. In most contract relationships, an expectancy default rule is no more appropriate with respect to damages than with respect to the price of any other good, service, or contract term for which there is no established market price. We suggest, moreover, that the particular salience of a damages default—particularly one founded on an entrenched compensation principle—discourages parties from writing explicit termination provisions and deters the courts from specifically enforcing them. Thus, we argue in favor of a bargain-facilitating, instead of a majoritarian, approach. Where commercial parties have failed to provide expressly for termination rights, we propose that the courts specifically enforce the exchange. In the context of consumer transactions, where merchant sellers typically draft the contracts, the default should give the consumer a free option if the parties fail to make an express provision regarding termination rights. [....]

Termination Rights and Call Options

Scholars who frame contract breach in option terms typically analyze the buyer as having purchased the good for the contract price, P, and a put option on the good with exercise price, x. In this paper, however, we prefer the equivalent characterization in which the buyer pays an option price, d, to acquire a call option to purchase the good with an exercise price, x. The sum of the option price and the exercise price is the contract price, $P = d + x$. If the buyer's promise is enforced by damages, then d is the damages liability and x is the difference between the contract price and those damages.

We prefer the call option characterization because it is more analytically revealing than the contract-plus-put combination. Consider, for example, a contract under which the buyer purchases a widget for $15 and can recover $11 if she returns it within thirty days. Under the put-call parity rule, the buyer's position can be characterized either as 1) the combination of the widget together with a put option with exercise price $11; or 2) a call option on the widget with exercise price $11. By using the call option characterization, we can describe the option by the pair (d, x) that isolates the price of the option in d: The buyer pays a price of $4 for a call with exercise price $11. If we used the alternative characterization, the price of the put would be embedded in the contract price and thus could not be isolated and compared to contract damages (the contract price of $15 in the example above reflects the value of the put together with the value of the widget).

The parties can choose from a set of alternative option contracts, (d, x). The values of d and x will tend to be inversely related, and the contract price will be higher the easier it is for the buyer to walk away from the contract. Consider first a contract in which the buyer agrees to buy a widget for $12 with no termination right, (12, 0). Now, suppose the seller offers the buyer an alternative contract under which the buyer makes a deposit, d, and holds an option to purchase the widget for $1. The buyer pays d to acquire a call option with exercise price $1. The deposit, d, is effectively the price the buyer pays for the option. If there is some possibility the buyer will value the widget for less than $1, she will be prepared to pay a deposit—effectively an option price—greater than $11. Writing this option may also be costly for the seller, but the parties will choose to trade the option if this cost is less than the value of the option to the buyer. If the seller has some bargaining power, she will be able to capture some of the surplus. It is therefore likely that the aggregate contract price will be greater than $12 when the seller writes a call option with an exercise price of $1. As a general matter, the sensitivity of the option price to changes in the exercise price is such that, for each dollar increase in the exercise price, the price of the option decreases by less than a dollar. Therefore, the aggregate contract price rises asymptotically with the exercise price as the parties approach (0, P^), where P^ is the maximum value for the contract price.

If we begin our analysis instead at the (0, P^) end of the spectrum, suppose that P^ = x = $18. The seller effectively has given the buyer a free call option with an exercise price of $18. We later discuss the possible motivations for giving such a free option. For now, note that if the seller offers to reduce the exercise price from $18 to $17, the buyer will be willing to pay an option price in the form of a deposit—but in an amount less than $1. Similarly, if the seller offers to reduce the exercise price further, the buyer will be prepared to increase her deposit, but by less than the reduction in the exercise price. Of course, the seller does not seek to maximize the contract price per se, but rather to maximize the surplus between the option price and the cost of writing the option.

The ways in which the price of the call option, d, is paid are as diverse as the forms of termination fees. The buyer may make a nonrefundable deposit, agree to a cancellation fee, or assume a commitment to pay damages in the event of breach. The common feature is that the buyer pays for the call option by incurring an initial cost specified by contract and can subsequently choose to incur an additional cost to execute the contract exchange. If the option price is in the form of a commitment to pay damages upon breach, then this price depends on the materialized loss from breach suffered by the seller. Consequently, the buyer faces a distribution of option prices during the term of the option. This uncertainty does not change the analysis. The option to breach and pay damages conventionally may be termed an exchange option: the right to exchange one asset of uncertain value (the damages liability) for another (the payoff from a completed exchange). For our expositional purposes, however, we will stick to the call option characterization whether the option price is fixed or uncertain at the time of contract.

Indeed, there may be other sources of uncertainty in the option price. The enforcement of breach damages may be less than perfect or the duration of the option may be uncertain. For example, many consumers purchase retail items where the return policy is unclear; retailers may be deliberately vague. The consumers' ability to walk away from the deal may need to be discounted, therefore, according to the probability that the retailer will permit a refund of varying amounts, and according to the distribution of negotiated or judicial outcomes in the event of any dispute. Practically, these factors are significant in many circumstances. We suggest in Part II.B.1 below that the buyer may be willing to pay a premium to avoid these risks. This premium may be in the form of liquidated damages that will be struck down by a court—inappropriately, in our view—as supercompensatory and a penalty.

In the discussion that follows, we distinguish between two sources of value of embedded call options: 1) preserving the real options given by nature (without the need for renegotiation between the parties); and 2) insuring the buyer against the risk of fluctuations in her valuation of, and in the cost of, the seller's performance. Consistent with conventional efficient breach theory, real options analysis suggests that expectation damages lead to the efficient exercise of real options. As we noted earlier, however, the embellishments to contract theory over the past twenty-five years have emphasized the significance of specific investments and the ability of parties to renegotiate their contracts. As a result, it is now clear that expectation damages are neither necessary nor sufficient for efficiency. The analysis that follows introduces important and widely applicable risk management considerations indicating that optimal termination provisions are highly context contingent and are determined by the factors of insurance and market conditions, rather than the compensation principles of contract law. [. . .]

Consider a venture that entails the production of a good at a cost, c, and value, v, where both variables are initially random. An integrated firm with this opportunity bears exogenous risks in the joint distribution of v and c that cause $v - c$ to rise or fall. The firm might preserve its option to be able to walk away if subsequent new information reveals that $v' < c'$. Now, consider that two parties might pursue the same project by a fixed-price contract with price, P: The seller produces the good at a cost, c, and delivers it to the buyer who values it at v. Under a specifically enforceable contract, the seller bears the cost risk, $(P - c)$, and the buyer keeps the value risk, $(v - P)$. The parties can preserve the real option that would be held by the integrated firm by choosing to enforce their contract by expectation damages. Each party shares in the value of this real option by being able to shed some of her respective downside risk (in particular, the risk that v falls at the same time as c rises) without passing any additional risk to the other party. When the parties agree to expectation damages, the seller does not write an option for the benefit of the buyer; it is given by nature.

Beyond the preservation of real options, however, the seller might also write an option in favor of the buyer that would further insure the buyer against the risks of the project. When the seller writes the option, the termination fee is not equal to the seller's realized loss from termination (i.e., expectation damages). Assume that the seller will always specifically perform (i.e., deliver the goods). Under our notation, a regime of expectation damages gives the buyer a call option, $(d, x) = (P - c, c)$; that is, the buyer incurs a liability of $P - c$ and can exercise its call by paying the balance of the contract price, c. Note that both the option price and the exercise price are uncertain at the time the parties enter into their contract, and these amounts will be judicially determined at a later date. Consequently, the buyer may be prepared to pay a premium in order to avoid the risk in the option price that is due to fluctuations in c. The seller may therefore write a call option with a fixed price (i.e., a liquidated damages provision) that the court would perceive as supercompensatory in the ex ante sense. [. . .]

Finally, recall that the parties also have the choice among different combinations of option price and exercise price, (d, x). By raising the exercise price, x, and reducing the option price, d, below the seller's expected profit, $P - E_0(c)$, the parties can shift a larger portion of the valuation risk, v, from the buyer to the seller. In this way, the buyer can escape more of the lower tail of the distribution by walking away from her call option when her valuation falls below the contract price. Of course, the buyer in return must agree to a higher exercise price. But if a court interprets the option price, d, as stipulated damages imposed in the event of the buyer's breach, these damages will appear to be undercompensatory even though they are a fair price for the call option with that exercise price. The discrepancy arises from the fact that compensation measures the seller's lost payoff given that there is no exchange. The option price takes into account the exercise price that the seller will receive in those states of the world in which the option is exercised. From this perspective, true damages more nearly approximate the seller's cost of writing the option than the seller's loss when the option expires without exercise.

The Right to Return*
EUGENE KANDEL

The choice of the optimal contract with the distributor is of great importance to most manufacturers. This is the subject of a large body of literature dealing with franchising, exclusive territories, exclusive dealership, resale price maintenance (RPM), and other types of contracts [. . .] This article examines yet another contractual issue, the allocation of responsibility for unsold inventory, provision for which is made either formally or implicitly in practically every contract between manufacturers and retailers. The two extreme cases are the consignment contract, which allocates all the burden to the manufacturer, and the no-return contract, in which the retailer purchases the merchandise from the manufacturer and assumes responsibility for the unsold inventory. Intermediate contracts, which divide the responsibility between the manufacturer and the retailer, also exist.

This contractual provision is relevant only when a significant degree of uncertainty about the retail demand is present. [. . .] Within the wide category of products facing uncertain retail demand, the marketplace presents a variety of contracts used: retailers of books, journals, newspapers, musical records and compact discs, jewelry, as well as dairy products and cigarettes generally have the right to return unsold inventory to the manufacturers. New products by upstart and even established firms are frequently sold on consignment as well. Distributors selling from manufacturers' catalogs as well as manufacturers renting retail space in department stores are essentially using the consignment contract. In contrast, the distribution of fashion clothing, produce, flowers, greeting cards, computer software and toys is not generally accompanied by the return option. Both types of contracts are found in the auto, auto parts, and office equipment industries, as well as in department store purchasing and movie distribution. Different contracts are used across different types of distributors selling the same products: book and record clubs cannot return the unsold inventory, whereas book and record stores routinely do so. Apparel stores cannot, in general, return the leftovers, yet manufacturers of high-priced designer items sold through boutiques frequently allow returns. Contract choices may change over time: a recent decision by Kmart to urge toy manufacturers

* 39 J. L. & Econ. 329 (1996).

to sell on consignment is against the established practice and has created much commotion in the industry. One of the main differences between the U.S. and the Japanese distribution systems is the much wider use of consignment contracts and catalog stores in Japan [. . .] The Japanese distribution system is currently undergoing dramatic change, an important aspect of which is the introduction of discounting accompanied by the gradual abolition of consignment. [. . .]

The book publishing industry in the United States is characterized by consignment contracts between the vast majority of publishers and retailers. [The following discussion] suggests that consignment evolved over time as the optimal contract between the publishers and the bookstores.

Book publishing has a large fixed component in the cost structure. Payments for manuscript rights, editing, typesetting, and other activities are made well before the first copy is printed. The printing process itself has significant economies of scale as well: the setup of printing presses is costly, making small print runs very expensive. It is desirable to concentrate printing in large batches, which are based on the retailers' backorders. [. . . E]very major publisher has to deal with a tremendous variety of book retailers, which means that nonlinear pricing contracts are not feasible. There are quantity discounts which are mostly designed to discourage small orders. Thus, the assumption of single-price contracts approximates this industry quite well. [. . .]

Scrap Values. Books which are not sold in a particular store during the initial demand period can be either discounted in the same store or returned to the publisher, where they are either shipped to another full-price store or remaindered. In-store discounting is not likely to significantly increase sales because it would signal lower quality of the book. The publisher can reallocate inventory more efficiently than the independent store because of specific knowledge about demand in other locations and because of economies of scale in coordination. [. . . I]t is likely that the manufacturer's scrap value is higher than the retailer's, which implies that consignment is likely to be optimal.

Size. Each of the largest publishing houses setting the norms in the industry is much larger than any independent bookstore. They also have a much larger market share. Both the risk-sharing and the contract determination arguments suggest that the consignment contract is the optimal one.

Information Asymmetry. Each new title is a new product facing a considerable uncertainty with respect to future sales. The publisher is the one picking the titles and therefore is likely to be more optimistic than the bookstores on the prospects of any particular title.

Promotions and Quality. Which party affects consumer demand the most? Success of most wide-audience titles depends on the quality of the book as perceived by consumers (and not necessarily by literary critics) and the amount of exposure it gets; the publisher seems to have an advantage in assuring both. First, the publisher can choose the title and encourage the author to improve the manuscript and to promote the book. Second, the publisher can exploit the economies of scale in advertising. Independent bookstores are ill-equipped to accomplish either of these tasks. They do provide an important service and affect the consumption patterns of their loyal customers, but this segment does not seem to be the main target of the major publishers. A consignment contract which allocates the incentives to publish quality titles and promote them is likely to be optimal.

As previous arguments suggest, the consignment contract is likely to be the optimal one between the publishers and the bookstores. This contract has indeed evolved since the 1940s as the norm in the industry, the distribution part of which was mainly composed of small independent stores. The explosive growth of large chains in the last 15 years has separated the market into two distinct segments. The consignment contract is still the optimal one for publishers selling to the independent bookstore segment, while it may not be for the chains. If this is the case, then the publishers should consider offering two types of contracts to induce self-selection of the two distributor types. Consistent with this prediction, Harcourt Brace recently unveiled a new contract with two choices to its retail and wholesale customers. One choice is the traditional contract, in which the wholesale price is 55–60 percent of the retail price, and returns are not allowed; the other offers wholesale prices of as low as 40 percent of the retail price, but does not allow returns.

Summary

This article identifies the determinants of a contractual provision between manufacturers and retailers: namely, who bears responsibility for the unsold inventory. The article focuses initially on the optimal inventory considerations and shows that under the base model assumptions, manufacturers prefer the consignment contract while retailers prefer the no-return one. Then it identifies additional factors affecting the contract choice. Those are specified in the form of testable implications:

1) If the manufacturer has better opportunities for the disposal of unsold inventory than the retailer, the consignment contract is more likely.

2) When manufacturers are larger than retailers, they are likely to choose consignment contracts. Larger retailers are likely to prefer no-return contracts.

3) Low price elasticity of the retail demand increases the likelihood of observing consignment contracts.

4) If the demand for the particular product can be more easily increased through advertisement and quality improvement, the

consignment contract is more likely. However, if retailers have an advantage in increasing demand through service and in-store promotions, the no-return contract is more likely.

5) In a dynamic setting, when the demand parameters are unknown to the manufacturer, the consignment contract is costly and thus unlikely. If, however, the parameters of stochastic demand are known and prices are stable over time, the likelihood of the consignment contract usage increases.

These implications can be tested when the data on cross-sectional variation of contracts become available. The predictions seem to be broadly consistent with the example of the book publishing industry presented in the article.

NOTES

1. Embedded options. Contract law enforces few promises by injunction. Therefore, most parties to contracts have the choice among more than one promise to perform; usually including the option to pay a monetary amount. Legal scholars are adopting this embedded option increasingly as a tool for analyzing liability rules, in contracts as well as other areas of law. See, e.g., George G. Triantis, *The Effects of Insolvency and Bankruptcy on Contract Performance and Adjustment,* 43 U. Tor. L. J. 679 (1993); Paul Mahoney, *Contract Remedies and Options Pricing,* 24 J. Legal Stud. 139 (1995); Avery Weiner Katz, *The Efficient Design of Option Contracts: Principles and Applications,* 90 Va. L. Rev. 2187 (2004); Ian Ayres, Optional Law (2005).

2. The purposes of termination rights and contract damages. The first excerpt in this section suggests that termination rights and contract damages serve the same purpose and differ only in the price that the promisor must pay to avoid the exchange contemplated by the contract. The key decision variable is to determine that price, and a range of variables affect that determination. Professors Scott and Triantis question the fixation of contract law with compensation. Nevertheless, compensatory damages have some virtues. Students of contract law are usually familiar with the principle of efficient breach: the promisor should breach if the benefit from doing so exceeds the cost of the breach to the promisee. Expectation damages also protect reliance investments, though they may induce overinvestment by allowing the promisee to recover the return on the investment even in the event of breach, when the investment goes to waste.

Professors Scott and Triantis focus on the objective of optimal insurance or risk management. When stipulated damages are fixed, the promisor does not bear the risk of fluctuations in the profitability of the contract to the promisee. And, the lower the damages, the lower the risk to the promisee of fluctuations in the value of the contract to her. Professor Kandel's article focuses on the binary choice between no-return and free-return (consignment) rather than the continuum of options described in Scott and Triantis. Kandel explores features of risk allocation that are particularly salient in contracts between distributors and retailers, such as comparative advantages in promoting or predicting sales, in disposing of unsold inventory and diversifying the risk of fluctuating consumer demand.

3.   The damages defaults of Article 2: the "lost volume" and related problems. Article 2 of the UCC provides for three default methods for measuring the damages of a seller when the buyer breaches. First, if the seller resells the goods, she can recover the difference between the contract price and the resale price, plus incidental selling expenses. Second, the seller may recover market damages, equal to the difference between contract price and market price (i.e., the retail price) *plus* incidental selling expenses (see § 2–710). Third, the seller sometimes can sue for its lost profits on the contract, measured by the difference between contract price and estimated costs (i.e., the wholesale price) *less* expenses saved. The three provisions each purport to measure the value of the lost sale to the seller. Yet, they rely on different information and yield different award amounts in some cases. If given the choice among these measures, the seller will choose the one that yields the largest award. With little guidance from the language of Article 2, the courts must decide which measure is most appropriate in different categories of circumstances.

The courts face this dilemma in the "lost volume" cases, illustrated in the following example. James, a manufacturer of bicycles, sells his product to 100 retailers. One of these retailers, Kevin, decides to breach on a purchase order for 20 of James' bicycles. James thereafter "covers" by finding Mike, a new distributor for those bicycles. When it comes time to determine damages, however, James might argue that he would have sold those bikes to Mike anyway. Therefore, the twenty bicycles James sold to Mike shouldn't be considered "cover" because pre-breach he could have expected to sell forty bicycles, whereas post-breach he will only be able to sell 20. Under the common law, this argument was rejected whenever there was an available market for the goods. See, for example, *Rodocanachi, Sons & Co. v. Milburn Bros.*, 18 QBD 67 (1886); *United States v. Burton Coal Co.*, 273 U.S. 337 (1927); Arthur Corbin, 5 Contracts Section 1100 (West, 1951). The choice between market damages and lost profits has attracted the attention of a number of legal scholars, who have analyzed cases such as Mike's breach. RICHARD CRASWELL & ALAN SCHWARTZ, FOUNDATIONS OF CONTRACT LAW (1994) has an excellent review of the issue. For further analyses of the issue, see Robert E. Scott, *The Case for Market Damages: Revisiting the Lost Profits Puzzle*, 57 U. Chic. L. Rev. 1155 (1990); Robert Cooter and Melvin Aron Eisenberg, *Damages for Breach of Contract* 73 Cal. L. Rev. 1434 (1985); Victor P. Goldberg, *An Economic Analysis of the Lost–Volume Retail Seller*, 57 S. Cal. L. Rev. 283 (1984); John A. Sebert, *Remedies Under Article Two of the Uniform Commercial Code: An Agenda for Review*, 130 U. Pa. L. Rev. 360 (1981); and William L. Schlosser, *Construing UCC Section 2–708(2) to Apply to the Lost–Volume Seller*, 24 Case W. Res. L. Rev. 686 (1973).

A similar issue arises in cases in which market damages exceed the post-breach economic loss of the injured party (where, of course, the seller claims for lost profits). For example, in *Nobs Chemical, U.S.A., Inc. v. Koppers Co., Inc.*, 616 F.2d 212 (5th Cir. 1980), Nobs contracted to sell 1,000 metric tons of cumene to Koppers at a fixed price of $540,000. Nobs arranged to acquire the cumene in Brazil for $400 per ton and to expend $45 per ton in transportation costs, for a total expense of $445,000. Koppers breached the contract when the market value of cumene dropped to around $220 per ton at the time of delivery. Nobs was able to cancel the Koppers order with its supplier, although it lost its volume discount and had to pay an additional $25 per ton on the balance of its order for other customers. At trial, therefore, the court confronted the choice between market damages of $320,000 and the $95,000 profit that, as matters turned out, the seller would have earned had the buyer accepted delivery and paid the contract price. Professor Scott has argued that, where parties have attempted to allocate market risks (as in *Nobs Chemical*, supra), lost profit awards and lost profit limitations distort their allocation and diminish the value of the contract surplus. In these cases, courts should take an ex ante perspective in awarding market damages rather than the ex post compensation of lost profits. Robert E. Scott, *The Case for Market Damages: Revisiting the Lost Profits Puzzle*, 57 U. Chic. L. Rev. 1155 (1990). Some courts have adopted Scott's argument. See Tongish v. Thomas, 840 P.2d 471 (Kan. 1992).

The ex ante perspective is important because it also reveals a fundamental flaw in the compensation objective that guides each of the measures of damages in the UCC. Compensation presupposes the right that is breached and, as discussed in the excerpt by Scott and Triantis, *supra*, contract rights are diverse and complex in the manner in which they embed cancellation and termination rights. Each measure of seller's damages presumes a termination right and, in practice, many contracts have termination rights that are different from those on which these measures are based. If the contract in question is not explicit about the termination right, then the courts may examine the context to select the appropriate default. But, this calls for an ex ante rather than ex post perspective. As a useful exercise, consider each default measure of damages provided by Article 2 and identify the circumstances and contracting objectives that are consistent with each respective measure.

4. Anticipatory breach. A promisor enjoys further flexibility in that she may make a decision to repudiate the contract before her performance is due (known as anticipatory repudiation or anticipatory breach). The promisor might thereby reduce its liability for damages, by inducing the promisee to take steps to mitigate his losses. But the promisor cannot revoke its repudiation if the promisee has taken steps in reliance on the repudiation (§ 2–611). Therefore, anticipatory breach also surrenders the promisor's right to the promisee's return performance. The timing decision for repudiation is correspondingly complex. This trade-off complicates the decision to breach early. Does the anticipatory breach default rule make sense? Does it comport with commercial practice as you understand it or with Llewellyn's approach to incorporation of industry norms? For discussions of the tradeoff between triggering mitigation and surrendering contract rights and the contrasting implications for contract law, see Richard Craswell, *Insecurity, Repudiation and Cure*, 19 J. Legal Stud. 399 (1990); Alexander J. Triantis and George G. Triantis, *Timing Problems in Contract Breach Decisions*, 41 J. Law & Econ. 163 (1998).

3.6 Good Faith Purchase

The Good Faith Purchase Idea and the Uniform Commercial Code: Confessions of a Repentant Draftsman*

GRANT GILMORE

One of the ideas I took from Llewellyn's bounteous store was that the good faith purchaser is always right and that the story of his triumph was not only one of the most fascinating episodes in our nineteenth-century legal history (which it was), but was also one of continuing relevance for our own time (which, I have belatedly come to believe, it is not). That attitude, which was shared by almost all—perhaps all—the people who became involved in the Code's drafting, explains a great deal about the Code's treatment of third-party rights. What I propose to do in this article is to review the ideas that we accepted and to explain why (as I now think) we were in large part (although not entirely) mistaken. I shall trace some of the ways in which the good faith purchase idea found its way into the Code's various articles. By way of conclusion, I shall indulge myself in some speculations about what courts should—or will—do with a mid-twentieth-century codification of a mid-nineteenth-century idea whose time has long since gone.

The good faith purchase problem first showed up in our rapidly improvised law of sales in connection with the distribution of goods from manufacturer to ultimate user. The conduit through which the goods traveled was the selling agent, or factor, who took goods on consignment, resold them, and (if he was honest) remitted the proceeds, less his commission, to the manufacturer. With the building of the rail network and the replacement of sail by steam in shipping, the geographical extent of the market constantly expanded. The selling factors became more and more independent of their principals, particularly because the technology of long-distance communications lagged a generation or two behind the technology of long-distance transportation. Not all factors were honest. Some absconded with the proceeds instead of remitting them; some pledged the consigned goods for their own account; some sold on credit when they were authorized to sell only for cash. When their frauds were discovered, who was to bear the loss? The true owner of the goods—that is, the manufacturer? Or the good faith purchaser for value who had bought the goods from the factor (or had taken them as security for a loan) in reliance on his possession and without notice of his intended wrongdoing?

The good faith purchaser won out, which seems odd in the light of what we think we know about the economic and political clout of large

* 15 GA. L. REV. 605 (1981).

manufacturers. In England and in the Eastern seaboard states in this country, Parliament and the state legislatures had to intervene on behalf of the good faith purchaser under so-called Factor's Acts. The midwestern and western states never bothered with Factor's Acts, presumably because the courts, as commerce and industry crossed the mountains, knew what was expected of them.

The theoretical explanation for the result in the factors' cases—apart from the fact that the legislatures had so decreed—came to be that the manufacturer had voluntarily entrusted the goods to the factor. Thus the factor, being lawfully in possession with power of sale, must have some kind of title upon which third parties were entitled to rely. The courts hit on the expression "voidable title," which meant that the "true owner" could get the goods back if he reclaimed them before the factor had resold (or pledged) them but could not pursue them in the hands of good faith buyers (or pledgees). The theoretical explanation broadened the range of situations in which purchasers from fraudulent middlemen could be protected against true owners. The owner who "entrusted" his property to someone else, at least in a commercial setting, thereby conferred on the "trustee" an effective power of disposition—*Ins disponendi,* as it was elegantly put.

Let me suggest some quite different conclusions that we could have deduced from our premises. In a society that recognizes property as something more than theft, you do not go around lightly destroying property rights; you must have a compelling reason for awarding *A's* property to *C.* Even in a contract-oriented law, you do not go around lightly telling people who have been tricked, cheated, and defrauded that they must nevertheless pay up in full; you must have a compelling reason for doing that, too. So, what could the compelling reasons have been which led the courts to reach, the better part of two hundred years ago, these extraordinary conclusions? Are those reasons equally compelling today?

In this country, after the Civil War, manufacturers began to distribute their goods through franchised dealers whose operations they were in a position to control—and did control—much more effectively than they had ever been able to control the independent factors. The factor, who quickly disappeared from the hornbooks and treatises, succeeded in maintaining himself only in a few isolated pockets of the economy—mainly in the distribution of agricultural products. With the disappearance of the factor, the principal reason for the protection of good faith purchasers of goods against defrauded owners also disappeared. The courts promptly began dismantling the good faith purchase idea in its sales version. "[T]he Uniform Sales Act ... was open-ended on the good faith purchase issue. Section 23 saved the old Factors' Acts (in the few states that had them) from repeal," and section 24 provided that a buyer with voidable title could convey good title to a subsequent good faith buyer but made no attempt to explain what "voidable title" was or how it was acquired. I have no idea whether this open-endedness was the result of inadvertence or of deliberate design on the part of the draftsman, Professor Williston. At all events, the courts in Sales Act states had no difficulty in getting on with their dismantling job, which was done by discovering or inventing more and more situations in which the fraudulent middleman who had somehow acquired possession of goods from the true owner was found to have acquired no title at all so that he had nothing to convey to anyone who took from him.

If, in the 1940's, we had paid any attention to what the courts had been doing for fifty or seventy-five years past, we might have come up with something like this: the good faith purchase idea was an intuitive judicial response to economic conditions that ceased to exist after 1850 or thereabouts. During the second half of the nineteenth century, the courts, losing their enthusiasm for the good faith purchase idea, began cutting back instead of further expanding it.... The courts were roundly condemned for holding (as they regularly did) that buyers who had obtained possession of goods by paying for them with bad checks had not thereby acquired the "voidable title" that would protect the people (usually second-hand dealers) to whom they immediately resold the goods. The Tennessee Supreme Court was made to wear the dunce's cap because of a case in which it had failed, in the full light of the twentieth century, to give an "expansive" reading to the old Factors' Act.

Let us turn to the Code. In article 2, the heart of the matter is section 2–403, captioned "Power to Transfer; Good Faith Purchase of Goods; 'Entrusting.' " The first subsection starts off as if it was merely going to restate the "voidable title" provision of the Sales Act: "A person with voidable title has power to transfer a good title to a good faith purchaser for value." That formulation is already broader than the Sales Act formulation in that it protects all subsequent "purchasers" from the voidable-title man instead of merely subsequent "buyers"; "purchaser," as defined in the Code, includes any security transferee. However, the Code does not, as the Sales Act had done, stop there. The following sentence tells us that anyone to whom goods have been delivered "under a transaction of purchase" has the power to convey good title even though

> (a) the transferor [*i.e.,* the original seller] was deceived as to the identify of the purchaser [*i.e.,* the fraudulent middleman], or

> (b) the delivery was in exchange for a check which is later dishonored, or

> (c) it was agreed that the transaction was to be a "cash sale", or

(d) the delivery was procured through fraud punishable as larcenous under the criminal law.

What are we to make of this a-b-c-d list? The official comment observes that, under the sentence just quoted, "subsection (1) provides specifically for the protection of the good faith purchaser for value in a number of specific situations which have been troublesome under prior law." For "situations which have been troublesome" read "situations in which the courts have been protecting the original transferor by refusing to expand the 'voidable title' concept." All the courts that had failed to appreciate the "mercantile approach" were being put in their places. At least as a matter of drafting, "troublesome" was a stroke of genius.

The section 2–403 draftsman was not content to rest from his labors at that point. The next two subsections resurrect nineteenth-century "entrusting" theory—which Williston had not found it necessary to mention in the Sales Act—and put it to some unsuspected uses. Subsection (3) defines "entrusting" as including everything short of armed robbery (larceny is expressly approved). When goods have been so entrusted to "a merchant who deals in goods of that kind," the merchant has power to transfer the entruster's title to "a buyer in ordinary course of business." (For some reason, the security transferees who were protected in the voidable title subsection by the use of the term "purchaser" do not qualify for protection under the entrusting subsection. I have no idea why the draftsman chose thus to narrow the protected class). The upshot of all this is that if you leave your watch to be repaired by a jeweler who not only repairs but sells watches, you lose the watch if the jeweler chooses to sell it. Goods, it is tempting to say, have at long last become fully negotiable—well, almost fully negotiable.

The final subsection of section 2–403 is a literally incomprehensible cross-reference to other articles of the Code (including article 9) which, it is suggested, may, with respect to some types of "purchasers" and to "lien creditors," contain provisions that supersede section 2–403. I do not believe that the cross-reference was meant to be incomprehensible. The drafting became terribly botched and no one ever got around to cleaning it up. The dividing line, however, between article 2 good faith purchasers and article 9 good faith purchasers is not an easy one to draw. . . .

[W]e may take heart in the fact that statutes, even if they are called codes, age even more rapidly than human beings do. The Code dates from the 1940's; it already qualifies for senior citizen status. Let us treat it with respect—even with a nostalgic affection—but there is no need, and with each passing year there will be less need, for us to be overborne by its quaint, old-fashioned ways. There may yet be a way out of the nineteenth century.

Markets Overt, Voidable Titles, and Feckless Agents: Judges and Efficiency in the Antebellum Doctrine of Good Faith Purchase*

HAROLD R. WEINBERG

This article seeks to determine the extent to which antebellum American judges employed economic efficiency as a criterion in formulating decision rules applicable to disputes between the owners and good faith purchasers of goods. It necessarily also considers the possibility of other judicial criteria including the redistribution of wealth.

The decisions selected for study generally arose in the following situation. A's goods come into the possession of B. After one or more additional transfers, the goods come to rest in the hands of C, a good faith purchaser. A then seeks to recover the goods (or their value) from C who was previously unaware of A's claim. Confronted with this situation, antebellum courts focused on the circumstances under which A and A's goods parted company. All permitted A to recover his goods when they had been stolen by B even if C would have been protected by the English doctrine of market overt. American courts developed the voidable title doctrine which permitted A to prevail over C when the goods had been taken from A by B through some, but not all, types of fraud. If A's transfer was to B as A's agent, recovery from C was dependent upon the application of principles of agency and estoppel.

In an earlier paper, this author employed economic analysis to explain this pattern of purchaser protection. Significant theoretical considerations in this study included each decision rule's impact on the demand for and supply of illegitimate goods in the marketplace and the comparative efficiency of owners and good faith purchasers with respect to their ability to prevent the risk that goods would move from the former class to the latter. However, the earlier paper analyzed the pattern under modern-day conditions and did not consider whether it was the product of judges who sought to announce efficient decision rules. This paper explores the pattern's antebellum roots.

Markets Overt

The market overt doctrine reached its fullest English development by the sixteenth century. It matured in a feudal and agrarian society in which periodic and carefully controlled chartered or customary markets and fairs provided significant opportunities for trade. Blackstone provided a description of the doctrine:

> Property may also in some cases be transferred by sale, though the vendor *hath none at all* in the goods: for it is expedient that the buyer, by taking proper precautions, may at all events be secure of his

* 56 TUL. L. REV. 1 (1981).

purchase; otherwise all commerce between man and man must soon be at an end. And therefore, the general rule of law is ... that all sales and contracts of any thing vendible, in fairs and markets *overt* ... (that is, open), shall not only be good between the parties, but also be binding on all those that have any right or property therein.... But if my goods are stolen from me, and sold, out of market overt, my property is not altered, and I may take them wherever I find them.... If the buyer knoweth the property not to be in the seller; or there be any other fraud in the transaction ... the owner's property is not bound thereby.... By which wise regulations the common law has secured the right of the proprietor in personal chattels from being devested, so far as was consistent with that other necessary policy, that purchasers, *bona fide*, in a fair, open, and regular manner, should not be afterwards put to difficulties by reason of the previous knavery of the seller.

An additional justification for affording limited negotiability to goods can be found in Coke, who wrote that "the common Law did hold it for a point of great policy, and [advantageous] for the Commonwealth, that Fairs and Markets overt should be replenished and well furnished with all manner of commodities ... for the necessary [sustenance] and use of the people." Markets and fairs were so beneficial that it was essential "to encourage men there unto."

Blackstone's and Coke's statements suggest an intuitive understanding of economic values, many of which were to be considered by antebellum judges deciding whether the market overt doctrine would be received in America. Their calculus reflects risks connected with the theft and the good faith purchase of stolen goods and the possibility that these costs might be reduced by both owners and purchasers through the adoption of protective measures. Their statements also recognize how a decision rule governing disputes between owners and good faith purchasers might affect criminal and legitimate commercial activity. All these considerations provide the ingredients for an economic rationale for or against good faith purchaser protection. Gains from trade must be balanced against the costs of increased criminal activity. The relative capacities of owners and good faith purchasers to reduce the risk that stolen goods might pass from the former group into the hands of the latter must also be considered.

Hosack v. Weaver, involved a lost or stolen horse discovered by the owner in the possession of a good faith purchaser. The horse was purchased in the Philadelphia public horse market after it had been shown for two or three market days. In charging the jury, the court distinguished Philadelphia markets from those in England as lacking any "ancient law or custom" protecting good faith purchasers. The charge also contained a justification for this lack of protection:

> We think these resolutions founded in honesty, and the soundest and best policy.... "They tend to the advancement of justice, to make men prosecute felons, and they will discourage persons from buying stolen goods, though in market overt; for under that pretence, men buy goods

there for a small value of persons whom they have reason to suspect,
which practise these resolutions will abate.''

This language may illustrate the court's awareness that insulating
good faith purchasers from owners' claims could reduce the costs of
engaging in thievery. An owner would be less inclined to try to recover
his stolen goods, and track down the thief in the process, if he knew that
his efforts would be wasted in the event that the goods were found in the
hands of a good faith purchaser. Further, the court seems to have
recognized that protecting good faith purchasers might enable purchasers who buy stolen goods under suspicious but colorably legitimate
circumstances to cut off owners' claims. This could decrease the risk of
this sort of purchase and, thereby, increase the demand for stolen goods.

Voidable Titles

Hosack [was] decided during the earliest stages of post-independence
economic growth. The unyielding owners' entitlement which [it] and
other market overt cases announced had the virtue of certainty. It may
also have imposed costs on wrongdoers, reduced demand for illegitimate
goods, and provided an incentive for production. But the entitlement
excused even the most careless owner and required good faith purchasers to determine in all cases whether goods had entered commerce
through the efforts of a wrongdoer. A purchaser could not meet this
burden without obtaining information concerning his seller's title or
taking other protective steps. The cost of these measures would often
exceed the purchaser's valuation of the risk of acquiring wrongfully
taken goods with the result that the risk which the purchaser was
compelled to assume was unavoidable in the economic sense.

The voidable title doctrine enabled courts to protect some good faith
purchasers without dishonoring the idea of an unqualified owners'
entitlement. The good faith purchaser would prevail if the court decided
that the defrauded owner had *intended* to transfer title to the wrongdoer. The owner could void this ill-gotten title and recover his goods so
long as they remained with the wrongdoer or were transferred to non-
good faith purchasers. However, the voidable title would become enforceable against the owner if the goods were acquired by a good faith
purchaser. If the court decided that the owner had intended to transfer
mere possession only and not title to the wrongdoer, then subsequent
transferees could only obtain a void title which could not be converted to
a good title under any circumstances.

Somes v. Brewer, decided by the Supreme Judicial Court of Massa-
chusetts in 1824, was the first case to consider the rights of a defrauded
seller and good faith purchaser under the voidable title doctrine in that
state. It dealt with realty, but Chief Justice Parker, the opinion's author,
stated that the decision would have been the same for personalty. The
plaintiff sought to recover two parcels of land in Boston that he had been
induced to sell through fraud and undue influence and without receiving

any consideration. The purchaser, appropriately named Skinner, had been the plaintiff's guardian until the plaintiff reached majority. Skinner obtained title to the parcels which he subsequently resold to a good faith purchaser. The opinion ... seems to incorporate and express an economic concept of negligence that requires risk to be placed on the more efficient risk preventer.

> Now it is said, that it is contrary to a fundamental principle of property, that the owner shall be devested of it without his consent. The answer is, that in this case he has consented; and though this consent was unfairly obtained, so that he may vacate the contract against the party who procured it, yet the policy of law and the security of innocent purchasers, who confide in the lawful evidence of property in the party of whom they purchase, and particularly in his having actual possession, accompanied with the legal proofs of property under the seal of the former owner, require that titles thus obtained should not be disturbed. Nor is it inequitable, or incongruous with the rules of law applied to other cases of misfortune in relation to property. It is a general and just rule, that when a loss has happened which must fall on one of two innocent persons, it shall be borne by him who is the occasion of the loss, even without any positive fault committed by him, but more especially if there has been any carelessness on his part which caused or contributed to the misfortune. A man can scarcely be cheated out of his property, especially of real estate, in such manner as to give an innocent purchaser a right to hold according to the principles which have been mentioned, without a degree of negligence on his part which should remove all ground of complaint.

Under this approach, the plaintiff was clearly negligent and the defendant clearly not contributorily negligent. Justice Parker noted that a more prudent owner could have reduced this risk through a variety of relatively low cost means such as seeking the advice of friends or counsel before executing the deeds, refusing to acknowledge the deeds even after they had been signed, or by recording a notice of the defect in Skinner's title. He also reasoned that the plaintiff had created such an appearance of ownership in Skinner that a good faith purchaser would reasonably believe that only routine self-protective measures such as examining the deeds and the public record would be required. These measures would not have revealed the fraudulent nature of the conveyance to Skinner. As a result, the risk could not be avoided at efficient cost by a good faith purchaser.

[W]hy did antebellum jurists afford any measure of negotiability to fraudulent goods? An answer may begin with *Somes'* demonstration that courts appreciated the limited capacity of good faith purchasers for efficiently investigating the quality of their sellers' titles to land and recognized that a rule favoring defrauded owners could inhibit realty transactions. Good faith purchasers' title investigative capacity would have been even more limited for goods sold in a dynamic and impersonal market in which they often would not have dealt face-to-face with the wrongdoer. Lack of title protection for good faith purchasers of goods might also exert a chilling effect on transactions in goods. A statement by the same judge who decided *Mowrey* suggests that these considerations did, indeed, underlie that case's formalistically crafted holding for the purchaser.

Feckless Agents

Antebellum courts protected owners' titles to stolen goods, but also protected good faith purchasers of goods taken through nonfelonious fraud. There is evidence that an intuitive concern for efficiency underlay these developments. There is also evidence that courts employed an extension of this calculus of costs and benefits in cases involving owners whose misplaced confidence in agents resulted in the acquisition of entrusted goods by good faith purchasers.

Nineteenth century American merchants necessarily relied on the services of ship's captains, commission agents, salesmen and others in order to engage in a world-wide commerce. The successful selection and management of these persons may have been the most important prerequisite to commercial success. Yet many of the factors which made the use of agents increasingly necessary, such as growth in the range and complexity of commercial enterprise, also caused the policing of agent behavior to be extremely costly with the result that merchants were forced to place a high degree of trust in their employees.

[T]he opinion of Gulian Verplanck in *Saltus v. Everett*, which became a leading case on the issue, reconciled a conflict between an owner who had selected a feckless agent and a good faith purchaser through the application of a cost-benefit calculus that reflected agency costs such as monitoring and considered the efficiencies obtainable through team production. Gulian Verplanck ... understood what twentieth century economics would come to teach: the risk of agent misbehavior can be reduced through means such as investigating an agent's honesty or monitoring his conduct, but also that at some point the cost of these means would exceed the value of the risk. Apparent authority and estoppel by indicia of ownership were tools to be employed in placing this risk on owners when their inefficient investigation or monitoring failed to reduce optimally the risk of feckless behavior that could result in a good faith purchase or when they intentionally accepted the risk. Voluntary acceptance would indicate that the owner considered the increased risk justified because of the benefits that would flow from the use of an agent clothed with indicia of ownership or authority to sell.

The good faith purchase of goods originating with feckless agents would often be unavoidable. The general placement of this risk on purchasers was justified under Verplanck's calculus because owners increased the output of their assets through the use of agents in team production. Placing the unavoidable risk of agent misconduct on owners would increase the costs of and thereby reduce the levels of owner production. . . .

[I]s it not a bit absurd to believe that judges deciding cases just a few years after the publication of the *Wealth of Nations* in 1776 would be concerned with economic efficiency? Their opinions suggest it is not. Antebellum judges, at least in the three sets of cases considered in this paper, did respond to the economic values they perceived by seeking to integrate them into the fabric of decision rules. Like the consumers and firms of microeconomic theory, they could do this without formal training in economic concepts. It would have been surprising to learn that judges were unconcerned with economic values in an era of judicial instrumentalism in which economic growth was a socially desirable policy.

NOTES

1. Good faith purchase and entrusting: The context and the issues.* The "problem" of third party rights in sales cases is easily framed: The original owner of goods delivers them to a debtor under a sales contract, a lease or a bailment. The debtor then wrongfully sells the goods to a third party, or permits a third party to encumber them. The debtor, however, does not pay the original owner for the goods. Since the debtor is judgment-proof, the original owner asserts rights to the goods in opposition to the claims of the third party. This question concerns the source of the property rights asserted by original owners and third parties. Third parties who deal with the debtor may obtain property rights in several ways. They may have purchased and taken delivery of the goods, taken security interests, or obtained judicial liens. The legal task is to rank the property rights that original owners and third parties have in the goods of an insolvent debtor. One approach is to ask whether efficiency analysis is helpful.

Assume that a seller sells goods to a debtor and takes a check as payment. The debtor resells the goods to a buyer. The check is subsequently dishonored. If the seller cannot recover the goods from the buyer in this case, she has an incentive to investigate potential debtors carefully, monitor debtors after delivery or insure against the risk of debtor misbehavior by raising prices. Alternatively, if the risk were assigned to the good faith purchaser, the purchaser could carefully investigate his potential seller (the debtor) and the seller's rights to the goods. To decide which risk allocation is efficient in this situation, contrast a simple and a more context-dependent rule: (1) either the sellers or buyers always bear the risk of debtor misbehavior, and (2) the risk is borne by the party who can avoid it or insure against it more cheaply. The second rule-which imposes the risk of debtor misconduct on buyers when they are able to reduce the risk more cheaply—is more efficient than a rule that always imposes this risk on buyers (or sellers), provided that the pertinent information is available to the court. A case-by-case determination is expensive, however, and may not yield the best

---

* This note draws on Alan Schwartz & Robert E. Scott, Commercial Transactions: Principles and Policies (1991).

incentives if the outcome is not predictable. Thus, an intermediate approach may be preferable. Since this task of identification is expensive, the wisest course may be to have a few general rules for allocating risks that impose risks on classes of parties—sellers or buyers—in cases when the parties in the class are likely to be able to bear the risk at least cost.

Does this analysis help you justify the good faith purchaser rules that are found in § 2–403? What criteria are relevant to answering the question as to which party has the comparative advantage in reducing the risk of debtor misbehavior? Do the Code rules generally reach efficient outcomes? Are you persuaded by Weinberg's argument that nineteenth century courts used these considerations in formulating the basic doctrines governing good faith purchase?

2.   Was Gilmore's "confession" necessary? Grant Gilmore became skeptical about the protections accorded good faith purchasers and buyers from a merchant to whom goods had been entrusted. His argument rests on the claim that the conditions that obtained in the 19th century—namely the practice of selling goods through factors, some of whom were dishonest— justified the good faith purchaser rules and those selling conditions no longer are prevalent. But does that mean that the protections are not justifiable? Certainly, if the economic considerations are important, wouldn't it be necessary to ask whether the more modern means of distribution of goods— through retailers, franchisees etc.—implied that buyers were now better able than sellers to prevent the fraud from occurring? Why might that be so?

3.   The "theft rule." One of the puzzles in justifying the good faith purchaser rules is to explain why a seller who obtains the goods from the original owner by theft obtains only a "void" title and thus cannot pass any property rights to a good faith purchaser. After all, what difference does it make in terms of the buyer's capacity to reduce this risk whether the original owner transfers possession of his goods by fraud or whether they are stolen from him? Moreover, even if a buyer *sometimes* has the comparative advantage in reducing the risk of wrongdoing in the case of theft, does it follow that buyers would *always* have such an advantage? This seems unlikely, yet the "theft rule" places the risk of stolen goods entirely on the buyer in all cases. Can you explain this? Weinberg suggests that the theft rule can be justified on the grounds that it reduces the incentives of wrongdoers to steal goods from original owners. Do you find this argument plausible? An alternative analysis is to focus on which rule in the case of theft would create incentives for any of the affected parties to reduce the risk of theft. Assume, for example, that owners of stolen goods assign a negligible value to the potential benefits of returned goods because the probability of recovery is so low *and* the value of recovered goods is also low because the goods are used and the thief may have abused them. On the other hand, assume that purchasers value those goods more than owners do, because a purchaser who surrenders stolen goods will have to replace them with new items. Given those assumptions, the theft rule can be justified on prevention grounds—purchasers will be more responsive than owners to the legal rule allocating property rights in stolen goods. If purchasers must yield the goods they will, given these assumptions, take greater precautions than owners to reduce the risk of surrender. This argument rests on several strong assumptions, however. Do you find them plausible?

3.7   Choice of Law

Contractual Choice of Law and the Prudential Foundations of Appellate Review*
DAVID FRISCH

The principle of "freedom of contract," popular among contract theorists in the nineteenth and early twentieth centuries, rests on the belief that respect for personal autonomy is a necessary complement to both the liberal political state and a free-market economy. More precisely, if the government enforces private agreements voluntarily entered into by parties seeking to order their business and personal affairs, then individual liberty is preserved, equality of opportunity is ensured, and the maximization of societal wealth can be achieved. Notwithstanding its waning acceptance, freedom of contract has been offered as an appropriate foundational approach to legislation as diverse as the Uniform Computer Information Transactions Act ("U.C.I.T.A."), the National Labor Relations Act of 1935, and state limited liability acts.

Even more generally, freedom of contract means that parties should be free to choose, as a strategic matter, the legal rules they consider to be most beneficial given their interests. The most familiar example of this strategy is a contract term that specifies that the parties' bargain is to be governed by the positive law of a given jurisdiction. However, the fact that a policy in favor of enforcing contractual choice-of-law clauses might have significant instrumental value for realizing the right to personal autonomy and other core elements of liberalism does not necessarily mean that courts will recognize and protect the parties' choice without restrictions. In fact, their unwillingness to do so has had a long history. Indeed, early-twentieth-century commentators attacked the very concept of party autonomy in choice of law as unacceptable "private legislation." After all, they wondered, how could private individuals "displace the law of the place where their acts are done by exercise of any choice of their own?" This recognition of territorial sovereignty accounts for the absence of any provisions in the Restatement (First) of Conflict of Laws, addressing the freedom of contracting parties to choose the law that will govern their relationship.

In this light, the decision by the drafters of the U.C.C. to include a general choice-of-law provision that provides for limited party autonomy can be seen as a major innovation in the law. Nevertheless, it was entirely consistent with the drafters' own embrace of freedom of contract as a fundamental Code principle. Section 1–105 provides, subject to eight

* 56 VAND. L. REV. 1 (2003).

exceptions, that "when a transaction bears a reasonable relation to this state and also to another state or nation the parties may agree that the law either of this state or of such other state or nation shall govern their rights and duties." [...]

Once released from the constraints of an outdated conception of party autonomy, the difficult issue for theorists became the appropriate scope of the parties' power to choose the applicable law. In this regard, the drafters of the Restatement (Second) of Conflict of Laws ("the Restatement"), conceptualized the matter quite differently than had the drafters of the U.C.C. Where the latter adopted and proceeded from a unitary view under which the law chosen by the parties is uniformly applicable to all the terms of the contract and aspects of the relationship, the A.L.I. identified two separate categories of contractual provisions. These consist of: (1) those addressing issues, such as sufficiency of performance and excuse, that are and always have been within the contractual capacity of the parties to determine; and (2) those addressing issues, such as capacity to contract and the statute of frauds, which are governed by immutable state law and are therefore of such a character that the parties could not have resolved them by explicit provision in their agreement. The A.L.I. believed that choice-of-law clauses would fare better and prove less troublesome if guided by recognition of this duality, which is not only more faithful to our conflicts history but also squarely confronts the interests at stake when a single contract has a connection to two or more states. The drafters of the Restatement therefore thought it critical to reject what they considered to be the harmful illusion that all contractual issues are similar.

As to the first category of issues, those traditionally resolved by contractual terms, the Restatement provides that the state law chosen by the parties will always be applied. In such a situation, no countervailing policy is implicated, because the parties could have accomplished the same thing by drafting a clause mimicking the attributes of the chosen law. By contrast, when the issue concerns a matter not amenable to regulation by contract, the Restatement significantly curtails the parties' autonomy. In such cases, the parties' choice will not be effective if:

> (a) the chosen state has no substantial relationship to the parties or the transaction and there is no other reasonable basis for the parties' choice, or

> (b) application of the law of the chosen state would be contrary to a fundamental policy of a state which has a materially greater interest than the chosen state in the determination of the particular issue and which ... would be the state of the applicable law in the absence of an effective choice of law by the parties.

Underlying this less generous grant of party autonomy is the drafters' reluctance to diminish the benefits that certain state policies were meant to ensure, as well as their desire to make certain that the parties had a legitimate reason for their choice of law. In effect, by rejecting the conceptual framework of the Code, the drafters of the Restatement have created a test that is both broader and narrower than the Code formulation. As one commentator has noted:

> It [is] broader in two ways. First, the parties' choice of law [is] in no way limited if the issue [is] one that the parties could have resolved in their contract. Second, although there [is] a requirement that the choice be reasonable, there [is] no requirement that the relationship between the transaction and the chosen law be reasonable.... The Restatement test [is] narrower, however, in that it provide[s] for a limitation on even a reasonable choice of law if there [is] a conflict with a fundamental policy of a state with a materially greater interest in the issue.

Several decades have passed since the Code and the Restatement shifted toward a more favorable view of party autonomy, and the future of choice-of-law clauses has once again become the center of a major policy debate. This change has occurred in part because codification has increasingly become the preferred method of shaping the development of commercial law. Aside from the process of periodic adjustments in existing U.C.C. articles to reflect fundamental changes in society, on several occasions supplementary articles have been enacted as formal amendments to the Code. In addition to these efforts to keep the Code responsive to contemporary needs, legislatures have also enacted auxiliary statutes covering limited subjects that are not consolidated into the Code. These drafting projects have stimulated the debate over contractual choice by creating an opportunity for those who have been critical of restraints on party autonomy to voice their displeasure and lobby for change, and for others who see party autonomy as a problem rather than a solution to advocate for greater statutory protections for those upon whom choice-of-law clauses are likely to be imposed (i.e., consumers and small businesses). At no time has the debate been more heated than it was during the drafting of U.C.I.T.A.

From the very beginning, the drafts of U.C.I.T.A. (and its forerunner, proposed U.C.C. Article 2B) contained a powerful endorsement of party autonomy that exceeded the contents of section 1–105 of the Code and the Restatement. Perhaps the most fundamental point is that the new framework created by the drafters of the U.C.C. and the Restatement called into question the need for any restrictions at all on the enforcement of choice-of-law clauses in commercial transactions. The U.C.I.T.A. drafting committee saw complete party autonomy as a necessary guarantor of the successful development of electronic commerce. Because the Internet recognizes no geographic borders, the committee concluded that the approach embodied in section 1–105 and the Restatement had to be rejected if electronic commerce was to flourish. In other words, the drafters of U.C.I.T.A. sought to leave nothing to judicial decision on the theory that, unless the parties selecting a jurisdiction to provide the governing law could be certain that their choice would be given effect, the unfortunate result would be that "even the smallest business would be subject to the law of all fifty States and all countries in the world."

It was inevitable that this hyperbolic claim would ultimately draw into question the drafters' notion that U.C.I.T.A. transactions were somehow different from ordinary commercial transactions and that the environment of cyberspace required special rules to govern the enforcement of choice-of-law clauses. Indeed, many argued that U.C.I.T.A. was so flawed in its structure and in many of its individual provisions that the entire project should be scrapped. The A.L.I. itself eventually withdrew from the project in the aftermath of this controversy. Nevertheless, U.C.I.T.A. was eventually approved by N.C.C.U.S.L. and sent to the states for adoption as a statute external to the Code. The provision on choice of law states:

> The parties in their agreement may choose the applicable law. However, the choice is not enforceable in a consumer contract to the extent it would vary a rule that may not be varied by agreement under the law of the jurisdiction whose law would apply . . . in the absence of the agreement.

Thus, at least in commercial cases governed by U.C.I.T.A., no relationship between the state law chosen and the geographic location of the transaction is at all necessary.

Of equal significance to the party autonomy debate are the recent revisions to U.C.C. Article 1. Here, too, significant changes to traditional choice-of-law doctrine outside the context of conventional consumer transactions are in the offing. Deference will be accorded to the parties' agreement when domestic law is selected, except to the extent that their choice is contrary to a fundamental policy of the jurisdiction whose law would otherwise govern in the absence of a contractual designation. Under this approach, the key issue ceases to be the existence of a "reasonable relation" (as in former Article 1) and becomes whether a conflicting policy is "fundamental" or something less. This distinction is not always sharp, and it will call for an exercise of judgment. In the vast majority of cases, however, it should be easily administered, and the parties' choice given effect.

A general conclusion emerges from the discussion and developments to date: The new choice-of-law framework resulting from these reform efforts will provide parties with an expanded menu of legal regimes from which to choose when selecting the law that will govern their contract. That flexibility will in turn lead to more frequent use of contractual choice-of-law clauses. Indeed, some have suggested that omitting such a clause may soon be considered malpractice by the commercial lawyer.

Intrastate Choice of Applicable Law in the UCC*
FRED H. MILLER

Except as explicitly provided otherwise in the Uniform Commercial Code, where a transaction bears a relationship to more than one jurisdiction, if there is an appropriate relationship to the jurisdiction where the issue is raised, the law of that jurisdiction may be applied. The parties may agree, however, that the law of any jurisdiction having a reasonable relationship to the transaction may govern their rights and duties. These rules determine the applicable law in a transaction involving more than one jurisdiction, either interstate or international, subject to possible conflicting and controlling foreign choice of law principles or any applicable international convention or treaty. The question presented here, however, is: what is the applicable law for a UCC transaction that takes place entirely in one jurisdiction that has enacted the UCC?

The facile answer seems to be, the appropriate Article of the UCC as enacted in that jurisdiction. Absent a contrary agreement, this answer is correct. This result is roughly equivalent to the analysis, absent agreement, under section 1–105(1) for transactions that do not take place entirely within one jurisdiction. But can an agreement change the applicable law within one jurisdiction similar to the way it may change the applicable law between jurisdictions pursuant to section 1–105(1)? It is submitted that generally the answer is yes. This article explores the details of that proposition.

Opt out

UCC sections 1–102(3) and (4) state that, even without the signal "unless otherwise agreed," the effect of a UCC provision may generally be varied by agreement, with certain limitations. The goal is flexibility. The parties to a transaction can design their own rules to fit their own particular situation, and need not be confined to rules premised on a particular norm that does not consider unforeseen or new circumstances and practices. Thus, by agreement, the parties can change the effect of the applicable, but not mandatory, statutory rules of law. Examples of these changes are limitless, but two illustrations will make the point. First, the parties may disclaim certain implied warranties if the goods are sold in circumstances where the warranties are not consistent with the bargain. Second, in modern leasing practice, the parties to a lease of goods often supply their own formula for damages in the event of default, rather than rely on the statutory remedy structure. When the parties do either of the above, or take similar action, they are essentially opting out of the so-called default rules of the UCC.

If the parties frequently opt out with respect to a particular transaction they have, in essence, written a particularized Article 2, Article 2A,

* 54 SMU L. Rev. 525 (2001).

or other UCC article for their use. Thus it seems logical to conclude that the parties could do this in a single provision, rather than by a step-by-step procedure. The agreement could provide that "the parties agree that the contract law of the State of ___, as found in its statutes and decisions, shall govern their rights and duties in this transaction, rather than the provisions of Uniform Commercial Code Article as enacted in the State of ___." This represents a complete opt out.

The parties, however, would seldom want to fully opt out. The UCC was created because the general common law of contracts and property was not fully suited to govern the transactions now covered by the UCC. For example, a major contribution of Article 2 on sales was to make the common law contract formation rules, like "mirror image" and the "last shot rule" in the "battle of the forms," more realistic for commercial transactions. To abandon the specifically tailored rules of the UCC for more general, and often outdated, rules is very different from adjusting some of those specifically tailored UCC rules to fit a particular transaction. In some circumstances, however, there may be sense in opting out. For example, there has been much discussion regarding negotiability since the UCC allows an assignee of a contract to take the assignment free of defenses to payment and claims to the instrument from parties the assignee has not dealt with. Many feel that this doctrine no longer serves a purpose, at least in a consumer context. Negotiability, however, comes within the rules of UCC Article 3. If the words "payable to the order of" are left out or struck out of a promissory note, Article 3 no longer applies and the normal rule that an assignee of the contract stands in the assignor's shoes applies. Thus, a person who wishes to preserve the ability to raise defenses against payment, even when the instrument is in the hands of an assignee who acquired it for value, in good faith, and without notice, may want to opt out of UCC Article 3 and take steps to avoid a similar outcome.

Nonetheless, this opt out analysis has generated some concern since it explicitly articulates the right to opt out found in UCC Article 1. Some fear that such an express permission could lead to malpractice liability if the opt out was not used and an unfortunate consequence occurred, even if it was unreasonable for the attorney to have researched the entirety of the law to determine if a more suitable rule existed. This argument is unpersuasive. Many believe another scenario, where opt out is used to reach a perceived bad result, poses an even greater danger. For example, in 1999, the National Conference of Commissioners on Uniform State Laws promulgated the Uniform Computer Information Transactions Act (UCITA). Section 104 contains the following explicit opt-out and opt-in provisions:

> The parties may agree that this Act, including contract-formation rules, governs the transaction, in whole or part, or that other law governs the transaction and this Act does not apply, if a material part of the subject matter to which the agreement

applies is computer information or informational rights in it that are within the scope of this Act, or is subject matter within this Act under Section 103(b), or is subject matter excluded by Section 103(d)(1) or (2).

This provision was designed to deal with the "mixed transactions" often encountered in this area of business. For example, a transaction might involve both computer software and hardware and, depending on the predominant interest of the transaction, the parties might desire to have the law applicable to the interest also govern the whole transaction. Some argue that, because UCITA's licensee protections are too limited, the ability for a seller/licensor to opt in to UCITA for the whole transaction, and thus opt out of the otherwise applicable Article 2 law for the hardware, is improper because it puts the buyer/licensee, and perhaps others, at greater risk. An explicit opt-out provision in the UCC would control if UCITA were not enacted, and would reinforce the UCITA provision if both statutes were enacted.

One safeguard against this situation is to limit a general opt out to a mixed transaction, which is the most justifiable case for opt out. Another possible safeguard is to make explicit what is implicit—that one cannot opt out of the mandatory UCC provisions that would govern in the absence of opt out.

Since the UCITA provision is a good example of how to employ safeguards, it arguably represents a better policy approach than current proposed UCC section 1–302. UCITA section 104(2) alters what otherwise would be the result under the freedom-of-contract rule; in short, an opt out agreement under UCITA is treated differently than an agreement to vary a provision of UCITA. This makes sense because the law that is opted into has its own protections, and a minimalist approach reduces chances of conflict and other confusion. An example of this complexity, albeit one that would exist under even the minimalist approach, is how an opt out of UCITA would nonetheless leave the obligations of honesty in fact and good faith in performance or enforcement in every contract that would be a mass-market transaction under UCITA. For example, if the applicable law after opt out were general contract law, in Oklahoma a statute would set the standard of good faith as essentially one of honesty. Under Oklahoma law, the UCITA definition would control, but this may not be as clear under the law of other jurisdictions. This clarity in Oklahoma puts great pressure on determining what a mass-market transaction is and the duties within the transaction.

Opt in

As the previous discussion shows, opt out and opt in are essentially two sides of the same coin. Nonetheless, there is some benefit in focusing on each individually. To make that point, opt in, in contrast to opt out, can be desirable in many contexts, and there already are several illustrations of this in the present UCC. For example, section 8–103(c) states that an interest in a partnership or limited liability company is not a security, and thus is not governed by Article 8, unless it is an investment company security or is dealt in or traded on securities exchanges or in securities markets, but if its terms expressly provide that it is a security and elect to be governed by Article 8, then that election is effective. The Official Comment to section 2A–102 provides that the parties to a transaction creating a lease of personal property other than goods, or a bailment of personal property, may provide by agreement that Article 2A applies. Likewise, Official Comment 2 to section 3–104 provides that the immediate parties to an order or promise that is not an instrument may provide by agreement that one or more of the provisions of Article 3 determine their rights and obligations under the writing. Such guidance might be useful in New York, which has not yet enacted revised UCC Articles 3 and 4. In New York, the law may still be that a promissory note with a variable interest rate is not a negotiable instrument, and thus might be governed by the common law, even though that law was superseded as inappropriate in many respects by specialized negotiable instruments law. Finally, opt in may be attractive for mixed transactions as well as transactions searching for more cogent law. For example, a seller who will install the product might wish Article 2 to cover both the sale and service aspects, presumably with an appropriate disclaimer of warranty at least as to the quality of the service.

Opt in, almost by definition, has a greater problem than opt out in determining to what extent it is legally permitted since the otherwise governing law is often vague on this issue. What is a mandatory, as opposed to default, rule is not clear. To illustrate, Oklahoma has many statutes on guarantees and suretyship, which unfortunately reflect a much earlier era in the law. A person drafting a guaranty for a modern transaction may desire to have it governed by some of the more up-to-date discharge rules and other UCC provisions. It is equally possible, in a contract not governed by Article 2A, that the seller might want to opt out of the stricter Oklahoma statutes on liquidated damages and opt into the more modern and clearer provision of Article 2A. Yet it is unclear whether the Oklahoma statutes in title 15 are mandatory, or whether, like the provisions of the UCC generally, their effect can be varied by agreement. Even an explicit opt-in provision, like UCITA section 104(1) cannot solve this difficulty. Only the law being opted out of can solve this by clearly stating which of its provisions are mandatory. Even the UCC is often not that clear.

This problem may not be critical since most laws, at least in the private law/commercial law area, are not mandatory. Moreover, little downside is perceived in an attempt to opt in since, if the opt in is held to be valid, the goal was achieved. If the opt in is held to be invalid, while some mandatory provision might not have been complied with because it was believed the agreement rendered it inapplicable, the consequence would seldom be serious. A perceived possible serious consequence for non-compliance would signal that the provision was non-variable in the first place, and an attempt to vary its effect by agreement should not be made. In this context, little seems lost by the decision of the drafting committee to delete its once proposed section 1–103, except perhaps a small amount of certainty due to an explicit authorization.

Conclusion

The draft of proposed revised Article 1 seems to correctly address the question of whether the parties may change the applicable law in an intrastate transaction by agreement in the context of the UCC. It will leave opt out to the general freedom-of-contract rules and limitations found in the UCC. This decision protects what is necessary and, while it leaves some doubt about an ability to opt out in one simple provision, encourages the parties to selectively opt out provision by provision. This selection process forces the parties to concentrate on the consequences of any such agreement, something that may not occur, or not occur as well, in a single, general opt-out provision. There are fewer, less compelling, reasons for general opt out. The safeguards that would exist if a UCITA-type approach were drafted can be important, but are largely unnecessary and difficult to draft due to the uncertainty regarding which provisions are considered mandatory, let alone "fundamentally mandatory" for the purpose of a minimalist approach.

On the other hand, opt in, where there are often reasonable or compelling reasons to do so, could be encouraged by an express provision, such as that found in the UCITA. Opt in is still possible, however, in the absence of such a provision. This could make the difference where there is doubt. Such an opt-in provision, however, would not be without difficulty or risk. It would seem a limitation on its use in mixed transactions, as in UCITA, could be unwise in many instances, but a lack of limitations could lead to instances of abuse.

Moreover, while the risk of unintended consequences exists in both opting in and opting out, any decision to opt out is more likely to be focused and occur after the attorney has reviewed the applicable laws and has concluded that the chosen law is better. In opt in, it is much more likely to be a wholesale choice, even though prompted by a reaction to one or more specific unfavorable provisions in the other law, and is more likely to occur without adequate consideration of its possible consequences. This problem flags the need for an attorney, who is familiar with the law to be abandoned, to carefully consider the matter, but that will be a very difficult task.

NOTES

1. Forum shopping in other contractual relationships. Scholars in corporate and bankruptcy law have identified forum shopping incentives and behavior, and assessed whether the competition among forums for incorporation or for bankruptcy cases leads to a race to the top or a race to the bottom, in terms of the efficiency of law-making. Particularly in the case of corporate charters, a robust literature has focused on the substantive benefits inherent in jurisdictional diversity—stimulating a "race to the top" as states compete among themselves to capture the economic rents from incorporation. See e.g., Roberta Romano, *Law as a Product; Some Pieces of the Incorporation Puzzle,* 1 J. Law, Econ. & Org. 224 (1985); William J. Carney, *The Production of Corporate Law,* 71 S. Cal. L. Rev. 715 (1998); Roberta Romano, *The Genius of American Corporate Law* (1993); Ronald J. Daniels, *Should Provinces Compete?: The Case for a Competitive Corporate Law Market,* 36 McGill L. J. 130 (1993). Do the same considerations apply to competition for "good" sales law? Some jurisdictions have explicitly marketed their commercial law as a superior product and eliminated or reduced jurisdictional barriers that would otherwise preclude commercial parties from taking advantage of their law. The state of New York, for instance, has enacted a statute permitting parties in a case involving more than $250,000 to choose New York law to govern their transaction even if that transaction has no other contact with New York (See N.Y. General Obligation Laws § 5–1401 (2001)).

2. The political economy of choice of law. Recall the discussion in Chapter 2 of the political economy of the private legislative bodies that formulate the UCC. The interest group clash that undermined the attempted revision of Article 2 has played out as well in attempts to secure adoption of the revised Article 1 which was approved for adoption by the states in 2001. The issues center on the language of revised section 1–301. As Professor Frisch suggests, 1–301 is both broader and narrower than the existing choice of law provision, section 1–105, that it would replace. Software, computer, and banking interests have proposed non-uniform amendments to section 1–301 that would eliminate the restrictions on choice of law provisions in consumer transactions. Gail Hillebrand, an attorney for the Consumers Union, advises state legislators that:

> The National Conference of Commissioners on Uniform State Laws has approved a revision of Uniform Commercial Code Article 1. This revision will be offered for enactment in every state legislature. Article 1 is important to consumers because it sets the basic ground rules for all transactions governed by the UCC, including personal property secured transactions such as car loans, sales of goods, personal checks and promissory notes.

> Two subsections in the choice of law provision of the new revised Article 1 protect consumers. The bill should be opposed if these consumer subsections are removed. New subsection 1–301(c) would substantially broaden choice of law rules for most transactions covered by the UCC. However, subsections (e) and (f) provide special protections for consumers. Subsection (f) protects any party from the choice of law selected in the contract if that choice would be contrary to a fundamental policy of a state's or country's law which would govern in the absence of the agreement.

Subsection (e) renders a choice of law clause ineffective in a consumer transaction covered by UCC Article 1 unless the transaction bears a reasonable relation to the state or country designated. In addition, a choice of law clause may not deprive a consumer of protections under a non-waivable consumer protection law. Standing alone, new subsection 1–301(c) is a dramatic expansion of choice of law for contract Medicare Modernization Acters. Subsections (e) and (f) restrict the application of subsection (c) in consumer contracts. In some states, industry may attempt to pass a revised UCC Article 1 with the expanded authorization for choice of law in subsection (c), but without the protections in subsections (e) and (f). This is a matter of such significance that advocates for consumers should oppose the entirety of revised UCC Article 1 in any state where subsection 1–301(c) is offered without subsections 1–301(e) and (f).

It could be useful to try to add an unconscionability provision to the revised UCC Article 1 in some state legislatures. Adding such a provision to UCC Article 1 would have the effect of applying an unconscionability rule to UCC Article 9, governing transactions secured by personal property (such as car loans), and Articles 3 and 4, governing negotiable instruments.

At the same time, academic reformers have proposed postponing promulgation of the revised Article 1 because of the broad language in section 1–301(c) that makes choice of law clauses effective without regard to whether the transaction had a "reasonable relation" to the designated state or country as required by existing section 1–105. Thus, Professor Jay Westbrook moved to table revised Article 1 stating that

> As Bill Woodward points out in his motion, the conflicts provisions of the proposed Article 1, section 1–301, represent a massive and important break with existing law. He addresses the domestic side of that break and I discuss below the unfortunate and unwise consequences internationally. Furthermore, adoption of section 1–301 will leave the Institute supporting two conflicting rules in the UCC and the Restatement (2d) Conflict of Laws § 187(2), creating confusion and serious boundary problems. In addition, the American Bankers Association has indicated deep concern about the consumer protection provisions of section 301, which may suggest substantial opposition to its adoption with those provisions.

This interest group clash has played out in the state legislative process. To date, 34 states have adopted revised Article 1 and a number of those adoptions have resulted in non-uniform amendments to section 1–301.

3. Choice of law and the political economy of international sales law. The dramatic growth of international trade has generated pressure for a uniform international sales law. The assumption is that the lack of uniformity increases the costs of writing contracts for parties to international sales transactions. Parties have to bargain over the legal regime (and the default terms) that will govern their transaction. The response to these concerns has been United Nations Convention on Contracts for the International Sale of Goods (CISG), the primary treaty that governs the international exchange of goods by contract. If adoption is a measure of success, the CISG has become the most successful of efforts to create uniform international commercial law. As of this writing, the CISG has been adopted by 74 states. They include most of the major trading nations, although the United Kingdom and Japan are not parties. Clayton Gillette and Robert Scott have argued, however, that the political economy that produced the CISG will lead to wholesale opting out of its provisions and that competition among states for "good" sales law is a preferable alternative:

> In many respects the drafting process of the CISG exemplifies all of the problems with the creation of sales law default rules by quasi-private legislative bodies. These bodies suffer from the same deficits as ordinary legislative bodies but, in addition, lack many of the constraints on legislative behavior that mediate the product of ordinary legislatures. Where the products of this drafting process are rules governing commercial sales transactions, there is no reason to expect interest group competition to emerge and influence the process, either negatively or positively. Parties to commercial sales transactions are both buyers and sellers, and thus there is little risk that one group or class will be distributionally disadvantaged over another. But, by the same token, the absence of interest group pressure generates a legislative product that is shaped primarily by the motivations and incentives of the drafters themselves. In the case of international sales law, the incentives to maximize initial adoptions generate default rules that are formally uniform but whose substantive terms are vague and ambiguous.

> Commercial parties value clarity and predictability, which they can achieve in their contracts by carefully drafted combinations of bright line rules coupled with broader standards. The promulgation of many vague default terms is inconsistent with the need to balance standards with rules. Thus, commercial parties frequently will opt out of the CISG's vague terms. This, in turn, will undermine one of the principal goals of a uniform ISL—to reduce the legal knowledge costs associated with different rules governed by different legal regimes. In the case of the CISG, the lack of meaningful uniformity is exacerbated by the failure to create interpretive mechanisms that, over time, might have given substantive content to the vague default standards.

> The upshot is a treaty whose provisions are likely to become less and less useful as time goes on. Indeed, we predict that CISG ultimately will lose out in competition with alternative legal regimes. The most likely competitors are prominent domestic law systems that offer the kinds of substantive rules preferred by commercial parties. Should that prediction materialize, then CISG would simply remain as a costly impediment to the sort of harmonization that has occurred in the common law of contracts in the United States. In the United States, a natural experiment with

multiple common law regimes has shown that economic and cultural forces over time produce a remarkable degree of harmonization around substantively uniform rules of contract law. It is unlikely that this phenomenon is unique to the American experience. Powerful market forces push toward harmonization across diverse cultures and jurisdictions. These market forces and not the normative preferences of bureaucrats and academic reformers will determine the ultimate shape of international sales law.

Clayton P. Gillette & Robert E. Scott, *The Political Economy of International Sales Law,* 25 Int'l Rev. L. & Econ. 446 (2005).

4.   Can parties opt out of the Code's parol evidence and interpretation rules? Professor Miller suggests that parties can opt out of the Code and have their transaction governed by the contract law of the state that governs the transaction except "that one cannot opt out of the mandatory UCC provisions that would govern in the absence of opt out." This statement begs an important question, however. Just what provisions are mandatory and thus not subject to opt out? Consider the Code's rules governing interpretation which abolish the common law plain meaning rule and adopt a "soft" parol evidence rule. Imagine two commercial parties wished to write a contract with a merger clause in such a way that they could reliably stand exclusively on the writing should any dispute subsequently arise. In other words, they wish to adopt a plain meaning rule of interpretation and to exclude any contextual evidence to interpret the meaning of their writing. They might wish to do so as a precommitment against costly litigation. By limiting evidence to the writing alone they can resolve any dispute at the summary judgment stage. If, instead, the court adopts the Code's rules governing parol evidence and interpretation, then the parties must necessarily anticipate evidence of relevant oral understandings, usages of trade and the like which would require a costly, full blown trial. Would a choice of law clause be enforceable if it opted out of the UCC and into the more traditional interpretation rules of the common law of contract law that are followed by many states? Should such a clause be enforceable? Alan Schwartz and Robert Scott have considered those question and they conclude that the answer to the first question is "no" and the answer to the second question is "yes."

> Courts making common law adjudications commonly take a Willistonian approach, while the UCC strongly urges a contextualist interpretive style. Courts in general, however, treat interpretation rules as mandatory. Judges are reluctant to invoke the coercive machinery of the state to require a party to perform a contract (or to pay damages) unless the judge is satisfied that the contract actually directed what the party failed to do. It seemingly follows that courts, not parties, should choose the rules that determine how contracts are read. This view is understandable but misguided. The law in general permits persons and firms to make choices in litigation that may lead courts to act on less than full information. For example, persons and firms may waive the right to counsel, agree to stipulated findings of fact, and use summary arbitration procedures whose results courts are required to enforce. In sum, the

law generally sacrifices accuracy in adjudication to parties' self interested choices. Similarly, parties should be permitted to realize the cost savings from contract interpretations on minimal evidentiary bases even if, in any given case, the odds of an accurate interpretation would be higher with a broader base.

Alan Schwartz & Robert E. Scott, *Contract Theory and the Limits of Contract Law,* 113 Yale L. J. 541 (2003).

5. UCITA. The story of the Uniform Computer Information Transactions Act (UCITA) reflects the interest group politics that have plagued recent efforts to revise the UCC. In 1991, acting upon the report and recommendation of a study committee, the ALI and NCCUSL appointed a drafting committee to begin work on a comprehensive revision of Article 2, that, among other things, would bring within the scope of Article 2 the provisions on lease transactions that were then embodied in Article 2A, and would also include provisions to address the unique characteristics of software licensing transactions. The Article 2 Drafting Committee worked for several years on this "hub and spoke" scheme for incorporating all relevant transactions within the Article 2 umbrella. But the effort was abandoned when key insiders concluded that the differences between the products, their markets and practices made the draft unworkable. The ALI and NCCUSL then decided to return leases to its own statute (Article 2A) and also to draft a separate UCC Article 2B for computer information contracts. Separate drafting committees were thus appointed for each of Article 2, Article 2A and Article 2B and the drafting work proceeded on parallel, but separate, tracks.

The first public indication that the private legislative coalition that had supported the UCC project for fifty years was beginning to unravel surfaced in 1999 when proposed Article 2B was brought forward by the drafting committee for final approval by the ALI and NCCUSL. The ALI declined to approve Article 2B on the ground that the drafting process, dominated by the software and information industry, had produced a "seller-friendly" statute. NCCUSL, on the other hand, decided to go forward with the project on its own, reissuing the statute as the Uniform Computer Information Transactions Act (UCITA). The controversy over UCITA centered on the provisions of the statute dealing with contract formation in standardized retail transactions. UCITA endorses current market practices in which consumers signify advance acceptance of subsequently disclosed terms. The subsequently disclosed terms typically have provisions by which sellers or licensors seek to limit their warranty liability and/or limit the buyer/licensee's remedies for "bugs" or defects in software or other "smart" goods. Thus, at bottom, the issue has to do with the extension of Article 2 warranty liability to software and computer information providers and the mechanisms by which that liability can be shifted (in whole or in part). See Jean Braucher, *Uniform Computer Information Transactions Act (UCITA): Objections from the Consumer Perspective,* 5 No. 6 GLCY Law 2 (2000); James C. McKay. Jr., *UCITA and the Consumer: A Response to Professor Braucher,* 5 No. 8 GLCY Law 9 (2000); Michael L. Rustad, *Making UCITA More Consumer-Friendly,* 18 J. Marshall J. Computer & Info. L. 547 (1999). UCITA has been adopted in Virginia and Maryland, but has encountered stiff opposition from consumer interests in other jurisdictions.

Chapter 4

Payment Systems

4.1 Introduction

Barter is rare because it is unlikely that an exchange of goods or services between any two given parties can optimally satisfy their respective needs. Suppose an economy has three individuals (Alan, Betty and Carl) and three goods (a toaster, a hair dryer and a skateboard). Alan owns the toaster but would prefer the hair dryer. Betty has the hair dryer but would prefer the skateboard. Carl owns the skateboard but would prefer the toaster. If only bilateral exchanges occur, the parties cannot achieve the optimal allocation of the goods without a medium of exchange. It is not surprising, therefore, that at least one party in almost all commercial transactions owes a monetary obligation (convention labels that party the buyer). In some cases, the buyer promises to pay at or before the time of the seller's performance. We address the form and legal attributes of the buyer's contemporaneous payment in this chapter. In other cases, the seller agrees to deliver on credit and the buyer's payment is due at a later date. Chapter 5 concerns the form and legal attributes of the credit instruments that evidence the buyer's obligation and particularly the role of sureties and guarantors.

Payment obligations may be satisfied by delivery of government-issued currency. However, buyers often pay in forms other than currency: for example, checks, drafts, commercial letters of credit, credit cards, debit cards or other types of electronic transfer. Articles 3 and 4 of the Uniform Commercial Code govern payments by drafts. A draft is a three party instrument. It represents an order by one person (the drawer) directed to a second party (the drawee) demanding that he pay a third

179

party (the payee). Unless the drawee indicates otherwise on the draft (for example, by signing it to indicate its acceptance), she assumes no payment obligation to the payee under the draft. § 3–409. Most familiar, of course, is the check, a draft payable on demand and drawn on a bank or similar deposit-taking financial institution. § 3–104(f).

The relationship between the drawer and the drawee in these cases is one of contract and Articles 3 and 4 contain several default provisions. The bank/drawee charges the drawer's deposit account the amount the bank pays on the check, with some exceptions noted below. § 4–401. If the check is properly payable and if the drawer has sufficient funds in its account to cover it, then the bank is liable for wrongful dishonor if it refuses to pay. § 4–402. Typically, a check will be deposited for collection by a payee in her own bank (the depository bank). Under standard check collection procedures, the depository bank forwards the check through banking channels to the drawee bank where it is presented for payment. The payee bank has a short period of time within which to decide whether or not to honor the check. Once it does (or the time passes) then the check is finally paid and the drawee bank can charge the customer/drawer's account for the amount of the check. As we will see in the excerpts below, however, this traditional collection process has been significantly affected by modern means of electronic transmission of checks.

Commercial letters of credit are often the form of payment in sales across long distances. Article 5 of the UCC governs letters of credit. (In addition to commercial letters of credit, Article 5 also governs stand-by letters of credit which serve a credit rather than a payment function. We consider those issues in Chapter 5.) A letter of credit requires that the beneficiary, or the one receiving the payment (usually the seller), present certain documents to the issuer of the letter, usually a bank, in order for the bank to honor the letter. The Uniform Customs and Practice for Commercial Documentary Credits (UCP) is another important source of letter of credit law on an international level. The latest version was adopted in 2007 (UCP 600). UCC Article 5 allows parties to opt for the rules of the UCP, with a few exceptions for terms that cannot be changed.

Negotiability

The central feature of letters of credit is the independence principle. The bank's obligation on the letter of credit is completely separate from any of the contractual obligations of the underlying transaction, either the obligation of the buyer to pay the seller or any obligation that the buyer might have to reimburse the bank for payments made on its behalf. This feature—the insulation of the liability to make payment from any alleged defects in the underlying transaction—is akin to the feature of negotiability that parties can assign to other payment mechanisms. The circumstances in which negotiability (or independence) is desirable is a core question in the field of payment mechanisms, and is the focus of Section 4.2.

As an example of how negotiability works, consider again the hypothetical economy consisting of Alan, Betty and Carl. If Carl buys the toaster from Alan by paying currency, Alan can then use the currency to purchase the hair dryer from Betty. (Betty, in turn can then use the currency to buy the skateboard from Harry and all three are better off). If Carl pays for the toaster instead with a check (or other type of draft), Alan might cash the check with the drawee bank and then pay cash to Betty for the hair dryer. Consider, however, that Alan might offer to pay for the hair dryer by transferring to Betty his rights under the check against Carl (the drawer). As the excerpts below from articles by Gilmore and Rosenthal indicate, the marketability of instruments was a crucial economic issue before state-backed currency became a widespread exchange medium. The marketability of an instrument depends on the degree to which Alan as the purchaser of the instrument needs to look beyond the face of the instrument and particularly to investigate the relationship between the original parties to the instrument. Negotiability is the term of art used to describe the immunity of Betty as the prospective purchaser of an instrument to defenses that could be asserted by Carl, the drawer, against Alan, the payee. This immunity allows Betty to value the check simply on the basis of the solvency of Carl, the drawer (and any other obligor). Cash is the extreme case of a negotiable instrument. Under Article 3, parties to a draft can make it negotiable, but less so than cash. But, as we discuss below, there are certain costs to "pure" negotiability that make the intermediate position attractive in many circumstances.

The rights of a purchaser of a negotiable instrument depend on his or her status. A *holder in due course,* for example, often will be able to enforce the instrument against the person liable on it, notwithstanding that the obligor has a defense against the original payee on the instrument. Holders in due course are vulnerable only to the relatively rare "real" defenses such as infancy, duress, lack of legal capacity, illegality, or certain types of fraud. § 3–302. Suppose Carl buys the toaster from Alan by delivering a negotiable draft that directs a drawee to pay the contract price to the seller/payee. After receiving the draft, Alan transfers it to a third party (e.g., Betty in our example) who seeks to collect first against the drawee and then against Carl. If Betty is a mere transferee of the draft, she acquires only the rights in the instrument possessed by Alan, her transferor, and is therefore subject to any defenses that could be asserted against Alan by the drawer, Carl (or by any other obligor under the draft). § 3–203(b). However, Betty becomes a *holder* of the negotiable draft if she has taken possession of it and if it was indorsed to her by Alan. If Betty also paid value for the draft, took it in good faith and had no notice of the types of defects listed in § 3–302, then she may qualify as a holder in due course. In the vast majority of cases, therefore, the single risk that a holder in due course must assume is the solvency of the various obligors on the instrument. While that risk is an inevitable consequence of the purchase of an obligation, it can be significantly mitigated by the purchaser's ability to look also to his immediate transferor (as to whom the costs of assessing the likelihood of default are presumably lower) for payment.

Legal certainty is highly important to the effectiveness of a purported medium of exchange. In particular, market participants need to be certain whether an instrument is negotiable or not. To this end, the law sets formal requirements to make an instrument negotiable: a draft must be in writing, signed by the person undertaking to pay, contain an unconditional order to pay a fixed amount of money (on demand or at a definite time); contain no other undertaking or instruction to do any act in addition to the payment of money except those authorized; and be payable either to order or to bearer. § 3–104. Thus, a potential purchaser can quickly discern from the face of an instrument whether it is negotiable: a simple promise or order to pay money on demand or at a designated future date. Retaining these basic characteristics, and preventing the obligation from being further qualified or conditioned, enhances the marketability of the instrument because it reduces uncertainty concerning the probabilities of payment.

The Finality Doctrine

A distinguishing feature of a payment instrument in contrast to a credit instrument, is its finality. Once a buyer "pays" for a good, she relinquishes the self-help remedy of withholding payment in the event that the seller's performance is deficient. The buyer must seek legal recourse in court or otherwise persuade the seller to pay a refund or compensating amount. This is the case with payments by cash. In contrast, a drawer of a check enjoys a brief period following delivery of the check during which she can stop payment. § 4–403. An individual who pays by debit card, in contrast, does not enjoy this right and is effectively treated the same as if she had paid with cash. A credit card holder has a limited right to withhold payment when the delivered goods or services are deficient. These varied rules of finality might influence the choice of payment mechanism by parties to an exchange. Yet, one might also question whether these differences reflect an incoherence in the development of payments law and whether, instead of broadening payment options, they simply give rise to costly confusion. The material in Section 4.3 provides an account and analysis of these differences.

Allocating the Risk of Loss, Theft and Fraud

The same features that promote the marketability advantage of negotiability also raise the risk of theft and fraud. Suppose that a cash buyer, on his way to close the deal with the seller, loses currency to a thief, who uses it to buy a laptop computer from a third party. Because cash is negotiable, the buyer cannot recover the cash from the third party. This is, after all, the consequence of the supreme negotiability of currency: a third party bears no responsibility for investigating the history of a cash payment, including theft and fraud. A check is somewhat less negotiable than cash, in the sense noted above that a third party purchaser is subject to some real defenses. This diminishes the value of a check as a medium of exchange, but it also gives some protection against theft, as well as against fraud and forgery. In this sense, a negotiable instrument occupies an intermediate position between goods and currency. A bank cannot charge a drawer's deposit account for a check paid over a forged drawer's or indorser's signature, unless the forgery is due to the negligence of the drawer. § 4–401, ct. 1; § 3–406. The excerpts in section 4.4 discuss the economic principles behind this and other allocations of loss. Financial institutions seem able to bear losses better than individuals, but there are other efficiency concerns that may qualify, such as the ability of the customer to prevent the loss.

On the other hand, to the extent that these rules have been adopted by legislatures, they may be influenced by political considerations, such as interest group activity by financial institutions. As we have seen in our discussion of Sales law in Chapter 3, the interests of discrete groups may be favorably or adversely affected by the particular rule adopted by the UCC. Even where parties are free to opt out of that rule, the party who dislikes the default rule will have to bear the costs of negotiating for an alternative. Thus, it is important once again to test the proposition that the rules of Articles 3 and 4 may not reflect a consensus on a common objective, such as risk reduction, but may instead reflect the interests of a particular group that was able to dominate the process of drafting the commercial law.

Political economy explanations have been particularly strong with respect to the recent revision of Article 3 and the Amendments to Article 4. Interest group influence is not necessarily in tension with efficiency objectives. If an industry obtains a statute that reduces its costs and the industry is competitive, social welfare is enhanced. On the other hand, firms sometimes use their political power to redistribute wealth from other diffused interests to themselves. Thus, the question is not whether much of Articles 3 and 4 advance the objectives of the banking industry. Rather, the question is which parts of payments law, if any, are efficient and enhance social welfare and which parts, if any, merely redistribute wealth from one interest group to another. New technological innovations in payment methods, such as electronic currency, remain mostly outside the current bounds of payment law and present the opportunity to consider what the optimal law, if any, should consist of and who should formulate it (see Arnold Rosenberg, *Better than Cash? Global*

Proliferation of Payment Cards and Consumer Protection Policy, section
4.3 and 4.4 infra).

Modern Payment Systems

While new forms of payment have rapidly increased in use, checks
remain the predominant form of non-cash payment in the United States.
But the ubiquity of checks is clearly on the wane. Technological advances
over the past half-century have led to paper-less payment forms that rely
on electronic transfers between the accounts of the payor and the payee.
Credit and debit cards are the most common of these new advances, but
other variations on traditional checking and bill payment methods are
emerging, such as stored-value cards, smart cards and electronic currency. Once the electronic transfer of funds from a payor to a payee is final,
the payee may use the funds to make a payment to a third party in a
new transaction. The third party is immune from the defenses of the
payor in the first transaction and the issue of negotiability does not
arise.

Federal consumer protection legislation governs the finality of payments and risk allocation in electronic fund transfers involving individuals. In particular, the Truth in Lending Act (TILA) and the Fair Credit
Billing Act regulate credit cards. The Electronic Funds Transfer Act
(EFTA) governs debit cards and the increasingly common automatic
clearing house (ACH) payment methods. Article 4A of the UCC governs
wire transfers between business entities and financial institutions.
Emerging payment methods, such as smart cards and electronic currency, are at this time largely unregulated by law. This new technology
offers a unique opportunity to weigh the benefits and costs of diversity
in the rules governing payment devices and thereby to evaluate the
justification for moving toward a more uniform and comprehensive
regulation (see section 4.3 infra).

The excerpts that follow first consider the relevance of the doctrine
of negotiability in the modern economy. Section 4.2 introduces three
complementary perspectives that question the relevance of the negotiability concept to contemporary commercial transactions. By contrast
Professors Merrill and Smith offer a principle that might be used to
justify the doctrine. We turn to the finality doctrine in section 4.3.
Professors Mann and Rosenberg survey the different degrees of finality
and the different regulatory regimes that govern modern payment
mechanisms, particularly credit cards, debit cards and other stored-value
cards. These issues have increased importance a the use of these devices
spreads around the world. Finally, in section 4.4 we turn to four excerpts
that focus on the liability issues that are endemic in the use of methods
of payment subject to theft, fraud and loss.

4.2 Negotiability and the Modern Economy

The Commercial Doctrine of Good Faith Purchases*
GRANT GILMORE

Good Faith Purchase of Intangibles: Negotiability

The good faith purchase idea takes on an extra dimension of complexity when intangibles and not goods are concerned. Goods have an ascertainable location in space and time. If they are in Connecticut it is obvious, even to the legal mind, that they are not in New York. If A, the owner, sells goods to B, then A, except for claims based on breach of warranty, has nothing further to do with them. Nor has anyone ever doubted that goods can be sold. Even if, theoretically, goods can be made the subject of the sort of future interests which make up so much of our real property law, they have never in fact been so burdened.

None of these truisms is safe when we come to intangibles. Intangibles are not in themselves property, in the sense that goods are; they are claims to property. Thus when A gives his promissory note to B who negotiates to C who in turn negotiates it to D, what is being bought and sold is not the piece of paper which physically changes hands but the right to collect a certain amount of money from A which is represented by the piece of paper. Furthermore two distinct types of dispute can arise on the transfer of intangibles, only one of which is possible when goods are sold. When C, having acquired A's note from B, sells it to D, D has to worry not only whether he has acquired good title to the note against B, the original owner, but also whether the claim against A was valid in the first place. When he buys goods from C and takes delivery, he may or may not get title (depending on whether or not C is a thief) but at least he can be sure that the goods exist. When he buys A's note and takes delivery of that, it is far from certain that there ever was a claim against A, whose signature may have been forged or extorted or who may be free of liability because of usury. Moreover, if A, a resident of Connecticut, mails the note to B in New York, and if C and D are residents of Florida and California, it may be far from clear, even to lay mind, exactly where the claim against A "is."

Finally in contrast to the idea that public policy favors the free alienability of chattels, the law relating to the transfer of intangibles starts from the proposition that claims—choses in action—are not assignable. It is hard for us to understand why this should ever have been the law. The rule may have come in at a time when intangible property was little known, insignificant as a form of wealth, and therefore could be summarily disposed of in a shorthand phrase. We like to say that it is no longer the law today.

* 63 YALE L. J. 1057 (1954).

The development of the law of good faith purchase in this field has thus had to take account of burdensome complexities which were not met with in the relatively simple case of goods. It has been necessary to work out a number of subordinate propositions in addition to the basic one that the purchaser in good faith and for value gets "title" or "good title" or even "perfect title." It is this network of good faith purchase rules that we mean when we describe paper as "negotiable."

Negotiable Instruments and Nonnegotiable Choses

"Negotiable" and "negotiability" are words rarely, if ever, defined. They mean not one but many things. The principle attributes of negotiability are these:

(1) The paper must be freely assignable; no restraints on alienation will be tolerated.

(2) The debt claim is "merged" into the paper evidencing the claim; thus the paper must be treated in many situations as if it were the claim itself:

a) Transfer of the claim can *only* be made by physical delivery of the paper, completed by evidence of the transferor's intent to transfer which is customarily given by his indorsement on the paper itself;

b) Discharge of the debt evidenced by the paper can be made *only* by payment to (or cancellation by) the holder—the person physically in possession;

c) Creditors of a holder can assert their claims against the paper (as part of the debtor's assets) *only* by getting possession of it through appropriate legal process, and not by serving a garnishment order on the obligor;

d) The situs of the debt is where the paper is.

(3) In pursuing his claim against the obligor, the holder receives the benefit of a series of presumptions which cast on the defendant the greater part of the burden of proof normally carried by plaintiffs in contract actions.

(4) On default by the obligor, the holder has an automatic right of recourse against prior indorsers.

(5) As to "purchase in good faith, without notice and for value":

a) a purchaser is "in good faith" as long as he is "subjectively" honest at the time he takes the paper; he is under no duty of inquiry; he may even have "forgotten" relevant information; he is merely required not to be actively in bad faith;

b) a purchaser is not put on notice by anything not contained in the paper itself; he is not subject to constructive notice from public recordation or to limitations contained in collateral agreements unless the limitations are actually known to him;

c) a purchaser has "given value" if he has given any consideration sufficient to support a simple contract; moreover a pre-existing debt constitutes value.

(6) Any holder, even though he took the instrument in bad faith, with notice of defenses, after maturity and without giving value, has all the rights of any prior holder in due course from whom his title derives (provided only that he himself is not a party to any fraud or illegality affecting the instrument).

(7) A holder in due course, or a holder whose title is derived from such a holder, holds the instrument free both of equities of prior owners of the instrument, and of defenses of the obligor except the so-called "real" defenses. The real defenses, which are nowhere defined in the Negotiable Instruments Law, cover essentially the cases where there never was a claim against the obligor on the instrument: forgery, insanity or other lack of capacity to contract, and duress.

Of the blessings which flow so bounteously for the holder in due course of negotiable paper, the assignee of the "ordinary," "simple" or nonnegotiable chose in action receives only a thin trickle.[...] The purchaser of nonnegotiable paper not only receives almost none of the protection accorded to the purchaser of negotiable paper, he receives less protection than does the purchaser of chattels. Here the original rules of property law have stood almost unchanged: equities of ownership are effectively maintained, defenses are sedulously preserved. We have a development in three stages: the purchaser of negotiable paper receives an extraordinary degree of protection; the purchaser of chattels gets less, without by any means being left naked to the elements; the purchaser of a nonnegotiable chose gets almost nothing. Why should not the development of the law of assignment have at least run even with the law of sales? The explanation lies in this inarticulate major premise: Negotiable paper is commercial property; nonnegotiable paper is noncommercial; goods can be either.

In sales law the expansion of the good faith purchase idea in commercial situations and its restriction in noncommercial situations was achieved by the manipulation of a set of concepts which did not purport to take "commerciality" into account. There was thus no need in sales law to develop nice distinctions between commercial goods and noncommercial possessions: the subtle accommodation to commercial needs and pressures was worked out at a deeper level. In the field of intangibles, however, we find a sharp distinction drawn between commercial and noncommercial property, between paper that is negotiable and paper that is not. In the growth of the law there came in as a matter of first importance the necessity of distinguishing between the two.

Negotiability—Who Needs It?*
ALBERT J. ROSENTHAL

The law of negotiable instruments has been painted with a very broad brush—in some respects perhaps too broad a brush. With minor exceptions, any kind of claim and any kind of defense will be cut off in favor of any kind of holder in due course. This happens under the Uniform Commercial Code (hereinafter referred to in text as the Code) regardless of the comparative equities of the holder vis-á-vis the person whose rights are cut off, and sometimes regardless as well of whether any genuine commercial needs are served thereby.

Apparently a negotiable instrument is a negotiable instrument is a negotiable instrument. And a holder in due course is a holder in due course is a holder in due course. Much can be said, of course, in favor of a broad, simple rule, easily understood and applied. There is a danger, however, that a rule which is too simplistic may lead to simple-minded results: it may operate unfairly and harmfully at the expense of some, while giving to others windfalls that serve no significant social or commercial need.

When a question arises as to whether a holder in due course can cut off defenses or claims, a decision must be made as to which of two innocent parties will probably bear the entire loss. The problem usually arises only because there is a third party who is dishonest, impecunious, or both. There is theoretically a right over against such a party, but exercise of this right is generally inconvenient and often worthless. While it would be possible to divide the loss between the two innocent parties, this type of solution rarely finds favor in our law. And where both have behaved decently and honorably, the allocation of loss can scarcely be based upon a calculus of comparative nobility of character. The decision therefore almost inevitably has to rest upon the collateral effects of the rule to be enunciated—for example, its effect upon commerce.

Promissory Notes

A Bank of England bearer note, while not yet legal tender in 1756, was, according to Lord Mansfield, "treated as money, as cash." In the leading case of Miller v. Race he concluded that when such a bearer note was stolen and subsequently sold to a bona fide purchaser, it had to belong to the purchaser rather than to the previous owner, because of "the consequences to trade and, commerce ... which would be most incommoded by a contrary determination."

While the negotiable character of certain kinds of instruments had earlier been given some measure of protection in specialized commercial courts in England, this decision seems to have been the first clear-cut

---

* 71 COLUM. L. REV. 375, 377–385, 394–396, 401 (1971).

holding of its kind by a common-law court. Several points should be noted. (1) A claim of ownership was cut off—no defense against payment of the instrument was involved. (2) The note in question was of a type customarily passed from hand to hand, serving many of the purposes of paper money, which did not exist in England at the time. (3) Without the free circulation of such "money," business would have been impeded.

The negotiable promissory note of today is quite a different instrument, serving different purposes, and the consequences of its negotiability are quite different in impact. By far the most commonly employed variety of the species today is the note given by the installment purchaser of goods to reflect the unpaid portion of the purchase price. Typically, such a note is transferred just once, from the dealer to the lender (usually either a finance company or a bank), and thereafter remains in the possession of the latter or its lawyers until it is either paid off or offered in evidence in court. Its negotiable character is of no importance with respect to claims of ownership, as it is unlikely to be lost or stolen. Even if it is, the last endorsement will have been a special endorsement to the order of the lender; without the genuine further endorsement of the latter there can be no subsequent holder, much less a holder in due course.

The only significant consequence of the negotiability of such a note is that it cuts off the defenses of the maker. If, for example, the purchaser gives the note in payment for a refrigerator, the finance company is entitled to full payment regardless of whether the refrigerator fails to work or whether its sale was accomplished through fraudulent misrepresentations or, indeed, whether it was ever delivered at all. And it may be small comfort to the buyer, forced to pay the finance company in full, to know that he has a cause of action against the seller, which may at best be collectible with difficulty and may in many cases be worthless because the seller is insolvent or has left town [. . .]

A promissory note of this kind, and a consequence of negotiability that works in this fashion, are a far cry from the stolen Bank of England note, and the protection accorded its purchaser, in *Miller v. Race*. Whether the finance company should be allowed to prevail free of the maker's defenses raises questions that ought to be decided on their merits, and not merely through the absent-minded application of a doctrine created to meet an entirely different situation [. . .]

Checks

The case of *Peacock v. Rhodes* came before Lord Mansfield twenty-three years after *Miller v. Race*. In *Peacock*, a bill of exchange indorsed in blank was stolen from the holder by a pickpocket and subsequently sold to a bona fide purchaser for value. As with the Bank of England note in *Miller v. Race*, such bills often passed from hand to hand as a substitute for paper money; this had indeed been true of the actual bill involved in the case. Here again, Mansfield held in favor of the bona fide purchaser of the bill; to rule otherwise, he said, "would stop their currency."

The modern term for a bill of exchange is a "draft" and a check is a type of draft, whose special characteristics are that it is drawn on a bank and is payable on demand. Does it therefore follow from *Peacock v. Rhodes* that all of the consequences of negotiability—including, again, the cutting off not only of claims but of defenses as well—ought to be applied to checks? To what extent does the reason for the rule of *Peacock v. Rhodes* apply to the modern check?

To begin with, negotiability normally plays almost no part with respect to checks. While some checks are cashed at a grocery store or across the counter at a bank, the overwhelming majority of checks are deposited by the payee for collection at his own bank, which, acting merely as the depositor's agent for that purpose, sends the check through banking channels to the drawee bank where it is presented for payment. If paid, the check is so marked and is ultimately returned to the drawer along with his monthly statement; if the check is dishonored, a slip setting forth the reason is attached to it and goes with it back through banking channels to the payee.

There is no holder in due course (except perhaps the payee himself) of such a check since, even though such other requirements as good faith and lack of notice may be met, the bank would not have given value for the check. Any dispute between drawer and payee will, therefore, simply be between themselves, with no one else in a position to assert special rights.

Let us now modify the case of a relatively poor buyer purchasing a refrigerator on installments, and substitute a middle-class consumer paying for it with his personal check. If the refrigerator fails to work properly, if its defect is immediately apparent, if the buyer's attempts to get redress from the seller prove unavailing, and if the buyer moves with sufficient alacrity, he can often stop payment on his check before it has cleared through his own bank. The buyer and seller will then be in a position themselves to resolve their dispute on the merits, with the buyer having the tactical advantage that the seller will have to bring suit in order to collect if the matter cannot be resolved without litigation.

Suppose, however, the bank in which the seller-payee deposits the check allows him to draw against it before it has been collected. This is not standard practice, but it does occur with some frequency. When the check is presented to the drawee bank for payment, it is dishonored because of the stop payment order. This time, however, the depositary bank is given the status of holder in due course "to the extent to which credit for the item has been withdrawn or applied," or "if it makes an advance on or against the item." To this extent, the drawer cannot assert against the bank the defense that the sale of the refrigerator was fraudulent. Although the stop payment order is effective, its utility to the drawer is defeated, since he is liable to the depository bank.

The Code achieves this result by having section 4–208(1) accord the depository bank a security interest in the check or its proceeds, and then declaring in section 4–209 that, for purposes of qualifying as a holder in due course, the bank is regarded as having given value to the extent that the bank has a security interest in the item. Even without these specific provisions the same result might be reached under the more general provision of section 3–303(a) that the instrument is taken for value "to the extent that the agreed consideration has been performed."

If the depository bank were to grant credit to the payee by allowing withdrawals before collection, and if it were to do this in reliance upon its knowledge of the drawer's financial standing or reputation, there might be good reason to protect the depository bank in this fashion. Typically, however, the depository bank pays no attention to the identity of the drawer; in fact, it does not even know whether the drawer's signature is genuine. It will often allow or refuse to allow withdrawals against the check before collection solely on the basis of its relations with and knowledge of the creditworthiness of its own customer, the payee. If payment is stopped, and the depository bank cannot recover its advances by charging the amount back against the payee's account, but is permitted to hold the drawer liable, the bank receives a windfall: in such cases, it picks up the liability of the drawer, which by hypothesis it had not counted upon when it made its decision to allow withdrawals before collection.

The fact that the depository bank would not normally be relying upon the drawer's credit may be seen in the improbable combination of circumstances that have to coincide for the drawer's liability to matter. First, the bank's customer, the payee, must have allowed his account to drop to the point at which some of his withdrawals cannot be charged against other funds in the account but must be regarded as advances against the uncollected check. Second, the payee must be insolvent, or at least his assets must not be readily amenable to collection. Third, the drawer has to be solvent and available, and his signature genuine. Fourth, the check must be dishonored. Finally, for the doctrine to make any ultimate difference, the drawer must have a legitimate defense on the check that is good against the payee, but is not of a type that can be asserted against a holder in due course. Only if all of these elements coincide is the bank's position improved by virtue of its becoming a holder in due course. It must therefore be a rare case indeed in which the bank's decision to extend credit before the check is collected can be regarded as having been made in reliance upon its ability to cut off the defenses of the drawer. Neither banks specifically, nor commerce in general, seem to need the rule declaring the bank to be a holder in due course. Where the bank relies entirely on the identity and credit of the payee in allowing withdrawals, it should shock no one's conscience if the bank were limited to the payee as a source of reimbursement.

Searching for Negotiability in Payment and Credit Systems*
RONALD J. MANN

The Irrelevance of Negotiability to the Modern Payment System

[T]he continued use of negotiable instruments in the checking system does not suggest that negotiability has any continuing significance. Rather, negotiability has little or no role in the practices by which payments are made and collected in the checking system. Although the system has retained the technical form of negotiability, it has abandoned in practice all of the major concepts by which negotiability can facilitate transactions. The reason for this change should be clear by now: In the modern checking system, negotiability is not an aid to the effectiveness of the system, but an obstacle for the industry to overcome.

The central premise of negotiability is that assets can be transferred more readily in a system that allows a physical object to represent all rights in the assets[...] [A]ll of the benefits that negotiability offers arise from the system's use of the document as the ultimate indicator of rights in the assets. The clearest evidence of the true irrelevance of negotiability to the checking system is the growing push to adopt "truncated" processing devices that rid the system of the physical document as much as possible.

The checking system faces the same technological pressures as the various payment and credit systems ... but it must deal with those pressures on a canvas of daunting size, in a system called upon to process more than sixty billion checks a year. The absurdity of reliance on the physical document is evidenced by the need for the banks where checks are deposited (depositary banks) to sort those checks and then have them transported (normally by truck or airplane) to locations designated by the various banks on whom the checks are drawn (the payor banks). One study concludes that the current collection process expends approximately 2.5 cents to process each paper check, but the costs can be much higher. For instance, the Federal Reserve in some cases may charge more than twenty-five cents per check. The fact is, in the checking system just as much as in any other payment system, the notion of centralizing legal rights in the physical document is no longer the benefit it might have been centuries ago: It is an albatross that drags down the entire system.

The key intellectual challenge is to realize that however central the "document" might be to a negotiability-based system, there is no reason

* 44 UCLA L. Rev. 951, 985–990, 994–998, 1004–1005 (1997).

for the checking system to continue to operate a document-based system for collection of checks. The collection process needs to facilitate two actions by the payor bank: a decision whether to honor the check; and transmission of payment or notice of dishonor to the depositary bank. Given the capabilities of existing technology, physically transporting the check from place to place is not the simplest way to perform those two functions. It makes much more sense and should be dramatically cheaper in the long run to perform those functions electronically—by a transmission from the depositary bank to the payor bank advising of the deposit of the check; and a return transmission from the payor bank agreeing or declining to honor the check. Indeed, the inevitability of the demise of the paper-based processing system has been obvious for so long that the revisers of Article 4 in the 1980s took several conscious steps to give the statute the flexibility to accommodate the truncated electronic system that should replace the current system over the next few decades.

Indeed, the beginnings of a truncated system already are in place. In 1994, some form of electronic presentment was used for over 650 million checks, which was just over one percent of the total volume. For checks cleared through the Federal Reserve system, truncation is even more common, in the range of two percent of all checks. Under that system, the check stops when it reaches the depositary bank. Instead of transmitting the check to the payor bank or an intermediary, the payor bank creates a record of the check, either a photographic image or a digital record of the relevant data. The depositary bank then transmits an electronic message seeking collection. Depending on the agreement between the parties (or, perhaps more likely in the future, on standardized rules implemented by the Federal Reserve), the message might consist of the entire image or simply include data summarizing relevant facts about the check, such as the payor bank, account number, amount, date, and payee. Ideally, the message would be sent directly to the payor bank, but currently many of those transactions still pass through an intermediary such as the Federal Reserve.

The payor bank receiving the message has the same options as it has under the conventional paper-based clearing process—it can honor the check or dishonor it. If it chooses to dishonor the check, it advises the depositary bank electronically of its decision. If the payor bank chooses to honor the check, it has no obligation to do anything. At the end of the month, the payor bank cannot return the actual checks to its customers because those checks are still at the depositary bank. Therefore, it sends its customers either images of the checks (much like the images of credit-card slips that come with American Express bills) or detailed statements describing the transactions reflected by the checks. Finally, the depositary bank retains the image of the check for a period of time sufficient to resolve disputes that might arise.

The outmoded nature of the document-based processing system is made even clearer by the burgeoning use of electronic cash letters, also known as electronic presentment. In that system, a depositary bank runs checks through a machine that produces a computer file containing the relevant information about the checks and sends that file directly to the payor bank by electronic mail. The payor bank then must decide on an expedited basis whether it wishes to honor or dishonor the checks. In accordance with customary practice, the paper copies of the check are transmitted later by ordinary procedures. Because the payor bank has made and communicated all of the relevant decisions long before the paper checks arrive at the depositary bank, the transportation of those checks expends a great deal of resources for no useful purpose. The physical transportation of the checks, the last surviving vestige of negotiability, should succumb to budgetary pressures in the immediate future.

But there is more at stake here than cost savings. An electronic system is not only cheaper than a document-based system, it should be much faster as well. An electronic presentment system should be able to clear checks nationwide on a same-day or same-hour basis, so that check recipients would receive final payment almost immediately upon deposit. The skeptic should consider how easily banks are able to process electronic payments made by debit cards. Although there are some differences, there is no fundamental reason why the system could not develop so that payor banks respond with the same promptness to payment directions made by way of check as they presently do to payment directions made by way of a debit card.

Of course, an electronic system would impose some costs on the entities that wrote checks, because they would lose the "float" they gain in the current system during the time that passes between their writing a check and the removal of the funds from their account. Unfortunately, however fond of float we may be as individuals, a system in which expedited processing minimizes the float available to check writers should improve the checking system as a whole by increasing the value of the check as a payment system. Presently, a merchant gets paid more when it gets immediate cash than when it gets a check, both because it gets use of the funds earlier, and because payment is far more certain. And the increase in certainty means that a system that provides contemporaneous clearing does something more than transfer the time value of the float from the consumer writing the check to the merchant that receives it. By increasing the certainty of collection, contemporaneous clearing lowers the costs of collection and thus increases the effectiveness of the system as a whole.

The ability of the system to develop such a completely electronic collection system does not prove the irrelevance of the document-based negotiability system, for current procedures still transport tens of billions of checks for physical collection each year. Nevertheless, the potential for a development that would eliminate physical collection entirely strongly suggests that the concept of negotiability no longer plays any useful role in the system. [...]

[I]t is not practicable for the payor bank to rely on a verification of the physical signature as a predicate for determining whether it will honor the check. The biggest problem is the sheer volume of checks that a payor bank must process. A large check-processing center will receive something on the order of one million checks each day. It would take an army of signature examiners to compare the signatures on that many checks with the signature cards for the relevant accounts. To be sure, some small banks still verify signatures on the checks their customers write. More commonly, however, banks limit signature verification to a small group of the checks that they receive. For example, one of the processing centers that I visited examines the signatures on 20,000 checks per day, less than one-half of one percent of the checks that it receives. Thus, although 20,000 checks per day might seem like a large number in the abstract, that sample is highly unlikely to include all of the fraudulently issued checks: the payor bank's evaluation of more than 99.5% of the checks proceeds without any examination at all of the drawer's signature.

The difficulty of determining whether a signature is valid heightens the impracticality of examining signatures. Absent a striking lack of competence, a forger with a sample of a valid signature should be able to provide a signature that would pass muster even if the check is in the small sample a bank chooses for examination. Thus, the bank cannot be sure that the signature is valid even on the few checks that it does examine.

In the end, banks are faced with a reality in which the signature provides little significant protection against losses from fraud. To have any realistic protection against those losses, banks must move beyond negotiability and develop other, nonsignatory devices to protect themselves. The most prominent of those devices are systems in which the drawer of the check directly authorizes payment so that the payor bank can rely on that authorization rather than the signature. For example, consider the "positive-pay" system of check verification that is coming into common use for large business accounts. In that system, the bank provides its customer with a software package that allows the customer to send the bank a computer file at the close of each business day that describes each check that the customer has issued. When checks are presented to the bank for payment, the bank can rely on computerized sorting and analysis of the checks to determine if the checks presented for payment match checks described in the daily transmissions. If the checks are described in those transmissions, then the payor bank need not examine the signature on the check because the bank has something better than a signature to evidence the drawer's willingness to pay—a direct electronic message from the customer verifying its willingness to pay. Conversely, a check that is not described in the transmissions can be dishonored even if it is such an excellent forgery that it appears on its face to be a validly issued check.

It is encouraging that the checking system has begun to move beyond reliance on the signature and to develop nonsignatory devices for verifying the drawer's authorization of the instrument. But those non-signatory verification devices do not solve the difficulty with physical signatures as much as they highlight two fundamental problems with a payment system that relies on physical signatures. First, a system that relies on physical signatures cannot even make a pretense of verifying the signature without comparing the signature to a specimen signature of the customer; and the logistics of getting the check to a place where it can be compared to the signature and of effecting that comparison are relatively time consuming. Second, even if the system goes to the trouble of making the comparison, the comparison of a physical signature to a specimen signature is necessarily inexact and cannot significantly deter a determined forger.

Those problems are directly attributable to the document-based system of negotiability out of which the checking system has developed. Nonsignatory verification systems may mitigate those problems, but they cannot solve them completely, if only because of the expense of grafting a universal nonsignatory verification system onto the current checking system. To completely solve those problems, the system would have to cut loose from the documentary moorings of negotiability and move to an entirely nondocumentary system, perhaps one that relies on digital signatures. A digital-signature system would fulfill the verification function much more effectively than the current system because digital signatures can be verified much more inexpensively and reliably than conventional physical signatures.

Payment Systems of the Future: The King Is Dead, Long Live the King!

The final interment of the negotiable instrument need not result in any serious dislocation for the credit and payment systems in which negotiable instruments have been used. Rather, as this Article suggests, the movement away from negotiable instruments has occurred with so little dislocation that it has passed largely unnoticed by the affected academic community.

In the generally large-dollar world of credit systems, the passage already has been completed. Negotiability is gone, not only practically but also as a matter of form. For high-credit borrowers whose obligations are publicly traded, negotiability has given way to more effective systems that record the issue, transfer, and satisfaction of the obligations electronically. Home-mortgage notes—susceptible of public trading only through securitization—have moved more slowly, but even there systems for electronic transfer are moving into place. Finally, in contexts involving nonuniform obligations that are not suitable for trading, the negotiable instrument has passed away for the less definitive but nonetheless forceful reason that negotiability has so little to offer the parties that they are better off focusing their attentions on more direct devices to diminish the likelihood that the borrower will become recalcitrant after the transfer.

The forces of advancing financial sophistication move just as surely to remove negotiability from payment systems. The only context in which it retains significance even as a formal matter is in the retail transaction where the payor "pays" the payee by transferring a claim against a bank. Even in that context it appears only in the checking system, not the functionally similar card-related systems.

Optimal Standardization in the Law of Property: The Numerus Clausus Principle*

THOMAS W. MERRILL and **HENRY E. SMITH**

A central difference between contract and property concerns the freedom to "customize" legally enforceable interests. The law of contract recognizes no inherent limitations on the nature or the duration of the interests that can be the subject of a legally binding contract. Certain types of promises—such as promises to commit a crime—are declared unenforceable as a matter of public policy. But outside these relatively narrow areas of proscription and requirements such as definiteness and (maybe) consideration, there is a potentially infinite range of promises that the law will honor. The parties to a contract are free to be as whimsical or fanciful as they like in describing the promise to be performed, the consideration to be given in return for the promise, and the duration of the agreement.

The law of property is very different in this respect. Generally speaking, the law will enforce as property only those interests that conform to a limited number of standard forms. As it is stated in a leading English case, "incidents of a novel kind" cannot "be devised and attached to property at the fancy or caprice of any owner." With respect to interests in land, for example, the basic forms are the fee simple, the defeasible fee simple, the life estate, and the lease. When parties wish to transfer property in land, they must specify which legal form they are using—fee simple, lease, and so forth. If they fail to be clear about which legal interest they are conveying, or if they attempt to customize a new type of interest, the courts will generally recast the conveyance as creating one of the recognized forms. Of course, the law freely allows customization of the more physical, tangible dimensions of ownership rights. Property comes in all sorts of shapes and sizes. But with respect

---

* 110 Yale L. J. 1 (2000).

to the legal dimensions of property, the law generally insists on strict standardization.[...]

The root of the difference, we suggest, stems from the in rem nature of property rights: When property rights are created, third parties must expend time and resources to determine the attributes of these rights, both to avoid violating them and to acquire them from the present holders. The existence of unusual property rights increases the cost of processing information about all property rights. Those creating or transferring idiosyncratic property rights cannot always be expected to take these increases in measurement costs fully into account, making them a true externality. Standardization of property rights reduces these measurement costs.[...]

The need for standardization in property law stems from an externality involving measurement costs: Parties who create new property rights will not take into account the full magnitude of the measurement costs they impose on strangers to the title. An example illustrates. Suppose one hundred people own watches. *A* is the sole owner of a watch and wants to transfer some or all of the rights to use the watch to *B*. The law of personal property allows the sale of *A*'s entire interest in the watch, or the sale of a life estate in the watch, or the sale of a joint tenancy or tenancy in common in the watch. But suppose *A* wants to create a "time-share" in the watch, which would allow *B* to use the watch on Mondays but only on Mondays (with *A* retaining for now the rights to the watch on all other days). As a matter of contract law, *A* and *B* are perfectly free to enter into such an idiosyncratic agreement. But *A* and *B* are not permitted by the law of personal property to create a *property right* in the use of the watch on Mondays only and to transfer this property right from *A* to *B*.

Why might the law restrict the freedom of *A* and *B* to create such an unusual property right? Suppose, counterfactually, that such idiosyncratic property rights are permitted. Word spreads that someone has sold a Monday right in a watch, but not which of the one hundred owners did so. If *A* now decides to sell his watch, he will have to explain that it does not include Monday rights, and this will reduce the attractiveness of the watch to potential buyers. Presumably, however, *A* will foresee this when he sells the Monday rights, and is willing to bear the costs of that action in the form of a lower sales price. But consider what will happen now when any of the *other* ninety-nine watch owners try to sell their watches. Given the awareness that someone has created a Monday-only right, anyone else buying a watch must now also investigate whether any particular watch does not include Monday rights. Thus, by allowing even one person to create an idiosyncratic property right, the information processing costs of all persons who have existing or potential interests in this type of property go up. This external cost on other market participants forms the basis of our explanation of the *numerus clausus* [...]

[T]he costs to potential successors in interest [to B, will be] mediated through the price mechanism and so will not require legal intervention. In the literature on fragmentation, it is often pointed out that the creation of novel interests can be difficult for later individuals dealing with the asset ... to figure out or to undo. Even interests that do not lead to fragmentation per se can be difficult for those in the distant future to understand and take into account, and this is a reason to adopt some degree of standardization in property rights. But these costs are not externalities to such decisions. If a fancy lowers the price that a future purchaser will pay for an interest in the watch over which A and B are transacting, the difficulties facing future [parties] who might purchase any interest in that watch—or who might lend to the owner of the watch while taking a security interest in the watch—will lead to a lower price than [they] might pay for an unrestricted watch. This lower price will be reflected in a lower market value the instant that the fancy creating such difficulties is created. Because the difficulties to the potential successors in interest ... are reflected in costs facing A (and B) now, there is no externality and no need to intervene.[. . .]

To return to our hypothetical world of one-hundred watch owners, suppose the value of creating the Monday-only right to A is $10, but the existence of this idiosyncrasy increases processing costs by $1 for all watch owners. The net benefit to A is $9, but the social cost is $90. As this example suggests, idiosyncratic property rights create a common-pool problem. The marginal benefits of the idiosyncrasy are fully internalized to the owner of the property right, but the owner bears only a fraction of the general measurement costs thereby created. Overall, the creation of external costs associated with this common-pool problem is likely to proceed beyond the optimal level. The problem cannot be resolved by side payments from the remaining ninety-nine to A, because the transaction costs are virtually certain to be prohibitive. Consequently, since an individual's interest in creating the nonstandard right—the extra benefit from using it rather than the next best alternative—is less than the additional measurement costs imposed on the other market participants, there is a rationale for the law to prohibit the creation of this kind of idiosyncratic right.

One way to control the external costs of measurement to third parties is through compulsory standardization of property rights. Standardization reduces the costs of measuring the attributes of such rights. Limiting the number of basic property forms allows a market participant or a potential violator to limit his or her inquiry to whether the interest does or does not have the features of the forms on the menu. Fancies not on the closed list need not be considered because they will not be enforced. When it comes to the basic legal dimensions of property, limiting the number of forms thus makes the determination of their nature less costly. The "good" in question here might be considered to be the prevention of error in ascertaining the attributes of property rights. Standardization means less measurement is required to achieve a given amount of error prevention. Alternatively, one can say that standardization increases the productivity of any given level of measurement efforts.

One would expect standardization to have the most value in connection with the dimensions of property rights that are least visible, and hence the most difficult for ordinary observers to measure. The tangible attributes of property, such as its size, shape, color, or texture, are typically readily observable and hence can be relatively easily measured by third parties. In the watch example, the watch can be a Timex or a Rolex and can be any size or color, and so forth. These physical attributes, and of course the price, are relatively easy for third parties to process using their senses, and thus there is less to be gained from standardizing them. The legal dimensions of property are less visible and less easy to comprehend, especially when they deviate from the most familiar forms such as the undivided fee simple. Thus, one would expect the effort to lower third-party information costs through standardization to focus on the legal dimension of ownership. [. . .]

In both language and property, standardizing the building blocks will cause some frustration of purposes, but the analogy to language suggests why this may be tolerable. If there were only one form of tailor-made property right for each objective people might have, then limiting such rights would have a severe effect on the objectives people could pursue with the law's aid. But if building blocks can be combined in many ways to serve objectives that cannot be served with the building blocks themselves, then the degree of frustration depends on how well and how easily the building blocks can be combined to serve those objectives. That is, it is important to know the generative power of the system of property rights.

In this respect, the set of outputs of the property system is potentially infinite for reasons analogous to those that capture the infinity of sentences of a language. The set of property rights bundles is potentially infinite because, like some of the rules of language, some rules for forming property rights are *recursive*: These rules can feed into themselves. For example, a fee simple can be physically divided and divided yet again, or a lessee can create a sublease and the sublessee a (sub)sublease, etc. Also leading to an infinity of outputs are rules that permit multiple owners; for example, a fee simple can be divided into tenancies in common with any number of concurrent owners or a single lease can be executed with multiple lessees. And the rules permitting physical and temporal division can be combined with the rules permitting multiple ownership. Thus, again as with language, relatively simple systems can potentially have great generative capacity or expressive power. If so, then the limitations on the vocabulary of property rights may not lead to as much frustration of parties' objectives as one might first think.

Quite complex structures—of property rights or sentences—can be constructed from a limited number of standard building blocks. Importantly, these complexes are easier to process for the very reason that they are built with the standard building blocks. In language, sentences that obey grammatical constraints are likely to be easier to parse than are ungrammatical sentences, something that Chomsky pointed out at the dawn of his research program on generative grammar. Similarly, in property, a complex of property rights built from a small number of standard building blocks is likely to be easier for third parties to process than functionally equivalent complex property rights for which third parties must figure out the nature of the building blocks.

As is generally true of analogies, likening the system of property rights to human language only gets us so far. The two networks resemble each other on the frustration cost side of the ledger: The generative power of each leads to great flexibility. Much can be done with a limited vocabulary. On the measurement cost side of the inquiry, however, the system of property looks like language only in certain specialized contexts. Everyday language is a flexible standard: It is permissible and often beneficial to coin new words, and this does not usually lead to a degree of confusion costs that requires standardization by a central authority. The grammar of a language is more standardized, but again this generally occurs spontaneously. Standardizing property and language may not create massive frustration costs because of each system's generative power, but the source of the standardization is different in the two networks

NOTES

1. The physical embodiment of intangible claims. Gilmore suggests that claims are difficult to transfer in their intangible form. Where transfers are valuable, the claims needed to be merged into tangible matter, specifically a paper document that provided the exclusive evidence of the claim. The exclusivity feature of this "paper principle" was essential to commercial transactions, he argues, such that a transfer of a claim could only be made by physical transfer of the paper and that discharge of the debt could only be made by payment to the person in possession of the paper. Do you think that this "paper principle" makes sense? Is tangible form necessary? Would your answer turn on whether the mechanism was being used by institutions or by individuals? Similarly, Mann says that "The central premise of negotiability is that assets can be transferred more readily in a system that allows a physical object to represent all rights in the assets." Thus, the physical embodiment of claims has been assumed to be a necessary requirement for the transferability of claims. As we discuss below, negotiability is a special subcategory of transfers that bestows on the transferee greater rights than those enjoyed by the original payee. A physical transfer is necessary but not sufficient for negotiability.

Mann questions whether the paper is needed or even desirable any more in light of technological advances that permit paperless evidence of claims. He focuses on the process of check collection, in which the claim and payment passes through several hands. Much of Mann's analysis derives from the increasing transaction costs endemic to the document-based payment system, such as verifying the signatures on checks. He observes that "Negotiability has given way to more effective systems that record the issue, transfer, and satisfaction of the obligations electronically ..." and, to the extent that physical transportation of checks is still present, he calls it "the last surviving vestige of negotiability." Why does federal law require expedited processing of checks? Who benefits? Would you expect some financial institutions to benefit more than others? Do Mann's arguments apply similarly to other forms of commercial paper?

When Mann speaks of the death of "negotiability," however, is he referring to simply the physical embodiment of payment claims or also the protection of the good faith transferee? With respect to the latter, is negotiability still relevant in modern transactions? We discuss this question in the notes below.

2. Is there a contemporary economic rationale for negotiability? Rosenthal presents a brief history of negotiable instruments to show how they facilitate the movement of capital to distant markets. By insulating purchasers in distant markets from potential claims of prior parties, bearer notes and other types of commercial paper increased the reliability of the payment obligations issued by debtors. Gilmore argues that negotiability was necessary in the commercial realm, but not elsewhere. *See* Beutel, *The Development of Negotiable Instruments in Early English Law*, 51 Harv. L. Rev. 813 (1938); J. Holden, *The History of Negotiable Instruments in English Law* (1955). Rosenthal argues that the rationale underlying negotiability is no longer applicable in today's economy. Does negotiability serve any contemporary purpose by cutting off the defense of the issuer of the commercial paper? Is the economic rationale for defeating defenses to payment different from the rationale for defeating claims to the instrument? One might argue that the problem of recovering payment may be more readily dealt with through substitute arrangements such as estoppel letters and warranties than the problem of non-ownership of the instrument (including attached collateral). Rosenthal writes that the courts weighed two distinct considerations: 1) equity as between the purchaser and the original maker, and 2) the efficiency losses that might obtain in an economy where the value of such a note might be discounted by the probability that any previous transfers were illegitimate. He suggests that the equitable considerations are more relevant today. Does it matter whether the paper serves a payment or credit function?

For other discussions of the contemporary relevance of negotiability in payment systems, *see,* James Steven Rogers, *The Irrelevance of Negotiable Instruments Concepts in the Law of the Check–Based Payment System*, 65 Tex. L. Rev. 929 (1987); Charles W. Mooney, Jr., *Beyond Negotiability: A New Model for Transfer and Pledge of Interests in Securities Controlled by*

Intermediaries, 12 Cardozo L. Rev. 305 (1990), James Steven Rogers, *An Essay on Horseless Carriages and Paperless Negotiable Instruments: Some Lessons from the Article 8 Revision*, 31 Idaho L. Rev. 689 (1995); James Steven Rogers, *Negotiability, Property, and Identity*, 12 Cardozo L. Rev. 471 (1990). Consider also the relevance of negotiability in innovative payment mechanisms introduced in Section 4.3.

3. Are payment instruments property or contract? Thomas Merrill and Henry Smith explore the distinction between contract and property in the excerpted article and in a sequel, *The Property/Contract Interface*, 101 Colum. L. Rev. 773 (2001). In light of the trade in payment instruments, is it more helpful to think of those instruments as contracts or property? If property, does Merrill and Smith's analysis of the value of standardization help to understand the rigidities in the requirements of negotiability? Negotiability seems to offer parties a binary choice between opting in or out. Can parties contract for an intermediate arrangement that insulates a future holder of the instrument from a subset of defenses but not others? Would they call it a "negotiable" or "nonnegotiable" instrument, and what effect would either strategy have on information costs of third parties?

In demonstrating the interface between property and contract, Merrill and Smith use as examples the hybrid institutions of bailment, landlord-tenant relations, security interests, and trusts. *The Property/Contract Interface*, at 809–51. Merrill and Smith refer specifically to negotiability in passing. They note that the rigidities of "numerus clausus" standardization give way to the greater freedom of contract as technology lowers the cost of information. They say:

> Notice is arguably easier to furnish (if not to process) when, for example, rights to digital content are being transferred, and notice of restrictions and other features of rights transferred are technologically not difficult to provide. Also fitting this pattern are recent criticisms of negotiability as being superseded by technology [e.g Mann, *supra*]. Negotiability imposes very strict formality requirements precisely in order to reduce the need to measure the reliability of an instrument. But when technology furnishes alternative means of promoting reliance (including lowering the need to measure risk), there is less need for the standardization provided for by the requirements of negotiability.

The Numerus Clausus *Principle*, at 42.

Do technological advances provide a justification for relaxing the formal requirements for negotiability? Do they also undermine the value of negotiability entirely? Suppose a party in Seattle purchases a payment obligation issued by a buyer in New York to a seller in Texas. Under payments law, the Seattle party is a holder in due course only if it takes possession of a negotiable instrument. The instrument must either say explicitly that it is negotiable or it must be expressly payable "to the order of" the Texas seller (and be appropriately negotiated). What is the information transmission capability under modern technology that makes the formal requirements for negotiation redundant?

4. Legal inertia. If there is doubt about the contemporary purpose or relevance of negotiability or the need for physical paper evidence of claims, why is the law slow to adjust? In a later article, *Formalism and the Law of Negotiable Instruments*, 13 Creighton L. Rev. 441 (1979), Gilmore offers a historical explanation for the contemporary law of negotiable instruments. He analyzes the development of bank lending policies, the attitudes of so-called "formalist" judges, and the theories of a few key scholars (such as Karl Llewellyn) to show why some types of commercial paper—which may or may not require the protections of negotiability—remain negotiable. Article 3 of the UCC, he concludes, is a "museum of antiquities." Once codified, the law tends to preserve itself. And once preserved, formalist judges tend to stick to the letter of the law, even when the commercial context that motivated the law has disappeared into the past. If Gilmore's argument had force when he wrote his article in 1979, how much more telling is it today, even after a newly revised Article 3 was promulgated in 1992? We have discussed similar questions of legal inertia in connection with other areas of commercial law. See Chapter 2, Section 2.3, supra.

5. The interplay between legal rules and industry practice. Commercial parties can contract into (or out of) negotiability simply by complying (or not). Payments law, and Article 3 in particular, reduce their cost of doing so by allowing the parties to contract for a full package of negotiability rights by satisfying several simple formal requisites, such as making notes or drafts out to bearer or to the order of the payee. Presumably, law makers have thought that a significant set of parties would want their payment instruments to be negotiable. Scholars cited above have suggested that this may no longer be the case. In a revisionist account of negotiability, James Steven Rogers presents a more extreme argument that negotiability and the holder in due course principle were never fundamental to merchant transactions. Rather, he suggests that they were the invention of legal historians and scholars, an invention that later became codified in the Negotiable Instruments Law in 1896 and subsequently in UCC Article 3. James Steven Rogers, *The Myth of Negotiability*, 31 B.C. L. Rev. 265 (1990). What kind of evidence would indicate that Rogers is correct? What motivation would lead legal historians to invent negotiability when it did not exist? Under what circumstances would merchants find negotiability unnecessary? Rogers predicts that "within another decade or so, this aspect of commercial law may have recovered fully from the myth of negotiability and become again what the classical law of bills and notes actually was—an exogenously defined law of the payment transactions actually used in commerce." *Id.* at 328. What is the effect of a commercial legal regime that is out of line with the needs of business practice? Even if Rogers is correct that the demand for negotiability is less of a historical fact than abstract scholarly creation, what is the harm of providing this option to commercial parties? In light of your thoughts about Note 2 supra, should negotiability be eliminated or revised?

4.3   The Finality Doctrine

A Payments Policy for the Information Age*
RONALD J. MANN

[. . .] The most difficult policy question for consumer payment systems is the question of finality: when does the consumer lose the right to retract the payment from the merchant? For cash payments, the rule is quite simple: if a consumer pays with cash, the "payment" is final at that moment, in the sense that the consumer cannot recover the cash. Of course the consumer might obtain a separate right to payment from the merchant by establishing some separate claim under the contract in question. But that is quite a different thing from a right to retract the payment itself. For cash payments, such a right of retraction obviously is impractical.

For non-cash payment systems, however, the situation is considerably more complicated: the different non-cash payment systems afford consumers differing rights to retract a payment made to a merchant without first proving a failure of the merchant's entitlement to payment under the contract in question. That right of retraction—and the system-to-system differences in its application—is the focus of this article.

Although the landscape is changing rapidly, three systems dominate the current world of non-cash consumer payments in the United States. As of 1998 (the last year for which complete statistics are available), checks still were delivered in 30% of all retail payment transactions, credit cards were used in about 17% of those transactions, and debit cards, although their use is increasing rapidly, were still used for only 5% of transactions. The following sections discuss the finality rules that apply in each of those three systems.

Finality with Checks

The checking system offers the customer what seems at first to be the broadest right to retract payment, a right to stop payment set out in UCC § 4–403(a). The customer's right to stop payment is absolute: the customer can act for any reason it wishes or even, it seems, for no reason at all. The general concept, as the comment to that provision explains, is that the right to stop payment is a basic right that should be incident to a bank account, even if the bank occasionally incurs some loss through the customer's exercise of that right.

However salutary that policy might sound in the abstract, technological developments have so overtaken it that in the contexts most important to consumers it has become almost a dead letter. The difficulty is in the last clause of the relevant sentence of Section 4–403(a), which limits the time within which the customer can send a stop-payment order.

* 93 Geo. L. J. 633 (2005).

Specifically, the notice must be sent at a time that gives the bank a reasonable opportunity to act "before any action by the bank … described in Section 4–303." That section, in turn, describes the points in the life of a check after which a third party cannot prevent a bank from paying a check; the key point for this discussion is the moment when "the bank settles for the item without having a right to revoke the settlement under statute, clearing-house rule, or agreement." Thus, the customer's right (under Section 4–403) to force its bank to stop payment on a check that the customer has written terminates when the bank's obligation to pay the check (normally to a depositary bank or some intermediary that has transmitted the check to the customer's bank) becomes final (under Section 4–303).

The problem for the customer is that current settlement mechanisms are likely to get the check to the customer's bank (the "payor" bank in the UCC's terminology) quite swiftly. For example, if the customer writes the check locally (that is, in the metropolitan area in which the customer's bank is located), the payor bank often would receive the check on the very day that the customer writes it. Because the federal Expedited Funds Availability Act (the EFAA) generally requires depositary banks to allow their customers second-business-day availability for funds deposited by local check, banks into which such checks are deposited have powerful incentives to process those checks rapidly. Responding to that incentive, large banks in major metropolitan areas have developed efficient local clearinghouses that typically get local checks into the hands of the payor bank around midnight of the date on which those checks are deposited. To protect depositary banks against the risk that their depositors will withdraw funds purportedly deposited by check before the depositary banks can learn which checks will be dishonored, the clearinghouses include draconian rules requiring payor banks to provide swift notice of dishonor, normally by early in the afternoon of the next business day (in normal cases, the day after the check is written).

To see what that means to the consumer, consider a typical check, written at ten in the morning to purchase a lawnmower at a store in the consumer's home town, in which the consumer's bank is located. The check might be deposited by the merchant late that afternoon, in which case it probably would reach a clearinghouse that evening and the payor bank sometime in the middle of the night. The payor bank, in turn, would become finally obligated to pay the check if it did not dishonor the check by early the following afternoon. Thus, the consumer's right to stop payment on the check would last little more than 24 hours.

Finality with Credit Cards

That summary might strike the casual reader as unexceptional. After all, when a consumer purchases something with cash, a bout of next-day dissatisfaction will not give the consumer the right to go back to the merchant and force the merchant to return the cash. If the consumer wants to retract the cash from the merchant, the consumer will have to convince the merchant of the validity of the complaint (or, at least, of sufficient sincerity in the complaint that the merchant will disgorge the cash even if it doubts the validity of the complaint). From that perspective, the limited practical effectiveness of the check-using consumer's right to stop payment is not likely to be upsetting.

For the second major non-cash payment system, however, the situation is quite different. If the hypothetical lawnmower purchaser had used a credit card, it would retain, for a period likely to extend several weeks, two overlapping rights to retract payment from the merchant. Those rights both arise not under the state promulgated Uniform Commercial Code—which has little or no application to credit-card transactions—but rather under the Truth-in-Lending Act (TILA), Title I of the federal Consumer Credit Protection Act.

The first appears in TILA § 170(a), which grants cardholders that make purchases with a credit card the right to assert against their issuing banks any defense that they could have asserted against the merchants from whom the purchases were made. In legal substance, Section 170(a) articulates a general anti-holder-in-due-course rule for credit-card transactions. Thus, the section protects the cardholder's defenses even when the claim for payment is transferred from the merchant, from which the purchase was made, to the bank that issued the credit card.

But the practical effect of the rule is somewhat broader, allowing consumers to retract payment from merchants essentially at will. The key is the internal network rules of the major credit-card systems. Under those rules, a card-issuing bank can (and typically does) unwind, or charge back, any credit-card transaction for which a customer disputes its obligation under TILA. Thus, as soon as the cardholder interposes a claim under Section 170(a), the issuing bank charges the transaction back to the bank that processed the transaction for the merchant; that bank, in turn, recovers the funds that it advanced to the merchant for the transaction in question. Thus, if the merchant wants to receive payment for the challenged transaction, the onus is on the merchant to take some action to substantiate its right to payment.

To be sure, Section 170(a) itself is subject to various limitations. For one thing, it does not apply to transactions that occur both outside the state of the cardholder's residence and more than 100 miles from that residence. For another, the right expires when the cardholder pays the charge in question. But even with those limitations, the right seems much more likely to have significance to the consumer than the stop-payment right described above. Assuming a four-week billing cycle, the average bill will not come for at least two weeks after the date of the transaction, and the date on which payment is due will be at least several days after that. Thus, even for cardholders that ordinarily pay their entire bills promptly each month, Section 170(a) affords an effective remedy, at least for local transactions, that extends a period of weeks after the transaction.

Moreover, the statute also provides a broader remedy for cases in which the merchant fails to perform entirely (as in the transaction from which this article began). If the case is one in which the goods or services were not delivered at all, the cardholder's complaint falls within the broad definition of billing errors in TILA § 161. That section is not covered by the geographic limitation in Section 170; thus, it can be applied to transactions of any location. More importantly, billing-error claims need not be presented to the issuing bank for months; the statute requires only that the cardholder provide written notice to the issuer within 60 days after the date on which the creditor sent the relevant statement to the cardholder. And the billing-error claim continues even if the charge in question already has been paid. As with the right to withhold payment under Section 170(a), the ordinary effect of a claim of billing error by a cardholder is a prompt retraction by the issuing bank of the payment that it previously made to the merchant.

* * * * *

In sum, the consumer that reaches for the credit card instead of the checkbook has a much more effective device for pressing subsequent disputes with the merchants from whom the consumer buys retail goods and services.

Finality with Debit Cards

The final consumer payment device of current significance is the debit card. Although the debit card looks much like an ordinary credit card, the cards are distinct in ways that legally are quite significant, largely because the debit card authorizes the merchant (and the issuing bank) to obtain payment directly from a designated bank account of the cardholder. Thus, the payment comes from the cardholder's bank account at the time of the transaction (or, at most, a few days later); unlike the credit card, there is no delay for the transmittal of a statement and payment of the monthly bill by the cardholder.

Like the credit card, the consumer protections for debit cards come from federal law, in this case the Electronic Funds Transfer Act (the EFTA). The rules under the EFTA, however, differ starkly from the rules under TILA. Specifically, the EFTA contains no analogue to either TILA Section 170(a)'s right to withhold payment or to the billing-error rules in TILA Section 161. Thus, payments made with a debit card are just as final as if they had been made with cash.

The Existing Policy Justification: Limiting Imprudent Borrowing

Stepping back from the details of the legal rules discussed above, it is easy to discern an overarching policy justification for the existing framework, rooted in the long-standing concerns of the Anglo–American legal system about the rationality with which borrowers evaluate credit transactions.

From that perspective, the existing rules divide consumer payments into two classes. The first class includes transactions in which the consumer makes substantially contemporaneous payment: cash, checks, and debit cards. Because the consumer at the time of the transaction understands that the payment is being made more or less immediately, the consumer is treated as adequately assessing the wisdom of the payment in question.

Credit cards, however, are quite different from that perspective, because the consumer that purchases with a credit card does not make immediate payment. Rather, although the merchant receives substantially contemporaneous payment, the payment by the consumer is deferred, automatically until a statement is received and, at the consumer's option, more or less indefinitely, as permitted by the strikingly lenient repayment options typical of the modern American credit card.

The Anglo–American legal system has a long tradition of protecting borrowers from the folly of imprudent borrowing. The most famous example surely is the centuries-long effort of English courts to invalidate a series of creditor devices that had the effect of granting mortgage creditors a broad right to take real-estate collateral from borrowers who failed to perform precisely as they had promised at the time of the loan. And that instinct continues to have broad application today, as courts steadily broaden the range of devices to which that invalidating rule extends.

Though it is a bit much to superimpose the insights of modern academic literature on the policy instincts of the medieval English judiciary, that policy finds broad support in the specific concerns of the nascent behavioral economics movement. Scholars in that field often point to an overlapping set of tendencies that generally lead a normal individual to underestimate the likelihood of negative future events that have not previously been salient in the experience of the individual's circle of personal acquaintances. A similar, related phenomenon leads to systematic underestimation of the likelihood that a negative event will happen to the estimating individual, even if the individual accurately understands the overall likelihood of the event. Both of those phenomena are exacerbated by the likelihood that consumers have higher discount rates for events perceived as likely to occur far in the future than they do for events likely to occur in the immediate future. Thus, those scholars would say, it is reasonable to worry that borrowers entering into credit transactions do not adequately weigh the likely harms to them from the difficulties that might come at the time that repayment is due. Also, with a little more subtlety, those who pay in advance might underestimate the likelihood that they will harm their strategic relations with the merchant by agreeing to pay now and receive the subject merchandise (or services) later.

What Policies Does TILA Serve?

As summarized in Part I, the practical impact of TILA is to alter the burden of going forward in a dispute about a retail purchase transaction. Without TILA—that is, in a cash or debit-card transaction—the merchant has the funds and the dissatisfied consumer can obtain satisfaction only through the exercise of some legal remedy or threatened non-legal sanction such as public outcry designed to harm the merchant's reputation. Conversely, if TILA intervenes, then the charge will be removed from the cardholder's account and the funds retracted from the merchant, at least temporarily. Thus, it is the merchant that will have to take action to obtain the disputed funds. In a world of zero transaction costs and perfectly balanced positions, that change would not matter. But the general imbalance in litigating capabilities between merchants and consumers at least suggests the possibility that the shift of the burden of going forward could improve the effectiveness of the system considerably.

At bottom, the consumer with TILA as a weapon is much better positioned in the dispute than the consumer without TILA. And if the improvement of the consumer's position seems appropriate, then the lesson of the earlier sections of this part is obvious: the improvement in the consumer's position should not depend on whether the consumer uses a debit card or a credit card. To put it bluntly, the distinction in consumer protections between credit cards and debit cards rests on a circumstance—the possibility that the consumer will fail to pay the bill at the end of the month—that is irrelevant to the basic transaction between the consumer and the merchant. Thus, it should be irrelevant to the procedures that facilitate the consumer's ability to obtain satisfaction in that transaction.

Collectively, those points are enough to persuade me—in the absence of any countervailing empirical evidence—that the TILA protections reflect a plausible intervention to redress a significant imbalance in litigation capacity. The question, then, is what policies that conclusion implies. Albeit with some trepidation, I propose an extension of those protections to all card-based payment systems.

It would be easy to push that rationale farther—to transactions that use cash or checks—but for several reasons that seems to me unwise. First, the most determined consumer advocate could not credibly claim that the TILA policies should be extended to all transactions and all payment instruments. There obviously is some category of transactions for which a lack of finality—some right to retract funds in the future—is completely incompatible with the expectations of the parties, if only because the purchased object is one for which the likelihood of a dispute is too low to justify such a remedy.... Checks are a harder problem, and thus a closer call, at least as a theoretical matter. On the one hand, consumers that use checks to make purchases often use them in transactions of a size and type quite similar to the transactions in which they use credit cards, with the choice depending more on personal predilection than anything else. Thus, there is every reason to expect that consumers that purchase with checks would benefit as much from a right to retract payment as consumers that purchase with credit cards.

On the other hand, a rule permitting check purchasers to retract payments would be almost as complicated as a rule that benefitted cash purchasers, because it would require substantial revisions to Article 4 of the Uniform Commercial Code and Regulation CC. Perhaps more importantly, checks resemble cash in the sense that the path of a cleared check is not nearly so easily retraced as the path of a completed credit-card transaction.... In sum, I tentatively propose an extension of the protections of TILA to other existing card-based payment systems. Checks and cash would be excluded, but transactions that used debit cards would include rights to interpose defenses to payment for a period of time in the range of 60 days, analogous to the period practically available under current TILA-based credit-card practices.

Better Than Cash? Global Proliferation of Payment Cards and Consumer Protection Policy*

ARNOLD S. ROSENBERG

Because of the global spread of payment cards, governments throughout the world need to adopt new laws protecting consumers who use them. The billions of people with low to moderate incomes who are being hurled from a cash economy into the era of electronic payments in emerging economies by the proliferation of debit and prepaid cards are particularly vulnerable to abuses by banks and merchants. Private lawmaking by Visa, MasterCard et al. will not protect consumers because the payment card associations' economic incentive is to attract merchants to make the necessary investment in equipment to be able to accept payment cards.

There is a risk that nations with emerging economies will uncritically emulate regimes of consumer protection adopted in the United States and Europe. These regimes lack a consistent conceptual foundation and fail to address problems—such as bank fees, access to banking services, and payment system insolvency—that are poorly addressed in developed countries if they are addressed at all. For example, debit and prepaid card transactions are both convenient means of obtaining cash and a substitute for cash, but this does not justify denying chargeback rights to

* 44 COLUM. J. TRANSNAT'L L. 520 (2006).

consumers who use debit and prepaid cards as if they had paid in cash
[. . .]

While the lack of anonymity inherent in the use of payment cards
entails risks for consumer privacy, it also makes possible greater transparency in payment systems. As billions of vulnerable consumers become
connected to electronic payment systems, the chargeback systems regulated and operated by Visa and other card networks become a possible
means of protecting them from merchant misconduct. Legislation should
be adopted requiring payment card associations such as Visa and Master-
Card not only to make their rules public—rules that they currently
refuse to disclose on the theory that they are "trade secrets"—but also
to compile chargeback data regarding specific merchants and make it
available to consumers, in the manner that eBay publicizes the complaint experience of its merchants.

Consumer problems associated with payment card use have changed
in the twenty or thirty years since developing countries established their
schemes of consumer protection law. For example, today, fees and
charges imposed on consumers for payment card services are one of the
most prolific sources of consumer complaints, yet they are not generally
regulated by existing laws except through the imposition of disclosure
requirements that are largely ineffective [. . .] Developing countries
newly inundated with payment cards confront problems of consumer
protection that differ in some respects from the problems experienced in
developed countries. Developing countries therefore should be wary of
emulating these schemes, which in many respects are aimed at the kinds
of abuses that predominated at another time and in another place.

Debit, Credit, and Charge Cards

Debit cards, sometimes issued as "ATM cards," "check cards,"
"cash cards,"or "Smart Cards" are proliferating worldwide at a stagger-
ing rate. Debit cards are distinguished from credit cards and charge
cards in that the use of a debit card results in a direct debit to the user's
bank account, while the use of a credit card or charge card results in an
extension of credit to the cardholder.

Although the volume of credit card transactions has grown, in 2003
debit cards overtook credit cards in aggregate dollar volume worldwide
at Visa, by far the largest of the payment card networks, representing
about half of the global payment card market. Debit cards are now the
dominant card-based payment system in most countries other than the
United States, Canada, and Japan, and the most widely used non-cash
consumer payment system in the world. Even in the United States, debit
card transactions have risen precipitously, and now represent a higher
percentage of Visa point-of-sale (POS) transactions than credit cards.

Debit and credit card transactions are governed by a series of
contracts. The underlying contract between merchant and consumer

gives rise to the payment obligation and authorizes the merchant to draw funds from the consumer's bank account to satisfy it. The consumer-card issuer contract governs the obligation of the bank to honor an authorized order to pay funds from the consumer's account. The merchant-acquirer contract governs the rights of the merchant to be credited with funds by the merchant acquirer once the merchant presents the transaction to the merchant acquirer, and the right of the merchant acquirer to deduct a fee, called a "discount." The merchant transfers its rights against the consumer to the merchant acquirer, who then transfers these rights to the card issuer in exchange for payment in accordance with payment card association rules that contractually bind both banks as association members. The card issuer then debits the consumer's account for the authorized amount in accordance with the payment order and its contract with the consumer.

The costs of processing payment card transactions generally are borne by merchants through discount fees paid per transaction to their merchant acquirers. The merchant acquirers are the merchant's banks, members of Visa, MasterCard, or another card association, which either own—as in the case of Chase—or are part of a bank association affiliated with, a processing entity, the largest of which in the United States is First Data Corporation. These banks are called "merchant acquirers" because by contracting with the merchant to accept payment through Visa or MasterCard they are said to have "acquired" the merchant for the Visa or MasterCard association.

Visa, the largest payment card network, is an association of banks governed by a common set of bylaws and operating regulations. It is organized as the Visa International association, comprised of six regional entities, the largest of which is Visa U.S.A., Inc. Each regional entity is owned by member banks in the region. Worldwide, Visa has about 21,000 member banks. Banks may join as card issuers, merchant acquirers, or both. However, the merchant acquirer business, as a practical matter, is concentrated in a few large banks while many smaller banks join so they can issue payment cards with the Visa logo. The regional entities provide member banks with clearing and settlement facilities for payment card transactions within their region and also with security technology and procedures. The MasterCard association has a structure similar to Visa's.

So-called "private label" credit cards are cards that can only be used at a particular retailer. These are common in the developing world at present, but have become a minor part of the American card market. Private label credit cards were common in the United States in the 1960s and 1970s, but today most credit cards offered by American retailers to their customers bear the Visa or MasterCard logo and therefore are usable anywhere that accepts Visa or MasterCard cards.

Debit cards are categorized as either personal identification number (PIN) debit, also called "online" debit, or signature debit, also called "offline." PIN debit card transactions require entry of a PIN into a keypad and normally clear through interbank networks such as the Star and Cirrus systems. Signature debit cards are mainly issued in the United States by Visa and MasterCard member banks and bear the Visa or MasterCard logo. In most other countries, such as Canada, all debit cards are PIN-based. A signature is required, as with a credit card.

Although most consumers do not know it, there are significant differences between the two types of debit cards. PIN debit card transactions clear and are debited to the consumer's bank account almost instantaneously. They are real-time transactions. In the United States, the consumer often will be charged a fee by her bank for using another bank's or a merchant's facilities to consummate the PIN debit transaction. Such fees are uncommon in many other countries.

Signature debit transactions, like most checks, take two to three days to clear and to be posted to the consumer's bank account. They are riskier for the merchant, who could go unpaid if during those two to three days the consumer closes or depletes his bank account. However, signature debit is favored by American banks, which receive higher fees from merchants, paid in the form of discounts from what is credited to the merchant's account, than they do in PIN debit transactions. In contrast, merchants benefit from PIN debit in the form of lower discounts, but American consumers have resisted PIN debit due to the fees passed on to them by merchants and banks.

Many newer debit cards are actually "Smart Cards." Rather than a magnetic strip, Smart Cards contain a microchip. This makes them capable of storing a greater volume of data and performing multiple functions. Smart Cards can have both debit and credit functions, of which the consumer can choose either at the point of sale. They can collect, utilize, and send data about purchases, benefit entitlements, and other information.

For the card issuer, Smart Cards represent an additional source of information about the consumer and a possible source of additional revenue through the use or sale of that information. For the consumer, there is a risk of loss of privacy in the collection of this information. This risk is not new; the ability to collect information about the consumer proved to be a selling point when Visa and MasterCard were building their bank networks in the United States in the 1970s. The inability to share customer information with other banks was one reason that, in the late 1960s, Bank of America ceded control of its BankAmericard franchise network, the predecessor of Visa, to what became the Visa International association.

Payroll, Stored Value, and Other Prepaid Cards

In a massive change that has accelerated during the past few years, instead of cash, millions of employees from Russia to Mexico—and increasingly in the United States—are now paid through prepaid cards called "payroll cards," which they can swipe at a store to make a purchase and have the price debited from an account funded by wages deposited by their employer.

Prepaid cards are not limited to payroll cards, but include phone cards, gift cards, benefit cards, and travel cards, among others. Prepaid cards also are increasingly used to pay public benefits, especially in the many countries in which checks are rarely used as a method of payment. Prepaid cards may be prepaid debit cards, the use of which results in a debit to a bank account opened for the benefit of the cardholder (e.g., by an employer), or they may be "stored value cards" in which value is stored on the card itself. While some prepaid cards—so-called "closed loop" cards, including most gift and phone cards—are usable only for purchases from a particular retailer or service provider, prepaid cards are increasingly network-branded "open loop" cards, transactions with which are processed through Visa, MasterCard, and other payment card networks.

Because prepaid cards do not require either creditworthiness or bank accounts, they are proliferating especially in areas such as Africa and parts of Latin America where relatively few people have bank accounts. Prepaid debit and stored value cards are a king of "poor man's credit card," allowing access to electronic payments networks for those who cannot qualify for credit or lack bank accounts. Even in the United States, prepaid phone cards have become popular and payroll cards are catching on as a way to pay wages to the many, usually low-income employees who lack a bank account, sometimes referred to as "the unbanked."

The Global Trend Toward Debit and Prepaid Cards

Several factors have contributed to the rise of the debit card and the prepaid card. Most developing countries never acquired the credit card habit. They lack the credit information and reporting systems necessary to support credit cards, and relatively few of their citizens have sufficient demonstrable income to qualify for credit. While computer use and e-commerce are growing in developing countries, they remain the domain of a small percentage of those populations. As a result, while the "Plastic Revolution" takes hold in developing countries like China, Brazil, and Mexico, it is not credit cards but debit and prepaid cards that are beginning to transform the cash economies of those countries.

The trend toward debit and prepaid card use is part of what some economists have erroneously called a trend toward "cashlessness." In fact, debit cards and many prepaid cards are not only a substitute for cash, but also a convenient means of obtaining it at an ATM. ATMs, which are already ubiquitous in developed countries, are rapidly spreading through the developing world. Cash payments still amount to an estimated seventy to 90% of global retail payment volume, though they are low in value compared to card transactions. In recent years, the growth in volume of debit card transactions has outpaced that of credit cards, indicating that payment cards—even credit cards—are primarily used as a cheap means of funds transfer rather than for credit purposes. Rather than curtail the use of cash, the spread of debit cards has revitalized cash economies by making cash more readily available.

Debit cards and "open loop" prepaid cards can be used either at ATMs or at the point-of-sale. Other ways by which consumers access and transfer funds electronically include automated clearing house (ACH) payments, home banking, electronic giros (e-giro) in Europe and parts of Asia, and internet-based "electronic cash." However, none of these other methods has approached debit cards in the volume or share of transactions, nor in worldwide growth.

Credit card use is not growing nearly as rapidly as debit card use. Globally, the ability to finance a purchase and carry a balance on a credit card seems to hold limited appeal, because most consumers use payment cards—even credit cards—for convenience, as a cash substitute or a way to obtain cash, not as a loan. Available data show that card use in retail payments has grown primarily at the expense of cash. This is even true in the United States, where of the purchases of goods and services for personal consumption in 1996, 57% were made by checks, 21% with cash, and 22% with payment cards. In 1984, however, 58% of purchases of goods and services for personal consumption were made with checks, 36% with cash, and only 6% with cards. While American consumers persist in the habit of maintaining large credit card balances and resist the use of debit cards for purchases, they remain an anomaly compared to consumers in most other countries.

The stakes involved in the proliferation of debit and prepaid cards may be much greater than the fees generated by payment card transactions. Recent studies suggest that the rise in mobile telecommunications and electronic payments each will generate an economic "growth dividend" in the developing world of about 0.6% of GDP. Mobile telephone service providers may also emerge as serious competition for banks and money remitters, as prepaid phone cards make it possible for consumers to pay for goods and services, and to transfer funds, using short mobile phone messages rather than checks, credit cards, wire transfers, and other services offered by traditional financial institutions. Technology is emerging in the economically developed world for the use of mobile phones to make payments at checkout counters. Mobile payments may become a common method to circumvent the cash register.

Despite the explosive growth in debit and prepaid cards, and to a lesser extent, in credit cards, few jurisdictions outside the United States, Canada, and the European Union have enacted consumer protection laws regulating the rights of card users with respect to card issuers or merchants. Within the United States, Canada, and the European Union, issues such as the reversibility of consumer transactions and the allocation of losses caused by unauthorized transactions are resolved in ways that are inconsistent and analytically unsatisfactory, unduly influenced by legal regimes designed to regulate the use of different payment technologies twenty or thirty years ago. . . .

Transparency: A Proposal

Transparency in the chargeback system could play an important role in redressing the existing imbalance of leverage between consumer and merchant. Private lawmaking by card associations has rejected transparency, yet policy makers seem to have given little thought to legislation that would mandate a degree of transparency for the benefit of consumers.

Private lawmaking by payment card associations has eschewed transparency for at least two reasons. First, competition for merchants is more keen than competition for consumers, especially in global markets in which payment cards are proliferating faster than merchants equipped to accept them. Second, as behavioral economists have observed, consumers tend not to consider the possibility of something going wrong at the time when they enter into a transaction, let alone when they apply for a payment card that will facilitate future transactions. Therefore, a transparent system for resolving disputes would not confer any significant advantage on card issuers in competing for consumer accounts.

The chargeback system lacks transparency in two particularly important respects. First, the rules of the system, and the right to participate in chargeback arbitrations, are open only to card association members. Second, and perhaps more importantly, card associations, merchant acquirers, and card issuers keep data about the chargeback experience of individual merchants confidential [. . .] Card associations compete, through merchant acquirers, for merchant memberships. Merchants presumably prefer to keep negative information about themselves confidential. Card associations therefore have an interest in promising merchants that they will keep chargeback information secret from the public.

Compare the card associations' incentives with those of eBay, the online auction service. eBay posts data about online merchants, including consumer ratings and complaints, that is available to consumers when they make a purchase. Online merchants have to overcome the remoteness of the transaction in gaining consumers' trust because consumers often must rely on a merchant's representations about merchandise they cannot hold in their hands even though they are unfamiliar with the merchant. eBay, anticipating this problem, chose to require merchants to consent to release of data about them.

Visa and MasterCard could compile the same data as eBay, but they do not, or, at least, they do not make such data accessible to the public. It is in consumers' interests to have access to such information. Most merchants would ultimately benefit from ratings based on chargeback experiences, even if they do not perceive the release of the information positively, because most have relatively few complaints [. . .]

Another means of deterring merchant misconduct would be experience rating of the discounts that are deducted from what merchants collect from credit and debit card issuers. Currently, industry practice is to standardize discount rates depending on whether the merchant engages in remote transactions, in which the card is not presented by the customer. Mail order-telephone order (MOTO) and Internet merchants, now collectively called "card-not-present" or "MO/TO/ECI" merchants, are at high risk for unauthorized charges and, hence, incur a higher discount rate than the roughly 1.6% discount that is deducted from what "card-present" merchants receive from card issuers for transactions with customers using credit and debit cards.

An alternative would be to set discount rates according to a chargeback experience rating system. Issuers and merchant acquirers would charge a higher discount rate to merchants that have a relatively high incidence of certain types of chargebacks that may indicate misconduct. The chargeback reason code would determine the types of chargebacks that would count in setting discount rates.

NOTES

1. Negotiability and the internet. In Section 4.2, we introduced the concept of negotiability. While negotiability has traditionally required a physical document, does the principle still have some application in largely electronic systems of payment? After having read about the basic mechanics of these systems, how would one apply negotiability to them? Are the holder in due course rules still necessary given technological advances? In short, isn't it the case that negotiability is relevant only so long as payment is not final? Negotiability and the HDC rules are designed, after all, to give a third party purchaser of commercial paper the same rights to receive payment as the original payee. But once payment has been made and it is final, then the paper obligation is extinguished along with the debt which has been "paid." Thus, negotiability and the HDC doctrine may have continued relevance in the case of negotiable notes, where credit is extended, but not in the case of check substitutes where payment is final almost immediately. In short, the need to make checks negotiable was a response to the technological limitations of the paper system. But with the advent of new payment systems, the negotiability concept loses much of its relevance.

2.   Finality and efficient litigation burdens. The time when a payment becomes "final" determines when the payor loses her right to retract payment in response to a grievance against the payor—such as a buyer who has paid for a good she claims is defective. Once the payment is final, the buyer must pursue other means, notably legal action to recover the payment or compensation for any harm. While valuable to the buyer, this right is costly to the seller. In particular, a seller who has fully performed his obligations and has been paid may still need to pursue legal action against a buyer who has withdrawn payment before it becomes final on the basis of a trumped-up excuse. Whether finality is delayed or immediate upon payment determines who must sue whom in the event of a dispute, and, accordingly, who must bear the burden of proof. Thus, all things equal, the buyer is likely to prefer a delayed time for finality and the seller is likely to prefer immediate finality. If left to bargain explicitly over finality, the seller may offer delayed finality in return for a higher contract price. One might predict in these circumstances that the parties will defer finality to the degree it is efficient for the seller to bear the burden of proof in any dispute. In short, a delayed finality is akin to a short-lived money-back warranty of performance. For a discussion of the effects of contract terms on litigation burden allocations, *see* Robert E. Scott & George G. Triantis, *Anticipating Litigation in Contract Design*, 115 Yale L. J. 814 (2006).

In addition to the burden of proof, the plaintiff also bears the risk that the other party will become insolvent before judgment is obtained. The risk of insolvency is clearly on the seller in the case where the buyer stops payment on a check. But does the same analysis apply to a credit card payment? Assume that the buyer pays by credit card, then disputes the charge, and the seller ultimately prevails in court. Can the seller recover directly from the credit card issuer (who must then file a claim against the buyer in a bankruptcy proceeding)?

3.   Finality in modern payments. An increasing proportion of transactions are for services and the internet has accelerated this trend by, for example, facilitating the sale and transfer of information and technology. As we noted in Section 4.2, the right of credit card holders to charge back and effectively cancel payment is a problem in service transactions because the card holder will usually have consumed the service and appropriated the value. Service providers who are concerned about this behavior might require cash payment. Internet service providers do not have this option because they rely on electronic payment by credit card. A number of entrepreneurs have attempted to fill the gap through "cash substitutes." For example, Duocash used long-distance phone cards to facilitate purchases on the internet. The customer at the seller's web site would type in the code found on his prepaid card. Duocash would then bill the card issuer and the issuer would accordingly reduce the value remaining on the customer's card.

Despite the apparent advantage of combining electronic payment with finality, Duocash was used in a narrow segment of internet commerce: "adult entertainment", where it yielded the added advantage of anonymity. "The [internet adult entertainment] industry has a high percentage of "chargebacks", or cancellations by credit card holders who claim that they did not authorize a purchase. In many cases, site owners complain, the credit card holder did in fact use his own credit card on a late-night-pornography cruise but cancelled the charge in the remorse of the day; others cancel when their spouses confront them with the strange charges, Mr. Fancher of Duocash said." John Schwartz, *New Economy: The steamy side of the Internet, pervasive and resilient to recession, is the underpinning of a new online cash venture*, The New York Times, April 9, 2001 (Late edition-Final), page C–4.

4. Evaluating diverse finality terms in payment mechanisms. Ronald Mann criticizes the variation in finality terms among checks, credit cards and debit cards. One might respond that the current scheme provides parties with the choice among different finality periods during which the payor can exercise self-help by retracting payment. The parties can thereby tailor the finality term to their circumstances, as described in Note 2 above. Mann's proposal to unify the terms across mechanisms would eliminate this menu.

Yet, recall from Section 4.2 that parties can opt easily only for a package of negotiability provisions; tailoring specific provisions is more complicated. Similarly, the choice among checks, credit cards and debit cards is among packages of terms, and it is difficult for the parties to mix and match. Therefore, while it may be valuable to have a "menu" of finality terms, does the packaging make sense? Recall, for example, the Merrill and Smith argument concerning the optimal standardization of property rights. Given the benefits of standardization, does it make sense for credit cards to accompany delayed finality and debit cards not to? After all, the "credit" being extended in the former case is by the credit card issuer, not the merchant. The merchant may value highly immediate finality because, for instance, he is selling a service that is immediately consumed. Yet, the buyer may not be able to pay for the service without credit from the card issuer. As a practical matter, the seller and buyer are unlikely to be able to tailor their respective agreements with the card issuer to reach the optimal packaging of rights.

As Mann indicates, credit cards continue to dominate debit cards as a payment mechanism in consumer transactions in the United States. Does this reflect a preference among merchants and consumers for delayed finality? Why do you suppose, as Rosenberg indicates, that debit cards and other similar products are more popular than credit cards in other countries, especially in developing economies? Is this just an example of historical path dependence or does it reflect differences in credit worthiness among the pool of consumers? What would be the effect of a federal regulation that restricts the ability of merchants to offer lower prices for cash payment than credit transactions? Assume a customer intends to pay the bill on his credit card in full when it is received and isn't using extended credit beyond the due date of the initial statement. Would these transactions still be treated as "loans" such that TILA would apply? Assuming that TILA does apply to this transaction, is the rationale for the lack of finality offered by Mann persuasive? Given the TILA rules, should merchants charge consumers more for using credit cards?

5.   "Finality" in commercial letters of credit. The ability of the buyer to impede final payment has long been an issue in sales between commercial parties across long distances because of the time it takes for goods to be shipped from seller to buyer. The buyer may hesitate to make a final payment before ensuring that the goods conform to her expectations and the seller does not want to send the goods as long as the buyer can retract her payment. Commercial letters of credit are often the form of payment in these transactions and the central feature of letters of credit is the *independence principle*. The bank's obligations on the letter of credit is entirely independent of the other contractual obligations on the underlying transaction. A letter of credit requires that the beneficiary, usually the seller receiving the payment, present certain documents to the issuer of the letter, usually a bank, in order for the bank to honor the letter. Contingent on the presentation of these documents, the buyer's payment is final at the time the letter of credit is issued and delivered to the seller. Often the documents are those that the carrier issues to acknowledge receipt of the goods. The buyer is therefore assured that payment will not be made until the goods are shipped.

The standard of compliance for a letter of credit determines the types of documents that must be presented and how closely they must conform to the documents specified in the letter. Most modern courts require strict compliance with the terms of a letter of credit. See, e.g., *American Coleman v. Intrawest Bank*, 887 F.2d 1382 (10th Cir. 1989). UCC § 5–108(e) states that "[a]n issuer shall observe standard practice of financial institutions that regularly issue letters of credit. Determination of the issuer's observance of the standard practice is a matter of interpretation for the court." Comment 1 elaborates this point:

> Strict compliance does not mean slavish conformity to the terms of the letter of credit. By adopting standard practice as a way of measuring strict compliance, this article indorses the conclusion of . . . [cited cases] holding that literal compliance is not required.

Thus, what may appear to be a bright line rule of strict compliance, at least in form, turns out to be a broad standard in its application. The motivation for determining compliance with a standard rather than a rule is to prevent issuers (and buyers) from escaping legitimate payment obligations on the basis of trivial defects. On the other hand, bright line rules are said to enhance ex ante predictability; is such predictability jeopardized by the rise of standards in letter of credit law? How important is predictability in this context? Is the hoped-for improvement in accuracy worth the reduction in predictability? And, given the prominent role of financial institutions as issuers of letters of credit, does legal enforcement play a significant role in the first place? *See* 3 James J. White & Robert Summers, Uniform Commercial Code (Prac. ed.) § 26–5, at 140–41.

6.   The durability of existing payment systems. Despite promises of "electronic money" and the creation of entirely different payment mechanism to replace credit cards, debit cards and checks, the new technology largely piggy-backs on these mechanisms rather than offering an entirely

new payment product. In *Regulating Internet Payment Intermediaries*, 82
Tex. L. Rev. 681 (2004), Ronald Mann explains that

> The Internet has produced significant changes in many aspects of
> commercial interaction. The rise of Internet retailers is one of the
> most obvious changes, but oddly enough the overwhelming majority
> of commercial transactions facilitated by the Internet use a conven-
> tional payment system. Thus, even in 2002, shoppers made at least
> eighty percent of Internet purchases with credit cards. To many
> observers, this figure has come as a surprise. The early days of the
> Internet heralded a variety of proposals for entirely new payment
> systems—generically described as electronic money—that would use
> wholly electronic tokens that consumers could issue, transfer, and
> redeem. But years later, no electronic-money system has gained a
> significant role in commerce.
>
> The continuing maturation of the Internet, however, has brought
> significant changes to the methods by which individuals make
> payments. Person-to-person (P2P) systems like PayPal now make
> hundreds of millions of payments a year between individuals. The
> most common purpose is to facilitate the purchase of items at
> Internet auctions, but increasingly P2P transfers are used to trans-
> fer funds overseas. Less far along, but gaining transactions rapidly,
> are a variety of systems for electronic bill presentment and payment
> (EBPP). Interestingly, both of these developments follow a less
> ambitious path than the still-hypothetical electronic-money systems:
> they involve the use of intermediaries to "piggyback" on existing
> systems to provide payment. Thus, in essence, they use the technol-
> ogy of the Web site to facilitate the use of conventional payment
> networks.

Id.

What explains the durability of the bank credit card? We consider, in
Note 7 below, whether government regulation can affect the development of
new payment mechanisms. Are there other non-regulatory forces that might
slow the acceptance of new technologies?

7. Should new payment technologies be subject to new regulation?
Since the commercial emergence of the internet in the 1990s, legal scholars
have debated whether new laws were called for to address novel issues raised
by the technology or whether existing legal principles could readily be
applied to them by courts. A similar set of questions are raised by the new
payment systems: are they covered by existing regulation, is there a need for
a new set of rules to govern them and if so, what should they be?

In *Internet Payment Systems: Legal Issues Facing Business, Consumers
and Payment Service Providers*, 6 Comm. Law Conspectus 11 (1998), Robert
Stankey argues that internet payments are not unregulated as commonly
believed. He suggests, however, that existing laws, regulations, and contract
rules need to be adapted to meet the needs of the new systems. Jeffrey Taft,
on the other hand, suggests in *An Overview of the Electronic Fund Transfer*

Act and Regulation E and Their Application to E–Commerce, 57 Cons. Fin. L.Q. Rep. 198 (2003), that the application of Regulation E to these new payment services is still an open question. Account aggregation and EBPP systems present good examples of internet payment activities which are partially governed by a variety of laws but which have regulatory gaps. In *Regulating Internet Payment Intermediaries*, supra, Ronald Mann addresses the specific problem of nonbank intermediaries who offer account aggregation and EBPP services as these intermediaries fall outside of current banking regulations. Mann considers three possibilities for addressing these currently unregulated entities: do nothing, directly regulate intermediaries, or regulate intermediaries through banks. What are the advantages and disadvantages to each approach? Mann concludes that:

> It is not plausible at this stage to offer a definitive "answer" to the problem of regulatory strategy that this Article addresses. For one thing, the industries are developing and changing so rapidly that the object of inquiry is a moving target. For another, information about how the systems in fact operate is scarce, and it is difficult to assess the weight of the competing concerns. We know next to nothing about the rates of fraud and error in these systems, the culture of data privacy in the industry, and the degree of compliance with regulatory responsibilities. Finally, because the possible risks of allowing unregulated access to consumer deposit accounts and of hasty intervention in a fluid competitive situation are not readily balanced against each other, an element of frank judgment is necessary to resolve a conflict between them.

Id. at 709.

How should the law react to rapid technological change? Is it a justification for leaving these new payment systems largely unregulated or for increased use of flexible standards rather than rules? Consider two objectives of payments regulation: protecting consumers and promoting payment efficiency. Do the new technologies raise additional concerns about consumer vulnerability or do they ameliorate old ones. For example, are consumers using new mechanisms likely to be more sophisticated than those using established ones? As Mann asks in the foregoing excerpt, do policy makers have sufficient information and experience to know how to achieve the desirable balance in the protection of consumers? Will regulation stifle innovation? Do the providers of these novel instruments have a greater incentive to regulate themselves in order to avoid governmental interference? Some have also argued that government involvement is necessary to build consumer confidence in certain payment technologies. *See* Sarah Jane Hughes, *A Case For Regulating Cyberpayments*, 51 Admin. L. Rev. 809 (1999). Many ventures were established to provide electronic money failed. Checks and conventional credit cards continue to occupy a dominant position in payments. Should the government be taking any measures to encourage the transition to more efficient, newer systems?

4.4   Allocating the Risk of Loss, Theft, and Fraud

A Theory of Loss Allocation for Consumer Payments*

ROBERT D. COOTER and **EDWARD L. RUBIN**

Every payment instrument imposes a variety of costs on the parties that use it. These costs include the financial institution's costs in operating the system, which the institution will generally transfer to its customers as a direct or indirect charge; the customer's costs of using the instrument, such as the time and expense spent getting to a financial institution; and the costs imposed by fraud, forgery, and error losses, the topic of the present discussion. All these costs belong to the economic category of 'transaction costs' because they are attached to an underlying transaction. This underlying transaction—typically an exchange of goods or services for value—is beneficial to both parties, but the transaction costs reduce the value of the exchange, and both parties to the exchange will want to minimize them. [. . .]

The Loss Spreading Principle

A basic characteristic of economic actors is their attitude toward risk. Most people are risk averse: when facing a possible loss, they will pay more than the loss's average value to eliminate the risk of it. In contrast, a risk neutral person places a value on risk equal to the loss's average value.

Whenever one person can bear risk at a lower cost than another, there is an opportunity for a mutually beneficial exchange, because risk averse people will pay risk neutral people to assume the risk of loss. For example, if there is a probability of one in one thousand of suffering a forgery loss of $10,000, then a risk averse consumer will pay more than $10 for the financial institution to assume it; in contrast, if the financial institution is risk neutral, it can profitably assume the risk if it is paid any amount greater than $10, plus a charge to cover the administrative costs.

Two conditions affecting a party's ability to achieve risk neutrality are the relative size of the loss and the party's ability to spread it. Most decision makers are risk neutral toward losses that are small in proportion to their wealth, and risk averse toward losses that are relatively large. In addition, financial institutions, unlike consumers, can achieve complete risk neutrality by spreading the resulting losses across their entire group of customers. To be spread, the losses must be sufficiently small and occur frequently enough to be predictable. For example, a financial institution often cannot know whether specific payment instruments are forged, but because it engages in a large number of transac-

---

* 66 Texas L. Rev. 63, 67–81, 84–86 (1987).

tions, it can accurately predict the number of forgeries that will occur in a given year. Once the institution makes that prediction, it can pass on the cost to its customers as a charge for its service, just as it passes on the cost of paying tellers or encoding checks.

These considerations suggest the first principle of efficient payment law, which is frequently called the loss spreading principle: assign liability for a loss to the party that can achieve risk neutrality at the lowest cost. In general, the party that can achieve risk neutrality at the lowest cost is the one that has greater economic resources and is in a position to spread the loss most effectively. This principle, therefore, suggests that liability for losses should fall on financial institutions rather than on individual consumers. The forgery or alteration of a single payment item, like a check, can involve a significant proportion of an individual's wealth, but will typically constitute an insignificant loss for a financial institution. Moreover, the institution can predict the total volume of its losses and spread them over a large group of consumers, whereas consumers will generally end up bearing the entire loss themselves.

The Loss Reduction Principle

Independent of their ability to spread payment losses, consumers and financial institutions often have the ability to reduce these losses, and one of them can often do so at less cost than the other. Efficiency requires that the legal rules create incentives for such loss reduction. The standard means for creating legal incentives is the assignment of liability, which suggests the loss reduction principle: an efficient legal system assigns liability to the party that can reduce losses at the lowest cost.

This principle is much more complex than the loss spreading principle. Loss spreading presumes that a loss already has occurred and assigns liability to the party that can more effectively spread it, but the loss reduction principle assigns liability for the more complex purpose of affecting human behavior. It thus raises empirical questions about the effectiveness of liability rules, adds a dynamic element because behavior changes over time, and produces a variety of moral concerns about the proper standards of behavior. In discussing these issues, this Article distinguishes four distinct elements of the principle's operation: precaution, innovation, responsiveness, and learning.

Consumers and financial institutions often can reduce payment losses by taking the precautions that are presently available to them. Consumers can do so through ordinary prudence and care in making payments, and financial institutions can reduce losses through internal measures similar to quality control in manufacturing. Precautions, however, entail costs in money, time, and effort, which discourage consumers and financial institutions from undertaking them. Legal rules that impose liability on consumers or financial institutions force them to include this potential liability in their calculus of costs, and thus weigh it against the cost of precaution. In economic terms, the liable party internalizes the social value of the precaution. To achieve internalization at the most efficient level, payment rules must assign liability to the party who, on the basis of its position in the process, is able to take precaution against the loss at the lowest cost.

This generalization encounters an immediate difficulty when more than one party can take precaution. If liability falls upon only one party, how can the liability rules motivate other parties to take precaution as well? This phenomenon is an example of the 'paradox of compensation,' which afflicts no-fault rules in all areas of law. Holding one party strictly liable for a loss erodes the other party's incentive to take precaution and to refrain from any action that would increase the loss. Economic analysis suggests that fault-based liability rules are a solution to this paradox. Any fault rule, including simple negligence, negligence with a contributory negligence defense, and comparative negligence, will motivate one party to satisfy the legal standard of fault in order to avoid liability, while inducing the other party to take precaution because it must bear any residual responsibility for the loss. Theoretically, if the legal standard of fault is set at the efficient level of precaution, then fault rules provide incentives for more than one party to take precaution, and will be preferable to strict liability or no liability rules in situations of bilateral precaution—situations in which more than one party can take precaution or restrain reliance at low cost [. . .]

Does the loss reduction principle, like the loss spreading principle, systematically favor one class of participants in the payment system over another? The answer will depend upon the relative importance of the principle's four elements—precaution, innovation, responsiveness, and learning. The precaution element is unrelated to the size and nature of the party; its determining factor is the party's position in the payment transaction. For example, when a bank incorrectly encodes the magnetic numbers on the bottom of a check, which results in an overpayment, the bank is clearly in the best position to prevent the loss, because check encoding does not involve consumers at all. On the other hand, a consumer is in the best position to avoid the loss that results when he gives a check to an impostor, who then cashes it and absconds with the proceeds.

The innovation element, however, modifies the effect of the precaution element. Innovations such as credit cards, wire transfers, automated clearinghouses, and automated teller machines have transformed the entire payment system in recent years, and point of sale systems and home banking are likely to produce further changes in the coming decades. Concurrently, researchers are developing a variety of technological mechanisms designed to reduce fraud losses, including the 'smart' card, signature dynamics, and fingerprint or finger-length recognition systems. All of this activity is being carried out by financial institutions: it is a rare individual who invests a few million dollars in the development of an innovative method to prevent check fraud. Payment rules that assign liability to financial institutions, therefore, act as an incentive for the continued development of anti-fraud innovations. While the course of technological innovation is unpredictable and future innovations could alter the situation, the innovation element presently favors the imposition of liability for payment losses on financial institutions.

The responsiveness element of loss reduction, like the innovation element, correlates with the size and nature of the party, particularly for losses that arise infrequently and involve esoteric laws. Because individual consumers engage in a very small number of payment system transactions relative to the average financial institution, consumers who behave rationally in economic terms are often ignorant of the details of payment law, whereas ignorance is irrational for financial institutions. Financial institutions, consequently, are more likely than consumers to respond to legal incentives. Indeed, the ignorance of consumers, which creates market failure and justifies legal intervention in the first place, also suggests that consumers will be unresponsive to liability rules designed to remedy that market failure[...]

The Loss Imposition Principle

The loss spreading and loss reduction principles indicate the party to which payment rules can most efficiently assign liability. The third principle in establishing an efficient payment law, the loss imposition principle, concerns the enforcement of this assigned liability. The enforcement process turns the law from a set of legal rules into a series of actual monetary transfers. Liability may be enforced through civil suits, criminal trials, or administrative proceedings, as well as through the many informal devices for settling disputes. One feature that all these mechanisms share is that they are costly; they represent a deadweight loss to the participants in the payment system. To achieve efficiency, therefore, the enforcement process should be as inexpensive as possible.

The most inexpensive approach to loss imposition would be to allow the losses to fall where they may. When a dispute arises over a payment, the initial loss generally falls upon the creditor—the party that advanced money to another. Allowing liability to rest on the party that bears the initial loss completely avoids the costs of enforcement. But this approach may result in inefficient loss spreading and loss reduction because the creditor is not necessarily the best party to spread losses or to take the actions required to avoid them.

If reallocating the loss is required for increased efficiency, then the most desirable enforcement process is the one that will shift liability as cheaply as possible from the creditor to the party that should suffer the final loss. This goal can be achieved by fashioning simple, clear, and decisive liability rules. Such rules discourage people from bringing merit-less lawsuits by decreasing the law's level of ambiguity. In addition, they simplify court proceedings and lower litigation costs by decreasing the number of issues, the amount of relevant evidence, the number of required court appearances, and the amount of prelitigation legal counseling. The mechanisms that will generate simple, clear, and decisive liability rules, and thus achieve these advantages, are familiar: strict liability rather than fault-based liability, single factor standards rather than multiple factor standards, objective rather than subjective tests, and statutory liquidated damages rather than damages based on individualized determinations of loss.

Of course, structuring the enforcement process in this way may deprive it of the flexibility necessary for loss spreading and loss reduction, because it represents a fairly rough allocation of liability, rather than the precise allocation that these principles would recommend. The choice ultimately depends on the relative economic impact of all three principles of efficient loss allocation. In weighing the impact of these three principles, loss imposition factors will tend to be extremely significant, much more so than the precaution-oriented rules of the UCC would suggest. The cost of making even a single factual determination would quickly surpass all but the most catastrophic losses on a consumer account. To determine that a consumer negligently left a checkbook in an open desk drawer or that a financial institution negligently cashed a check for a man with a pasted-on, Fu Manchu mustache demands at least one deposition, one set of interrogatories, and a one-day trial. The legal bill for even this modest fact-finding procedure would probably require a consumer to write a check that is substantially larger than the one at issue in the litigation.

Not only do the costs of loss imposition represent a deadweight loss to payment system participants, but they can also distort the underlying allocation of losses, and thus impede the operation of the loss spreading and loss reduction principles. Because enforcement in payment law depends primarily on private litigation, the most significant distortion in the process arises from the costs of asserting legal rights, which often exceed the amounts in dispute. Potential litigants, therefore, will make the decision to sue, if they are acting rationally, by balancing the possible gain from winning the suit against the certain costs of litigating it. When the costs exceed the possible gain, they will not take action, and thus absorb the loss themselves. In that case, the loss falls upon the creditor; thus consumers are likely to under enforce their rights involving losses from checks, electronic transfers, and point of sale transactions, whereas financial institutions are likely to under enforce their rights for credit card losses. This under enforcement distorts the allocation of liability suggested by the other two principles, thus generating inefficiencies.

Economically rational financial institutions and consumers decide whether to assert their legal rights in the same way, but the likelihood of under enforcement is higher for consumers than financial institutions. Because individual consumers have little at stake in the resolution of the principle at issue in the dispute, or in the effect of the dispute on their general reputation, they are unlikely to derive any benefit from the suit beyond the cash value of the possible award. The interests of financial institutions, however, go beyond the award because these institutions must continue to operate in the payment system under whatever rules or lack of rules emerge from the lawsuit. Moreover, financial institutions have a continuing reputation in the business world to protect. They may want to be regarded as sensitive and generous in their dealings with consumers, but they may also seek the reputation of merciless ferocity in the assertion of their legal rights. Financial institutions also benefit from economies of scale in obtaining legal services. The staff attorneys in a financial institution provide an extremely convenient source of counsel, and their repeated contacts with officers of the financial institution eliminate the burdensome start-up costs that consumers generally incur in lawyer-client relationships. Because of consumers' lesser stake in the outcome of a lawsuit and relatively higher costs in pursuing one, even consumers who are distrustful and litigious, as economic rationality demands, may be reluctant to assert their legal rights in a payment dispute.

The Interaction of the Principles

The loss spreading, loss reduction, and loss imposition principles identify the major considerations for framing legal rules to allocate losses in an efficient manner. When the principles converge, the best rule is obvious, but when they diverge, their relative economic effects must be compared to determine which legal rule minimizes their combined effect. In many cases, comparing these effects requires empirical data, which is costly to obtain, with the unfortunate result that public policy proceeds by guesswork. Careful examination of the relationship among the three principles, however, can identify the data needed to choose the best rule, and in the absence of data, improves our ability to guess what that rule should be.

The loss spreading principle unambiguously assigns liability for payment losses to financial institutions, because an enterprise can spread losses among its customers. In contrast, the loss reduction principle's assignment of liability depends upon which of its various elements predominate. If technological innovation is the cheapest way to eliminate a particular type of loss, liability should be assigned to the financial institution. Similarly, if consumer responsiveness to liability rules is low, the financial institution should once again be liable. However, if existing precautions provide the cheapest mechanism to reduce losses, and if both parties are responsive to liability rules, then the principle either assigns liability to whichever party can more cheaply take precaution to prevent the loss, or divides liability according to each party's capacity for precaution. This consideration is generally neutral between financial institutions and consumers; the outcome depends upon the type of payment loss at issue.

The third principle, loss imposition, suggests that the rules allocating losses should be designed to avoid costly litigation and to overcome under enforcement, especially for small losses by consumers. Thus, this principle favors rules that are simple and unambiguous, such as a rule of strict liability for a fixed amount. The loss reduction principle favors a fault-based liability rule that can provide incentives for efficient precaution by several parties at once. But the loss imposition principle virtually precludes such a solution in the payment system; determinations of fault or negligence are likely to be so complex, and thus so expensive, that the overall cost of imposing fault-based rules invariably will exceed the advantage gained in loss reduction.

Rules, Standards, and Precautions in Payment Systems*

CLAYTON P. GILLETTE

Given the similarity of function and objective, it is curious that the law concerning fraud in payment systems varies among payment devices. The law of checks employs a relatively complex and nebulous negligence standard that requires ad hoc investigation into the reasonableness of each party's conduct. Different transactions require different levels of care; insofar as what is negligent depends on the size of the potential loss, the law of checks implicitly considers the amount at issue in determining the liability of the parties. The law of cards, on the other hand, employs highly-tailored rules such as caps on customer liability. These provisions ignore the circumstances of the individual transaction, the level of care practiced by parties to the transaction, and the amount at issue.

The law of payments, therefore, contains a puzzle. Why should regulations that govern functionally equivalent payment devices—checks and cards—vary in both form and substance? One might imagine that payment devices that serve a common objective would be susceptible to an optimal form of regulation that is applied across the board. Several candidates for the optimal form might exist. For instance, if we believe that risk allocation rules should minimize the total costs of fraudulent use and its prevention, and if we further believe that customers are typically in a superior position to accomplish that objective, we could select among several statutory forms to codify those beliefs. We could, for instance, impose strict liability on customers and deny all defenses

* 82 Va. L. Rev. 181, 181–187, 221–227 (1996).

not specifically contracted for, perhaps linked with limits to avoid imposing crushing liability on the occasional customer who would otherwise suffer massive losses. Alternatively we could impose negligence liability on customers, on the assumption that fraud is facilitated by negligent consumers. Or we could impose liability on customers in an amount that we believe would be appropriate to induce optimal care by the average customer. But unless one believes that the variety we see is a response to uncertainty about the optimal form of regulation, the question arises: Why would legislatures not select similar regulations to govern all payment mechanisms?

The commercial requirements of payment systems add another element to this puzzle. Precise risk allocations create clear liability rules that can minimize the costs of the enforcement process. In addition, clear ex ante allocations make legal doctrine more accessible to those untrained in legal nuance. Both of these characteristics will be favored by commercial parties, and thus will stimulate the commercial activity that payment systems are intended to serve. Thus, one would anticipate that doubts about the form of optimal payment regulations would uniformly be resolved in favor of precise rules. After all, an underlying assumption of payment devices is that they solve coordination problems between trading partners by providing a medium of exchange; widely accepted payment devices, whether cash or one of its alternatives, thicken markets that would otherwise be subject to the obstacles to trade implicit in a barter economy. Precise rules facilitate coordination by ensuring that transactors follow similar patterns of behavior. The apparent benefits of uniformity generally, and of precision in particular, make the current coexistence of precise rules with vague appeals to customer negligence all the more perplexing.

The Appropriateness of Rules and Standards in Payment Systems

The literature of rules and standards suggests that the choice of form should depend on whether it is appropriate to give content to the law ex ante or ex post. Rules are typically characterized by ex ante formulations of the requirements of compliance. Thus, rules impose relatively large costs in the creation of the regulation in order to ensure that the correct indicia of care are included. But the relative precision of rules typically facilitates identification of proscribed conduct, and thus translates into relatively small costs in enforcement. Rules, therefore, make sense where the regulated activity occurs frequently. In this situation, which Louis Kaplow considers the most important determinant for using a rule or a standard, costs incurred in making an ex ante investigation and disseminating the results can be amortized over a large number of events, and the aggregate costs of enforcement are minimized. Savings are realized for target actors (those whose conduct the rule seeks to regulate), for victims who seek to determine whether they have suffered a legally cognizable harm, and for administrators of the law. Target actors find it easier to conform their conduct to appropriate patterns once a rule has been announced, victims can determine whether they are entitled to legal redress, and officials, judges and juries can enforce at lower costs because compliance or noncompliance is more readily ascertained.

Standards present a mirror image of these considerations: they are easy to formulate, but costly to apply. For example, it is easier to express a general requirement of "good faith" than it is to delineate the behaviors that might constitute good faith across a range of situations. If the circumstances that would determine whether there has been compliance are highly idiosyncratic, so that the results of any investigation are applicable only in a small number of subsequent situations, the costs of regulation might be minimized through ex post investigation under a broad standard. Similarly, if information gathered at an initial period would be dated or otherwise unusable to determine whether a target actor had subsequently violated the social norm embodied in the regulation, ex post decisions would be preferable.

Once formulated, both rules and standards are subject to errors at the implementation and enforcement stages, but errors of differing sorts. Rules are susceptible to the possibility that they may proscribe behavior that does not really track the underlying objective the rule was intended to achieve. For instance, technological developments may make a rule obsolete because behavior that was once antisocial is now less so (imagine that safer and more accident-resistant automobiles render current speed limits obsolete), or behavior once proscribed with mild penalties turns out to be more serious than originally thought because activity levels have increased (imagine escalation in drunk-driving cases, and a related increase in deaths of pedestrians). Standards permit flexibility in enforcement that avoids the inaccuracy of a rigid rule, but at the expense of requiring target actors to guess about compliance and allowing ex post decision-makers substantial discretion to define a violation. The inevitable result is that the decision-maker will (more frequently than in the case of a rule) misapply the standard, sometimes by imposing liability where no violation has occurred and sometimes by failing to discover actual violations of the behavior that the standard was intended to avoid.

Kaplow's use of activity levels as an indicator of whether we want to incur the costs related to rules or to standards has an initial appeal insofar as it suggests that those costs will systematically depend on the frequency with which errors in formulation or application occur. Frequent activity provides opportunities for amortizing the initial, high costs associated with rules and thus suggests a context for favoring rules over standards. [. . .]

Variance may exist either in the costs of precautions that can be taken to prevent a harm from materializing, or in the expected costs that are generated should the harm materialize. Of course, the two are somewhat related. Target actors have incentives to invest in developing additional precautions as the expected losses from an activity increase. An activity that creates a risk of injury with an expected value of $100, but that can be avoided by investments of $50, $200, $500 or $1000, might still exhibit little variance among precautions, because only the form of precaution requiring a $50 investment is cost-effective. Should the expected losses rise to $1200, however, one might expect substantial variation in precautions for the same activity.

Where there is little variation within the scope of desirable precautions, i.e., optimal precautions are essentially the same across persons and situations, and where all instances of the activity may be considered sufficiently similar (at least from the perspective of possible precautions), a rule mandating the desired precautions is likely to be more appropriate than a standard. If, for instance, essentially all drivers, regardless of experience and expertise, and all cars, regardless of weight or safety features, could only be driven safely on highways at speeds up to sixty miles per hour, then a rule prohibiting driving above that speed would be appropriate. Such a rule would create a safe harbor that reduced investigation costs for individuals without creating substantial social costs for those who could drive safely beyond that speed (because, by hypothesis, such individuals are few in number). At the same time, the existence of the rule (assuming speed could be tested with accuracy) would allow less costly adjudication of unsafe driving cases than a standard that imposed liability on those who drove "unreasonably."

Alternatively, consider the possibility that the same activity can produce wide variations in expected losses. In this case, even if precaution costs for all target actors were identical, desirable behavior would not necessarily be the same. Assume, for instance, that truck drivers are essentially equal to non-truck drivers in skill and precaution costs, but that accidents involving trucks are more likely to result in death or substantial property loss. It might then be appropriate either to have separate safety rules for cars and trucks or to replace the "one size fits all" speed limit rule with a standard that allowed an ex post adjudicator to take into account whether the violator of the standard was driving a car or a truck.

Consideration of the variations in cost of precautions and of losses for cards and checks suggests that different treatment of these payment devices may be appropriate. Recall that the effect of current regulations is to induce check users to investigate what constitutes due care with respect to the maintenance of their checks in all cases, but not to induce card users to investigate or take precautions for expected losses in excess of $50, regardless of their comparative ability to do so. Check and credit card transactions are both sufficiently numerous that ex ante investigations can be amortized over a substantial number of activities. And the conditions under which each is used appear to be sufficiently static that variance in precautions appears to be limited. Precautions for both checkbooks and cards consist of maintaining possession or control over the physical entity, although, as noted above, possession of a credit card is not a complete guarantee against fraud. Indeed, because (at least in the case of consumers) checkbooks and cards are frequently kept together, e.g., in a pocketbook or jacket, it would appear that precautions for each are identical. Thus, from the perspective of precaution costs, rules may or may not be appropriate, but there seems little justification for differences in the form of regulation affecting checks and cards.

Variance in expected losses poses a more complicated issue. Recall that if losses vary widely for an activity, then a flexible standard might be superior to a single, "one size fits all" rule of precaution. A rule in such a situation might induce some of the negative behavior associated with a safe harbor, e.g., inducing overinvestment in precaution by risk averse individuals who will spend more than is warranted by their level of the activity or the expected losses generated by their engagement in the activity. Alternatively, a rule in such a situation could induce underinvestment in precautions. For instance, if the cost of taking efficient precautions exceeds expected losses permissible under the rule, cardholders will not invest more than the minimum required, and thus will not take adequate precautions. Low variance suggests that even where these losses occur, they will be outweighed by the savings from avoiding ad hoc determinations of care. Thus, a $50 cap on liability that is intended to induce precautions by cardholders makes sense if expected losses tend to exceed $50 (thus justifying some precautions by cardholders), but not by so much that the customer who is faced with the cap would otherwise efficiently expend more resources in precaution. For instance, if expected losses systematically ranged between $100 to $150, if customers could avoid these losses with an expenditure of $75 (but not less), and if non-customers (merchants or card issuers) could avoid these losses with an expenditure of between $75 and $100, the $50 liability cap would deter efficient precautions. Just as a safe harbor might induce some overcompliance with the law because the resulting certainty of avoiding penalties outweighs the personal overcompliance costs, so too may a safe harbor induce under-compliance from the perspective of efficient precaution if the rule sets the liability cap too low. Similarly, if the range of precaution costs were narrow and steeply peaked, a liability cap that reflected that peak would be an appropriate approximation of average precaution costs. The "one size fits all" rule, in essence, makes sense if there are few midgets and giants.

There is a credible argument that this explanation justifies different forms of regulation (if not the substance of current regulations) for checks and cards. Loss from credit card fraud is limited by the amount of the cardholder's available credit line, and ATM card fraud is limited by a maximum amount that the customer can withdraw within a given period (usually a day). Check fraud, on the other hand, is limited by the amount in the customer's checking account. If checking account balances are subject to greater variations than losses from credit cards or ATM cards, it could be appropriate to have a "one size fits all" rule for cards, but not for checks, the very situation that current law reflects. The greater variation for check losses might warrant ad hoc determination of whether the customer should have taken advantage of more costly precautions, whereas a specific investment in precautions against losses with low variance (e.g., losses resulting from card fraud) might suitably avoid ad hoc inquiries.

One might infer that check fraud would not tend to involve large amounts, so that the variance of losses would seem to be within a narrow range. The reason for this intuition is that, although the cost of the engaging in check fraud (taking steps to avoid detection, printing one's own checks) may be so high that it is not worth the effort for trivial amounts, the risk of detection will increase with amounts at stake. Paying banks are far more likely to take steps to verify checks of high amounts than those of low amounts. Similarly, merchants are more likely to seek preacceptance authorization for checks of high amounts than low amounts. Thus, even if variance in the value of checking accounts is more substantial than with cards, it may be that the variance in the value of forged checks is not.

Better Than Cash? Global Proliferation of Payment Cards and Consumer Protection Policy*

ARNOLD S. ROSENBERG

Fraudulent and Unauthorized Transactions

In the United States, fraudulent transactions are the consumer problem of greatest concern in payment systems and the greatest concern overall. Identity theft is particularly concerning. Thirty-nine percent of consumer complaints to the FTC in 2003 were for identity theft, and U.S. consumers rate it as their highest priority among consumer issues, although the incidence of identity theft through credit cards actually has begun to level off. On the other hand, debit card fraud in the United States is growing rapidly. Debit card fraud is already at high levels in Canada.

The high level of fraud in Canada occurs despite the fact that Canadian debit cards are entirely PIN (online) debit. The linkage of all ATMs to a single network, Interac, in Canada and more frequent use of debit cards there are related causes. By comparison, in the United States there are twenty-five different networks. On the other hand, signature debit, unique to the United States, has two-to three-day delay in clear-

* 44 COLUM. J. TRANSNAT'L L. 520 (2006).

ance and settlement and entails greater risk of loss due to non-payment in cases of insufficient funds and closed bank accounts.

The problems of debit card users are similar to those of users of credit cards and checks, particularly with respect to the allocation of loss due to unauthorized use, identity theft, and fraud. However, laws in many countries establish divergent rules and standards for debit card users and the users of credit cards, checks, and cash.

If a consumer in the United States loses a blank check on the bus, and a thief forges the consumer's signature, the loss normally falls on the payor bank absent fault on the part of the consumer, but if the loss of the check was caused by the consumer's negligence, the consumer bears at least part of the loss on comparative fault principles.

However, if the same consumer lost a credit card along with the check, and the same thief used the credit card to make a purchase, the consumer's liability would be limited by law to a maximum of $50, regardless of the amount of the purchase, the consumer's negligence in losing the card, and the consumer's further negligence in failing to review credit card statements. In the case of a credit card, the loss ultimately would fall on the merchant, barring the merchant's insolvency and assuming that the card issuer pursued its right of chargeback under association (Visa or MasterCard) rules.

The $50 ceiling was originally put forth in a seminal article by Roland Brandel and Carl Leonard in 1971 as an "arbitrary" figure that they selected as a boundary between small purchases in which credit cards normally would be used for convenience as a cash substitute, and larger purchases which a consumer normally might expect to carry as a revolving credit balance. The United Kingdom adopted a £50 ceiling, in Section 84 of the Consumer Credit Act adopted in 1974. Again, however, transfers from deposit accounts were excluded. Section 84 was said to be an exception to the general rule of Section 83 of the Consumer Credit Act that a debtor under a regulated consumer credit agreement is not liable for loss "arising from use of the credit facility by another person."

In the case of debit cards, American law attempts to have it both ways. The consumer's liability for unauthorized debit card transactions is limited to $50, but only if he or she reports the loss to the issuer within two business days after discovery. For the consumer who fails to report promptly, the ceiling is raised to $500 for charges beyond the two business days, and to unlimited liability for charges on the lost card once a consumer has had sixty days to review a credit card statement reflecting unauthorized charges and still has failed to report the loss. The consumer's duty is to be a prompt reporter and careful reader of statements from her bank, but not to prevent the loss or theft of the card (apart from the now-minor risk of a $50 liability, which may be waived by the issuer). The law leaves the merchant's duty entirely up to its contract with the merchant's bank and to association rules.

Other countries have taken a variety of approaches to the consumer's liability for unauthorized debit card transactions. In some, a negligence standard applies, and in others, a combination of rules and standards is applied. For example, in Australia, under codes of practice adopted by the banking industry and enforced through the Australian Banking Ombudsman, a cardholder is absolved of liability beyond fifty Australian dollars (AUD) for unauthorized transactions occurring before notification of the issuer that a card has been lost or stolen, provided that the cardholder was neither negligent nor contributory to the loss of the card.

The EC issued a recommendation in 1997 on the subject of electronic payment instruments, which applies to debit cards. The EC recommended that Member States adopt a liability ceiling of one hundred and fifty European Currency Unit (ECU) for the holder in case of loss or theft of the card for unauthorized transactions prior to the holder's reporting the loss or theft to the issuer, "except where he acted with extreme negligence or fraudulently." It included a recommendation that in case of a dispute, the issuer should have the burden of proving that a transaction was accurately recorded and entered into accounts. However, only two Member States of the European Union had adopted laws following that recommendation as of 2002 [. . .]

Debit cards, on the other hand, confer access to cash. The liability ceiling for unauthorized use of a debit card in the EFTA was a compromise, the outcome of a battle between advocates of a negligence standard, including the banking industry, and consumer advocates who advocated the same $50 ceiling that applied to credit cards. Consumer advocates argued that the $50 ceiling was adequate incentive to consumers to exercise sufficient care with respect to their cards, and that making the issuer liable for losses over $50 would incentivize consumers to implement security measures to minimize their losses. Banks, on the other hand, argued that unlike credit cards, which have a fixed credit limit, debit card losses depended entirely on the amount of money the consumer had in his bank account. However, at that time debit cards were only usable to access ATMs, which have dollar limits for cash withdrawals.

Compare these rules to the rules pertaining to cash. Because cash is both negotiable and anonymous, containing no internal means of identifying the person entitled to it, a consumer has no recourse with respect to stolen cash, except to sue for conversion if he or she can identify the perpetrator. A merchant who receives payment in lost or stolen cash has no duty to restore it to the consumer who owned the cash. The reason for this misallocation of loss is primarily the anonymity of cash, and secondarily the cost of time. If cash was identified by owner—e.g., if a dollar bill had an electronic tag stating in bright neon letters who owned it at any given moment—then would the merchant, receiving tagged cash from the thief, still be held to no duty with respect to the identified owner of the cash? Possibly not, but only if the legislature considered the transaction costs in terms of time that would be incurred by the merchant in examining the bills and asking for identification to be too significant.

For purposes deemed sufficiently important and amounts sufficiently significant, the legislature has restricted the anonymity of cash by imposing reporting requirements on its recipient. For example, money laundering rules adopted pursuant to the Bank Secrecy Act require banks to file Currency Transaction Reports for cash transactions of $10,000 or more. Cash transactions of $5000 or more under suspicious circumstances require the filing of Suspicious Activity Reports.

American consumer law thus incorporates divergent rules and standards of loss allocation for four instrumentalities of payment, all of which are usually used by consumers as cash or cash equivalents. The Visa and MasterCard associations ultimately decided to waive the $50 in all cases. Presumably the transaction costs and loss of goodwill incurred by card issuers in collecting the $50 from card holders who had been the victims of loss or theft proved to be more costly than the amounts collected.

This action by Visa and MasterCard speaks eloquently to the folly of attempting to read precise legislative judgments about optimal loss allocation into rules and standards adopted at different times under different political conditions. Fifty dollars was picked as an "arbitrary figure" to establish a boundary between transactions intended by the credit cardholder as convenience transactions and transactions intended as credit transactions, not as an attempt to optimize anything. This "arbitrary figure" was established on the theory that up to that amount the lost or stolen card would have been used as a "convenience card" in place of cash, so that the loss should be treated as if cash had been lost. The differences in the liability ceilings for debit and credit cards reflected a political compromise between those who wanted to treat credit cards and debit cards the same, and those dissatisfied with the low credit card liability ceiling who wanted to import a fault concept into the rule. The rationale for the small-dollar exclusion is further weakening as consumers increasingly use credit cards as convenience cards even in the United States, and as the functional differences between debit and credit cards correspondingly diminish....

The use of payment cards makes it feasible in most cases to correct this [problem] through the intervention of the financial institutions that operate the payment system. Those institutions are capable of protecting themselves through security procedures. Since most debit cards do, or should, require use of a PIN, allocation of loss to the consumer should be limited to cases in which the consumer negligently or culpably divulged the PIN to the wrongdoer or in which the consumer's negligent or culpable conduct otherwise compromises a security system implemented by the issuer to protect against unauthorized use of the card. If American banks want to promote signature debit because the interchange fees are higher, and thereby forego password protection of card transactions, they, and not the consumer or merchant, should bear the losses that could have been prevented by the use of a PIN.

Efficiency, Equity, and the Proposed Revision of Articles 3 and 4*
EDWARD L. RUBIN

The final area of market failure is loss allocation. Here the market failure is probably the most extreme, given the unpredictability of the occurrence and the complexity of the issue. The most efficient way to allocate losses, which usually appears in negotiated contracts between parties with equivalent information, is to place liability for clearly avoidable losses on the party responsible for the loss and divide liability for other losses between the customer and the financial institution. [. . .]

The original loss allocation rules in Articles 3 and 4 did not embody these principles of economic efficiency, and the revisions do little to alter this situation. The concept of loss spreading does not occur in the revised Code at all; parties are assigned liability on the basis of their actions, with no regard to their economic status. Revised Article 3, which still contains the bulk of the loss allocation rules, does not even acknowledge that banks are involved. It continues to use the generic terminology of "person," "drawee" or "payor," as if we still had a group of individuals with interchangeable roles, as we did in eighteenth century mercantile practice. This obscures the basic policy choice of loss spreading. When we assign liability to a bank, we are not imposing a loss on that "person" as an individual entity. Instead, we are deciding that the loss should be spread across the entire customer base, instead of letting it fall on the particular customers who happened to be victimized. In many cases, such loss spreading will be more efficient, but the Code does not reflect that fact.

The Code and its revision do embody the second principle of economic efficiency in loss allocation—that the loss should be assigned to the party who is in the best position to avoid it. This is achieved through use of the fault principle. If there is a forged drawer's signature, liability is assigned to the drawee; if there is a forged indorsement, liability is initially assigned to the drawee, but can be shifted to the person who first took the fraudulent instrument from the thief. This is the venerable rule of Price v. Neal.

It is preserved in sections 3–416, 3–418, and 3–419, which replace former section 3–417 with mercifully clearer language and a separate treatment of transfer and presentment warranties. Although this rule

* 42 ALA. L. REV. 551, 564–569, 576–578 (1991).

imposes strict liability on banks in certain circumstances, the banks
remained faithful to the sponsors' agreement and made no attempt to
eliminate this liability. The fault principle enters, however, through
former sections 3–405 and 3–406, which are essentially preserved in
sections 3–404 to 3–406 of the revision. Former section 3–406 allowed
the drawee bank to shift liability to any person who contributes to a
fraud or forgery by failing to exercise ordinary care. Here (and in revised
section 3–405), the bankers were unable to resist temptation and de-
manded a new provision that relieves them of the obligation to examine
checks. The revision achieves this result by declaring that failure to
examine does not constitute a lack of ordinary care, thus overruling
Medford Irrigation District v. Western Bank. In addition, certain actions
are deemed negligent per se, and automatically shift liability to the party
at fault. In former Article 3, these actions are defined in section 3–
405(1). The revision retains this definitional approach and also adds a
new section on employer liability. Unlike the treatment of fictitious
payees in former Article 3, this new section is clear, but it does expand
the existing liability of employers. That may well be efficient, however,
given that an entity with employees is generally a business, and is thus
unlikely to suffer from information asymmetries. But the relationship of
this section to the other liability provisions is obscure [. . .]

An even more serious problem with these liability provisions, however, is that fault does not quite correspond to the economic principle that
the loss should be assigned to the party who could have avoided it most
readily. To begin with, the U.C.C. fault principles impose unnecessarily
large losses on consumers—larger than is necessary to induce them to
take whatever precautions they are likely to take. For example, consumers can avoid losses by taking precautions against the theft of their
checkbooks, and they will do so if they are at risk of losing some
meaningful sum of money, for example a hundred dollars, and of
undergoing the inconvenience of closing their old account and opening a
new one. Providing that they can lose the entire account balance, as the
U.C.C.'s fault principle does, is unlikely to induce any additional precaution. The person who carelessly leaves a checkbook on the hardware
store counter will still do so, even with all this additional liability,
because his action is the result of carelessness, not a conscious weighing
of the costs and benefits. Beyond a certain point, liability simply punish-
es the consumer without achieving any increased level of loss reduction.

The second way that the fault principle deviates from economic
efficiency is by ignoring the role of systematic planning. Consumers
virtually never devise long-range loss avoidance strategies, and they have
no opportunity to alter the nature of the check collection system. Banks
design the system, and banks can avoid losses by restructuring it, by
training their employees, or by developing new technologies. For example, banks assert that they cannot check the signatures of all checks
drawn upon them, but they are currently experimenting with optical

scanning devices that may ultimately do exactly that. Such precautions will often be the most cost-effective means of loss reduction, but they are not captured by our concept of fault. Courts rarely hold that a bank was at fault, in a particular case, because it failed to engage in a five year planning process to develop a new security device.

But the most serious problem with the fault principle that Article 3 embodies, and that the revision perpetuates, is the enormous cost of its effectuation. Determining fault requires a complex, fact-based adjudication that will rapidly devour the amount at issue in all but the largest cases. The reporters were aware of this problem. While they never abandoned the fault principle, they did propose that the loss simply be divided in half in situations where both parties were negligent. Even this modest effort to reduce loss imposition costs troubled the banking industry, and the provisions were dropped. Instead, sections 3–405 and 3–406 now contain a comparative negligence provision to deal with cases where both parties are at fault. This is even worse, of course; with the contributory negligence or dual contributory negligence of the existing law, only the fact of negligence must be established. Under the revision the precise amount of negligence becomes important, so every fact is relevant, and the agonizingly expensive process of discovery and trial can go on even longer [. . .]

Social Equity

Another set of social equity problems involves the U.C.C.'s loss allocation provisions. As indicated in the previous discussion, the basic allocation of losses in Articles 3 and 4 is economically inefficient. By following the fault principle, the Code assigns too much liability to customers: more than is consistent with the loss spreading principle and more than is necessary to induce consumers to take whatever precautions they are likely to take. This does not necessarily create a social equity problem. The concept of fault is deeply embedded in our collective moral sensibility. People who leave their checkbooks on store counters or who write checks to impostors probably feel that they deserve to lose whatever amount is extracted from their accounts as a result. One can readily imagine explaining to such people that there would have been no loss but for their actions, and that they should be responsible. In fact, it is the instinctiveness of these feelings and the persuasiveness of this explanation that makes an economically efficient loss allocation scheme difficult for many people to accept.

The real social equity problem involving loss allocation lies in the process of resolving disputes and imposing losses. When a loss occurs and the bank disagrees with its customer about who should be responsible, the bank can resort to self help, by simply deducting the disputed amount from the customer's checking account. The customer must then endure the expense and aggravation of hiring a lawyer and filing a complaint before she can even compel the bank to answer. In many consumer checking cases, it would be impractical for the consumer to hire a lawyer because the amount at issue is minimal. Even if a lawyer is retained, the chances of winning may be limited, because that lawyer will be facing experienced bank attorneys whose client, the bank, will want to maintain a reputation for effectiveness and avoid disadvantageous precedents. The result is that most consumers are powerless when the bank resorts to self help, even if they feel they are right and even if they really are right. This is the paradigmatic case of unfairness: to feel that one is right but know that one has no redress. How can we explain to people why the checking system has been designed so that both parties are not equal in their ability to present their claim?

A special and particularly piquant case of this social inequity involves stop orders. A stop order is a device that enables consumers to counteract the social inequity of loss imposition vis-a-vis vendors of goods or services. Suppose a consumer pays for merchandise, brings it home, and discovers or believes that it is defective. If she has paid by cash, she must initiate the lawsuit against the merchant, a lawsuit attended by many of the difficulties just described. If she has paid by check, however, she can simply contact the bank and stop the check, leaving the unpaid merchant to initiate the suit. The stop feature was not designed for consumer protection purposes; it is merely a logical consequence of the rule in former section 3–409 (section 3–408 in the revision) that a check is not an assignment. However, it has turned out to be one of the few truly effective mechanisms for consumer redress. Moreover, the stop payment no longer need be tied to the assignment rule; any payment system could provide a reversal procedure.

Former Article 4 granted the customer a "right to stop payment" and the revision perpetuates this feature. Suppose, however, the bank pays a check despite the fact that the customer has issued a valid stop order. Former subsection 4–403(3) provided that the burden of proving that this bank error resulted in a loss rested with the customer. Thus, the bank maintained the debit against the customer's account, and the customer had to go to court against the bank to prove that she was legally justified in stopping payment on the check. This provision, of course, vitiated the entire value of the stop order when such an error occurred.

Once again, the customer was required to initiate the suit and, once again, it was unlikely that she would be able to do so. Article 4 said, in effect, that there were perfectly good reasons to allow consumers a self help remedy when dealing with vendors, but not when dealing with banks, even banks that have concededly made an error. It would be difficult to devise a legal rule that produces a greater sense of felt injustice, or that is more difficult to justify. In the initial revisions of Article 4, section 4–403 was modified. The reporters provided that the bank must recredit the customer's account and would then have the burden of proving that no loss to the customer had resulted from its error. Since the bank is subrogated to the customer's rights against the merchant-payee in this situation, by virtue of existing section 4–407, it would not necessarily absorb the loss. If the customer was justified, and the bank was required to reimburse her, it could assert her rights in a suit against the payee. The customer was required to cooperate with the bank in such a suit by providing an affidavit about the reasons for stopping payment of the check, and that doing so would be a precondition to obtaining the recredit. But the banks objected to this revision; they argued that they usually recredit a customer's account anyway, so no legal requirement was necessary This position prevailed and the revision now continues subsection 4–403(3) essentially unchanged.

NOTES

1. Efficient liability rules for payment systems. Recall the allocation of loss from the fraud of the rogue merchant seller who delivers a defective product, receives payment in the form of a paper such as a note, transfers the paper to a buyer and then disappears with the cash. The loss must be borne either by the buyer of the good who pays for a defective product or by the purchaser of the note who would be unable to recover the full claim. Rules that promote efficient loss allocation thereby increase the value of the initial transaction and may therefore be preferred by the two innocent parties who deal with each other. The rogue in this section steals money by forging a signature on a check or by using a credit or debit card without authorization. The loss is typically borne either by the rightful owner (of the checking account or the card) or the financial institution. Here again, a guiding principle may be efficient risk allocation that might be preferred by the parties to the initial instrument.

Risk bearing capacity is a function of three factors: 1) the relative ability to reduce the probability and severity of the materialization of the threatened loss, 2) the relative knowledge concerning the probability and severity, and 3) the ability to spread the risk of loss. Contracts often allocate risks of loss. Consider, for instance, a contract for fire insurance. The insurer can better spread the risk. But, the parties' respective abilities in preventing the loss, limiting its severity, or in predicting either the probability or severity, are not always clear. The insured can take precautions against fire, and has some private information about the condition of her home and about her habits. Then again, an insurer has the advantage of knowing the system-wide probabilities of losses from fires and can even take some precautions to reduce the risk (e.g. educating the community about fire prevention). Yet another important factor governing the optimal contractual allocation of risk is the minimization of the cost of enforcing the risk allocation in the contract, particularly when factors are costly to verify.

Returning to the problem of the rogue, the allocation of forgery risk differs somewhat from the earlier discussion of negotiability because one of the parties is typically a financial institution that enjoys some risk spreading and risk reduction advantages owing to its size and expertise. After all, we see plenty of examples of financial institutions bundling insurance with payment services: credit cards often offer insurance connected to purchases of travel (e.g. lost luggage), car rental (liability for damage) and even ordinary goods (against damage in the first month after purchase). Despite these advantages, it is not optimal to allocate the entire loss to the financial institution because of the consequent dilution of incentives of the other party to act with the efficient degree of care. Finally, the cost of enforcing loss allocations might outweigh the benefit and that it might even distort the intended incentive effects by deterring enforcement (particularly by consumers against financial institutions). See Robert D. Cooter and Edward L. Rubin, *A Theory of Loss Allocation for Consumer Payments*, 66 Texas L. Rev. 63, 67–81, 84–86 (1987).

2. Rules v. standards. Recall from the previous section, Ronald Mann's concern about the diversity of finality rules across payment mechanisms. Clayton Gillette makes a similar point about the rules allocating "rogue" losses in checks, credit cards and debit cards. Are the considerations that produce different loss allocation rules as between checks and credit cards the same as those that lead to different finality rules? Cooter and Rubin's analysis, summarized in Note 1 above, suggests that the efficient allocation of such losses is quite context-dependent: a function of the expected size of payments, the comparative advantage in precaution-taking of the institution and the consumer. As a result, there may be an advantage to making a menu of risk allocation available to the parties. But, as we asked in connection with finality, does the bundling of features make sense in the case of each of these payment mechanisms?

Gillette points out the difference also in the legal process of risk allocation: namely the preference for rules or standards in each case. Cooter and Rubin suggest that rules reduce loss imposition costs but that standards may be superior in assigning to both parties the efficient incentives for taking precautions. Gillette reviews some of the factors governing the choice between rules and standards that were raised earlier in this book, in order to speculate why standards might be more appropriately used in the case of check forgeries than unauthorized use of credit or debit cards. He suggests, for example, that fixed caps on liability fit better with credit or ATM cards because they have set credit limits. Yet, many people's credit card limits exceed the amounts available in their checking accounts. Moreover, as Gillette notes, the financial institution can adjust its precautions when it sees checks or card charges in particularly large amounts.

Gillette seems more strongly opposed to standards in the allocation of "rogue" losses in payments than Cooter and Rubin. Gillette recites the virtues of predictability and certainty both ex post (in reducing enforcement costs) and ex ante (in enhancing the value of the payment as a medium of exchange). These considerations arise repeatedly in commercial law, so you might take a moment to review their weight in this context. For instance, would government-issued lottery tickets succeed as a medium for exchange?

3. Allocation of rogue losses. Does the Cooter and Rubin framework described in Section 4.4 apply to prescribe the efficient allocation of "rogue" losses? Are different loss allocation rules appropriate or, given the pace of technological innovation, is there a stronger case for standards? Review the website for Ecash Direct (a company in the UK) that provides the licence agreement at http://www.ecashdirect.net. How does the allocation scheme compare to those for checks or credit cards? Are the differences justified by contrasting contexts?

Consider the example of liability limits with debit cards which Rosenberg discusses above. Recall that under TILA, a consumer is only liable for $50 of losses on a lost or stolen credit card. EFTA, however, caps losses for debit cards at $50 only if the consumer reports the card lost or stolen within two business days; if unreported, liability is capped at $500 and is potentially unlimited if the customer never gives notice to the financial institution. One of the major criticisms of current payment law is the different treatment of similar types of payment methods. For example, the liability rules governing credit and debit cards are different despite the fact that each is a card-based system which many consumers use interchangeably. What justifications can you think of for the differing rules? Does it (or should it) matter whether the transaction is in the "physical world"(either a point of sale of telephone transaction) or on the internet? For further commentary on credit and debit card differences, *see* Ronald Mann, *Regulating Internet Payment Intermediaries*, 82 Tex. L. Rev. 681 (2004).

To some extent these regulations can be varied by contract, at least if they substitute more consumer-friendly terms. MasterCard brand debit cards, for example, have a self-imposed $50 consumer liability cap regardless of when the loss is reported to the financial institution. Visa has similar rules with an exception for gross negligence on the part of the cardholder. Rosenberg also documents several attempts by Congress to modify EFTA, but notes they are largely unnecessary since financial institutions have imposed the limits themselves.

4. Contracting behavior and the problem of market failure. If the choice between rules and standards and, more broadly, among different loss allocation rules, is highly context dependent, then why not let the parties agree to the approach that best suits their circumstances? To what extent do the loss allocation provisions allow parties to contract for different arrangements? In *Efficiency, Equity and the Proposed Revision of Articles 3 and 4,* Edward Rubin proposes that a "perfectly functioning market will minimize transaction costs, such as the cost of payment, by competitive pressure" Rubin, *Efficiency* at 561. Do you need perfect competition to reach the efficient term, or would we see it offered even by a regional monopoly? If market structure does not impede the evolution of provisions for optimal risk allocation, what is the source of the market failure that justifies the establishment of mandatory terms? How do Article 3 and 4 attempt to address these market failures?

5. The political economy of payment systems law. As described in the last excerpt from Rubin, Articles 3 and 4 were the product of a legislative process that required a compromise between competing interest groups. Both the public and private legislatures that might consider reforms to the payment system are subject to interest group pressures that were discussed earlier in the book. See Chapter 2, Section 2.3 and notes following Chapter 3, Section 3.6. See also, Christopher Termini, *Return on Political Investment:*

The Puzzle of Ex Ante Investment in Articles 3 and 4 of the U.C.C., 92 Va. L. Rev. 1023 (2006).

In his excerpt, Arnold Rosenberg contrasts the debit card rules for loss allocation with those of credit cards and checks, and reveals a hybrid approach in the U.S. as well as variations across countries. Can these diverse approaches be reconciled more appropriately as reflecting different views as to efficient risk allocation, or different political environments?

Therefore, in addressing market failures in the provision of payment terms, we have a choice between an imperfect market and an imperfect political process. This is a difficult choice to assess because it entails not only the identification of imperfections, but also their quantification for the purpose of comparison. Moreover, one might investigate whether the public rule-making process might be improved. For example, should more issues be left to the courts to decide rather than the legislatures (public or private)? In light of ongoing reform initiatives, we should also ask about the wisdom of piece-meal implementation of legal reforms. To what extent does the entire scheme of rules have to be implemented so that its constituent parts operate as anticipated?

Chapter 5

Credit Instruments, Suretyship and Standby Letters of Credit

5.1 Introduction

Debt (or credit) contracts lie at the intersection of commercial law and corporate finance. Financial capital bridges the temporal gap caused by the fact that businesses incur costs before they collect revenues. Financing is often bundled with a contract for goods or services. For example, a business may buy its inventory on credit or pay its employees and contractors monthly for their services. Or, the business may receive capital under pure financing contracts with investors, such as the sale of stock or a bank loan. In either case, the creditor's right to be paid may be evidenced either by simply the terms of the contract or, more formally, by an independent instrument, such as a note. Notes and drafts serve different purposes in modern transactions: the note is a credit instrument and draft a payment instrument. Yet, Article 3 regulates them in similar fashion because, historically, notes and drafts (known as bills of exchange) both circulated as payment mechanisms.

Suppose a buyer purchases goods on one-year credit. The buyer may execute a promissory note in favor of the seller, at least partly because the seller does not wish to bear the default risk and therefore intends to discount the note to a third party prior to its maturity date. The seller/payee can thereby obtain prompt payment from the third party. Recall that we explored the feature of negotiability in Chapter 4. If the buyer made the note negotiable and if the third party becomes a holder in due course, the third party has an action for payment against the buyer, the note's maker, and is free of defenses the buyer would have against a suit by the seller-payee. The buyer thus faces the following dilemma. By making the note negotiable and thereby more marketable, the buyer increases the note's value to the seller, who is therefore likely to give the buyer a better price. However, the buyer will lose her defenses arising from, for example, the receipt of a defective good. This reduces the value of the good to the buyer. Concerns with the ability of a consumer buyer to understand the downside of negotiability has led the FTC effectively to abolish the holder in due course doctrine in consumer transactions.

Sureties and guarantors

A debtor may also reduce the default risk borne by the seller or its assignee by arranging for a third party to agree to become obligated on the debt, particularly if the debtor defaults. The material in this chapter raises several questions about the forms and legal attributes of sureties and guaranties, and indirectly the efficiency gains from credit default insurance. Another mechanism for reducing default risk (without the express participation of a third party) is the use of security interests, which is the topic of Chapter 6.

A person who assumes secondary liability on a debt may be known as a surety or a guarantor. "A 'surety' is typically jointly and severally liable with the principal obligor on an obligation to which they are both bound, while a 'guarantor' typically contracts to fulfill an obligation upon the default of the principal obligor." Restatement of the Law, Suretyship and Guaranty § 1 ct. c (1995). Nevertheless, the term surety often encompasses both sureties and guarantors, unless the context indicates otherwise. § 1–201(40). The UCC imports general suretyship law under § 1–103, but several important provisions in Article 3 apply to one type of surety, the accommodation party, who becomes a surety by signing a negotiable instrument.

A third party surety may become an accommodation party on a negotiable instrument that evidences the primary obligation: for example, by signing as a co-maker or indorser on the primary debtor's promissory note. By incurring liability on the instrument without being a direct beneficiary of the value given for the instrument, the third party becomes an accommodation party under Article 3. § 3–419. If the surety signs the instrument as a co-maker, then the surety is primarily liable on the instrument and must pay the obligation when due, regardless of whether the holder has pursued the principal debtor. If the surety signs the instrument as an indorser, then she only incurs secondary liability on the instrument, meaning that the holder must first present the instrument to the maker and give notice of dishonor to the surety. § 3–419(b). If the surety pays the debt, she has the right to recover the payment from the principal debtor under the doctrines of subrogation and reimbursement. § 3–419(e). An accommodation party may raise many of the primary debtor's defenses to payment, such as a failure of consideration by the seller. But the accommodation party cannot assert the primary debtor's defenses of insolvency, infancy or lack of legal capacity. § 3–305(d). The accommodation party may also have additional defenses arising out of modifications in the contract between the payee and the principal debtor. § 3–605.

Alternatively, a third party's agreement to act as a surety may be found in a writing separate from the principal debt contract or instrument. One example is the *standby* letter of credit. We described the *commercial* letter of credit in the Introduction to Chapter 4. The holder of such documentary credit is typically a seller of goods who is paid by the issuer of the letter upon presentation of documents specified in the letter of credit. Under standby letters of credit, the issuer (such as a bank) agrees to make a payment to the beneficiary if the applicant for the credit fails to perform. The performance due is often the payment of money, but might also be the performance of a non-monetary obligation (e.g. in the construction and other service industries). There is an important difference between the obligation of an issuer of a letter of credit on the one hand, and a guarantor or conventional surety on the other. Due to the independence principle of letters of credit, the issuer cannot assert the defenses on the underlying deal that would be available to the debtor. Even if the beneficiary has fundamentally breached its contract with the applicant, the issuer must nevertheless pay under the letter of credit.

In the realm of corporate finance (as opposed to commercial sales on credit), insurance against credit risk comes in a number of other forms that raise similar issues. One form that has acquired particular notoriety in recent years is the credit derivative known as a credit default swap (CDS), which emerged in the early 1990s as a tool for commercial banks to transfer excess lending risks. See Charles Smithson and David Mengle, *The Promise of Credit Derivatives in Nonfinancial Corporations (and Why It's Failed to Materialize)*, 18(4) J. App. Corp. Fin. 54 (Fall 2006). A CDS is a promise by the seller of a CDS (the insurer) to pay a fixed amount to the buyer of the CDS upon the occurrence of an adverse credit event that affects a "reference entity" (a debtor) or its obligation. The credit event might be a loan default or a specified change in the debtor's condition, such as a lower credit rating or bankruptcy filing. CDS contracts are based upon standard master agreements and definitions published by the International Swaps and Derivatives Association, Inc. (ISDA). They typically require the seller to post collateral, or a margin, that may vary during the life of the CDS according to changes in the debtor (such as credit rating or securities prices).

The common practice of transferring pieces of credit risks to third parties, whether by sureties or otherwise, raises several economic puzzles regardless of the chosen form. In Section 5.2, the excerpts by Professor Baird and Professor Katz ask how sureties add value in credit transactions: why are two obligors more efficient than one? It is true that the creditor's default risk is lower as a result and she therefore charges a lower interest rate. However, the creditors of the *surety* bear a higher default risk and they are likely to increase the interest they charge that person when she undertakes the secondary obligation. Without knowing more about the characteristics of the surety, we would expect the changes in interest rates to offset each other, thus begging the question of why the parties would include a surety. What would you expect to be the relative magnitude of these effects?

In Section 5.3, the excerpt from Avery Katz raises a more specific question about sureties. Suppose a creditor lending to A wants B to be secondarily or jointly liable on A's repayment obligation. Why would the creditor choose a surety arrangement over the simpler arrangement under which the creditor lends to B, who then makes a separate loan to A? Katz offers two explanations, and the notes encourage the reader to search for others.

5.2 Motivations for Sureties and Standby Letters of Credit

Standby Letters of Credit in Bankruptcy*
DOUGLAS G. BAIRD

Background of the Letter-of-credit Transaction

As recently as twenty years ago, letters of credit were used principally in international sales. No seller willingly sends its goods across national borders unless it is confident it will be paid, because no seller welcomes the prospect of having its goods in the care of unknown parties in a foreign port, where finding a new buyer may be impossible and bringing a legal action extremely difficult. The letter of credit as we now know it arose in the middle of the nineteenth century in response to this problem.

Although letter-of-credit transactions vary, their basic structure can be stated briefly. In a typical letter-of-credit transaction, a seller specifies that payment be made with a letter of credit in its favor. The buyer (known as the 'customer' in the letter-of-credit transaction) contracts with the bank to issue the letter. The bank, knowing the creditworthiness of its customer, is willing to issue the letter for a small fee, typically some fraction of one per cent of the price of the goods. The bank sends the letter to the seller, promising to pay the full price of the goods when the seller presents it with a draft and the documents specified in the letter. These documents typically include a negotiable bill of lading.

* 49 U. Chi. L. Rev. 130, 135–143 (1982).

This arrangement benefits all parties to the transaction. The seller can manufacture goods to the buyer's order, confident it will be paid regardless of what befalls the buyer, because it can rely on the bank's commitment. The buyer that secures the letter of credit is better off than if it had advanced cash to the seller, because it does not become liable for the price until a trustworthy party (the bank) has possession of a negotiable document of title. The bank, in turn, earns a fee for issuing the letter and exposes itself to only a small risk, because it can readily assess the creditworthiness of its customer and, as the holder of a negotiable bill of lading, it has a perfected security interest in the goods involved in the transaction.

The linchpin of the letter-of-credit transaction is the unique legal relationship between the bank and the beneficiary. Unlike a guarantor, the bank is primarily liable whenever the beneficiary presents a draft and documents that conform to the letter. Unlike its counterpart in a third-party beneficiary contract, the bank may not invoke the defenses its customer might have on the underlying contract. Moreover, the status of a beneficiary of a letter of credit is radically different from that of a payee of a check, who has no right to compel payment from the drawee bank. In the letter-of-credit transaction, the beneficiary does have the right to compel payment, and once the letter of credit is issued, the customer is powerless to stop payment in the absence of fraud. This difference exists because a letter of credit, unlike a negotiable instrument such as a check, is a binding and irrevocable obligation of the bank itself, not of the customer who procured it. The legal relationship between bank and beneficiary is governed by special principles which, like the law merchant in an earlier era, are nearly uniform throughout the world.

The Standby Letter of Credit

The archetypal letter-of-credit transaction described above is the means by which the parties pay one another if the underlying transaction takes place as planned. Standby letters of credit, in contrast, are never drawn upon if the transaction runs smoothly. For example, a builder might require a developer to have a bank issue a letter of credit in its behalf to ensure payment if the developer defaults. Such a letter of credit might require that the bank honor the builder's draft when accompanied by an architect's certificate that the building was finished and a statement by the builder that it had not been paid. In this kind of transaction, the bank usually will issue the letter only if the developer gives it a security interest in some property to which the bank will have recourse if the letter is drawn upon. If all goes well, the builder never presents its draft because it has been paid on schedule by the developer. If the developer defaults, however, the builder is still assured payment under the letter of credit. The bank then must seek reimbursement from the developer or enforce its security interest.

The parties to this transaction might employ a standby letter of credit in a different way. The developer might want to ensure that any money it advances to the builder is used to build the building. The developer could require the builder to have its bank issue a letter of credit in the developer's favor. Such a letter might provide that the developer's draft, accompanied by its statement that the builder had defaulted on its obligations, would be honored by the bank. Unlike the negotiable document of title specified in the usual commercial letter-of-credit transaction, the documents in the standby letter-of-credit transaction have no intrinsic value. For this reason, the bank is likely to insist that the builder give it a security interest as a condition of the letter's issuance.

Standby letters of credit also are used in transactions involving sales of goods. A supplier of raw materials, for example, might prefer to have a letter of credit in its favor from the buyer's bank rather than a security interest in the goods. Alternatively, a buyer of manufactured goods might want to protect itself when it advances money to finance its seller's purchase of raw materials. Such a buyer risks more in the event of default than one who sells on credit, because the buyer cannot easily acquire a purchase money security interest in the raw materials its seller uses. As the beneficiary of a standby letter of credit issued by the seller's bank, however, the buyer obtains equivalent protection.

A business that wishes to raise money may issue commercial paper backed by a standby letter of credit. This type of transaction involves larger dollar amounts than other uses of letters of credit. The business's bank may be more willing to accept the risk of its customer's insolvency than will the buyers of commercial paper. The buyers, however, may be willing to extend cash to the business if they can rely on the bank to ensure repayment. The letter of credit makes it easy for all of the parties to allocate among themselves the risk of the business's failure. The business acquires the cash it needs, the bank lends its credit to the business without having to supply cash, and the buyers of commercial paper enjoy a relatively safe investment. As in the other letter-of-credit transactions, all parties directly involved benefit. [. . .]

Letters of Credit as a Financing Device

[Suppose a] seller owns a high-speed digital computer with a value of one million dollars, but it wishes to purchase another more suited to its current needs. It has found a buyer for its old computer, and (to keep the example simple) both parties want an outright sale. An important element of their bargain will be the method of payment. Cash payment, of course, would be simplest, but the buyer may not have the purchase price in cash, and its bank may not be willing to lend it that amount. For its part, the seller may be cash rich and have no immediate need to be paid in full. If it were willing to defer payment, the seller could, in principle, fully protect itself with a purchase money security interest in the computer. The seller then would have priority with respect to the computer over all other creditors, and its security interest could not be set aside by a trustee in bankruptcy if the buyer became insolvent.

In practice, however, this arrangement might leave the seller insufficiently protected. The computer might depreciate at a rate faster than the buyer's payments, making the right to repossess an imperfect protection. To protect itself, the seller might seek a security interest in other property of the buyer, but other secured parties might have priority over it. Moreover, although the bankruptcy petition does not destroy a secured creditor's rights, the automatic stay and cram down powers of the trustee can disrupt them. Because of these risks, the seller might seek additional protection by introducing a third party into the transaction.

A third party can decrease the seller's risks by cosigning the buyer's promissory note as a guarantor. If the third party who is willing to bear the risk that the buyer will default is a bank, however, it must issue a standby letter of credit rather than a guarantee. Before issuing such a letter, the bank usually requires its customer (the purchaser of the computer) to grant it a security interest in property to which it will have recourse if it is forced to pay on the letter and the customer is unwilling or unable to reimburse it. [. . .]

An Economic Analysis of the Guarantee Contract*
AVERY W. KATZ

The Standard Guaranty Relationship

Guaranties and suretyships take many forms, but the essence of the relationship is a contract among three parties: a creditor, C, who is owed a duty, a debtor (D) who owes the duty, and a guarantor or surety (G) who promises to perform or pay damages on D's behalf. Depending on the context and the applicable body of law, however, these three parties are designated by different labels, as illustrated in Table 1. In the terminology of the Third Restatement, for example, C is the "obligee," D the "primary obligor," and G the "secondary obligor." As this terminology suggests, ordinarily D is expected to bear the burden of performance, and if G is called upon to perform or pay in D's stead, it is ordinarily expected that D will reimburse her if he is able. The arrangement can be achieved through a single contract or through multiple contracts; in the latter case, G may contract with D alone, with C alone, or with both. A guaranty may even be created without the knowledge of D or C, though in this case the parties' rights and duties will be altered in order to protect the uninformed party[. . .]

* 66 U. of Chic. L. Rev. 47, 52–62 (1999).

Standby Letters of Credit

D, a software design company, wishes to borrow funds for a new project from C, a commercial bank with whom it has not dealt previously. Because a regular loan would entail a new credit investigation and require C to familiarize itself with a new type of business, C would have to charge D more than the prime rate of interest. C, however, will loan the funds to D at or below the prime rate if D approaches G, a bank with whom it has a longstanding relationship, and obtains a standby letter of credit naming C as beneficiary. This letter of credit provides that if C presents G with documents attesting that D has defaulted on C's loan, C will be entitled to draw on the credit up to an agreed limit. In exchange for a fee proportional to the amount of the standby credit, G issues the letter to D, who presents it to C in exchange for the desired funds.

The Law Governing Guaranties

Because a guaranty relationship can be achieved through a variety of contractual devices, the precise body of law that governs the relationship will depend on the particular device used. Generally, the parties' relationship will be governed by the common law of contracts and suretyship, the latter of which has recently been recatalogued by the Third Restatement. If a guarantor (G) acquires her status by making or indorsing a negotiable instrument, however, the parties' relationship will be governed first by Article 3 of the Uniform Commercial Code ("UCC"), which provides special rules for "accommodation parties," and next by any common law rules that the UCC does not specifically displace. If the guaranty takes the form of a standby letter of credit, which is routine when the guarantor is a commercial bank, the relationship is governed in part by Article 5 of the UCC, in part by the common law, and—if the transaction has an international element—in part by the International Chamber of Commerce's Uniform Customs and Practice for Documentary Credits. If the guarantor provides collateral to secure the underlying secondary obligation, or if the guaranty arises out of a sale or assignment of accounts, then UCC Article 9 governs the transaction. Finally, as indicated above, if the U.S. government or U.S.-sponsored institutions guarantee a loan, then federal statutes—and, ultimately, implicit political contracts among Congress, the executive branch, international actors, and American voters—provide the basis for liability.

Whatever body of law, commercial practice, or political understanding creates the guaranty, the functional issues are much the same. Guaranties are a response to potential moral hazard and adverse selection problems: they help protect creditors against some of the risks of debtor misbehavior or insolvency by shifting those risks to guarantors. In so doing, guaranties enlist the guarantor's efforts in reducing or managing those risks. As with any other insurance arrangement, however, guaranties themselves are subject to various types of moral hazard and adverse selection. Each party to the transaction can impose losses on the others by failing to take precautions or by withholding information. For example, guarantors have the power to hurt creditors (and debtors as well) by incautiously offering guaranties where the underlying financial situation does not warrant a loan, or by failing to monitor the debtor after money has been lent. Creditors may hurt guarantors (and debtors) by provoking debtors to default, by failing to collect from the debtor when possible, and by impairing the guarantor's ability to seek recourse from the debtor after the fact. Debtors can injure guarantors and creditors alike by taking excessive risks and making inadequate efforts to meet their primary obligations. Moreover, the very creation of a suretyship can itself raise incentive problems, particularly when one of the parties to the underlying primary contract had not anticipated that a three-corner relationship would arise.

Because of these common functional problems, all bodies of formal guaranty law provide the three archetypical parties with various rights and duties that, on the whole, are designed to discourage opportunism and encourage all persons involved to take reasonable precautions against economic loss. All regimes of guaranty law provide a default rule giving G a right of recourse against D in the event D does not perform his primary obligation and G has to make good on her guaranty.

The common law of suretyship, for example, protects this right of recourse in three ways. First, G is entitled to the right of reimbursement for any funds she actually pays out, plus reasonable expenses. Second, and alternatively, if G satisfies D's obligation to C in full, she is equitably subrogated to C's rights against D. This subrogation right is valuable if C has some special status (such as that of holder in due course) that gives her immunity against claims and defenses that D could otherwise raise (and specifically, that D could raise against G). It is also useful if C has priority over D's other creditors through a lien or other interest in specific property. Finally, G has a right to D's performance itself—that is, the right of exoneration. This last right is valuable because G can assert it before her duty to pay anything out has arisen, and such early action may increase the chances that D will still perform. Depending on the circumstances, the right of exoneration may entitle G to receive specific performance from D, pursue an action against D for creating insecurity along the lines of the right of adequate assurances under Section 2–609 of the UCC, or declare the contract in default.

Conversely, guaranty law provides a number of rules designed to protect guarantors against creditor action that materially increases guarantor risk. Thus, if the debtor's breach was occasioned by a countervailing breach by C—as when a credit buyer of goods withholds payment after discovering that the goods are unmerchantable—the traditional common law rule permits G to treat C's breach as a defense to her secondary liability to the same extent it would provide a defense to D's primary liability. Similarly, she may be able to assert D's unrelated claims against C by way of set-off.

Beyond such derivative claims, G is also entitled to raise certain rights and defenses against C that D could not raise—the so-called "suretyship defenses." For instance, if C modifies D's underlying obligation, extends D's time for performance, unreasonably refuses a tender of performance by either D or G, or fails to supervise or preserve rights against collateral or against co-sureties or sub-sureties, G may avoid liability to the extent she suffers resulting loss. Indeed, if C fails to disclose events that would support a good suretyship defense under conditions where it should know that G is ignorant of such events, G has a right to recover any amounts she has unnecessarily paid out.

The specific content of these various rights and duties, however, depends both upon the particular factual setting and the governing body of law. The substance of suretyship defenses and the duties of care owed by the creditor, for instance, are different under the common law of suretyship, Articles 3 and 9 of the UCC, and the law of letters of credit. The remedies that follow from a breach of C's duty to G are also different, as are the procedures for contracting around the default rules within various legal regimes. As a result, the content of guaranty obligations depends primarily on the parties' choice of transactional form. A person guaranteeing a promise embodied in a promissory note can opt into the rules of Article 3 by signing the note as an accommodation party or into the rules of the common law of suretyship by signing a separate written agreement. She can opt into Article 5 by casting her guaranty in the form of a letter of credit or opt into Article 9 by offering specific property as collateral. Even within these broader transactional forms, furthermore, she can vary her rights and duties by using particular terms of art, relying on the Article 3 distinction between guaranty of collection and guaranty of payment, or by providing specific conditions for transfer and presentment in a letter of credit. By issuing a limited rather than an unlimited guaranty, she can mimic various risk-sharing devices common in insurance markets, including liability caps, deductibles, and copayments. And apart from a few exceptions, she can contract around the default rules of suretyship whatever the applicable legal regime. Indeed, such waivers of default are the norm in many lending markets. [. . .]

When are guaranties efficient?

C would plainly prefer adding G to the transaction if there were no costs associated with doing so. But of course there is a cost—the risks and obligations that will be imposed on G in her role as guarantor. To the extent that C is relieved from the responsibility for monitoring, G is burdened with it. To the extent that C can recover from G following D's default, G (and G's other creditors) are at risk. Thus, many, though not all, of the costs saved by C on a guaranteed loan are simply shifted to G [. . .]

[A] loan made by C and guaranteed by G is cheaper than a simple unguaranteed loan from C if, and only if, the expected savings achieved by shifting some or all monitoring, enforcement, and default risk costs from C to G outweigh the increased transaction costs that arise from having to maintain three relationships among the parties instead of just one. In short, guaranties are profitable when the guarantor holds a sufficiently great comparative advantage in investigating, supervising, or collecting from the debtor in the event of default—in other words, when the guarantor is the least-cost monitor. The creditor and debtor engage the guarantor to do this monitoring and enforcement, either explicitly or implicitly, and the guarantor either keeps the proceeds as her compensation or allows the debtor to keep them as a gift [. . .]

The general practice of standby letters of credit can also be understood in such terms. Commercial banks will have a comparative advantage in monitoring their existing credit customers, as their prior relationships with such customers allow them to obtain and evaluate relevant information at low cost. They also have many more ways to influence such debtors' behavior after a loan is made. For instance, they can call in, refuse to renew, or exercise covenants on separate loans. In addition, they may have established general "floating liens" on the debtor's property—that is, mortgages or security interests that cover after-acquired property or that provide that existing collateral will also serve to secure future advances. Such cross-collateralization clauses improve the bank's ability to collect on any advances it makes pursuant to a guaranty; they also give the bank substantial leverage over the debtor by making it difficult for him to engage in subsequent borrowing without the bank's permission. Perhaps most importantly, the prior relationship gives the bank the power to ruin the customer's reputation with other lenders. Because an unfavorable credit reference from a longstanding creditor carries great weight in underwriting decisions, the bank can credibly threaten to raise the customer's cost of borrowing for the foreseeable future. Such a threat serves as a powerful incentive for D to repay. For all these reasons, then, bank guaranties—cast in the form of standby letters of credit—can substantially cut the expected costs of monitoring, default, and collection relative to unguaranteed loans. [. . .]

A guaranty, in short, is a credit transaction in which one party—the guarantor—specializes in information and monitoring, and another—the creditor—specializes in obtaining loanable funds. [. . . For example, consider our] example of the standby letter of credit. At any given moment, the marginal cost of interest and liquidity varies among large commercial banks. Such banks have different mixtures of long-term and short-term loans in their asset portfolios, and different risk exposures based on the specific commercial activities of their customers and on the particular investment products they have decided to back. Therefore, it can make sense for a bank with relatively heavy exposure in the area of commercial real estate, for instance, to decide that its marginal cost of liquidity is too high to justify a new loan to a longstanding client at market rates. If the client can obtain liquid funds elsewhere, however, the bank can trade on its informational investment in him by issuing a standby letter of credit in his favor. Conversely, another bank with temporarily superior access to a pool of liquid funds due, for instance, to a special relationship with an institutional depositor, may find it worthwhile to make a loan to an untried applicant if that applicant's current lender is willing to stand behind him. The standby letter of credit thus allows the debtor to benefit from the low monitoring cost that comes from establishing a long-term financing relationship while still retaining the option of shopping around for the best pure price on liquid funds [...]

NOTES

1. Problem. Happy Planet, Inc., a company that develops environmentally-friendly technology, wishes to borrow $1M for a new hydrogen fuel cell project from Big Bank, a commercial bank with whom it has not dealt previously. The prime rate of interest is 5%. Because a regular loan would entail a new credit investigation and require Big Bank to familiarize itself with the complicated business of hydrogen fuel cells, Big Bank would have to charge Happy Planet 7% interest. Big Bank, however, will loan the funds to Happy Planet at 5.25% if Happy Planet approaches Little Bank, a bank with whom the company has a longstanding relationship, and obtains a standby letter of credit naming Big Bank as beneficiary. This letter of credit provides that if Big Bank presents Little Bank with documents attesting that Happy Planet has defaulted on Big Bank's loan, Big Bank will be entitled to draw on the credit up to $400,000. In exchange for a fee of $20,000, Little Bank issues the letter to Happy Planet, who presents it to Big Bank in exchange for the desired funds. Applying Katz's analysis, what are the costs of credit in this transaction? Why is it, according to Katz, that Big Bank is willing to cut the applicable interest rate in return for Little Bank acting as a guarantor? To answer these questions one might first ask what each party brings to the transaction. Happy Planet brings an growth opportunity that has net present value. Big Bank brings a reserve of available capital and an ability to distribute financial losses among a broad customer base. And Little Bank brings knowledge of Happy Planet's past business successes (and failures) and an ability to monitor Happy Planet as it develops the fuel cell technology. What other features of Little Bank are important to Big Bank? Does Little Bank's involvement simply mean that Big Bank must monitor Little Bank rather than Happy Planet?

2. Irrelevance propositions. Irrelevance propositions are common analytical tools for understanding the motivation behind a behavioral pattern, particularly in finance. Indeed, several Nobel Prizes have been awarded to recognize such propositions. One well known example among law students is the Coase theorem that provides, loosely stated, that the assignment of legal rights does not affect the efficiency of outcomes in a world without transaction costs. Ronald H. Coase, *The Problem of Social Cost,* 3 J. Law & Econ. 1 (1960). The starting point for the modern analysis of a firm's choice between debt and equity financing is the Modigliani–Miller irrelevance proposition that holds under the assumptions they specify in their article, Franco Modigliani & Merton Miller, *The Cost of Capital, Corporation Finance, and the Theory of Investment,* 48 Am. Econ. Rev. 261 (1958). Similarly, Avery Katz begins with an irrelevance proposition for sureties: although a surety can reduce the borrowing cost to the debtor, the surety's liability raises the cost of her own credit by depleting her assets and thereby increasing the risk that her creditors may not get paid. Therefore, guaranties cannot be explained simply by stating that lenders charge lower rates of interest when they benefit from guaranties. Without more to the story, the cost of capital cannot be reduced in this way. In fact, the parties may be worse off to the extent that they incur transaction costs in establishing the surety relationship.

3. Imperfect information, screening and monitoring. One necessary assumption supporting the irrelevance of financial decisions is perfect information. In other words, financial decisions are often motivated by informational concerns. One category is agency problems (alternatively referred to as private action or moral hazard). Under this category, the existence of debt in the capital structure of a firm gives rise to three forms of misbehavior: (a) the distribution of assets to insiders or shareholders, (b) investment in risky, but unprofitable ventures (overinvestment), (c) the failure to exploit low-risk, profitable ventures where the payoffs would accrue to existing debtholders (underinvestment or debt overhang). Debt contracts seek to address these incentives in their covenants. *See* Clifford W. Smith, Jr. & Jerrold Warner, *On Financial Contracting: An Analysis of Bond Covenants,* 7 J. Fin. Econ. 117 (1979). The violation of covenants is typically an event of default that entitles the creditor to accelerate the maturity of the credit and enforce its claim. Often, covenants are quite broad, effectively giving the creditor the rights of a demand loan. Compliance with covenants, however, must be monitored, as must the financial condition of the borrower. Monitoring is costly and Katz suggests that sureties may be selected to undertake monitoring tasks at lower cost than the creditors.

4. Surety defenses. As we noted in the introduction to this chapter, there are a number of defenses that a surety (or an accommodation party under Article 3) might raise when called upon to pay the principal debtor's obligation. These defenses fall into two categories. Initially, the surety is entitled to raise a number of the defenses to payment that are available to the principal debtor against the creditor. For example, if the creditor has failed to perform its contract with the principal debtor, permitting the surety to raise the defense of failure of consideration removes the unnecessary circularity of allowing the creditor to recover from the surety, who would then recover from the principal debtor, who would then seek recovery from the creditor. But the second category of defenses is more puzzling. Under UCC § 3–605 the surety is discharged if the creditor agrees with the principal debtor to alterations in the terms of the original transactions, including extensions of time or other modifications of the debtor's obligation.

Why should an agreement to give the principal debtor more time to honor his obligation be an occasion for discharging the surety? To be sure, sometimes these actions will increase the surety's risk of not being able to recover reimbursement from the debtor. But other times, such modifications might actually increase the likelihood that the obligation will be repaid without default. Is this an example of a bright line rule that is unavoidably over and under-inclusive?

5. Menu of legal rules. Katz observes the flexibility that parties to surety or guarantee agreements have in providing for their respective rights and obligations. He also writes that "the content of guaranty obligations depends primarily on the parties' choice of transactional form," and he contrasts the law governing accommodation parties (Article 3), common law sureties under separate written agreements, and issuers of letters of credit (Article 5). Is the law serving a valuable function in providing for these alternatives, or should we be concerned with the inconsistencies across forms as Mann and Gillette were in connection with the rights associated with various payment instruments in Chapter 4?

5.3 Sureties versus Alternative Lending Arrangements

An Economic Analysis of the Guarantee Contract*
AVERY W. KATZ

Consider a situation where a would-be debtor, D, seeks funds from two potential creditors, C and G. There are several ways to provide funds to D.... First, D could borrow from C alone, leaving G out of the transaction entirely.... Second, D could borrow from C and supplement it with a guaranty from G. [Here] the extension of credit is contingent rather than unconditional. Specifically, if D does not repay the primary loan, then G will become indebted to C and D will become indebted to G. Third, G could borrow from C and then on-lend to D.... In this case both obligations are unconditional. C would then have no direct claim against D, though G's claim against D would be one of the assets to which C could ultimately look for satisfaction if G falls into default with C.

For each of these three possibilities there exists an alternative and symmetric arrangement with G and C switching places. For instance, D could borrow the entire amount from G rather than from C, and so on. Additionally, the parties could provide part of the desired funds through one form and the rest through another, as when C and G separately and independently lend D half of what he requests [. . .]

Why doesn't the guarantor simply act as an intermediary?

The guarantor's comparative advantage in monitoring, risk assessment, and collection explains why she should bear the residual risk of

* 66 U. of Chic. L. Rev. 47, 52–62 (1999).

the debtor's default; the creditor's comparative advantage in liquidity explains why it should obtain the funds. But neither explanation tells us why the relationship should take the form of a guaranty, for these same advantages could be achieved through pure intermediation or on-lending. Specifically, C could obtain funds and lend them to G, who could then turn around and lend to D.

Under such an arrangement, G would bear the costs of monitoring D and dealing with any default on his part, since she would remain liable to C whether or not D managed to repay. C would bear the costs of liquidity, since it would be the one who obtains the funds. There would, moreover, be only two relationships to manage instead of three. What, then are the advantages of guaranties as opposed to intermediation? Or to put the question differently, what are the advantages of giving C a direct right of recovery against D as well as against G?

It turns out that there are two answers to this question, which I take up in sequence. First, G's comparative advantage in supervising D may be incomplete, so that it pays for G to undertake some aspects of monitoring, risk assessment, or collection and for C to undertake others. Second, there is always a chance that G herself may default on her obligations to C. If she does, giving C a direct right against D allows C to avoid sharing the proceeds of D's loan with G's other creditors, in much the same way that a security interest confers priority over rival creditors.

Specialization in different types of monitoring or enforcement.

Recall that monitoring, as we have used the term, incorporates a wide variety of distinct business functions: underwriting, credit investigation, drafting and executing contracts, auditing, and the like. Similarly, collection may involve pursuing legal or nonlegal sanctions against the debtor, locating and gathering his assets, salvaging and reselling them, and, ultimately, bearing the risk that the proceeds will be inadequate to cover the debt. It is quite possible for G to have a comparative advantage in some of these tasks and C to have a comparative advantage in others. If so, it is efficient to have C and G specialize in different types of monitoring or enforcement. Consider, for example, a loan made for the purposes of financing a startup enterprise. The borrower's family members may be better able to assess his overall honesty and industriousness, keep track of his personal assets, and collect from him in the event of a business failure. On the other hand, they may know relatively little about the specific line of business he is contemplating or may lack experience in evaluating whether such startup projects have what it takes to succeed. For these reasons, they may not wish to incur the risk of financing the project out of their own funds. Once a commercial lender with background in the relevant industry has evaluated and underwritten the project, however, the residual risk to the family members from guaranteeing the borrower's debt is substantially lowered.

One way to achieve such specialization, of course, is through direct subcontracting of the relevant activities—one party could make the loan and hire another party to conduct underwriting or collection. Indeed, such subcontracts are not uncommon, as the existence of the credit reporting industry illustrates. But the very fact that one party has a comparative advantage in some aspect of monitoring or enforcement may make it difficult for the other interested parties to tell whether he or she is carrying out such tasks effectively. For that reason, monitors and enforcers are typically allocated some portion of the risk of default; for instance, a collection agency hired to hunt down delinquent accounts might be paid a commission based on the amounts it actually manages to extract from recalcitrant debtors. Thus, to make use of C's and G's comparative advantages, it is necessary to provide both with incentives to perform their assigned tasks.

A guaranty promotes such dual incentives better than pure intermediation. Under intermediation, the risk of D's default is borne almost entirely by G and hardly at all by C. C has no direct connection with D and no specific obligation to monitor him; indeed, so long as G retains other assets sufficient to repay her loan, C is fully protected against loss. Under a guaranty contract, in contrast, both G and C have good incentives to engage in monitoring. G's incentives to monitor D are obvious—absent some excuse or defense, she will be liable for his default. C's incentives, however, arise from the fact that if it fails to act reasonably or to live up to its other contractual obligations, G will acquire just such an excuse or defense, for under the law of suretyship and guaranty, C owes special duties toward G—duties it does not owe to other ordinary creditors or debtors. These are the so-called "suretyship defenses." Failing to perform duties owed the debtor, failing to maintain rights against the debtor or against any collateral, granting the debtor unreasonable extensions or modifications—all operate in the guaranty context to release the guarantor from her obligation. As Section 37 of the Third Restatement provides: "If the obligee acts to increase the secondary obligor's risk of loss by increasing its potential cost of performance or decreasing its potential ability to cause the principal obligor to bear the cost of performance, the secondary obligor is discharged."

The law of suretyship, accordingly, provides both C and G with incentives to engage in monitoring, in the same way that negligence law provides dual incentives to take precautions against accidents and contract law provides dual incentives for parties to mitigate damages. Under each of these regimes, one party—the guarantor in surety, the victim in tort, the promisor in contract—is presumptively liable for a loss, and so has optimal incentives to take care to prevent it. The presumption is reversed, however, if the other party breaches a legal duty of care. The threat of that reversal gives that other party—the primary creditor C, the potential tortfeasor, the contract promisee—strong incentives to take care. This result has been called "double responsibility on the margin."

Of course, it is not always efficient for law or contract to try to give both parties incentives to take care. If there is relatively little that one side can do to influence the underlying risk, or if the tribunal charged with enforcing the relevant duty of care is not good at determining whether it has really been breached, then the attempt to provide dual incentives may be more costly than it is worth. This is why, for instance, strict liability in tort is sometimes more efficient than a negligence rule. Similarly, if one of the parties already has good incentives to take care based on extralegal considerations such as reputation, it may be better for that party to disclaim liability for negligence or similar breaches of duty, reserving legal sanctions for the purpose of motivating the party not subject to such extralegal incentives. For all these reasons, then, it may be desirable in some cases to cast a credit transaction in the form of an intermediation rather than as a guaranty. Such factors can also help explain why it might be efficient for guarantors to waive their rights to assert the standard suretyship defenses; indeed, such explicit waivers are routine in many important commercial settings.

Risk of G's insolvency or recalcitrance.

A second and equally important reason why guaranties may be preferable to intermediation is that G herself may fall into default and prove uncollectable. In this event, a guaranty contract gives C an alternate means of expedited collection, as well as partial priority over G's other creditors. Indeed, from a functional perspective, a guaranty is analogous to a secured loan by C to G, with D's promise to pay operating as the collateral. Specifically, in the event that G defaults or becomes insolvent, guaranties and intermediation have different consequences. Under intermediation, C will have no contract or property claim allowing it to reach any of G's assets in particular. In order to collect directly from D, it would first have to win a lawsuit against G for breach of contract and then obtain and enforce a judgment lien against G's interest in D's loan. Such remedies can be costly; more importantly, in the time it takes under state collection law to pursue them, any value remaining in the loan may have dissipated. Furthermore, if G actually turns out to be insolvent, C will be forced to participate in bankruptcy proceedings and will have to share any proceeds arising from D's debt (and from G's other remaining assets) with all of G's other creditors on a pro rata basis.

Under a guaranty, in contrast, C gets an expedited collection procedure and an effective priority in D's debt over G's other creditors, through its option to obtain repayment directly from D. Of course, giving such an option to C is not costless; to the extent that C is able to satisfy itself out of the proceeds of D's debt to G, there will be fewer assets left for G's other creditors. Whether it is efficient to give C a priority in these proceeds, however, depends on whether that priority is more valuable in C's hands than in the hands of G's other creditors—or equivalently, whether C gains more from the priority than the other creditors lose.

But a well-established account of how one should allocate priority among creditors in the event of insolvency already exists; it can be found in the economic literature on secured credit. This account begins with the observation that secured credit has higher direct transaction costs than unsecured credit: it is necessary to write a special contract, file a public notice, restrict the use of collateral, and so on. Security is only worthwhile, on this account, if its other advantages justify these costs. This can be the case only if the secured lender places a higher value on a specific interest in the collateral than do the debtor's other creditors; otherwise the cost the debtor will pay when seeking other financing after having encumbered his assets will more than outweigh the benefits he receives in exchange for granting a security interest. The secured lender's higher value in specific collateral can arise from various factors: from superior information regarding its market or use-value, from a comparative advantage in salvage, from superior ability to monitor the collateral's whereabouts or to prevent it from being diverted to other uses—or from a relatively inferior ability to monitor, evaluate, or make use of the debtor's other assets. If any of these factors are present, value is created when the secured lender takes priority in the collateralized asset, leaving other, unsecured creditors to take their compensation through other property or through an increased price or risk premium.

The advantages and disadvantages of guaranties, when viewed as devices for gaining leverage and priority in the event of default, are precisely analogous. Guaranties have higher direct transaction costs than intermediation. While no public notice is required to create a guaranty, one does need to write a special contract, keep track of the rights and duties of three parties, and restrict the manner in which the guarantor and creditor deal with the debtor.

Accordingly, guaranties are worthwhile compared to intermediation only if C places a sufficiently higher value on having a direct claim against D than do G's other creditors; otherwise the costs that G incurs in her dealings with these other creditors will outweigh any benefits she gets when giving or selling the guaranty. This condition will be satisfied if C has superior information regarding the value of D's obligation to G, if C has superior ability to supervise D's behavior, or if C has superior ability to collect from D—in short, if C has a sufficient comparative advantage over G's other creditors in monitoring or enforcing against D.

This condition seems to be satisfied in most cases in which guaranties are used. Because C generally has had some prior dealings with D, has investigated D, enjoys some special leverage over D, or expects to do any of these things in the future, it makes sense for C to look directly to D for repayment or at least to have the option to do so. If C instead lends to G on an unsecured basis, it loses all the advantages that flow from its relationship with D [. . .]

Guaranties are more efficient than pure intermediation, in short, when C has some special interest or comparative advantage in monitoring D—either relative to G or to G's other creditors. The former comparison will be relevant in the event that G is solvent, and the latter comparison will be relevant in the event that she is not. Intermediation, in contrast, makes sense when the ultimate creditor has no comparative advantage in monitoring or collecting from the ultimate borrower. As a stereotypical example, consider commercial banking as it has traditionally been practiced: the bank obtains liquid funds from various individual depositors and lends them out to various business and consumer borrowers. Here the plainly efficient arrangement is for the bank to act as a pure intermediary. Since the depositors are in no position to evaluate or supervise the bank's lending decisions, there is no reason for them to take priority in or to have a direct claim against any particular loan or group of loans. The transaction costs of doing so—including, most importantly, the substantial inconvenience to the depositors of having to concern themselves with the bank's lending portfolio, and the corresponding inconvenience to borrowers of having to deal with inquiries from a multitude of small, scattered creditors—would simply be wasted.

NOTES

1.   The guaranty-vs-intermediary puzzle. Katz suggests that monitoring is a multi-faceted activity, so that different parties may have comparative advantages in monitoring different aspects of the debtor. Thus, he argues that lending relationships with guarantors harness the respective monitoring advantages of each of the lender ("C") and the guarantor ("G"). Moreover, he suggests that it does so better than the alternative of intermediation, under which G borrows directly from C in order to lend to D. The reason is that C may not have sufficient incentive to monitor D if she can collect her debt from G's other assets. Yet, could the parties exploit the same joint monitoring advantages simply by splitting the aggregate amount invested in D? Thus, C would lend part of it directly to D and the other part indirectly through G. Indeed, this arrangement would have the advantage over the surety alternative of allowing the parties to fine-tune monitoring incentives by varying the portion lent directly by C. Moreover, as we will explore in Chapter 6, the parties could use security interests to further exploit comparative monitoring advantages.

Katz advances another explanation for why C would prefer to lend with the benefit of G's guaranty rather than through G as an intermediary. Although the risk of G's insolvency may be more remote than that of D's, it is nevertheless a risk borne by C. If G became insolvent, C would have first priority over the debt owed by D. Katz notes that "from a functional perspective, a guaranty is analogous to a secured loan by C to G, with D's promise to pay operating as the collateral." In other words, the guaranty effectively gives C a security interest in the receivable from D to G. Here again, Katz acknowledges the puzzle raised by the irrelevance proposition. If C has a prior claim against D, then the claim is not generally available to G's other creditors. As Katz indicates in the foregoing excerpts, this is efficient

> "only if C places a sufficiently higher value on having a direct claim against D than do G's other creditors ... This condition will be satisfied if C has superior information regarding the value of D's obligation to C, if C has superior ability to supervise D's behavior, or if C has superior ability to collect from D—in short, if C has sufficient comparative advantage over G's other creditors in monitoring or enforcing against D."

This may be the case because C is D's lender, so she is likely to have better information about D than G's other creditors. We will see a similar argument advanced to explain why a creditor might receive a security interest in a specific asset: that asset can serve as a focal point for the creditor's monitoring of the debtor and the security interest can thereby exploit the creditor's advantage in monitoring that asset. See Chapter 6.2, infra.

2.   A distributional explanation. We might ask whether the creditors of the surety would be adequately informed about the new liability in order to adjust the rate they charge. In the intermediary example, G would incur an outright debt to C and this would appear as a liability on its balance sheet. Any creditor who could adjust would have the information enabling it to do so. Where G's liability, however, is contingent on, for example, D's default, the accounting principles are less clear. Guarantors must recognize a liability for an obligation at the inception of the guarantee if it is a non-contingent, immediate obligation to stand ready to perform. If the guarantee is contingent on the occurrence of specific conditions, however, then the fair market value of the contingent liability should be recognized and measured as directed by *FASB Statement No. 5, Accounting for Contingencies*, March 1975. *FASB Interpretation No. 45, Guarantor's Accounting and Disclosure Requirements for Guarantees, Including Indirect Guarantees of Indebtedness of Others: an interpretation of FASB Statements No. 5, 57, and 107 and rescission of FASB Interpretation No. 34*, November 2002. Despite the guidelines on measuring fair market value of a contingent guarantee, there is sufficient room for subjective estimation that a reader of the guarantor's financial statements might underestimate the risk of extending credit to that entity.

Chapter 6

Secured Credit

6.1 Introduction

Chapter 5 discussed the role of sureties in reducing the default risk borne by a creditor. This chapter focuses on another feature: the debtor may grant security interests in her assets (that serve as "collateral"). A security interest may be defined along two dimensions. First, it secures specific obligations of the debtor—most commonly, the obligation to pay an outstanding debt. Second, the security interest covers a group of assets, the collateral. For example, a debtor firm might borrow $5 million from a bank to finance its operations, and secure its repayment obligation with its inventory and receivables. Article 9 of the UCC governs security interests in most personal property. Some personal property interests fall under federal statutes (for example, aircraft or telecommunication licenses). And, security interests in real property (mortgages) are governed at the state level by real property statutes. The academic literature on secured credit tends to be set in the context of personal property, perhaps because of the greater scope for creative financing offered by Article 9. The federal Bankruptcy Code is important because it alters the rules governing security interests when the debtor is in bankruptcy. In light of the fact that security interests become most relevant when the debtor is in financial distress, bankruptcy rules are an important part of the law of secured credit.

Article 9 permits broad security interests along both dimensions described above. A security agreement may provide that collateral secures future advances by the creditor and the security interest can cover assets currently held by the debtor or acquired in the future. § 9–204(a), (c). A typically broad secured credit arrangement is a loan, under which the debtor grants a security interest in all its present or after-acquired assets, that secures all its current or future obligations to the lender (often designated as a "blanket lien").

A security interest gives the creditor two types of rights. First, upon default, the creditor may proceed directly to seize and sell the collateral in order to satisfy the outstanding indebtedness. § 9–609. In contrast, unsecured creditors must first obtain judgment against the debtor and then request that an officer of the court (typically, the sheriff) proceed against the assets of the judgment debtor. In fact, however, the enforcement right of the secured creditor is not as valuable as it might appear initially because the creditor may seize the collateral only if she can do so without breach of the peace. § 9–609(b)(2). If the debtor resists turning over the asset, the secured creditor must move in court for a replevin order and obtain the assistance of the sheriff.

The second right of a secured creditor is a priority right. It is typically the more valuable right, and the one that has given rise to more debate among academics. Creditors have fixed claims against the assets of their debtor. Until they take steps to enforce their claims and obtain liens, unsecured creditors share pro rata against the debtor's assets. Secured creditors, in contrast, enjoy priority over unsecured creditors so long as they publicize their rights by "perfecting" their security interests as Article 9 prescribes. This is because their priority dates from the time of perfection rather than, as in the case of unsecured creditors, from the time they take steps to obtain a judicial lien against the debtor. In short, the priority of secured creditors is asset-based rather than debtor-based, and thus it is limited to the secured party's collateral.

In addition, Article 9 specifies a priority scheme among secured creditors. The priority of a secured creditor hinges on the time at which she publicizes her lien. Assuming a security interest is enforceable against the debtor, a secured creditor enjoys priority over the collateral if it perfects the security interest by taking one of the prescribed steps to publicize it. Secured creditors typically perfect either by taking possession of the collateral or by providing public notice by filing a financing statement with the registry kept by the state. The registry merely puts a searcher on notice that the debtor may have granted a security interest in specified groups of assets to the identified creditor. § 9–502 ct. 2. The searcher may obtain further information from the secured party. UCC § 9–210. Priority among secured creditors is determined by a pure race system, rather than actual notice: a subsequent creditor with notice of an earlier claim can nonetheless prevail unless the prior creditor has fixed its priority by public filing.

In the commercial realm, most of the legal rules governing security interests concern the priority scheme: the priority of a secured creditor against other creditors and buyers. The policy justifications for this priority structure have fallen into two camps: (a) security interests mitigate information problems in debt contracting and (b) they redistribute wealth from unsecured to secured creditors and may create incentives for inefficient investment decisions by the borrower. In the former case, security interests might address two types of information problems: (i) The debtor has better information about its financial prospects, including the risk of default (information asymmetry or private information), and (ii) after borrowing, the debtor has an incentive to engage in activity that increases the risk of default (agency problems or moral hazard). In turn, the agency/moral hazard risk can be split into two subcategories: First, the borrower has the incentive to invest in high risk projects and will substitute high-risk for low-risk assets, even if the expected return from the new investment is negative. This misbehavior is referred to as *risk substitution* or *overinvestment*. Second, the borrower may find it difficult to finance a low-risk project even if it is profitable because, unless the new investor is given priority in the new project, that investor will be compelled to share the payoff from the project with the existing creditors of the same or higher priority. This problem is called *underinvestment* or *debt overhang*. The manner in which security interests may mitigate these various information problems is discussed in the material of the next three sections. The reader should consider the circumstances in which security interest provide plausible solutions to each problem.

In section 6.2, the authors suggest that the allocation of security interests among creditors with heterogeneous monitoring abilities can exploit comparative monitoring advantages and thereby reduce a debtor's cost of capital. Section 6.3 examines the provisions that increase the breadth of security interests by attaching to proceeds and after-acquired property, and by securing future advances. The readings in section 6.4 concern the allocation of security interests over time in order to both discourage overinvestment and mitigate underinvestment. Section 6.5 discusses the merits of a state-run registry and the perfection requirement as a mechanism for communicating the existence of secured credit to third parties dealing with the debtor.

In Section 6.6, several authors explore the distributional impact of secured debt on less sophisticated or smaller creditors who either are unaware or cannot adjust their credit terms to the amount of priority claims issued by their debtors. The result may include the misallocation of resources, leading authors from diverging perspectives to call for regulatory restriction on the freedom to contract for secured credit.

6.2 Why are Some Creditors Secured and Others Not?

Secured Credit and Priorities Among Creditors*

THOMAS H. JACKSON and **ANTHONY T. KRONMAN**

The price a creditor charges for extending credit—the interest his debtor must pay for the privilege of borrowing—varies directly with the riskiness of the loan itself. There is almost always some risk that a loan will not be repaid. As this risk increases, the interest rate set by the creditor making the loan will also increase. Once a creditor has agreed to make a loan at a specified rate of interest, however, that rate normally cannot be changed during the period when the loan is out-standing. Because the interest rate is fixed, the debtor has an incentive to increase the riskiness of the loan, since, by doing so, he effectively obtains a higher-risk loan at an interest rate reflecting the lower risk level anticipated by the creditor when the loan was made. By behaving in this way, the debtor gets something for nothing (ignoring, for the sake of argument, any reputational loss he may suffer as a result). We shall refer to this phenomenon, a species of opportunism, as the "threat of debtor misbehavior."

Naturally, a creditor will take this threat into account before agreeing to make his loan. One possible response the creditor may make is simply to increase the interest rate on his loan above what it would be in the absence of a threat of misbehavior. Alternatively, he may attempt to reduce the risk of misbehavior itself. One way to do this is to monitor the debtor's conduct after the loan has been made, or to require the debtor to assume contractual responsibilities, such as the preparation of periodic financial statements, that make it easier for the creditor to assess the financial consequences of the debtor's actions. We shall refer to a strategy of this sort as a "monitoring" or "policing" strategy.

The degree to which a creditor will rely on monitoring, rather than simply demanding increased compensation for bearing a greater risk, is determined by two factors—the cost of monitoring, and the magnitude of the risk that the debtor will misbehave. Assume that by spending $X on monitoring a creditor can entirely eliminate the risk of debtor misbehavior. If $X is less than the additional interest the debtor would have to pay in the absence of any monitoring, it will be to the debtor's advantage to be monitored. The debtor will in fact have an incentive to propose such an arrangement, and to pay the creditor something for agreeing to it. However, if $X is greater than the additional interest the creditor would demand in the absence of any monitoring (which might be the case if the creditor believes the risk of misbehavior to be very low, and

* 88 YALE L. J. 1143 (1979).

the cost of monitoring is very high), both parties will be better off without any monitoring.

Similar considerations will determine the allocation of monitoring responsibilities between the two parties. If the creditor can monitor his debtor by gathering relevant financial information at a cost of $X, but the debtor himself can produce the same information and the creditor can verify its accuracy for a total cost of $X + 1, there will be a cost saving to be shared between the parties if the debtor assumes contractual responsibility for producing the information in question. In a credit transaction of any complexity, it is reasonable to think that creditors will engage in some monitoring themselves, will require their debtors to undertake some monitoring-related responsibilities, and will also demand additional compensation for whatever risk of misbehavior remains after all cost-justified monitoring steps have been taken. Consequently there are three costs associated with the risk of debtor misbehavior: first, the cost of the creditor's monitoring activities; second, the cost of whatever monitoring the debtor undertakes himself; and finally, the cost of the increased compensation the creditor will demand for assuming any risk of misbehavior that cannot be eliminated by cost-justified monitoring. Both parties will have an incentive to arrange their transaction in a way that minimizes the sum of these three costs, since they can share any savings between them.

One can gain a general understanding of the utility of secured financing by considering the hypothetical case of a debtor with only two creditors, each of whom is contemplating some form of credit transaction with the debtor. Suppose that in negotiations between the debtor and one of his creditors, C1, a question is raised as to whether C1's loan should be secured by property of the debtor, for example, his equipment or inventory. The creation of a security interest in C1's favor will benefit him in two ways. First, it will reduce the riskiness of his loan by making it more likely that the loan will be repaid in the event of the debtor's insolvency. Second, the existence of collateral is also likely to reduce the cost of the monitoring required to guard against the debtor covertly increasing the riskiness of the loan.

Obviously, the mere existence of a security interest does not eliminate the risk of debtor misbehavior, since the debtor can still dissipate the collateral and thereby demote his creditor to unsecured status. But so long as the particular items of property securing his loan remain intact, a creditor will be immunized from the effects of his debtor's misbehavior. Consequently, the monitoring required to prevent the debtor from increasing the riskiness of a secured loan is likely to be significantly less than that required when the loan is unsecured. A secured creditor can focus his attention on the continued availability of his collateral and is largely free to disregard what the debtor does with the remainder of his estate. By restricting his attention in this way, the secured creditor can reduce the number and complexity of his monitoring tasks and thus achieve a substantial savings in monitoring costs.

If C1 and the debtor agree that C1's loan will be secured by an interest in specific items of collateral, C1 will charge a lower interest rate than he would charge if the loan were made on an unsecured basis. To some extent, this reduction in the interest rate will reflect the reduced riskiness of the loan, and to some extent it will reflect the lower monitoring costs that C1 must now incur or impose upon the debtor to protect against debtor misbehavior. Were it entirely costless for the debtor to give C1 a security interest in his property, the debtor would almost certainly do so, in order to take advantage of this interest-rate reduction. In fact, however, granting a security interest to C1 will have a costly impact on the debtor's relations with his other creditor, C2. If the debtor grants C1 a security interest in his property, he reduces the expected value of C2's recovery in the event of the debtor's insolvency. Consequently, if the debtor agrees to secure C1's loan, C2 will charge a higher interest rate to compensate for the increased risk of his own investment in the debtor's enterprise, and C2 will also be likely to spend more in monitoring the debtor's conduct, since the effects of misbehavior will now fall more heavily on C2 than they would if he had a pro rata claim to the debtor's entire estate.

Weighing these effects together, the debtor can be expected to give a security interest to C1 when the resulting decrease in the cost of C1's loan more than offsets any increase in the cost of borrowing from C2. This is most likely to be the case when the two creditors have different monitoring costs—when C2 either needs to do less monitoring, or is able to monitor more cheaply, than C1. To see that this is so, let us temporarily eliminate monitoring costs from consideration by assuming the risk of debtor misbehavior to be zero, in which case neither C1 nor C2 will devote any resources, or require the debtor himself to devote any, to monitoring the debtor's conduct. Even on this unrealistic assumption, the interest that the debtor must pay on C2's loan will rise if he grants C1 a security interest in his property, since the riskiness of C2's loan will increase at the same time that the riskiness of C1's decreases. However, in a world without monitoring or other transaction costs, the increase in risk borne by C2 should exactly offset the corresponding decrease in the risk to which C1 is subject. Therefore, any change in the interest rates charged by the two creditors should just offset one another and leave the total cost of credit to the debtor unchanged. With transaction costs eliminated from consideration, it is difficult to see why the debtor would prefer giving C1 a security interest in his property to granting each creditor an equal right to satisfy his claim from the entire estate, or how the welfare of the debtor and his two competing creditors could be increased by doing so.

Reintroduction of monitoring costs changes the picture dramatically, however. If the additional monitoring costs that C2 must incur due to the creation of a security interest in favor of C1 are less than the accompanying reduction in C1's monitoring costs, there will be a total cost saving to be shared among the three parties if C1's claim is secured. [. . .]

It might be true that even greater cost savings could be realized if both C1 and C2 had security interests in different assets. Although this possibility raises additional complications involving the effect of each creditor's security interest on the riskiness of the other's loan, it poses no new theoretical problems. The same would be true if the number of creditors were increased from, say, two to twenty. The simple model set out here would be more difficult to apply in a complex, multiparty situation of this sort, but the validity of the basic principles on which it rests is not dependent upon the number of competing creditors who happen to be involved. The key idea is a simple one. If we assume that the sum of all parties' monitoring costs depends on the priority of creditor claims, there are likely to be some situations in which everyone concerned, including the debtor, will be better off if the interests of certain creditors are subordinated to those of others than they would be if all creditors were given equal priority.

This approach suggests a more satisfactory answer to a question considered earlier: why does the law permit debtors to prefer some creditors over others by encumbering assets in their favor? Returning to the example, it should be clear that even if the debtor is prohibited by law from granting either of his creditors a consensual security interest in his property, both C1 and C2 will stand to gain by agreeing, between themselves, that C2's claim will be subordinated to C1's, at least with respect to certain assets of the debtor, in the event of insolvency. Such an agreement would allow the creditors to reduce their total monitoring cost, making each better off than he would be if both had an equal pro rata claim to the debtor's property. Consequently, if the law denied debtors the power to prefer some creditors over others through a system of security agreements, a similar network of priority relationships could be expected to emerge by consensual arrangement between creditors. Permitting debtors to encumber their assets achieves the same result, but in a simpler and more economical fashion. If a debtor has more than two or three creditors, free rider and holdout difficulties are likely to plague any attempt on the part of the creditors to work out a set of priority relationships among themselves. These transaction costs can be avoided by allowing the debtor himself to prefer one creditor over another. The rule permitting debtors to encumber their assets by private agreement is therefore justifiable as a cost-saving device that makes it easier and cheaper for the debtor's creditors to do what they would do in any case. This justification for the rule supplements and reinforces our earlier argument from the general principle of freedom of contract and suggests—as the idea of freedom of contract alone does not—why secured credit is such a widespread phenomenon.

Security Interests and Bankruptcy Priorities: A Review of Current Theories*

ALAN SCHWARTZ

Firms issue and creditors buy secured debt when the private gains from doing so exceed the costs. An efficiency explanation of secured debt must show when this is so and also that the social gains from security exceed the social costs. The conventional efficiency story is that high risk firms prefer issuing security because it enables them to borrow, and creditors prefer buying it because it enables them to make loans they otherwise would refuse. Security has these properties because it reduces the risks of creditors in the event of default, largely by allowing the secured party to take the property subject to its security interest and sell it to reduce or eliminate the debt. As we have seen, the power to seize and sell often survives the debtor's bankruptcy.

This conventional story seems unpersuasive if creditors (i) can learn of and react to the existence of security; (ii) can calculate risks of default reasonably precisely; (iii) are risk-neutral; and (iv) have homogeneous expectations respecting default probabilities. To see why this is so, it is helpful to consider more precisely just how secured financing reduces a creditor's risks. A lender that extends credit on an unsecured basis looks not only to the debtor's earning capacity for repayment but also to the debtor's assets. When a creditor becomes secured, however, certain (or all) assets of the debtor are set aside to help insure that this creditor is paid; in consequence, its chance of collecting its debt are much increased. And when these assets are removed from the general pool, the chance that the debtor's unsecured creditors will collect their debts correspondingly decreases. If all creditors are informed, the secured creditor will charge a lower interest rate because it is secured, whereas the unsecured creditors will charge higher interest rates because the pool of assets available to satisfy their claims has shrunk. The debtor's total interest bill is thus unaffected by the existence of security. Since the issuance of secured debt is itself costly, however, the debtor would be worse off with security than without it. Firms would never sell secured debt. [. . .]

A way to show that security can reduce a firm's net credit costs is to focus on the methods by which a firm can behave in a more risky fashion after a loan is made. Sometimes, taking greater risks requires a firm to exchange assets for other assets. A firm that wants to switch from making lathes to making amphibious cars, for example, will need different machinery. A security interest in the firm's property would impede such a substitution of assets by drying up the market for the firm's equipment. The code provides, in § 9–306(2), that "a security interest continues in collateral notwithstanding sale, exchange or other disposition thereof unless the disposition was authorized by the secured par-

* 10 J. Legal Studies 1 (1981).

ty...." In consequence, people would be deterred from purchasing equipment from misbehaving firms. Since asset substitution is an important method of behaving more riskily after a loan is made, security reduces the risk of a debtor's misbehaving. Most significantly, it reduces this risk not only for secured parties but for anyone who extends credit to the firm. The increase in monitoring costs that unsecured creditors experience as a result of security may thus be less than the decrease in monitoring costs that the secured party incurs; indeed, where asset substitution is the principal method of behaving more riskily, the absolute level of monitoring by unsecured creditors could decline.

This explanation of the existence of secured debt, however, is unpersuasive when applied to short-term financing because the kind of monitoring for which security is supposedly a substitute often seems unnecessary in this case. Suppose that creditors can observe at relatively low cost the significant asset substitutions by a debtor that materially alter the riskiness of the debtor's enterprise. A creditor can react to the possibility of such substitutions in two ways: it can monitor its debtor fairly extensively to reduce the likelihood of the debtor's misbehavior, or it can rely on the sanction of lost good will to induce the debtor not to misbehave. A firm that behaves in a riskier fashion after a loan is made shows itself to be untrustworthy, and its ability to obtain future loans is impaired. Lost good will would seem of particular concern to a debtor that primarily uses short-term financing. Such a firm must enter the credit market frequently and is likely to regard the good-will cost from asset substitutions as high in relation to the retroactive interest-rate reduction that those substitutions produce on existing loans. Thus the creditors of such a firm probably would choose to incur the relatively low cost of invoking the good-will sanction by observing whether significant asset substitutions have occurred, rather than the relatively high cost of policing to prevent this form of misbehavior. Security interests are expensive, however, and seem substitutes only for the high cost version of monitoring—that is, policing for preventive purposes. Creditors have an incentive to engage in this form of policing during long-term financing situations, where the debtor's good-will costs from misbehavior are relatively less. The monitoring-cost explanation therefore predicts that firms may issue secured debt when much of their financing is long-term but will seldom do so when they primarily use short-term credit. The relatively large amount of short-term secured debt issued by retailers thus constitutes a serious counterexample to the monitoring-cost theory.

That short-term debt sometimes has many of the characteristics of long-term debt is an insufficient response to this difficulty. Short-term debt is considered long-term debt for some purposes when a debtor and particular creditor form a relatively permanent association. As an example, a bank may finance a particular retailer for many years, taking security interests in its (ever-changing) inventory and accounts receivable. Banks, however, extend funds on a periodic basis in such relationships and will terminate if the firm behaves more riskily. Moreover, such a creditor can conveniently learn of important changes in its debtors' businesses. Thus, even in these "long-term" financing situations, the good-will costs of debtor misbehavior seem sufficiently high to make questionable the monitoring-cost explanation for the existence of secured debt.

This explanation also fails to hold because the danger of asset substitutions that secured debt is supposedly meant to prevent varies with the length of the loan. A short-term creditor would commonly perceive significant asset substitutions to be of relatively low probability. Firms, it is true, sometimes do significantly alter their affairs during the course of their lives, but such fundamental changes take time. A creditor holding a one-year note, for example, is therefore likely to assume that is debtor would be in roughly the same line of work at year's end. Thus again short-term creditors would have little incentive to take security as a substitute for incurring high monitoring costs.

A second explanation for the existence of secured debt that also is consistent with the assumption made about creditor knowledge, ability, risk neutrality, and homogeneity of expectations is that firms issue security as a "signal" to creditors of their prospects. Signaling explanations for the financing decisions of firms are becoming common and seem promising. At this stage in their development, however, signaling models are unsatisfactory because it is difficult to know whether a particular activity is a signal and whether a particular signaling outcome is efficient.

To perceive the promise and problems of a signaling explanation for the issuance of secured debt, first suppose that at a given time firms seek to finance a set of projects whose outcomes are highly variable. Firms know the "quality"—for example, the outcome mean and variance—of their own projects, but creditors cannot distinguish among firms on a the basis of quality. This asymmetry of information could occur because the quality of a particular project is a function of facts and prospects that outsiders can observe only with great difficulty. Further, the firm has an incentive to overestimate the likelihood of favorable outcomes. In this circumstance, interest rates in the loan market would reflect average project quality. Moreover, were the market to set interest rates that reflect a relatively high average quality (higher than the average risk of projects), firms would supply large numbers of low quality projects. This is because firms with low quality projects could borrow at rates that reflected risks below the actual risks their projects faced; such firms would make substantial gains at the expense of creditors. Creditors, however, are aware of this possibility and, when they lack information about the quality of particular projects, will suppose average project quality to be relatively low. In this event, firms with projects of higher quality than the market average could not get credit on accurate terms. These firms thus have an incentive to inform creditors of—that is, to "signal"—their relative status.

An effective signal must enable its observers to sort out the signalers by some criterion that the observers consider relevant. This signaling property probably exists in credit markets if the cost of signaling a firm's risk status declines as the quality of the firm's projects increases. This is because, if project quality were uncorrelated with signaling costs, firms with low quality projects would send out signals of high quality and creditors would learn to disregard the signal as a mark of quality.

A security interest might be such an effective signal. Security interests restrict future borrowing opportunities, give secured creditors greater leverage over firm behavior, and make it more difficult for a firm to reschedule debts in the event of hard times. A firm willing to encumber its assets is, thus, "signaling" that, in its view, its prospects justify these potential costs. Further, signaling costs apparently vary inversely with project quality because they are partly a function of the likelihood that the firm will experience financial difficulty. A firm likely to earn high profits may worry little about the future restrictions on its ability to borrow that a security interest may create or about the power that a security interest gives to a creditor to influence firm decisions if no profits are realized. Firms expecting not to do well, on the other hand, may regard the expected costs of issuing secured debt as high because those costs could well be incurred. The apparent property of secured debt to communicate accurately to creditors a firm's true estimate of its expected earnings indicates that the existence of secured debt may be explained as a signaling phenomenon. The information conveyed by the issuance of secured debt enables firms to borrow on terms that more accurately reflect their risk classes.

Monitors and Freeriders in Commercial and Corporate Settings*
SAUL LEVMORE

The Impact of Freeriding

The shortcomings of current monitoring cost theory derive in part from its lack of attention to the problem of freeriding. Consider again the need for C1 [one of two parties extending credit to a debtor] to be wary of debtor misbehavior. Why should C1 expend resources attempting to discover such misbehavior? C2 is also affected by such misbehavior and C1 may well expect C2 to monitor the debtor. Similarly, C2 may anticipate that C1 will perform the necessary monitoring. This situation, like others in which one activity benefits numerous parties, poses a freeriding problem. The two creditors may engage in duplicative moni-

* 92 Yale L. J. 49, 53–58 (1982).

toring efforts or they may rely on each other's efforts and fail altogether
to monitor the debtor. Although it is possible that one creditor will be a
brave bluffer and the other a conservative pessimist and that the debtor
will then be monitored in an ideal manner, such a result can hardly be
expected. Moreover, a suboptimal result is more likely the more numerous the creditors. [. . .]

Debtors might, however, solve the freeriding problem by offering
security interests to certain creditors. Consider, for example, a simple
debtor with assets consisting of some petty cash, accounts receivable, a
company car, and common office supplies. Although there is an imagin-
able threat of risk alteration, the most serious potential misbehavior
would seem to be the sale of the car followed by a conversion of the
proceeds for the debtor's personal use. Creditors may be unaware of such
misbehavior because each might hope that the other will monitor the
ownership of the debtor's vehicle. In this setting, the benefits of secured
financing are clear. The freeriding problem is largely avoided if one
creditor can be assigned to monitor the debtor's car, as a secured
creditor, with little expectation of effort on the part of other creditors.
To be sure, if an available creditor is a relatively talented monitor, the
security interest (and the attached monitoring task) can be assigned so
that the freeriding problem is solved and the monitoring talent put to
good use. Accordingly, the Jackson–Kronman model, which depicted the
talented monitors as assuming positions as unsecured creditors, seems
flawed in its failure to recognize the freeriding problem among creditors.

A monitoring theory that includes freeriding considerations is consistent with the casual evidence commented upon by Professor Schwartz
and meets the major objection to the Jackson–Kronman model. A typical
commercial bank, for example, appears to have excellent monitoring
ability. It is experienced, enjoys economies of scale, is financially sophisticated, and has ready access to many of the assets and records of the
debtor and its business associates. That banks are frequently, if not
exclusively, secured creditors thus fits the suggested monitoring theory.

Freeriding considerations also explain the Code's somewhat puzzling
and different treatments of two other contributors to the firm's financial
structure: the financer of a new asset and the "financing buyer," who
advances funds for the production of desired goods. The Code offers a
"purchase money security interest"—and therefore a relative priority
(with a grace period for filing)—to the former, but no similar arrangement to the latter. This treatment may reflect an expectation that the
financer of new equipment will be a more talented monitor than the
financing buyer and therefore better suited to a unique assignment as a
secured creditor. If this financer is a commercial bank, its suitability is
clear; and if the financer is the vendor or manufacturer of the new asset,
it will often also be a talented monitor because of its familiarity with the
use and maintenance of the asset in question. [. . .]

Given their monitoring roles, it is fair to wonder why secured creditors are not further encouraged to use their talents (and freedom from the freeriding problem) to monitor the debtor. The "secured monitor" could, for example, be given a priority to the extent of the particular security interest but then actually be subordinated to the unsecured creditors for any part of its claim not ultimately satisfied in bankruptcy by the assigned collateral. In the prevailing Article 9 system, the secured creditor's incentive to monitor derives solely from the premium it has paid in the form of agreeing to lend at a lower interest rate, and it consists of the right to satisfy its claim with the agreed-upon collateral. Still, if the secured creditor could satisfy its claim only with the assigned collateral or were subordinated to the unsecured creditors for any amount not satisfied by the collateralized asset, it seems likely that the secured creditor might have an additional incentive to monitor.

A creditor priority system that sought to increase monitoring incentives in this way would, however, face two obstacles. First, consider that among the risks assumed by the secured creditor is the possibility that the collateral will depreciate despite the creditor's monitoring efforts. If the secured creditor in bankruptcy has recourse only to the collateralized asset, then the secured creditor will be unlikely to agree to an interest rate lower than that agreed to by unsecured creditors unless the collateral's value were considerably greater than the loan extended to the debtor. But if this were the case and the asset did not depreciate significantly, the secured creditor would have a sizeable cushion against both depreciation and debtor misbehavior, and its incentive to monitor would consequently be reduced. Unsecured creditors are then unable to rely on the single monitor and are left to deal with their freeriding problem.

A separate difficulty with a system intended to stimulate monitoring efforts by denying the secured monitor a fallback position as an equal of the unsecured creditors arises because the assets that are available for security interests are not always perfect "focal" (observation) points of debtor misbehavior. Although the efficiency of the monitoring arrangement depends on the link between the concerns of the secured creditor and those of all creditors, this link is an imperfect one. Not all potential debtor misbehavior fits the secured monitor scheme as neatly as does the company car hypothetical. What if, instead, another form of misbehavior affects the value of all the debtor's assets and is more easily detected by an unsecured creditor, such as an employee? It is hardly sensible to discourage this (unsecured) monitor from expending some policing effort by constructing a system that places a cushion of inadequately secured creditors behind the unsecured ones. Moreover, suppose the secured monitor is in the best position to discover the debtor's misbehavior but refrains from doing so because its collateral is entirely dissipated, although other assets can still be salvaged. Again, it seems unwise to establish a priority system that sometimes reduces the secured creditor's incentive to monitor.

NOTES

1. What assumptions support the irrelevance proposition? We introduced the analytical tool of irrelevance propositions in the notes to Section 5.2. In this Section, Jackson–Kronman and Schwartz begin with an irrelevance proposition for the granting of security interests: under restrictive assumptions, a borrower cannot reduce its aggregate cost of capital by securing some of its creditors. Irrelevance propositions are useful only to the degree that they expose all necessary assumptions. Schwartz is more explicit than Jackson and Kronman about the necessary assumptions. Are there any other necessary assumptions to support the irrelevance result?

2. The relevance of imperfect information. One necessary assumption for most financial decisions is perfect information. In other words, financial decisions are often motivated by informational concerns. One category is agency problems (alternatively referred to as private action or moral hazard). Under this category, the existence of debt in the capital structure of a firm gives rise to three forms of misbehavior: (a) the distribution of assets to insiders or shareholders, (b) investment in risky, but unprofitable ventures (overinvestment), (c) the failure to exploit low-risk, profitable ventures where the payoffs would accrue to existing debtholders (underinvestment or debt overhang). Debt contracts seek to address these incentives in their covenants. *See* Clifford W. Smith, Jr. & Jerrold Warner, *On Financial Contracting: An Analysis of Bond Covenants,* 7 J. Fin. Econ. 117 (1979). The violation of covenants is typically an event of default that entitles the creditor to accelerate the maturity of the credit and enforce its claim. Often, covenants are quite broad, effectively giving the creditor the rights of a demand loan. Compliance with covenants, however, must be monitored, as must the financial condition of the borrower.

3. Comparative advantages in monitoring. The explanations in this section suggest that debtors issue security interests to exploit differences in the comparative monitoring abilities of their creditors. Jackson and Kronman contend that some creditors may be able to monitor the debtor more cheaply than other creditors, and security allows for monitoring costs to be assigned to the party who can bear those costs most efficiently. What does monitoring entail and what features of creditors makes one a better monitor than another? Is Citibank a better monitor than the local plumber or electrician? Levmore suggests that the "talent" for monitoring may be a function of location, experience, specialization, or expertise. Levmore, *Monitors,* at fn. 16.

A similar explanation exploiting heterogeneous abilities in screening borrowers is provided in Frank H. Buckley, *The Bankruptcy Priority Puzzle,* 72 Va. L. Rev. 13939 (1986). Security will reduce uncertainty that creditors have about the value of the assets upon default because a secured creditor need only predict whether sufficient assets will be available to satisfy his claim while the unsecured creditor must attempt to predict the priority of his claim to these assets. Furthermore, secured lending will also reduce screening costs where the secured creditor can exploit economies of scale in valuing secondary uses of firm assets for various differing outcomes. Unsecured creditors, who may require this information for only one purpose, need not invest at all where the asset has been removed from the available pool and granted to the secured creditor.

4. "Specialized" versus "general" monitors. One might test the Jackson–Kronman model by observing whether secured creditors are inferior monitors than unsecured creditors. Levmore points out that "many, if not most, actual unsecured creditors appear to be relatively inferior monitors." Levmore, *Monitors* at 53. In response to such criticism, Professors Baird and Jackson refine their comparative advantage theory in several respects. First, they incorporate Professor Levmore's free rider argument: better monitors take security interest in assets that are focal points for their specialized monitoring services. Second, they argue that these "specialized" monitors co-exist with "general" monitors. Some of these general monitors—such as local banks—remain unsecured so as to exploit their comparative monitoring advantage, while other general monitors—such as banks located in distant cities—take security in specific assets in order to reduce their monitoring costs. Douglas Baird & Thomas Jackson, Cases, Problems, and Materials on Security Interests in Personal Property 361–67 (1984).

5. Encouraging efficient monitoring. Monitoring yields positive externalities. Monitoring by one creditor reduces the risk of debtor misbehavior and thereby the risk of insolvency. This enures to the benefits of all creditors. Levmore suggests that the better monitors will take the priority of security as compensation for the tendency of less efficient creditors to free ride on their policing efforts. Even when the secured lender exits its relationship with a borrower by calling the loan, this action provides a valuable signal to other creditors that something is amiss with the borrower. George G. Triantis & Ronald J. Daniels, *The Role of Debt in Interactive Corporate Governance,* 83 Calif. L. Rev. 1073, 1082–1103 (1995). Professor Adler makes a similar argument with respect to screening activities: that screening by unsecured creditors benefits shareholders. Barry E. Adler, *An Equity–Agency Solution to the Bankruptcy–Priority Puzzle,* 22 J. Legal Stud. 73 (1993).

What kind of security interests motivate the secured creditor to monitor on behalf of all creditors? A security interest in an asset with a stable value is likely to deter active monitoring efforts. Appropriate focal point collateral under Levmore's approach are assets whose value is risky and closely related with the enterprise as a whole, as a matter of both correlation and causation. See George G. Triantis, *Secured Debt under Conditions of Imperfect Information,* 21 J. Legal Stud. 225, 243–5 (1992).

6. Organizations as monitors. What alternatives other than security interests are available as a means of exploiting comparative monitoring advantages? Hansmann and Kraakman argue that organizations, such as firms, may do a better job in monitoring than security interests. They present an example of an enterprise that includes a hotel and oil refinery. If the two lines of business are placed in separate corporations, the creditor lending to each unit can focus its monitoring expertise on that operation, without worrying about the other. Thus, the partitioning of assets into two corporations exploits monitoring specialization efficiencies. Henry Hansmann and Reinier Kraakman, *The Essential Role of Organizational Law,* 110 Yale L. J. 387 (2000). Similarly, monitoring explanations have been applied to securitization, where corporations and trusts are used to separate receivables from other firm assets. Edward M. Iacobucci and Ralph A. Winter, *Asset Securitization and Asymmetric Information,* 34 J. Legal Stud. 161 (2005). See, generally, Steven L. Schwarcz, *The Alchemy of Asset Securitization,* 1 Stan. J. L. Bus., & Fin. 133 (1994).

7. Signaling explanations of security. Alan Schwartz's article presents a signaling theory explanation for security. A particular debtor can, by issuing secured debt, signal to others in the market that it is a better credit risk than competing firms and thus obtain a lower interest rate. This signal will effectively separate the high quality debtor from the pool only if the lower quality creditors do not find it feasible to mimic the signal. The cost of secured credit includes the fact that the creditor can remove assets much quicker after default than in the case of unsecured debt. Triantis, *Imperfect Information,* supra. If low quality debtors do not mimic high quality debtors, capital markets are better informed and the signaling debtor can enjoy a lower cost of capital than others. See also David Besanko & Najan V. Thakor, *Collateral and Rationing: Sorting Equilibria in Monopolistic and Competitive Credit Markets,* 28 Int'l Econ. Rev. 671 (1987); Helmut Bester, *Screening vs. Rationing in Credit Markets with Imperfect Information,* 75 Am. Econ. Rev. 850 (1985). Otherwise, there may be a pooling equilibrium in which all debtors signal and creditors charge each a blended interest rate. No debtor can afford to stop signaling because they would be thereby identified as a low quality debtor. This yields an inefficient outcome in which the signaling costs are incurred but no information is produced to the creditors. Schwartz, *Alchemy,* supra.

Signaling theories have been advanced to explain a range of financial phenomena, including the issuance of debt and the payment of dividends. Usually, they yield the opposite predictions from agency cost theories. In the case of secured credit, agency theory predicts that secured credit will be issued by higher risk debtors; while signaling theory predicts it will be more common among lower risk debtors. Triantis, *Imperfect Information,* supra; Alan Schwartz, *Priority Contracts and Priority in Bankruptcy,* 82 Cornell L. Rev. 1396, 1413–4 (1997). When tested empirically, signaling explanations fare poorly, particularly in comparison to agency cost explanations. Michael J. Barclay and Clifford Smith, *The Priority Structure of Corporate Liabilities,* 50 J. Fin. 899 (1995).

8. Enforcement and rent-seeking. In Chapter 1, we emphasized the importance of incorporating the mechanism by which contracts are enforced, into the analysis of contract design. Litigation, in particular, is a rent-seeking activity in which parties expend resources in an effort to capture a larger share of the amount at stake. Their investments have no social benefit other than their ex ante effect on incentives to perform the contract. The enforcement of debt claims against an insolvent debtor has elements of rent-seeking as well that might inform the ex ante allocation of priority. Consider the following excerpt from Ivo Welch, *Why is Bank Debt Senior? A Theory of Asymmetry and Claim Priority Based on Influence Costs*, 10 Rev. Fin. Stud. 1203, 1204 (1997):

> The expected deadweight lobbying and litigation expenses, associated with a fight for preferential treatment (priority or side awards) in financial distress, can be lower if one awards the potentially stronger creditor ex post (the bank) the position with more power ex ante. That is, to maximize the 'deterrence' to avoid a fight between creditors involved in *rent-seeking* activities, it can be efficient to promise the stronger contender priority.... It is important not to interpret the litigative and lobbying costs too narrowly: such expenses should include the costs of organizing the creditor class, free-rider problems, reputation benefits in future restructuring negotiations (both positive and negative), and management time and hassle. Because of our wide interpretation of expenses, banks are likely to have a lower cost than public debt ... of "litigative/lobbying activity." (Italics in original)

6.3 Proceeds, After–Acquired Property and Future Advances

Rethinking Proceeds: The History, Misinterpretation and Revision of U.C.C. Section 9–306*

R. WILSON FREYERMUTH

Introduction

On its face, the Uniform Commercial Code (U.C.C.) attempts to provide a straightforward rule governing the rights of the debtor and the secured party when the debtor disposes of some or all of the secured party's collateral. Under U.C.C. section 9–306, the secured party not only maintains its security interest in the collateral following disposition, but also obtains a security interest in any identifiable proceeds of the collateral. Within the definition of "proceeds," the U.C.C. includes anything received upon the "sale, exchange, collection or other disposition of" the collateral. This continuing proceeds coverage is a default rule; under Section 9–203(3), the secured party automatically obtains continuing coverage against proceeds unless the security agreement specifies otherwise. Through these provisions, the U.C.C. seeks to achieve efficiency in secured transactions by codifying the ex ante bargain of the hypothetical reasonable debtor and secured party, who would expect the secured party's lien to continue against whatever property the debtor receives upon disposition of the collateral.

* 69 Tul. L. Rev. 645, 647–50, 692–707 (1995).

Despite the drafters' functional scheme, however, judicial interpretation of Section 9–306(1)'s proceeds coverage has been anything but straightforward. During the thirty-plus years following the adoption of Article 9, opportunistic debtors and bankruptcy trustees, eager to find unencumbered funds to finance a reorganization or to pay administrative expenses, have urged courts to construe Section 9–306(1)'s definition of proceeds narrowly. Debtors and bankruptcy trustees have raised this interpretive issue in a variety of contexts, as shown by the following examples:

- Debtor owns a car subject to a security interest in favor of Secured Party. Following Debtor's bankruptcy, the car is destroyed by an insured casualty. Upon receiving the insurance moneys, Trustee argues that Secured Party has no lien upon those funds because there has been no sale, exchange, collection, or other disposition of the car.

- Debtor owns a machine subject to a security interest in favor of Secured Party. Prior to filing for bankruptcy, Debtor had leased the machine to Lessee for $500 per month. During bankruptcy, Debtor argues that the lease rentals do not constitute Secured Party's cash collateral because there has been no sale, exchange, collection, or other disposition of the machine.

- Debtor owns 500 shares of stock in ABC Company, subject to a security interest in favor of Secured Party. Following Debtor's bankruptcy, ABC Co. pays a cash dividend of $1 per share. Trustee seeks to use the cash dividend to pay administrative expenses, arguing that the funds do not constitute Secured Party's cash collateral because there has been no disposition of the stock.

- Debtor borrows $10,000 from Secured Party and grants Secured Party a security interest in its upcoming corn crop. Instead of planting the crop, Debtor signs a payment-in-kind (PIK) contract and receives a government subsidy, in the form of PIK certificates, for agreeing not to plant corn. After Debtor's bankruptcy, Trustee argues that the PIK certificates are unencumbered because they are not proceeds of Debtor's crops, since there was no disposition of Debtor's crops.

In each of these examples, the disputed asset represents a return of the economic value or productive capacity of the bargained-for collateral. Thus, in each case Secured Party can argue persuasively that the Debtor received the disputed funds upon a disposition of collateral within the meaning of Section 9–306(1). [. . .]

The PEB Report and Its Recommendations

[A] report commissioned by the U.C.C.'s Permanent Editorial Board recommended a systematic revision of Article 9. Several of the recommendations in the PEB Report attempt to address the proper scope of the term "proceeds." The PEB Report recognized the crabbed judicial interpretations to which courts have subjected Section 9–306(1), noting that "the concepts 'sale, exchange, collection or other disposition' found in the current definition may not be broad enough" to demonstrate clearly the proper scope of the term "proceeds." The commentary in the PEB Report, however, spoke in relatively broad strokes and did not propose specific amendatory language. Further, the commentary did not attempt to establish one unifying concept underlying the true scope of the term "proceeds." In its discussion, the PEB Report separated the universe of proceeds cases into two categories: the "exchange and replacement" cases and the "close association" cases.

Within the "exchange and replacement" cases, the PEB Report placed those transactions in which something is "received in place of and in substitution for the original collateral, which has been disposed of or reduced in value." Under this paradigm, the PEB Report placed the casualty insurance cases, the lease rental cases, cases involving tort claims and breaches of sales contract warranties, and cases involving a debtor's licensing of intellectual property. Consistent with PEB Commentary Number 9 and its rejection of the Cleary Brothers analysis of lease rental payments, the PEB Report recommended revising Section 9–306(1) to make clear that lease rentals constitute proceeds. Likewise, the PEB Report acknowledged that tort claims and breach of contract warranty claims "replace the value of collateral that would have (or should have) been available to a secured party" and are thus so "similar to insurance proceeds" that Section 9–306(1) should treat them as proceeds of the collateral.

Within the "close association" paradigm, the PEB Report placed cases that it believed did not fit naturally within the exchange and replacement paradigm. Here, the PEB Report included cases involving "all forms of distributions on account of securities, partnership interests, ... government subsidies, and other payments that do not involve an 'exchange.'" In suggesting that these sums constituted proceeds of collateral, the PEB Report concluded that they were "so necessarily and obviously associated with an interest in the original collateral that a security agreement and financing statement ought not to be required to mention them explicitly." Without suggesting precise amendatory language, the PEB Report concluded that Section 9–306(1) should be "revised so as to embrace this 'close association' concept."

Toward a Unitary, Coherent Conception of Proceeds

By distinguishing between exchange and replacement proceeds and close association proceeds, the PEB Report creates the impression that there is no coherent, unified conception that provides a basis for classifying assets as proceeds. As further discussed below, this impression is mistaken. In fact, the PEB Report's definition of close association proceeds—"those things that are so necessarily and obviously associated with an interest in the original collateral that a security agreement and financing statement ought not to be required to mention them explicitly"—encompasses all varieties of proceeds.

    1. Protecting Against Diminishing the Collateral's Economic Value

In any secured transaction, the debtor and secured party bargain to provide the secured party with a property interest in the debtor's "collateral." But exactly what is the collateral over which the debtor and secured party bargained? As security law concerns itself with interests taken for security purposes, the real subject matter of the secured transaction is the economic value of the collateral. In order to respect the expected ex ante bargain of reasonable debtors and secured parties, security law generally should protect secured parties against actions and events that effectively reduce the collateral's economic value [...]

    2. Protecting Against Diminishing the Collateral's Productive Capacity

Once the inquiry focuses upon economic value as a key to proceeds classification, one must recognize that a debtor can consume the value of collateral in different ways. The debtor may consume the value of collateral via its own direct use (e.g., Cleary Brothers uses its crane on projects for which it serves as general contractor), by making the collateral available to third parties for their use permanently (e.g., Cleary Brothers sells the crane to a competitor), or by making the collateral available to third parties for their temporary use (e.g., Cleary Brothers leases the crane to another contractor for its use on other sites). Stated differently, the debtor's acquisition of title to the collateral naturally brings with it the collateral's future productive capacity, which the debtor captures through using the collateral (either in its own business or by transferring some or all of that use to third parties). In reality, the economic value of business collateral is nothing more than the net present value of what that collateral can produce in the future. Thus, to the extent that Section 9–306's proceeds coverage protects the secured party against events that exhaust the collateral's economic value, that coverage is incomplete unless it also addresses the exhaustion of the collateral's productive capacity [...]

Within the U.C.C.'s present framework, Section 9–306's proceeds coverage provides the logical conceptual mechanism for dealing with the exhaustion of collateral's productive capacity. Properly characterized, proceeds of collateral include whatever assets the debtor receives as a consequence of the consumption of that collateral's future productive capacity. Such a definition would provide a coherent and unitary framework for classifying proceeds in a manner consistent with the ex ante bargain of the reasonable debtor and secured party [. . .]

The Logical Limit of Continuing Proceeds Coverage

At first blush, one might attempt to criticize this unitary conception of proceeds by suggesting that under such a conception, everything becomes proceeds. The PEB Report implicitly made this same criticism in attempting to define the logical limit of the term "proceeds":

At some point, the acquisition of assets by a debtor, in part as a result of a diminution in value of collateral, will be too attenuated for those assets to be considered proceeds. For example, accounts generated by a construction contractor should not be considered proceeds of the contractor's construction equipment, even though the equipment depreciates as a result of its use in generating the accounts. Nor should inventory fabricated by a debtor's factory equipment be considered proceeds of that equipment. Cash earned from music or video machines presents a case closer to the margin. Has the equipment merely provided a service, or is the better analogy that of a short-term rental? The Committee is inclined to leave such marginal cases to the courts [. . .]

The PEB Report's attempted limitation on the scope of the term "proceeds" misses the mark, however, for two reasons. First, the PEB Report fails to explain as an economic matter how these derivative assets are functionally different from other derivative assets, such as sale proceeds and lease rentals, that clearly constitute proceeds. Second, the PEB Report confuses the question of whether to classify an asset as proceeds with the question of whether the security interest continues in that asset [. . .]

"Identifiability" as the Logical Limit of Proceeds Coverage

The hyphetheticals that the PEB Report uses to try to limit the scope of the term "proceeds" demonstrate a clear result orientation. The PEB Report assumes the correct result-that the secured party in the construction contractor hypothetical should not have a continuing security interest against the contractor's accounts. The PEB Report then chooses the most apparent solution that achieves that result-treating the contractor's accounts as nonproceeds.

The PEB Report errs, however, because it fails to recognize that the present language of the U.C.C. already achieves this result without placing a formalistic and commercially unjustified limitation upon the scope of the term "proceeds." In attempting to limit the scope of the term, the PEB Report confuses two unrelated questions: first, whether to classify an asset as proceeds and second, whether the security interest continues in that asset. As Section 9–306(2) makes clear, these are separate inquiries. The fact that an asset constitutes proceeds of collateral does not mean that the secured party automatically takes a continuing security interest in that asset. Depending upon the circumstances, an asset may constitute proceeds of collateral within the economic, value-based conception of that term, and yet a security interest will not continue in that asset because the asset is not identifiable proceeds of the collateral under Section 9–306(2).

One can see the coherent interaction of Section 9–306(1) and Section 9–306(2) by again considering the hypotheticals from the PEB Report. As demonstrated above, the contractor's accounts properly constitute proceeds of the equipment under Section 9–306(1), just as lease rentals would also constitute proceeds of the equipment if the contractor leased the equipment to a third party. Both the accounts and the lease rentals would be assets that are derivative of the equipment, functionally comparable to each other in an economic sense. Therefore, Section 9–306(1) should not distinguish them.

Section 9–306(2), however, should distinguish them. While the secured party would have a continuing security interest in the lease rentals, the secured party would have no continuing security interest in the accounts under Section 9–306(2). When the contractor uses the equipment by leasing it to a third party, there is no substantial question about the secured party's continuing interest in the lease rentals, which can be identified precisely to the lease of the equipment. When the contractor uses the equipment to generate accounts on its own jobs, however, the accounts are proceeds but cannot be identified precisely to the equipment. While the accounts are proceeds of the equipment, at a minimum they are also proceeds of any materials the contractor used on the job and the contractor's labor and expertise. Since the accounts are not identifiable precisely to the equipment, the secured party's lien should not extend to the accounts under Section 9–306(2) [. . .]

Conclusion: A Proposal for Revising Section 9–306 and Accompanying Commentary

The conception of proceeds presented in this Article is the only conception that is sufficiently coherent to rescue the term from the morass of ambiguity caused by judicial decisions focusing upon the passage of title and nonexistent collateral distracters. To give the term "proceeds" a coherent, functional meaning, one must define that term to include all assets received upon the occurrence of events that exhaust the collateral's economic value or productive capacity. At the same time, Article 9 should extend continuing proceeds coverage no further than those proceeds that are identifiable precisely to the secured party's collateral. This conception of the term "proceeds" most closely approximates the expected ex ante bargain of the reasonable debtor and secured party, and thus should form the basis for any revision of Section 9–306.

A Relational Theory of Secured Financing*
ROBERT E. SCOTT

[C]ertain debtors can best finance growth opportunities with private debt. Unfortunately, such debt contracts inevitably reduce the debtor's incentives to develop [some types of] business opportunity as fully as it would if the project were financed with equity. The leverage given to the creditor under a blanket (or "floating lien") security agreement ameliorates this conflict by motivating the debtor to maximize the joint interests of both the creditor and the debtor, thus enabling the parties to capture additional gains from the project. Exclusive financing agreements coupled with blanket security interests are superior to alternative mechanisms principally because they alone enable the creditor to threaten effectively to "turn off the spigot" if the debtor fails to cooperate. The external benefits of this financing arrangement derive from the valuable financial planning and coordination provided by the creditor. The financial inputs are a "public good" that will not be provided unless the creditor can structure the relationship so as to capture a share of the returns from the venture. [. . .]

How does the introduction of security affect the financing relationship? The conventional view of security is that it functions as a priority claim to designated assets, thus protecting the creditor's investment should the debtor default. Under this narrow conception, security serves no clearly identifiable role in resolving the relational dilemma. Even with a priority claim to specific assets, no rational creditor would finance a prospect, the proceeds of which are the source of repayment, where the creditor knows that some or all of the growth opportunity will not be realized. Indeed, the conventional focus on security as a method of protecting against default tends to obscure the possibility that security instead serves to enhance the many more frequent instances in which the business venture succeeds.

Monitoring cost theorists have expanded the traditional conception of security by linking it to the creditor's attempt to control debtor-creditor conflict through monitoring. But the focus on asset substitution and conversion has similarly deflected the analysis. If all the creditor is doing is watching focal points (such as a key piece of equipment or specific items of inventory) in order to facilitate supervision of the debtor, then security offers only marginal advantages over traditional loan covenants. After all, even without security the creditor can still scrutinize the debtor for evidence of misbehavior. Furthermore, the focal point conception of security does not address the underinvestment problem at all. Focusing monitoring efforts on particular items of collateral may well aid in reducing the risk of asset substitutions, but it offers no assistance in encouraging greater efforts from the debtor who fails to

---

* 86 Colum. L. Rev. 901, 925–930 (1986).

pursue fully the planned expansion. A creditor who carefully monitors a specific piece of equipment will still not know whether the equipment is being used productively.

What is required, therefore, is a broader conception of the means by which security acts to control debtor-creditor conflict. [... Instead of taking security interests in specific, discrete assets, many bank financers hold broader security interests: for example, in all of the debtor's accounts receivable and inventory presently held and after acquired. This interest typically secures an initial advance as all future advances, even where the subsequent advances are made without commitment.] Any student of Article 9 will understand that this is no extraordinary transaction. Indeed, rather than the security interest in specific focal points, the "floating lien" in a general pool of assets securing both present and future advances is the financing paradigm underlying Article 9.

By granting the exclusive financing creditor a blanket security interest, the debtor is better able to sell claims to the payoffs of the new project. Thus, not only does the creditor purchase an investment in the venture (in the form of an interest premium), but also a specific claim to the resulting accounts. Beyond the familiar notion of security as an asset cushion upon default, this relational security arrangement serves two related functions that enhance the prospects for a successful venture. First, combining exclusive financing with a blanket security interest provides the creditor with critically important leverage or strategic influence over the debtor's operational decisions. Second, relational security serves as a credible commitment, evidencing the debtor's resolve to develop the prospect fully. Each of these functions needs to be separately analyzed.

Leverage: The Value of Strategic Influence.

Relational security serves the obvious function of controlling the various types of active misbehavior by debtors. Thus, for example, a security interest in all the debtor's accounts and inventory supports the creditor's efforts to deter conversions, improvident risky business ventures, and the dilution of the claim through wrongful issuance of subsequent debt. These risks are well-understood, however, and often can be curtailed equally well by substitute measures such as restrictive loan covenants. Much less obvious is the phenomenon of leverage. By taking an interest that wraps around the debtor's business, the bank gains important influence over the debtor's strategic planning and operational decision making. The creditor's power comes from the ability to veto any proposed actions by withdrawing either financing or assets from the enterprise. A floating lien that supports an exclusive option to make future advances gives the creditor the power both to seize the debtor's assets (for example, through self-help repossession, and direct collection) and to terminate the financing necessary for the operation of the business. This power to "turn off the spigot" permits quick and decisive responses to the threat of disfavored behavior.

As with any lever, the power to prevent a disfavored action generates the power to compel a second, desired action. Leverage is important to the creditor in two respects. First, it mitigates the problem of end game behavior by debtors facing default. The synergy between the risk of business failure and the risk of misbehavior diminishes the reputational restraints that short-term financing exerts. To the extent that business failure is a product of managerial incompetence, leverage permits the creditor to ensure that strategic planning is not ill-advised or ill-conceived. Economies of scale give the relational creditor a particular advantage in financial planning and the coordination of investment decisions. In addition, leverage encourages the debtor to develop projected investment opportunities fully and thus has a unique role in solving the underinvestment dilemma. Relational security arrangements enable the creditor to influence the nature and timing of the debtor's production inputs. Insufficient or misdirected efforts are extraordinarily difficult to detect and to sanction. While the creditor must continue to monitor the debtor's activities to discover such errors of omission, the leverage of blanket security encourages prompt compliance when such errors are uncovered. Thus, even under severe time constraints the relational creditor can ensure that production is increased, or inventory built up, or even that the order and timing of raw material inputs is reconsidered. In each case, the creditor's influence comes from the extraordinary potency of the combination of exclusive financing and blanket security.

Credible Commitments: Security as a Hostage

In order to exercise leverage the relational financer must monitor the debtor's operational decisions. Direct supervision of these activities involves substantial administrative costs in hiring investigative personnel, training auditors, etc. When monitoring costs, such as direct supervision, are high relative to actions by the debtor that reassure the creditor, both parties will agree ex ante to substitute cost-effective bonding alternatives.

The relational security device serves the additional function of a bond given to ensure faithful efforts toward accomplishing the venture. By offering his assets as a hostage, the debtor invites the creditor to exercise actual operational control should he default on the agreement. For all practical purposes, the entrepreneur places his business in escrow, with the creditor serving as the escrow agent. The effectiveness of the bond derives from the severity of the sanction should any misbehavior be detected. This form of reassurance is particularly appropriate where the risk of misbehavior is difficult to detect as in the case of inadequate efforts or underinvestment. The debtor agrees to the arrangement because the threat of legal liability similarly constrains the creditor from misbehaving. Although the creditor retains the power to exercise control should the debtor misbehave, there are significant costs in actually assuming control that will deter any frivolous or bad faith action. A controlling creditor incurs enhanced risk of liability under both securities law and the common law of torts. Furthermore, should the debtor subsequently be reorganized in bankruptcy, the creditor's control will cause it to be designated an "insider" and subjected to more rigorous (and often disadvantageous) scrutiny.

The additional role of relational security as a valuable precommitment strategy for certain debtors enhances its effectiveness. By granting security, owner/managers [...] may grant security in order to reduce their opportunities to misbehave when events generate unanticipated stresses. Relational security limits the debtor's options when responding to the subsequent threat of business failure. While standard economic theory maintains that debtors would prefer to retain all their choices including the choice subsequently to misbehave, a precommitment analysis suggests that such security may simply be some debtors' method of protecting their present decisions against future temptations. Furthermore, the debtor's willingness to constrain his future decision making in this way signals the creditor of his resolve not to violate the terms of the debt contract. Because the debtor bears the cost of misbehavior ex ante, he has an incentive to agree to mechanisms that will limit his own ex post opportunities to cheat or otherwise misbehave.

NOTES

1. Monitoring Proceeds. A security interest automatically extends to identifiable proceeds of collateral. Section 9–315(a)(2). As Professor Freyermuth indicates, there has been considerable debate about the appropriate scope of "proceeds", a debate that has turned on concepts such as "exchange and replacement" for, "close association" with, or the "economic value" of the collateral. The recent amendments to Article 9 expanded the definition of proceeds in Section 9–102(64). In the excerpt of this section, Professor Freyermuth argues for an even broader definition of proceeds that encompasses "all assets received upon the occurrence of events that exhaust the collateral's economic value or productive capacity." He asserts that this conception most closely approximates the expected ex ante bargain of the reasonable debtor and secured party. If the objective is to reflect the expected ex ante bargain, however, the irrelevance proposition might here again be a good place to start. The secured creditor would charge a lower interest rate if her collateral included proceeds, and would drop the rate further if proceeds were defined broadly. However, the debtor's other creditors would charge an offsetting premium to compensate them for the correspondingly higher risk.

Can monitoring or screening considerations provide a justification for determining how far the concept of proceeds should be extended to aid the secured creditor of the original collateral? Note that this collateral is defined not by its intrinsic features or use (e.g. inventory, equipment, etc.) but rather by its relation to collateral expressly granted to the creditor. Is it likely that the debtor's actions with respect to proceeds will be best monitored by the creditor who has priority in the original collateral that gives rise to the proceeds? If, for example, a lender is granted a security interest in a piece of equipment because of a monitoring advantage, it is plausible that she has a related advantage in monitoring the cash proceeds received if that equipment is sold or leased. These may be "economies of scope" in monitoring. However, is this true if the equipment is used in the manufacture of inventory that is then sold? If monitoring is the reason for the automatic extension to proceeds, then the boundaries of the definition should be related to the existence of such monitoring economies.

While expanding greatly the definition of proceeds, Freyermuth advocates that the restriction on the scope of the security interest should come primarily from the requirement that the proceeds be identifiable. This is consistent with the monitoring motivation: the secured creditor's interest extends to proceeds only if she can trace them in a court, thereby giving her the incentive to keep track of them as they change location or form.

2. What explains the blanket lien? The automatic interest in proceeds is redundant in the case of a relational secured lender (described in the excerpt by Professor Scott) who takes an explicit blanket floating security interest in all the assets of the debtor. Scott suggests that this very common financing pattern is difficult to explain through monitoring specialization alone. In the excerpt, Scott emphasizes that blanket liens, particularly over "flow" assets such as inventory and receivables, give the relational lender the tools to perform its governance role. He observes that the security held by a relational lender "signals other creditors that a policeman is walking the beat, and thus they can relax their vigilance in taking individual precautions."

3. Conflict between secured and unsecured creditors. In some instances, the conflict between secured and unsecured creditors is muted because they operate in substantially different markets. For example, larger borrowers with substantial track records and good credit ratings can raise capital directly from capital markets through public issues of equity or debt securities. Smaller and younger borrowers rely more on trade credit and on financial intermediaries, notably banks. *See e.g.,* Douglas W. Diamond, *Monitoring and Reputation: The Choice Between Bank Loans and Directly Placed Debt,* 99 J. Pol. Econ. 689 (1991).

Yet, in other ways, the interests of secured and unsecured creditors conflict. As Professor Scott points out, broad security interests give financers substantial leverage over the decision making of their debtors. Scott suggests that the lender may use his leverage to dampen risk taking by the debtor, even when profitable. Or, under some conditions, the lender may induce breach and declare default too quickly when the collateral has a ready resale market. When a debtor is in financial distress, how else might a secured creditor influence decisions to improve its lot at the expense of the general creditors? *See generally,* George G. Triantis & Ronald J. Daniels, *The Role of Debt in Interactive Corporate Governance,* 83 Calif. L. Rev. 1073 1082–1103 (1995).

6.4 Priority Allocation Over Time: First–in–Time versus Later–in–Time Priority Rules

Explaining Creditor Priorities*
HIDEKI KANDA and **SAUL LEVMORE**

The Potential Advantage (and Problem with) Late-in-Time Priority

As a debtor's business plans and behavior unfold, the debtor may approach successive creditors, C1 and C2, for capital. Clearly, there is more information available later in time, and, to the extent that the debtor seeks capital for a new project, an up-to-date look at the debtor will be especially valuable to potential lenders. Some debtors will not seek out C2 but will instead return to C1 for additional funds in the later time period. Indeed, C1 normally will have a first-mover advantage over other creditors in learning about the debtor's latest plans. Other debtors, however, will choose to use multiple sources of capital, which may result in priority conflicts. It therefore is useful to focus on the stark case where the debtor first borrows from C1 and then turns to C2 for additional funds. C2 may well be the more informed lender, or more efficient decisionmaker, in many of these situations. The priority rules applicable to the debtor's potential insolvency are obviously relevant—in both private and social terms—to this bargain between the debtor and C2.

From an efficiency perspective, we might want bankruptcy or other priority rules to encourage C2 to consider the expected return from the debtor's planned investment. Put differently, one cost of a legal system that gives C1 priority over C2 is that C2 may decline to lend even when the debtor proposes to use new capital profitably (in expected value terms). Knowing that revenues must first satisfy C1, C2 may decline to lend unless there is either a fairly substantial margin of safety or a promise of a substantial interest rate—in which case the debtor may decline to borrow. A better rule therefore might be one that granted C2 priority over C1 in return for injecting new money, if only to encourage all investments that are passably profitable and marginally efficient. Put simply, it may be desirable to give the incentive to lend to the most recent lender, who is likely to be in the best position to assess the profitability of the debtor's present business plans.

If C2 is instead made last in right, this "marginal creditor" sometimes will be inclined not to support plans that are profitable, socially efficient, and even in the aggregate interest of all creditors. Such reasoning might explain the priority commonly granted to purchase-money lenders—that is, to certain C2's—and to various other injectors of

* 80 VA. L. REV. 2103, 2114–2121 (1994).

new money. On the other hand, if the late-in-time decisionmaker, or injector of new money, is given priority over previous lenders, the cushion of earlier money will inefficiently encourage lending with too little concern for the debtor's use of these marginal funds. In some situations it may be possible to limit the late-in-time claim, or superpriority (if it is that), to the very project that the debtor undertakes with the new funds. But it normally will be difficult to trace profits and losses in the manner necessary for such a scheme. A first-in-time priority rule will therefore squander the better information often available to the late-in-time lender, whereas a late-in-time priority rule, rather than encouraging efficient marginal decisionmaking, will encourage the latecomer to view old money as a cushion that forgives overlending.

When the problem is framed this way it becomes apparent why most preferred late-in-time lenders are given priority only with respect to a particular asset and not with respect to the debtor's estate as a whole. A late lender is an inefficient decisionmaker only when there is a cushion (formed by funds provided by other creditors) for a marginal project financed by this creditor that proves disappointing. The cushion problem is largely mitigated, however, to the extent that the prevailing scheme gives some late-in-time lenders priority only for a given asset, such as equipment that the lender finances or payments received from an account debtor after a surety completes its obligation under a performance bond. The optimistic explanation is that late lenders have more information than their predecessors and are thus encouraged by the priority system to consider the marginal profitability of the undertaking enabled by the new funds. In short, late lenders are likely to be better decisionmakers if given priority (only) with respect to the project or asset they decide to finance late in time.

We have seen that late-in-time creditors might be given limited priority in order to encourage better marginal decisionmaking on their part. But each bit of additional credit still increases the risk alteration problem. A scheme that gives priority to C2 will disadvantage C1 and bring on the risk alteration problem discussed in Part I. There is thus a tension between risk alteration, which suggests a first-in-time rule, and the later creditor's information advantage, which suggests at least occasional late-in-time priority.

A pro rata rule would not solve this tension between first-in-time and late-in-time advantages. Under such a rule we would still expect C2 to charge a higher interest rate than C1, and we might again expect the credit market to unravel as creditors avoided (or charged for) the position of C1. Both C1 and C2 would fear further borrowing and risk alteration by the debtor after their advances. But C2 would be likely to have more or better information about C1's previous commitment than C1 would have about C2's. C2 therefore would seem to occupy a more enviable position than C1 even though the hypothetical pro rata rule would apply to both claims. This perspective is obscured, however, because C1's relative disadvantage is one of uncertainty, and C1 might be compensated for this uncertainty through a higher interest rate.

Another way to think of the relative positions of C1 and C2 is to focus on the fact that C1 is likely to be worse off each time the debtor takes on more debt from C2 or other lenders. At its extreme, the debtor's behavior presents a "lemons problem": spiraling adverse selection forces C1 to charge an infinitely high interest rate because debtors drop out of the credit market as rates rise, until those who remain are those who plan to borrow and alter risk to the hilt.

Non-Risk-Altering, Late-in-Time Lenders

We have described early lenders as concerned with risk alteration and later lenders as enjoying informational advantages about the debtor's likely inclination toward risk and sometimes about the debtor's prospective investments. These factors alone suggest that the ideal priority system must balance first-in-time and late-in-time priorities. The balancing act becomes more precarious once we recognize that new money does not always generate a risk alteration problem for the early creditor.

Consider, for example, a creditor quite outside of Article 9, the salvor who rescues a vessel in distress. Admiralty law recognizes the monopoly (or perhaps bilateral monopoly) problem that would infect any bargain between a potential salvor and the master of a vessel in distress, often in a location far from other entrepreneurs who may wish to compete for the rescue task. The salvor's reward is therefore determined after the fact and is designed to encourage an efficient level of entry into the field. As for the priority of this reward in the event of the vessel owner's insolvency, all admiralty schemes of which we are aware give the salvor's claim priority over those of other creditors, including registered mortgage holders, who look to the vessel for security for their earlier advances. The conventional view of this priority is that but for the salvage operation there would be no vessel for other creditors to feast on. But this is only a partial explanation because other late-in-time claimants also might show, with the benefit of hindsight, that but for their contributions all other creditors would have been worse off. Similarly, the argument that the salvor can retrieve his money ahead of earlier claimants because he injected new money is insufficient; virtually all latecomers provide new money, yet very few can emerge from the ranks and defeat even prior, secured creditors.

Note that the salvor does not generate a risk alteration problem. Once the vessel is saved, the owner-debtor does have a new debt in the amount of the salvage award (and thus some temptation to increase the riskiness of future projects), but the salvor's advance does not enable the debtor to do anything new or unexpected. Although we have described first-in-time priority as a solution to the risk alteration problem, it seems plausible (but unconventional) to connect the late-in-time exception for salvors to the fact that these particular claimants do not create risk alteration problems for the creditors that have preceded them. Indeed, the connection is even closer if there is reason to think that earlier creditors would prefer to be subordinated to the later salvor, for in that case our argument is of the hypothetical-bargain variety. If, for instance, a potential salvor knew that there were substantial liens against a vessel, a first-in-time rule might deter the salvor from investing in a salvage operation. A court might be convinced to apply a multiplier to salvage awards based on the risk of both the salvage operation and the collection of the salvage award in bankruptcy. This award, however, is an ineffective incentive if its hypothetical low priority causes the potential salvor to stay away.

The salvor therefore may be a "better-informed" C2. He is both better situated and better equipped than earlier creditors, and the project funded by the salvor does not alter risk in a way that harms earlier creditors. And, as already noted, it is possible that the salvor would decline to act if not granted high, and of course late-in-time, priority. The salvor is thus a near-perfect example of a late-in-time creditor that is both non-risk-altering and a superior marginal decision-maker.

It is interesting but perhaps less useful to add that another advantage of giving priority to salvors and to other non-risk-altering latecomers is that priority discourages them from investing in information about the debtor's creditworthiness. Low priority, combined with whatever premium or multiplier is necessary to encourage potential salvors, will cause these actors to inquire into the debtor's history. Because this inquiry produces no social gain, it is arguable that high priority is more efficient.

Although the case of the salvor neatly illustrates the interaction between risk alteration (or the lack thereof) and late-in-time, superior decisionmaking, few transactions are this uncluttered. We suggest that Article 9 and related law seek to balance the advantages of first-in-time and late-in-time priority. The more a lender exhibits the qualities of a salvor, the more likely an exception to the first-in-time solution (to the risk alteration problem) will be made. Moreover, Article 9 attempts to work with categories rather than with case-by-case instructions. The scheme that emerges, then, is almost necessarily peppered with close (but plausibly correct) call.

Financial Slack Policy and the Laws of Secured Transactions*

GEORGE G. TRIANTIS

A manager's discretion depends on the firm's internal funds and its capacity to issue low-risk debt (together "financial slack"). The optimal amount of financial slack is a challenging problem in corporate finance. Too much slack encourages managerial misbehavior and exacerbates corporate agency problems. Too little slack prevents the firm from exploiting profitable investment opportunities.

Secured financing has a large impact on financial slack. The first-in-time priority right of an outstanding security interest impairs the ability of a debtor to issue low-risk debt and thereby restricts the firm's access to external finance. At the same time, the provision for later-in-time priority for certain categories of indebtedness restores some of this capacity. The property right of a security interest impedes the sale or other disposition of many types of collateral and thereby constrains the availability of internal funds. Yet, various rules loosen this property right to enable dispositions of firm assets in the ordinary course of the firm's business. Against this collection of legal rules, a firm decides when to create a security interest and over what assets. By deferring the decision to secure debt and borrowing on an unsecured basis, a firm pays a premium today in order to preserve its option to issue low-risk secured debt in the future.

The firm thereby chooses the amount of financial slack in the firm and the future discretion of its managers. The optimal amount of financial slack permits a firm to finance its profitable investment opportunities, but no more. By themselves, the categorical rules in Article 9 of the Uniform Commercial Code (U.C.C.) that govern the attachment and priority of security interests cannot yield this optimum when firms face uncertain periodic cash flows and investment prospects. Therefore, the capital structure of healthy firms allows a buffer of financial slack and relies on midstream monitoring of the excess. Creditors are important monitors of a firm's use of liquid assets. Scholars acknowledge that the granting of security interests implicitly allocates monitoring functions among creditors and thereby avoids free riding and duplicative monitoring efforts. The most significant focal point for creditor monitoring is the debtor's liquid assets. Therefore, secured transactions law, particularly relating to proceeds, creates important incentives for creditor monitoring of cash and other liquid assets.

The rigidity of categorical rules in this area becomes most problematic when a firm is insolvent. Almost by definition, insolvent firms have little liquidity and very limited access to external financing. At the

* 29 J. LEGAL STUDIES 35, 35–37, 46–59 (2000).

same time, they are threatened by a wide divergence between the interests of managers and their investors. As a result, the stakes are much higher when it comes to tailoring financial slack to meet the circumstances of each distressed firm. Bankruptcy law abandons the combination under Article 9 of the U.C.C. of rules that determine the amount of financial slack and rules that allocate ex post monitoring responsibilities among creditors. In their place, the law gives bankruptcy courts direct control over the debtor's access to internal and external funds. The standards provided in the Bankruptcy Code—notably, the requirement of adequate protection of a secured creditor—should lead the court to create financial slack only when it is likely to finance value-creating investment. As with any legal standard, however, its success in achieving the efficient result relies on the faithful and competent application by the judiciary and the effective production of information through the adversarial process [. . .]

Outside Bankruptcy: Priority Rules under U.C.C. Article 9

Suppose that a firm has assets worth $100 and owes $80 to its initial lender (C1) who enjoys the highest priority as a first-in-time lender. Lender C1 holds a perfected blanket lien over all the firm's current and after-acquired assets. One year from today, the firm has equal chances of being in one of two possible states. In the good state, the firm's current assets would be worth $150; in the bad state, they would be worth $50 (that is, the firm is insolvent in the bad state). The firm now has an opportunity to invest in project A, which is a risk-free, profitable project that requires an investment of $20 and will yield $30 a year from now (a certain profit of 50 percent). The firm cannot capture the value of this venture by selling it to another entity because, for example, it has no property right protection in the opportunity. It also has no available liquid assets to invest. Suppose for the moment that C1 cannot finance the investment. Shareholders will not invest $20 in new equity because the debt overhang from C1's priority claim in the bad state would absorb their investment, and their payoff from the good state is $30, which yields an expected payoff of only $15. Given C1's first-in-time priority, a new creditor C2 would also recover nothing in the insolvent state, and, therefore, C2 would lend only if the firm promised it at least $40 in the good state (an expected value of $20) to compensate for the effect of debt overhang in the bad state. The project pays only $30 in the good state, however, and the balance must come out of the value currently owned by the shareholders. Therefore, the shareholders and C2 would not reach an agreement to finance the project. If, however, C2 were given priority, the debt could be paid in full in both states. The shareholders and C2 could therefore agree to split the gains from project A in the good state. In this example, therefore, later-in-time priority for C2 is necessary to exploit the profitable project.

In contrast, suppose that the firm has the opportunity to invest in project B, which has a negative expected value. Project B requires an investment of $20 and yields $30 in the good state and nothing in the bad state. Although they are not willing to finance the project, the shareholders would encourage the firm to take the gamble because it improves their payoff in the good state without making them worse off in the bad state. If C1 has priority over all subsequent lenders, its priority effectively precludes the firm from obtaining financing to fund the gamble. However, if the new investor C2 enjoys priority, it will be paid in full in either state and can be enticed into the coalition by the promise of a portion of the shareholders' gain in the good state. Similarly, given later-in-time priority, C2 would also be prepared to finance other forms of misbehavior, such as distributions to shareholders, perquisites to managers, or a reserve pool of cash that insulates managers from the discipline of product or factor markets. In each case, C2 facilitates and participates in the inefficient transfer of wealth from C1.

The foregoing illustrates the trade-off between first-in-time and later-in-time priority rules when the priority is debtor based (that is, applies to all assets of the firm) rather than asset based. First-in-time priority hinders managers' efforts to raise cash with which to misbehave because a new creditor cannot be compensated in good states for the losses it incurs in insolvent states. Yet, the first-in-time rule also obstructs efforts to finance profitable investments like project A because it prevents later-in-time lenders from participating in the profits of the project in the event of insolvency (debt overhang problem). Various partial solutions might be available without qualifying the first-in-time priority rule. First, the tension described above depends on the assumption that C1 cannot finance the new project. If C1 is unconstrained, it has the appropriate incentive to finance project A but not project B. Moreover, as an existing creditor of the firm, C1 has an informational advantage that might allow it to offer the debtor financing at a lower cost than C2.Second, C1 may subordinate its claim to C2's claim if C1 believes that C2 would thereby finance project A rather than project B. In either of these two cases, however, the debtor must bargain with C1 in order to finance its profitable opportunities. These costs can be even larger in other examples where the debtor seeks external financing after having granted priority claims to numerous earlier creditors. The bilateral negotiation entails strategic maneuvering and other transaction costs that, if unchecked by reputational discipline, may frustrate the financing of marginally profitable opportunities. Moreover, even in the case of more lucrative projects, the debtor will be compelled to pay C1 a supercompetitive return for either a new advance or the agreement to subordinate. This may deter the firm's investment in the risky search for such opportunities. A third alternative is also consistent with the first-in-time rule. Unless the firm's contract with C1 penalizes prepayment of the loan, C2 might agree to provide sufficient funds to enable the firm to repay its outstanding indebtedness to C1. This alternative avoids the inefficiencies of bilateral negotiations described above because a number of creditors can compete to be C2. However, C2's information and transaction costs are higher than under the subordination alternative because C2 must finance not only the new project but the entire firm. As a consequence, profitable projects may not be funded at the margin.

A fourth solution is the exploitation of the new venture in a separate legal entity. For example, the firm's shareholders might establish a new firm that finances the project by borrowing from C2. This solves the problem of C1's overhang without allowing C2 recourse to the firm's old assets. If the new firm is a subsidiary of the old firm, this structure effectively subordinates C1's claim to the new venture to the priority of C2. The disadvantage of this solution is the cost of creating a new corporation, which may be sufficient to offset the expected gains from smaller projects. In some cases, the use of later-in-time priority financing described below may be more efficient.

In light of the foregoing transactional obstacles, the law might provide rules that remove the need for agreement between the debtor and C1 or that cast a clear shadow that deters opportunism and facilitates agreement. A solution to the trade-off between allowing profitable opportunities to be exploited and deterring investment in unprofitable ventures is to provide for later-in-time priority that is project based: in particular, the restricted priority that accompanies project financing. Thus, C2 enjoys priority with respect to the payoff from the new project and either has no recourse to or remains subordinate with respect to the other assets of the firm. By tying C2's payoff to the value of the proposed investment, project financing makes C2 an efficient gatekeeper in deciding whether to allow the firm to exploit the investment opportunity. Project financing of this sort mimics the alternative of exploiting the opportunity in a new, separately financed firm. The debtor and C1 can provide for this later-in-time priority in their initial contract and thereby avoid the inefficiencies of ex post negotiations. The ability of the parties to carve out the efficient later-in-time priority, however, depends on the ease with which C2's priority can be linked to the value created by its contribution and the absence of any adverse impact on the value of original assets. This is easiest to accomplish if C2 funds the purchase or manufacture of a discrete asset (purchase money credit) and somewhat less convenient if the newly acquired item is installed in or affixed to existing goods (for example, an accession). It is significantly more difficult if the new item thereby loses its identity (commingling) and least tractable if C2 finances expenses such as labor or electricity that enhance the value of existing assets.

Inside Bankruptcy: Priority Rules under Bankruptcy Code §§ 552, 364

The initiation of a bankruptcy proceeding brings quite a distinct regime to bear on the financing and investment decisions of the debtor. The problems of both overinvestment and debt overhang are more severe in bankruptcy. Bankruptcy law addresses overinvestment by giving the court powers to oversee the activities of the debtor. The court has the authority to determine whether the debtor should be reorganized or liquidated, and, if the debtor continues to operate, the court must authorize decisions made outside of the debtor's ordinary course of business. It is relatively more difficult for a court to compel investment in positive net present value opportunities than to block unprofitable projects. Therefore, the overhang problem is addressed by creating room at the top of the pecking order or, in other terms, opening financial slack by judicial intervention. Bankruptcy courts have the authority to increase the availability of cash flow (discussed in Section VC below) and the ability of the debtor to issue secured or senior debt to postpetition lenders. The later-in-time priority available in bankruptcy is broader than the purchase money security interest priority described in the previous section because the new funds can be used to pay wages, utility bills, and other operating expenses that enhance the value of existing inventory, plant, or equipment. The justification for making a broader later-in-time priority available in bankruptcy is that (1) the debt overhang problem is more severe when the firm is insolvent and (2) the affairs of the debtor are being overseen by the court and by creditor committees, which signals a shift in emphasis from ex ante constraints in the capital structure to ex post discipline under the bankruptcy process.

NOTES

1. The effects of secured credit: misuse of free cash. A secured creditor's priority has two caps: the amount of the secured indebtedness and the value of the collateral. Suppose a debtor borrows $1,000 and gives the lender a security interest worth $1,000. Several authors note that there should be no prejudice to unsecured creditors from this transaction because the assets of the firm rise by the same amount as the priority debt (in this case, $1,000), leaving the unsecured creditors with the same assets as before the transaction. Steven L. Harris & Charles W. Mooney, Jr., *A Property-Based Theory of Security Interests: Taking Debtors' Choices Seriously*, 80 Va. L. Rev. 2021 (1994). The readings in this section suggest that the efficiency of the secured transaction depends on what the debtor does with the credit or advance. *See* George G. Triantis, *A Free–Cash–Flow Theory of Secured Debt and Creditor Priorities*, 80 Va. L. Rev. 2155, 2161–2 (1994). Professor Schwarcz recognizes that existing creditors can be hurt by new money liens: "For example, they could be prejudiced by the debtor's misuse of loan proceeds. Such misuse, however, is more appropriately governed by fraudulent conveyance and preference laws and, in certain cases, by monitoring the use of proceeds."; Steven Schwarcz, *The Easy Case for the Priority of*

Secured Claims in Bankruptcy, 47 Duke L. J. 425, 431 (1997). All states have fraudulent conveyance (or fraudulent transfer) laws that entitle debtors to recover transfers made for less than reasonably equivalent value while the debtor was insolvent or undercapitalized. E.g., Uniform Fraudulent Transfer Act, §§ 4, 7. Federal bankruptcy law provides for avoidable preferences: a debtor (or its trustee) can recover transfers made on account of antecedent debt while the debtor was insolvent and within 90 days before the bankruptcy filing. Bankruptcy Code § 547(b). Both fraudulent conveyance and preference laws are limited in their ability to prevent the misuse of proceeds referred to by Schwarcz, however, by the requirement that the debtor be insolvent (or near to it) at the time of the transfer. (Fraudulent conveyance does offer the alternative, but difficult, avenue of proving intent to impair creditors). Suppose the debtor invests the $1,000 in a highly risky (and unwise) venture and later loses the investment, which leads to insolvency. The secured lender then recovers its debt from the remaining assets of the debtor. Do the other creditors have any legal recourse? Schwarcz suggests that they might avoid this result by monitoring the use of the proceeds. Yet, what should/could the creditors have done if their monitoring detected the unwise investment?

2.   The effects of secured credit: forestalling liquidation. The academic literature contains a concern that the priority of secured claims may permit inefficient projects to be financed or allow a firm to continue operating when it should be liquidated. *See* Barry E. Adler, *A Re–Examination of Near–Bankruptcy Investments Incentives,* 62 U. Chi. L. Rev. 575 (1995); John Hudson, *The Case Against Secured Lending,* 15 Int'l Rev. L. & Econ. 47 (1995); Thomas H. Jackson & Robert E. Scott, *On the Nature of Bankruptcy: An Essay on Bankruptcy Sharing and the Creditors' Bargain,* 75 Va. L. Rev. 155 (1989); Michelle J. White, *Public Policy Toward Bankruptcy: Me–First and Other Priority Rules,* 11 Bell J. Econ. 550 (1980); Lucian A. Bebchuk & Jesse M. Fried, *The Uneasy Case for the Priority of Secured Claims in Bankruptcy,* 105 Yale L. J. 857 (1996).

First-in-time priority would appear to be the antidote to these concerns, at least where a firm issues secured credit while financially sound, because the existence of a secured claim discourages the financing of new projects. George G. Triantis, *A Free–Cash–Flow Theory of Secured Debt and Creditor Priorities,* 80 Va. L. Rev. 2155 (1994); Oliver Hart & John Moore, *Debt and Seniority: An Analysis of the Role of Hard Claims in Constraining Management,* 85 Am. Econ. Rev. 567 (1995). Yet, as noted in the excerpt from Triantis, the overhang of the secured claim also impedes the financing of profitable opportunities.

3.   The effects of secured credit: underinvestment. Underinvestment is often due to the reluctance of new investors to contribute to even profitable ventures that are pursued by debtors who have outstanding debt, particularly when it is secured. Anticipating this difficulty, debtors are reluctant to fully encumber all their assets. They may decide to defer issuing secured debt to preserve the option to get easier credit later. This option is particularly valuable if the firm faces financial difficulty. *See* George G. Triantis, *Secured Debt Under Conditions of Imperfect Information,* 21 J. Legal Stud. 225, 258 (1992); Steven L. Schwarcz, *The Easy Case for the Priority of Secured Claims in Bankruptcy,* 47 Duke L.J. 425, 446–52 (1997). Yet, this same liquidity is what enables the financially distressed firm to pursue risky and unprofitable projects.

The tension between the problems of overinvestment and underinvestment lies at the core of the trade-off between first-in-time and later-in-time priority rules. Consider the following example. A bank finances the debtor's purchase of a truck. The truck is now several years old and the debtor's mechanic reports that it could use some reconditioning. At this time, the truck is worth $14,000 and the amount outstanding to the bank is $20,000. The mechanic says that the repairs will cost $5,000. Suppose first that the repairs would increase the value of the truck by $6,000. Would the mechanic be willing to provide parts and labor on credit (a) if the bank has priority, (b) if he shares priority with the bank, or (c) if he enjoys priority over the bank? Alternatively, suppose that the mechanic is simply trying to fabricate business for himself and the repairs will add no value to the truck. Under the same three priority scenarios listed above, would he provide parts and labor on credit? Does any priority ranking achieve the desired result in both cases: that is, the mechanic performs the work when, but only when, it is efficient? Would giving the mechanic a purchase money security priority achieve the best outcome? Would it help if the debtor filed for bankruptcy? Or, should the debtor move the truck to a separate corporation?

4. Project financing. Project financing limits the claim of a lender to the project that it helps finance. This feature provides a solution to the twin problems of overinvestment and underinvestment. It can be implemented by a variety of alternative techniques. In the face of a broad priority claim held by an existing lender, a new lender can take priority in the new project, but only in that project. The purchase money security interest might provide such later-in-time priority, but its scope is limited (as discussed in the excerpt from Triantis, supra). Alternatively, a firm might issue secured, but non-recourse debt to finance discrete projects to prevent the overhang of outstanding claims. Project-type financing might also be achieved by placing discrete projects or assets in separate trusts or corporations. *See* George G. Triantis, *Organizations as Internal Capital Markets,* 117 Harv. L. Rev. 1102 (2004). This approach is complementary to Hansmann and Kraakman's asset-partitioning justification of organizational boundaries based on monitoring efficiencies. See Note 6 in Section 6.2 supra. Indeed, this benefit from separate legal entities may be generalized in that the financing of and governance over each project may be tailored to their respective efficiency needs. This feature stems from the fact that the law treats each firm as a distinct legal entity, with distinct property rights. Edward M. Iacobucci and George G. Triantis, *Economic and Legal Boundaries of Firms,* 93 Va. L. Rev. 515 (2007); George G. Triantis, *Entity Property,* in KENNETH AYOTTE AND HENRY SMITH, RESEARCH HANDBOOK IN THE ECONOMICS OF PROPERTY LAW.

6.5   Notice Filing and Disclosure Alternatives

Perfection Hierarchies and Nontemporal Priority Rules*
RANDAL C. PICKER

Perfection and Priority

Perfection is just one of Article 9's instruments for describing a legal status and keying consequences to that status. Perfection is often described as being related to priority, but there is no simple relationship between perfection and priority. Priority may exist even without perfection. In other cases, priority is tied directly to perfection and is both necessary and sufficient for priority. Yet, in other cases, perfection is necessary but not sufficient for priority. To be more concrete, consider a contest between a secured creditor and an unsecured creditor. An unperfected secured creditor is senior to an unsecured creditor, so perfection is not necessary for priority, as the secured creditor will be senior without being perfected. Perfection, though, is sufficient for priority, as the perfected secured creditor is senior to the unsecured creditor. In contrast, in a competition between a secured creditor and a lien creditor, an unperfected secured creditor is junior to a lien creditor, while a perfected secured creditor has priority over a lien creditor as to all funds advanced by the secured creditor at the time the previously unsecured creditor becomes a lien creditor, and for at least forty-five days thereafter. Perfection is both necessary and sufficient for priority against the lien creditor, but even then only for funds advanced by the secured creditor during a particular time period. In a third case, perfection is necessary but not sufficient to establish priority. An unperfected secured creditor loses to another perfected secured creditor. Perfection is necessary for the first secured creditor to have superior rights as against the second perfected secured creditor but is insufficient standing alone to establish priority. For two perfected secured creditors, priority is generally dated by the earlier of first to file or perfect. As this should make clear, perfection says nothing necessarily about priority against a given competing creditor: either way, perfected or unperfected, the secured creditor can win or lose, depending on the competitor.

That said, it would be a mistake to lose sight of how important perfection is for the secured creditor. Although the unperfected secured creditor would triumph in a competition with an unsecured creditor, it is unlikely that the contest will be so framed. The unsecured creditor can—and will—take steps to improve its position by becoming a lien creditor. As a lien creditor has priority over an unperfected secured creditor, an unsecured creditor always has a route available that will enable it to change the momentary priority of the unperfected secured creditor.

* 74 CHI.-KENT L. REV. 1157, 1165–1172 (1999).

Perfection is the way that the secured creditor ensures that it maintains any priority that it enjoys against an unsecured creditor. First and foremost, to say that a secured creditor is perfected is to say that an unsecured creditor cannot jump ahead of the secured creditor. Perfection is also essential for the secured creditor to compete successfully with other secured creditors. Again, this is not literally true: Revised section 9–322(a)(3) provides a rule of priority based on the time of attachment to resolve priority disputes between attached but unperfected secured creditors. Nonetheless, it is highly unlikely that a dispute would arise in that context; one or both of the creditors would try to perfect, and Revised section 9–322(a)(3) would cease to apply.

Origins of the Ostensible Ownership Problem

So step back and ask again: why do we require an additional act for the security interest to be effective against third parties? The traditional explanation focuses on the problem of ostensible ownership. Consider the analysis in Clow v. Woods, a Pennsylvania case decided in 1819. Hancock and Poe formed a partnership. At some point thereafter, Hancock granted a mortgage on property to Clow, who had guaranteed certain of Hancock's debts. The mortgage covered all those goods and chattels now in [Hancock's] tanyard in Liberty street, in the Northern Liberties of Pittsburg (to wit), all the bark and tools and implements of trade of the party of the first part, all his calf-skins in bark, and all his sides of leather in bark, with the appurtenances. We are told nothing about whether this property was related to Hancock's partnership with Poe or wholly separate. That partnership dissolved and was settled through an "amicable suit" for the adjustment of their accounts. Sheriff Woods levied on the material in Hancock's tanyard to enforce the judgment obtained from the suit. Clow sought to divert the proceeds of that levy away from Poe to Clow based on the mortgage and sued the sheriff to force that result. Poe had no notice of the mortgage until the levy was made and Sheriff Wood received notice of it only after he had arrived on Hancock's premises. The mortgage had not been recorded. The legal issue presented was whether the mortgage was good against Poe notwithstanding that failure.

The court held that the mortgage transaction was a per se fraud against creditors and was void under the statute of 13 Elizabeth. That statute rendered void any conveyance made to the end, purpose, and intent of defrauding creditors. Both judges, Gibson and Duncan, issued opinions. The opinion of Gibson cut to the heart of the problem quickly:

> The law will not and ought not to permit the owner of personal property to create an interest in another, either by mortgage or absolute sale, and still continue to be the ostensible owner; and where the creating of such an interest is the sole object, the conveyance will be fraudulent, whether it contain a stipulation for retention of possession or not; for to indulge the motive that led to the arrangement would be against true policy.

Which policy? The clear concern was the ability of the borrower to cheat subsequent creditors: But where, from the nature of the transaction, possession cannot be given, the parties ought in lieu, to do every thing in their power to secure the public from that deception which the possession of property without the ownership always enables a person to practice. Duncan's opinion emphasizes the same issues and forecasts the death of credit were a contrary outcome to obtain.

In chattels, possession is the strongest evidence of ownership. That a secret mortgage to secure a creditor, without any change of possession, the debtor in the daily and constant occupation of the goods, without valuation or inventory or specification accompanying the instrument, should be valid and bind the property against creditors, or sales made by the debtor without notice, would be a reproach to the law. It ought not, it cannot be so. If it were so, it would put an end to all credit. Credit is given on the possession, on the faith, that the man who was once the owner of goods, continues the owner, until he parts with the possession. Note what this says before turning to whether it is right. The vision presented is that prospective creditors rely on the appearance of ownership of property in making lending decisions. Unlike the real estate system, where the public records provide a chain of title to establish ownership, evidence of ownership of personal property is tied directly to possession of that property. An unrecorded mortgage is, therefore, a secret lien, and it purports to divide the ownership of the property in a way that is incompatible with the possession of the property.

Problems with the Ostensible Ownership Problem Analysis

Now step back to see if this analysis holds up. There is a certain internal incoherence to this system: the problem of mistaken inferences from possession is to be solved by requiring that an effective security interest be created by turning over possession of the property to the secured creditor. This, of course, was the pledge system, where the secured creditor took possession of the property but did not become the owner of the property. This is the separation of ownership and possession that Clow decries and that defines the pledge system.

We should also question the informational assumptions made in Clow. The public record is hardly the only source of information about a debtor. Even though Dun & Bradstreet did not have an online service available in 1819, there was probably much "public" information known in small, closely-knit communities. And, we should not discount too quickly the possibility of learning valuable information from the debtor itself. A prospective trade creditor meets with the debtor and inquires about whether the debtor has any outstanding security interests. The assumption in Clow must be that the debtor will deny such interests in an effort to lure the trade creditor into providing credit at a lower interest rate than would otherwise be available were the security interest made known. While this may seem obviously right, closer examination suggests that the analysis is less straightforward. First, we should consider the possibility of explicit contractual provisions addressing preexisting security interests, with penalties attached to the breach of such a provision. Many creditors will require an affirmative covenant about the existence of security interests ("Debtor hereby covenants that, as of this date, there are no outstanding security interests against its property"). Although a penalty provision may be of little solace if the debtor is indeed insolvent, we students of failure should not lose sight of the fact that some businesses actually succeed. The unsecured creditor may learn of the breach eventually—by happenstance or, more systematically, by searching periodically for new financing statements against the debtor—and stick the debtor with the penalty when it has the wherewithal to pay. A sufficiently large penalty—paid when the debtor is solvent—may be enough to induce the debtor to act truthfully.

Penalty clauses have been notoriously difficult to get enforced in the courts, notwithstanding the substantial benefits that might flow from doing so. We should instead ask whether there are other ways to get the debtor to report its situation honestly. We could, for example, as was once contemplated—apparently briefly—impose a duty on the secured creditor to take care to ensure that the debtor tells creditors of the secured creditor's interest. A breach of that duty would give rise to an action for damages against the secured creditor to the extent of the harm suffered and caused by the breach. The existence of the duty should cause the secured creditor to act aggressively to ensure that the other creditors of the debtor learn of its security interest. Implementing this, though, would force litigation over the ever slippery questions of what did the debtor tell to the suing creditor, what did the creditor otherwise know, and what would the creditor have done had the required knowledge been created. These are not questions one could litigate with any confidence, and a legal system should be reluctant to tie outcomes to questions it cannot answer well.

So speak not of duties but incentives. It is possible that creditors would derive substantial comfort from the knowledge that a secured creditor was paying close attention to the debtor. As Gilmore puts it, the other creditors might "benefit[] from the fact that a professional with a substantial stake in the enterprise was acting as their policeman." Other creditors can reduce their efforts to police the debtor's behavior if they can piggyback on the steps taken by the secured creditor. This means that we can eliminate many steps taken in parallel by trade creditors, for example, and replace them with the efforts of the secured creditor. In this story, the savvy debtor wants to disclose that it has a secured creditor as a way of ensuring other creditors that the debtor will be policed. Debtors, in the fashion of modern homeowners, should post signs stating, "These premises protected by Secured Creditor Co."

Inferences and Information Revelation

We have focused so far on whether a debtor with a preexisting security interest would disclose that interest when faced with the inevitable request for a disclosure of all such interests. Another possibility has been put forward: namely, that debtors without preexisting security interests will be eager to show prospective lenders that they have no such interests and that the activities of these debtors will sufficiently distinguish security-interest free debtors from debtors with encumbered property so as to reveal the latter. Imagine a world with two types of borrowers, those with encumbered property and those without. The assumption here—and this is the same assumption that we saw in Clow—is that debtors would like to be seen as unencumbered so as to borrow at lower rates. These unencumbered debtors will make every effort to demonstrate that they have no outstanding security interests. They will open their books, give copies of their correspondence, do anything necessary to convince the prospective lender that there is no prior security interest in place. Debtors with preexisting security interests, goes the story, will not be eager to open their books for inquiry and, in so doing, will signal to the lender that they indeed do have outstanding security interests. Here, silence speaks volumes.

The problem with this, though, is that the borrower with a security interest may not remain silent but may instead aggressively misrepresent the facts. For the lender to be able to learn who does and does not have an outstanding security interest, the lender must be able to separate borrowers who actually have no outstanding security interests from those who claim to have no outstanding security interests. This is very much in the nature of trying to prove a negative. The lying borrower will have taken steps to hide evidence that would otherwise exist, and, as we have discussed above, penalties tied to a misrepresentation may or may not work. Beyond this, as noted before, the debtor may want to disclose its secured creditors as part of a bonding effort to assure its other creditors that they are protected. Of course, you might think, if this story is true, debtors would be in the business of lying about the existence of a preexisting security interest rather than its nonexistence. (We switch from the horror of the secret lien to the problem of the trumped-up secured creditor.) An answer is that a trade creditor can verify the secured creditor's existence once it has been disclosed, and only if the secured creditor is colluding with the debtor will we have the problem of fake secured creditors.

We have been considering whether the ostensible ownership problem identified in Clow is as substantial as that case suggests and whether its solution—continued reliance on the pledge—makes sense given the problem. The pledge creates an ostensible ownership problem, though one that might be surmounted by widespread knowledge of the customs of secured creditors. We have also looked at the informational assumptions embedded in the ostensible ownership problem analysis.

There are certainly ways that contracts might shrink the problem through penalty clauses, though the law itself has rendered this an ineffective approach. In addition, the debtor may be a source of information, either voluntarily through verifiable disclosures or involuntarily by comparison with the acts of other debtors in like circumstances. Taken together, this suggests that there may not be a central, unalterable information vacuum about the debtor and that we may not need to be able to infer ownership from possession in the way envisioned by the judges in Clow. All of that would support greater reliance on a system of security interests without a separate act of public notice. Whether we would want to move to such a system would clearly depend on the relative costs of running a system of public notice versus the type of private information gathering described above.

A Theory of Loan Priorities*
ALAN SCHWARTZ

This article analyzes priorities among lenders in an insolvent debtor's personal property. Current law regulating these priorities rests on three "priority principles": First, if the first creditor to deal with the debtor makes an unsecured loan, it shares pro rata with later unsecured creditors in the debtor's assets on default. Second, if this initial creditor makes an unsecured loan and a later creditor takes security, the later creditor has priority over the initial creditor in the assets subject to the security interest. Third, if the initial creditor makes a secured loan, it generally has priority over later creditors in the assets in which it has security. There are several exceptions to this third principle of "first in time is first in right," of which probably the most important is the purchase-money priority; a later creditor whose funds enable the debtor to purchase designated assets and who takes a security interest in these assets will have priority in them despite an earlier security interest that would otherwise have granted senior rank to the initial secured lender.

The legal rules that these three priority principles imply also hold independently of the contract between the initial financer and debtor. For example, if this creditor makes an unsecured loan but obtains from the debtor a covenant not to make future secured loans—a negative pledge clause—the covenant will not affect the debtor's power to grant security and, thus, senior rank to a subsequent lender. The second priority principle still controls, and it grants the later secured creditor priority over an earlier unsecured creditor.

This article's first substantive claim is that *if* initial financers and borrowers would agree to give initial financers senior rank even when the financers are unsecured, the law should enact this as its priority scheme even though unsecured lenders commonly do not give public

* 18 J. Legal Studies 209 (1989).

notice of their interests. There are two reasons for this conclusion. First, as just said above, to enact a priority scheme that gives the initial unsecured financer senior rank necessarily ranks the claims of later lenders junior to this lender's claims. Second, the two ways to ensure that these junior creditors are aware of earlier loans are to require all substantial initial debt—not just secured debt—to be filed or, alternatively, to rely on an unregulated market to generate sufficient information about prior claims in a borrower's property. The latter method, it is argued below, is as effective as the former, and cheaper. Therefore, to answer the question of which priority scheme borrowers and initial lenders would prefer is largely to answer the question of which priority scheme the state should adopt. There is no need to modify any preferred scheme on the ground that it would permit parties to the initial loan to deceive later creditors by concealing senior liens.

This article's second substantive claim is that the optimal priority contract—the typical acceptance priority proposal—actually would rank the initial financer first, whether it is secured or not. The one important exception allows later purchase-money-secured credit to have senior rank up to a specified fraction of the borrower's assets. Parties to typical debt contracts thus would reject the first two "priority principles" set out at the beginning of this article and alter the third one substantially. The Uniform Commercial Code and the Bankruptcy Code should be amended to implement this preference as the legal priority scheme.

This proposal would alter the current priority scheme primarily in favor of initial lenders that hold substantial amounts of a borrower's debt when the debt is expected to be outstanding for a considerable time. Such lenders, it will later be shown, would have senior rank in the likely credit market equilibrium. This article does not propose a priority scheme that ranks every creditor of an insolvent debtor according to the time of its credit extension. Many creditors, such as trade creditors, would not contract for such a ranking scheme. Therefore, under the proposal made here, initial lenders that hold substantial debt commonly would take first; later creditors that took security would rank second to the initial lender but ahead of creditors that came after; and most other later creditors would continue to take pro rata [. . .]

Common Loan Covenants

Practice varies sharply from the legal priority scheme contained in the three regnant priority principles: commercial parties typically contract out of the legal scheme to the extent the law allows. Apart from trade credit, which contains few covenants, firms borrow from four sources: finance companies, banks, insurance companies, and the public (through debt issues). Lenders in the first three categories commonly require covenants that restrict the debtor's ability to borrow elsewhere. These covenants sometimes explicitly bar all future debt. More frequently, they require the debtor to maintain a specified ratio between current earnings and fixed charges, which has the effect of permitting ordinary trade credit while barring substantial future financing. Similar covenants require the debtor to maintain a specified ratio between debt and net assets. When the initial loan is unsecured, typical covenants explicitly mention subsequent secured debt as falling under the ban of later borrowing but often permit purchase money debt up to a specified fraction of the debtor's assets. Initial lenders who are secured seem less concerned to bar future debt but do restrict or altogether eliminate the debtor's ability to incur future secured obligations. Restrictions to this effect commonly require the debtor to maintain a "cushion" between the value of the collateral subject to the earlier security interest and the amount still due on the loan. This provision is then policed by requiring the debtor who wishes to borrow further to supply independent appraisals of the collateral's value. Initial secured parties say they regulate later security to avoid being pressured by junior lienors to foreclose when the debtor is in difficulty. Rather, the seniors want the power themselves to decide whether the debtor should be allowed to continue in business or not.

Creditors enforce all of these restrictive covenants by making their violation an act of default and by monitoring their debtors. A senior lending officer of a large lender recently gave what apparently is the industry view respecting the purpose of these covenants. He is reported to have said "that covenants assure stability and continuity in the company being funded. If a company decides to change its operating strategy in the middle of the [debt] issue's life, investors should have the opportunity to rescue their principal, perhaps even at a premium, he said. A change in corporate strategy 'wasn't what we contracted for' when the investment was made, he maintained."

Public debt issues also restrict the debtor's ability to incur future debt but are less binding than private loans. For example, secured public debt issues may not bar later secured debt but will require this debt not to be senior to the prior debt. Public debt issues bind borrowers less closely than private debt for two reasons. First, it is relatively simple for a debtor to renegotiate with a single private lender when it wants to finance a later project, but it is inconvenient to renegotiate with the public. Hence, the debtor requires more freedom. Second, detailed covenants are enforced by monitoring. Public debt issues are widely held; thus monitoring is a public good to individual public debt holders and will be underproduced. Two consequences follow from this. Initially, public debt will be less risky than private debt because borrowers can induce lenders to forgo the protection from monitoring only for relatively safe loans. Further, the few covenants that public debt contains make their conditions turn on easily observable events that a bond trustee can police. Consistent with this last view, well over 90 percent of unsecured public debt issues contain negative pledge clauses; the giving of security, on account of registration, is easy to observe. Many public issues also contain nontrivial restrictions on the debtor's ability to borrow elsewhere.

Notice and Default Rules

The loan covenants just described suggest that initial financers and debtors commonly prefer to give the initial financer senior rank. Under current law, this preference cannot be made fully effective. A debtor has the legal power to vitiate covenant protection by borrowing elsewhere (in breach of its promises). If the optimal contract between the debtor and the initial financer were similar to the covenants described above, in that this contract also would give the financer senior rank, the law should adopt such a contract as its default rule and make it fully effective. To make the contract fully effective is to eliminate the debtor's power to vitiate covenant protection. All later lenders, under the legal rule now under consideration, would take behind the first. Adopting such a rule would create a difficulty that is the subject of Part II.

The difficulty concerns how later creditors should be informed that prior, senior debt exists. At present there is not public recording system for unsecured debt. Therefore, if the law held that the initial financer and debtor could subordinate later creditors just by entering into a loan contract, then these later creditors could be surprised by the appearance—in an insolvency proceeding, for example—of prior, superior claims in the debtor's property. Call a legal rule that confers senior rank on the initial financer who just enters into a loan contract a "true first-in-time (FT) rule." Then, to use a phrase familiar to commercial lawyers, a true FT rule seemingly would permit the parties to the initial loan contract to create secret liens. As shown above, a distaste for secret liens underlies several UCC rules, including the rule that secured lenders subordinate prior unsecured creditors. There is an alternative to adopting a true FT rule. The law could require the initial financer to file— that is, publicly record—its loan contract as a condition of obtaining first priority position. The question is whether to adopt a true FT rule and thereby permit parties to create secret liens or to incur the expense of a new filing regime.

Part II next argues that the secret lien objection to conferring an effective senior rank on initial financers by means of a true FT rule is weak. Rather, a potential lender operating under a true FT rule would know, because borrowers will tell it, of the existence of substantial prior debt. This disclosure obviously would not be free. Thus the choice whether to adopt a true FT rule or a new filing system should turn on the comparative costs of "private disclosure" and public notice. Part II also argues that private disclosure likely is cheaper than creating a new filing system. These arguments are made to show that if typical initial financers and senior lenders would find it optimal to confer senior rank on the financer, there is no valid objection—based on the likelihood of secret liens—against making this preference fully effective by adopting a true FT rule as the legal priority scheme.

The argument against the secret lien objection begins with the perception that debtors bear the costs of uncertainty concerning title to their property. A simple example illustrates this perception. Suppose that borrowers come in two types, those that have substantial prior debt and those that have none, and that the legal priority scheme is a true FT rule. Potential lenders, assume, cannot distinguish borrowers by type if the borrowers are silent about their debt status. No lender will voluntarily lend to a "bad" debtor type—one with substantial prior debt—without being compensated or its low priority rank; later lenders in this example, recall, take behind the first, not pro rata with the first. The sensibly conservative strategy for a lender operating in this legal environment is to assume that each borrower it faces is bad with a high probability. If lenders do pursue this obvious strategy, all borrowers will be charged an interest rate that is almost as high as the rate that would be exacted by a lender that believed with certainty that it was dealing with a bad debtor. As a consequence, "good" debtor types, rather than lenders, would bear the costs of any uncertainty concerning property rights that a true FT rule would create.

Good debtors could avoid paying the high interest rates that uninformed lenders would charge by informing the lenders that they had little or no prior debt. Were these borrowers able to make credible disclosure, the loan market would segment. The good types would receive the low interest rate that reflected their debt-free status, and the bad types, who would be revealed to be bad because they could not prove they were debt free, would be charged the highest interest rate. Such segmentation would be desirable because it is efficient. Each borrower would be charged the interest rate that reflects the social costs of lending to it, and the creditors would be compensated accurately for the risks they bear. The key question is whether good borrowers can make credible communications of their debt status at acceptable cost.

There are several reasons to believe that these credible communications would be made. Initially, it is cheap to disclose debt status. The extent, if any, of a firm's debt is revealed by audited financials and the firm's own books. As firms routinely have audits and keep books, the marginal cost to them of revealing these records to lenders is low. Such records typically are reliable indicators of a firm's situation. Also, firms that have debt take the tax deduction; hence, tax records that reveal no debt are credible and cheap to provide. Further, publicly held companies now are required to report substantial debt to the Securities and Exchange Commission (SEC); these reports are public information and are used by potential creditors and acquirers. Finally, borrowers have incentives to make credible communications of their debt status today. Under current law, an unsecured financer takes pro rata with prior creditors. Financing thus is risky when substantial prior debt exists.

Therefore, lenders now have an incentive to use the strategy, just described, of supposing there to be prior debt with a high probability unless the borrower shows otherwise.

The nature of commonly used loan contracts, described in Part IB, suggests that good borrowers routinely solve the disclosure problem that use of this likely financer strategy would create. These contracts give lenders covenant protection that would be useless if the borrower had substantial initial debt. For example, a covenant requiring a debtor to maintain a specified ratio of current earnings to fixed charges would be pointless were the current loan itself to cause the ratio to be exceeded because the debtor had borrowed extensively elsewhere. The ubiquitous presence of elaborate covenant protection suggests that those who obtain it plausibly believe that they are initial creditors. In sum, though a financer would have no reason to know of *all* prior credit transactions to which a potential borrower is party, it would learn of any transaction of sufficient magnitude as to affect materially the likelihood that its loan will be repaid.

Since good debtors conveniently can separate themselves from bad debtors, the secret lien objection to the adoption of a true FT rule is weak. Credit markets would appropriately segment even though initial financers did not give public notice of their loans. There is an apparent difficulty with this conclusion that seems best put in this way: when the question concerns priorities among unsecured creditors, the analysis above may be persuasive because all such creditors look primarily to the debtor's general earning power for repayment, not to its possession of specific unliened assets. Hence, unsecured creditors are concerned only that a portion of the debtor's income stream has not been dedicated to earlier lenders. A secured lender, in contrast, looks to repayment out of the debtor's assets and so wants these assets to be unencumbered when it lends. The aspect of current law that authorizes secured creditors to subordinate prior unsecured creditors permits a secured lender to satisfy this preference relatively cheaply and, so, should be retained.

This argument rests on a false assumption, namely, that secured creditors are unconcerned with a debtor's earning power so long as they have priority over identified assets. Given the low returns on secured debt in the event of insolvency, secured lenders much prefer repayment to foreclosure. Consequently, they make the same credit investigations that unsecured lenders make and will be informed about the existence of prior debt in the same ways. It thus is no more expensive to inform secured creditors of the existence of prior claims than it is to inform financers generally of the existence of earlier debt. Put another way, secured creditors do not have a unique need for a filing system.

To summarize, because private disclosure seems both cheap and common, there is no good case for retaining current law on the sole ground that implementing a new priority scheme would prohibitively increase the necessary costs of notifying creditors of the existence of prior claims in a borrower's property. Rather, if the optimal loan contract gives the initial financer first priority, then the choice is between a true FT rule and a system requiring initial loan contracts to be filed in a public office. This choice depends on the social costs of the two legal regimes. There is no easy way to make this comparison, but intuition suggests that a true FT rule would be cheaper. Under a filing system, the parties would bear the same costs of contract creation as they would under a true FT rule and the additional costs of filing. The state would bear those costs of creating standard filing forms and operating filing systems not recovered as user fees. In addition, there would be considerable litigation until the exact contours of the new scheme are established. Experience with filing litigation under the UCC suggests that litigation costs may be high. For example, though the UCC has been in existence for almost two decades, each new volume of the UCC Code Reporter routinely contains cases concerning whether the Code's filing requirements have been met. The expense to the parties of observing the borrower's books, which is the primary marginal cost of a true FT rule, seems cheaper than the costs of a new public system. Thus it would be best to implement the proposed default rule respecting priorities, if it actually is optimal, by means of a true FT rule.

The conclusion that a true FT rule is preferable to creating a new filing system does not imply that the existing filing system should be abolished. To see why, consider a possible problem for initial financers under a true FT rule, that is, that the debtor will sell off major assets after the loan is made. The new law could provide that the true FT rule gives the initial financer priority over later buyers, or that it does not. If the rule's application is limited to conflicts among creditors, then the option available under current law of subordinating later buyers to initial financers by giving public notice of a financer's claim would be lost unless the filing system is retained. Since there seldom is good reason to create legal constraints where none previously existed, the policy choice is to subordinate later buyers to initial financers through the FT rule or to restrict the rule's scope to creditor conflicts. The former choice implies that later buyers lose to financers unless a financer waives its priority position; the latter choice implies that financers lose to buyers unless the financers contract out (by taking a security interest and using the retained filing system to publicize it). The question is whether debtors would prefer to bear the costs of buyer or financer uncertainty. Despite what was said above, debtors probably would prefer the latter because it may be inconvenient—that is, expensive—always to disclose the extent of prior debt to later buyers, which would have to be done under a broad true FT rule; buyers do not routinely make credit investigations and may lack the expertise to evaluate financial data. Consequently, the FT rule should apply only to creditor disputes, and the filing system should be retained to regulate conflicts between financers and later buyers.

NOTES

1. Disclosure and the securities acts. Both Professors Picker and Schwartz explore the value added of a public registration system for security interests, compared to an alternative regime that would rely on private disclosure. Schwartz refers in passing to the disclosure regime under securities laws, and similar analysis has been applied in evaluating the case for mandating financial disclosure. The disclosure of information to investors in securities is central to corporate and securities laws, much like the registration of securities interests is central to their enforceability. The Securities Act of 1933 and the Securities Exchange Act of 1934 set the foundation for an elaborate scheme by which public companies are compelled to disclose information to their prospective and existing investors. Scholars and policy makers have debated whether disclosure needs to be mandated and, if so, the extent and form of the disclosure regulation. Some scholars argue that firms have adequate private incentives to disclose and that the existence of information intermediaries such as auditors, investment bankers and rating agencies, together with basic anti-fraud laws, obviate the need for mandatory disclosure rules. *See e.g.,* Frank H. Easterbrook and Daniel R. Fischel, *Mandatory Disclosure and the Protection of Investors,* 70 Va. L. Rev. 669 (1984). As Alan Schwartz suggests in the excerpted text, a similar critique can be developed about the personal property security system. Indeed, anti-fraud rules would be even more effective in policing statements about whether assets are encumbered because this is a more readily verifiable fact than the projected returns from a new project.

2. The social value of standardized disclosure. The law might enhance social welfare by standardizing the form of the disclosure. In questioning the need for mandatory disclosure in securities regulation, Easterbrook and Fischel state:

> "Sometimes firms simply will not find it in their interest to disclose adequate industry-wide, comparative, or standardized information. Because securities are not homogeneous products, and direct inspection of business prospects by investors is not cost-effective, there may be gains from collective insistence on certain disclosures."

Merrill and Smith emphasize these gains from standardization in discussing personal property security regulation: Article 9 standardizes the form of notice of security interests. A secured creditor enjoys priority against future lien holders or bankruptcy only if she provides notice by one of the permitted methods. Later creditors know, in general, that an asset is unencumbered by security interests if it is in possession of the debtor and no financing statement covering that asset has been filed against the debtor in the state registry. Thomas W. Merrill & Henry E. Smith, *The Property/Contract Interface,* 101 Colum. L. Rev. 773, 838–43 (2001). Compare this with the protection of good faith buyers without notice under § 2–403, where the adequacy of notice is left as a standard to be applied by the court. Id. at 840.

If there are indeed benefits to standardization of disclosure to prospective creditors, why are they exploited in some contexts but not others. Disclosure is regulated in some cases (public companies, information about security interests), but not in others (the financial health of private company debtors). Consider the types of information that creditors typically require in screening the debtor and setting the price for credit. The secured debt of a borrower is a relatively small item compared to all the other information that is disclosed, including the total amount of liabilities, the projected cash flow, the potential tort claims against the borrower? What theory rationalizes the boundary between standardized and non-standardized disclosure?

3. The function of notice filing. A distinctive feature of the Article 9 registry is that a financing statement puts a searcher on notice that the debtor may have granted a security interest in some or all of the identified assets to the identified creditor. The searcher must obtain further information from the debtor and the secured party. To what extent does this provision reduce disclosure costs? In the end, the disclosure of the existence and scope of the security interest is still private, leading one to wonder about the information cost saving generated by Article 9. Perhaps the cost saving is the externality that Merrill and Smith focus on in the excerpt in Section 4.2. Third parties who deal with debtors that have encumbered none of their assets still need to verify the absence of a security interest. The significant benefit yielded by Article 9 is in this context (or in the related case where the debtor needs to convince the creditors that some assets are free of security interests).

4. Do creditors rely on the filing system? James J. White speculates about the credit-check practices of lenders and the degree to which they rely on the filing system in fact:

> [The] encomiums of the Article 9 filing system rest on two assumptions that are seldom challenged. First is the assumption that a significant percentage of lenders, secured and unsecured, rely on the state of the filing records to find out about prior perfected secured creditors. Second is the assumption that the behavior of these creditors would be different if there were no such system. For many creditors in modern industrial society, these assumptions are not accurate. It would come as some surprise to find that the mine run trade lender in the Bronx ever checks the files in Albany. It is similarly doubtful that the plumber, the carpenter, or even the general or subcontractor, checks the files or collects data from the files through a reporting service such as Dun & Bradstreet. Surely, the mainline secured creditors, the banks, GMAC, GECC, who file to perfect their own interests must also check the files. One would expect any filer to have checked the files.
>
> But what reliance do these filers place on the filing system? And more to the point, how would they behave in the absence of a filing system? Any creditor that is to be the principal inventory, equipment, or account receivable lender to a substantial mercantile enterprise will have many sources of information about the prospec-

tive borrower; the filing system is unlikely to be the most important source. The debtor and the debtor's records are obvious sources of information. Even if the debtor is not forthcoming, there may be signs in its books and records. Doubtless creditors collect information from one another. None of these is a perfect source of information, but of course neither is the filing system. That secured financing can flourish in modern industrial European economies in the absence of an effective filing system should also cause us to question our assumptions. Because filing is usually necessary to defeat a trustee in bankruptcy, one cannot even infer from the large number of filings that filers rely upon the system to defeat other secured creditors. Their filings may be mostly insurance against bankruptcy. [. . .]

I raise these questions not because I believe there are no creditors who rely on the filing system, but because by hyperbole I hope to emphasize our ignorance about the behavior of creditors [. . .] Recognizing that there are effective and apparently efficient lending systems in Europe, in countries that do not have filing systems like our own, and understanding that there are alternative sources for much of the information that a filing system provides, the drafters should approach the assertions of secured creditors with some skepticism, and should at least understand that they are drafting law based on assumptions about and in considerable ignorance of creditor behavior.

James J. White, *Reforming Article 9 Priorities in Light of Old Ignorance and New Filing Rules*, 79 Minn. L. Rev. 529, 531–2 (1995).

5.   The negative pledge clause. Professor Schwartz refers to the common use of negative pledge clauses in private lending agreements, under which borrowers promises not to grant any future security interests in its assets. As with any contractual promise, it is important to assess the remedy for breach. Consider the following observation made in an article published in 1965:

> While negative pledges sometimes stand alone, careful corporate draftsmen . . . accompany a negative pledge with an affirmative covenant. The promisor agrees that if he violates the negative pledge by creating a lien in favor of a third party, that lien will automatically also secure any indebtedness due to the promisee.

Peter F. Coogan, Homer Kripke & Fredric Weiss, *The Outer Fringes of Article 9: Subordination Agreements, Security Interests in Money and Deposits, Negative Pledge Clauses, and Participation Agreements*, 79 Harv. L. Rev. 229, 264–5 (1965).

In fact, however, the negative pledge clause is not enforceable against a future creditor who obtains a security interest in violation of the clause. Some commentators argue in favor of giving negative pledge clauses a broader effect. Yet, when a contractual provision is enforceable against a third party, one might view it as giving rise to a property right and therefore wish to condition such enforcement on prior disclosure. *See* Carl S. Bjerre,

Secured Transactions Inside Out: Negative Pledge Covenants, Property and Perfection, 84 Cornell L. Rev. 305 (1999). Is the property versus contract distinction helpful in determining what features of a borrower must be publicly disclosed?

6. Notice to buyers. A security interest in personal property generally follows the collateral into the hands of a transferee, such as a buyer. Private disclosure is less cost-effective in the case of a simple sale than an investment by a creditor. So, the Article 9 registry may yield greater value in providing notice to buyers than creditors. What types of information does a *buyer* of an asset typically require? Under Article 9, the buyer may be able to find out whether a seller has granted a security interest in any of her assets. However, a buyer is concerned about all third party interests and claims against the asset and the problem of ostensible ownership extends to this full range of possible encumbrances. Article 2 provides for a warranty of title and against infringement (§ 2–312), but what is the buyer's recourse if the seller is insolvent? As we suggested in Note 2 above, the puzzle about the disclosure scheme for Article 9 extends beyond the justification for mandatory disclosure: once the justification is established, we need to ask why the scheme stops where it does rather than cover other interests in assets, such as leases.

7. Related literature. For other discussion and analysis of disclosure systems and the Article 9 filing process, *see* Douglas G. Baird, *Notice Filing and the Problem of Ostensible Ownership*, 12 J. Legal Stud. 53 (1983); Douglas G. Baird & Thomas H. Jackson, *Information, Uncertainty, and the Transfer of Property*, 13 J. Legal Stud. 299 (1984). See also the symposium issue, Managing the Paper Trail: Evaluating and Reforming the Article 9 Filing System, 79 Minn. L. Rev. 519–964 (1995).

6.6 Distributional Consequences of Secured Credit

The Unsecured Creditor's Bargain*
LYNN M. LOPUCKI

Involuntary Creditors

The few data available suggest that a substantial portion of all unsecured creditors do not consent to their status in any meaningful sense. They become creditors only by the wrongful acts of their debtors. For example, Professors Teresa Sullivan, Elizabeth Warren, and Jay Westbrook found that twenty-three percent of the unsecured debt of persons filing bankruptcy under Chapters 7 and 13 of the Bankruptcy Code was owed to what the researchers called "reluctant creditors."

By that they meant that those creditors were not in the business of extending credit and did not seek credit relationships. In the cases studied by Sullivan, Warren, and Westbrook, the debtors were principally consumers and their reluctant creditors were (1) tort victims, (2)

* 80 Va. L. Rev. 1887, 1896–1899, 1963–1965 (1994).

former spouses and children with unpaid support orders, (3) government agencies, (4) educational lending agencies, (5) health care providers, (6) tax authorities, (7) landlords, and (8) utilities.

Corresponding data with regard to business debtors do not exist. But on the basis of the data that are available, I would speculate that money owed to reluctant creditors constitutes an even larger portion of the debt of financially distressed companies. In the business cases, the categories of reluctant creditors include (1) product liability claimants; (2) victims of business torts, ranging from negligence to intentional interference with contractual relations; (3) victims of antitrust violations, unfair competition, and patent, trademark and copyright infringement; (4) environmental agencies that perform clean-ups; (5) taxing authorities; (6) creditors who became such through the debtor's fraud, including securities fraud; (7) government agencies, such as the Pension Benefit Guarantee Corporation; and (8) utility companies. Regardless of where one draws the line among these creditors, involuntary unsecured credit clearly exists in substantial amounts.

The ability to victimize involuntary creditors may in significant part explain "why secured credit is such a widespread phenomenon." Simply by entering into a security agreement, the debtor and a favored creditor can expropriate for themselves value that, absent the agreement, would go to involuntary creditors. To take the simplest example, assume that Debtor has assets of $100 and debt of $100 owed to a creditor ("C"). Debtor then inflicts a tortious injury of $100 on a victim ("T"). Debtor becomes liable for the tort, but does not gain from it, so that Debtor has assets of $100 and debt of $200. Debtor is then liquidated. If the debt to C is unsecured, C and T each receive distributions of $50. If the debt to C is secured, C receives $100, and T receives nothing. Because C collects $100 with security and only $50 without it, Debtor's cost of borrowing from C likely will be lower if the loan is secured. The cost saving thus achieved is not offset by higher costs of borrowing from T, because T had no opportunity to bargain. Professor David Leebron refers to the phenomenon described here as the "externalization of tort risk."

Any debtor who either has, or expects in the future to have, involuntary unsecured creditors will find economic advantage in "selling" secured status to its voluntary creditors. The use of an all-equity capital structure exposes the shareholders of the tortfeasors to liability to the extent of the capital they contributed to the enterprise. Critics have argued that such a structure is already too generous to the shareholders of the tortfeasor. When unsecured debt is introduced into the capital structure of a potential tortfeasor, the shareholder's real exposure to tort liability declines further. When all assets, including the future income stream of the tortfeasor, are encumbered to their full value, the company's real exposure to tort liability can be almost eliminated. Because of this "expropriation effect" of secured debt on involuntary unsecured creditors, debtors will tend to issue secured debt to reduce their real exposure to tort liability.

The tort example illustrates the fundamental nature of security. It is not, as Jackson and Kronman present it, a contract among debtor, secured creditor, and unsecured creditor. Only the debtor need sign; the "consent" of the unsecured creditor is implied in the best case and a blatant fiction in the worst. Security is an agreement between A and B that C take nothing . . .

Conclusion

Article 9 artificially and unjustifiably advantages the institution of security over unsecurity. It holds involuntary unsecured creditors to an entirely fictitious bargain. It holds voluntary unsecured creditors to the terms of security agreements to which they did not in fact agree and to which they do not even have access. The terms of those agreements are binding regardless of how unreasonable they may be. This bizarre scheme subsidizes the institution of security, causing more secured lending than is optimal.

With regard to involuntary unsecured creditors, the solution is becoming increasingly obvious to legal scholars. The priority of secured creditors over involuntary unsecured creditors cannot be justified by any coherent theory and should be abolished. Involuntary creditors should have priority over voluntary creditors, whether secured or unsecured.

To describe the voluntary unsecured creditor's bargain, I began by distinguishing two very different kinds of unsecured lending. The first, which I have referred to as "asset-based" unsecured lending, is characteristic of loans from large and powerful lenders to large and powerful borrowers. The arrangement effectively bars the debtor from granting security and gives the unsecured creditors nearly all of the advantages of security. The second, which I refer to as "cash-flow surfing" is more common. Sophisticated cash-flow surfers extend credit in relatively small amounts for relatively short periods of time. They expect to be paid ahead of secured creditors, from the secured creditors' collateral, so long as the debtor's business survives. If the debtor's business fails, most do not expect to be paid at all.

Because it was designed to serve only the information needs of secured creditors, the Article 9 filing system fails to supply the basic information that cash-flow surfers need. The principal categories of omitted information are information on the default status of the loan, the balance remaining available under a line of credit, and the secured creditor's intentions with regard to calling the loan. All are highly time sensitive. Instead of guaranteeing access to these kinds of information, Article 9 goes to the opposite extreme, insulating secured creditors against liability that they otherwise would incur under general principles of contract law. The secured creditor can permit and encourage the debtor to induce cash-flow surfers to furnish additional collateral by misleading them, defrauding them, and feigning to pay them with worthless checks. So long as the secured creditor avoids direct contact with the cash-flow surfer, whatever property the debtor can gather by these means, the secured creditor can keep.

In this Article, I have proposed two mechanisms for serving the information needs of cash-flow surfing unsecured creditors. First, the law should cease to bind unsecured creditors to the terms of agreements to which they are not parties and do not have access. Instead, cash-flow surfers should be presumed to know or assume only what reasonable persons similarly situated would in fact know or assume. What that is should be determined by a judge or jury as the trier of fact.

Under the scheme I propose, secured creditors who sought to bind unsecured creditors to a subordinate position would have to take whatever steps were reasonable to communicate their intentions to those unsecured creditors. To facilitate that communication, I have proposed that the Article 9 filing system be redesigned to serve the information needs of all who are to be bound by the secured creditor's bargain. Legal theory should take its cue from architecture and highway design. Those disciplines assiduously avoid assuming that the users of buildings and roads know what they in fact do not. Instead, the designers seek to supply ignorant users with the information the users need, when and where they need it. When particular kinds of accidents are predictable, they do not blame the drivers and wait for the market to learn; they redesign the road. If we create systems to supply the information relevant to the unsecured creditor's bargain through easily accessible media, unsecured creditors will have powerful incentives to listen to the information and act on it. Once they do, the unsecured creditor's bargain will cease to be a figment of the legal and economic imagination and will become a bargain in fact.

Making Policy With Imperfect Information: The Article 9 Full Priority Debates*

ELIZABETH WARREN

[In 1997, Cornell Law Review hosted a symposium on 82 Cornell L. Rev. 1279–1567 (1997). The following excerpt from Professor Warren's essay in that volume refers to two other contributions to that symposium: Steven L. Harris and Charles W. Mooney, Jr., *Measuring the Social Costs and Benefits and Identifying the Victims of Subordinating Security Interests in Bankruptcy*, 82 Cornell L. Rev. 1349 (1997); Alan Schwartz, *Priority Contracts and Priority in Bankruptcy*, 82 Cornell L. Rev. 1396 (1997).]

* 82 CORNELL L. REV. 1373, 1377–1379, 1385–1388 (1997).

The Burden of Proof

Professors Harris and Mooney described Article 9 of the Uniform Commercial Code as "the most successful commercial statute ever [written]." It is certainly well-loved, at least by those secured creditors who use it. But what makes it so great?

Professors Harris and Mooney admit that, without empirical evidence, it is hard to estimate the actual effects of a full priority system. There are no studies of the efficiency, distributive consequences, or any other aspect of Article 9. No studies show who benefits and who loses. No studies show the consequences of highly leveraging businesses. No studies show larger economic effects of Article 9. Although a number of Article 9 missionaries carry the message of Article 9 to foreign countries, as Americans have actively pushed the adoption of a UCC-style full priority system throughout Europe, Asia, and South America, the benefits of the system are asserted rather than proved.

According to Harris and Mooney, however, the absence of any empirical testing of the impact of Article 9 means that not only should secured creditors continue to enjoy full protection, but also that both Harris and Mooney should put their own efforts as reporters to the Article 9 revision process—and the considerable resources and prestige of the American Law Institute and the National Conference of Commissioners on Uniform State Law—to the task of expanding the reach of secured creditors. Without evidence, Harris and Mooney assume they should work to make it even more difficult for unsecured creditors to challenge security interests, to leave fewer assets on the table for the unsecured creditors to divide, and, in short, to make the world a more comfortable place for the downtrodden class of asset-based lenders.

Evidently there has been some sort of burden shift in the past forty years regarding changes to the status quo. The first Article 9 Drafting Committee, headed by Professor Gilmore, devised the scheme that made security interests in personal property cheap and reliable. The first Committee brought order out of chaos, turning assets in which no security interest could reliably be enforced at state law into valuable collateral. For his efforts, Professor Gilmore was featured in Time magazine and achieved near-saint status in the world of commercial law.

What about the empirical questions back in the 1960s? Gilmore's changes were heralded as "radical," "sweeping," and "monumental." Everyone knew the changes would promote secured lending on personal property, but no one suggested that an empirical inquiry into the effects of such increased secured lending should precede such a powerful change. No one asked whether such easily available security devices would expand secured credit precipitously, foster the formation of risky businesses, dramatically increase the leverage of one class of lenders, or disadvantage the class of unsecured creditors. Why were these arguments not part of the debate?

Harris and Mooney remind us that those who offer change should bear the burden of offering evidence that change is needed. Where was the evidence just thirty-five years ago when the current system radically reformed the state law collection system? Why do Professors Harris and Mooney press further expansion of the priority rights in Article 9 with no empirical examination of its effects? Do only those who quarrel with the powerful bear the burden of producing empirical evidence, while those who promote their interests get a free ride on empirical questions?

How Creditors Use Priority

Professors Harris and Mooney assert that empirical studies will tell us about the costs and benefits of secured credit. They suggest two approaches to such studies. The first is based on an analysis of current credit practices in "market segments in which anecdotal evidence and common knowledge indicate that secured credit plays an important role." They suggest surveys and questionnaires, but they do not explain what the questions are. "Do you like secured credit?" It is difficult to imagine a secured creditor dumb enough to say no, unless the question were framed in terms of whether the creditor could get even more protection. Nor is it possible to hypothesize an unsecured creditor who lost a fortune while the secured creditor walked away with all the assets of a business saying much more than no.

Perhaps there are other items to study in the Harris and Mooney survey, such as whether there were many failures in which the unsecured creditors took substantial losses. But again, the question lingers about what this inquiry would show. If the proportions of losses were small, would this mean that some constraint on full priority is unnecessary, or would it mean that some constraint would not be particularly disruptive to current business practices? Conversely, if the unsecured creditors' losses were high, would that support or undercut full priority? Until the hypothesis is clarified, such a study is useless. Harris and Mooney's second empirical test is an abstract model that "reliable data [to] inform the example" could fill in. Once again, the hypothesis to be tested remains unstated. Modest constriction might support either policy conclusion.

If we are to wait for law reform until these two studies are carried out, the wait will be long. Even if the lucky day comes when someone does these studies, it is unclear what they will tell us about the reform process. Here lies the crucial question as the debaters keep batting about unknown empirical assumptions: What can be learned about a restricted priority system by studying a full priority system? A definitive test of a restricted priority system is virtually impossible within the regime of full priority. The behavior of the parties provides a crucial example. Some creditors will lend only on a secured basis. Does that mean that they would not lend in a "no-priority" system? Not necessarily. So long as a system exists that permits others to take priority over them, they will insist on defensive priority. In a priority system, many creditors will decide that even if they did not want to beat out others, they must make sure that no one can beat them. Some creditors might be satisfied with pro-rata priority, but that is unavailable in the current scheme. Defensive security interests are essential in a world that subordinates the unsecured.

This does not mean that efforts to frame empirical questions are worthless. They are enormously useful, if only to serve as a reminder about how little we know as we draft laws to govern billions of credit transactions. In the Article 9 reform process, three observations about empirical studies are important: 1) we cannot wait for the definitive study before we make policy decisions, 2) we have to acknowledge that any empirical evidence is likely to be indirect and only suggestive, and 3) we have to be more creative in our approaches to gathering empirical data.

Creative Alternatives

Professor Schwartz continues his efforts to give the definitive answer to the question he posed more than a decade ago: Why have secured credit? In the latest incarnation of his answer, he focuses on the role of negative loan covenants and the creditor's paramount concern over debt dilution. Admirably, he looks for—and even finds—empirical evidence consistent with his view. The creativity of his approach to looking for supporting evidence suggests that even if direct measures of priority systems do not yield much information, indirect measures may be quite revealing.

If Professor Schwartz is right in his view that the lender is trying to prevent the debtor from shifting investments toward higher risk-taking over time, and that secured debt priorities further this restriction, and if his evidence is adequate to support his interpretation, then another perspective on lending priorities might be in the offing. But Schwartz's view of the reasons for secured debt offers a very different perspective on the accompanying system of full priority.

If, as Schwartz suggests, secured creditors contract with reference to the intended acquisition of future trade debt, then perhaps an efficient priority system would provide a lower priority for subsequent creditors who are not ordinary course creditors. Instead, such a system should logically provide a first priority for routine trade credit. According to this view, the parties who would be bound by priorities would be those who put the first lender at risk—the creditors who offer out-of-the-ordinary financing that permits the debtors to shift investment strategies. Incidentally, these are also the creditors who can best protect themselves by making informed lending decisions in the context of subordinated priority. For those who offer only the contemplated, routine trade debt that the secured creditor knows is essential to the survival of the business, and who have no hand in fostering subsequent risky investment decisions, perhaps first priority status would be in order. At a minimum, the Schwartz analysis raises the question why such trade debt should be subordinated to subsequent lenders who also take security interests and who finance the risky business operations that cause the trade creditors to lose out.

There is another implication from Professor Schwartz's argument: If creditors are mostly concerned about debt dilution, then it does not follow that these creditors should take priority over tort claimants. Tort creditors have not contributed to the subsequent risky investments. They are, at worst, merely its co-victims. If the point of Schwartz's analysis is to try to control the post-lending, risk-taking decisions of debtors, there is no justification for the last-place treatment of the victims of that risky behavior. [. . .]

When the Efficiency Answer Quits

There are a number of possible empirical questions that could inform the debate on full priority. Who are the creditors who profit from the current system, and who are those who lose? How much do the subordinate creditors lose? What are the effects of these losses on their businesses? What are the economy-wide effects of encouraging overleveraged businesses to continue operations? What are the effects of insulating secured creditors from the need to monitor the business operations of their debtors? The list grows quickly. Nevertheless, one empirical question drives the debate. The question that arises again and again, both in the scholarly literature and public debates, is whether a partial priority system would reduce credit availability. The empirical question quickly turns into the empirical assertion that credit availability would diminish, thereby harming all business interests. The credit-constriction claim is the most forceful weapon in the arsenal of the proponents of full priority.

While there may be no way of testing the credit-constriction assertion directly or measuring the magnitude or direction of the changes that would occur with partial priority, it is interesting to note how the assertion is treated as a debate stopper. If credit is reduced, the assumption runs, it will hurt commercial lenders and their borrowers, as well as their potential trade creditors. It will even threaten a robust economy.

The argument proves too much. If the only test of any part of a commercial law system were whether it promoted or constricted credit, then our system would look very different. Why not return to the days of debt servitude? There were efficiency concerns about servitude, but the bottom line was that servitude made credit available to people who otherwise could not obtain it. Nonetheless, it was gone by the early 1800s.

If the goal of a commercial law system is expansion of credit, then perhaps the revisions of Article 9 should reflect changes in medical technology since the 1960s. Why not permit security interests in body parts? Any debtor who promised her liver or her heart would surely have strong incentives to perform on the loan. It would be possible to restrict security interests to body parts that leave the debtor diminished, but alive, such as offering a kidney, skin for a graft, a womb, or a cornea as collateral. It appears that the expansion of credit notion has not been embraced fully.

The idea here is not to give the current Article 9 drafters new ideas. Instead, the point is to note that even if a security device promotes lending, reasons not to support it may exist. Some of the reasons may be grounded in efficiency arguments. Some may be naked applications of paternalism. Some of the arguments may refer to community sensibilities and fairness. These concepts may be hard to quantify in an equation full of sigmas and betas, but they have to do with our collective confidence in the commercial law system.

Even when the discussion is solely about money, the argument that full priority is justified whenever it promotes more lending still proves too much. Taxing authorities often take priority over secured lenders. For example, if property taxes are not paid, the government can foreclose on the property, hold a sale, and demand first distribution from the sale. In other cases, the government agrees to come second behind perfected secured creditors, even when such arrangements upset the priority scheme established in Article 9. Surely such priority disturbances constrict credit extension. What lender would not claim that it would lend more, if only it did not risk being primed by a government authority?

In addition to the federal tax laws, state laws abound with priorities that permit certain protected groups to take priority over secured creditors. Statutory liens for everyone from automobile repair persons, to launderers, to cattle feed suppliers, may trump the rights of the secured creditor. The full priority system gives full priority against only the unfavored groups who failed to persuade a legislature to pass a friendly statutory lien.

Federal bankruptcy law is the ultimate partial priority system. The rights accorded the trustee in bankruptcy to stop foreclosure and repossession, to strip down security interests, and to distribute the debtor's remaining assets pro rata in contravention of a security agreement, create perhaps the most frequently encountered partial priority scheme in commercial law. A few scholars would like to see bankruptcy laws amended to permit parties to contract out of bankruptcy, and thereby contract into the full priority scheme of Article 9. Nonetheless, the idea has attracted little attention outside the rarified atmosphere of academia.

The incursions on priority in tax law, in statutory liens, and in bankruptcy, make clear that fostering as much lending as possible is not the only goal of any commercial law system. The goal is always one of balance. Taxing authorities get priorities, in part because of a judgment that a business that cannot meet its tax obligations should not be operating. Cattle feed suppliers get a priority, in part because they add value in a way that makes it virtually impossible for them to take a protected interest through any other method. Employees may take priority because they are poor risk spreaders. And so on. Bankruptcy law takes precedence over contractual agreements, in part because the rights of third parties to pro rata distribution at liquidation cannot be negotiated away without consent.

The ultimate question is not whether a partial priority scheme might cause some constriction in lending. That empirical question remains open, although there are strong arguments both to refute and to support the idea that available total credit would remain the same. The real question is how the efficiency arguments, even if they were unambiguously true, stack up against other considerations.

Security Interests and Bankruptcy Priorities: A Review of Current Theories*

ALAN SCHWARTZ

The "Offensive" Distributional Explanation

Distributional explanations for the existence of secured debt are of two related kinds—the "offensive" and the "defensive." The former relaxes the assumption made in Part II–A that a firm's unsecured creditors are aware of security and react to its issuance by raising their interest rates. Suppose that some of these creditors fail to do this. Firms would then have an incentive to issue secured debt because they would benefit from the lower interest rates secured creditors would charge but not be harmed by higher interest rates charged elsewhere. In this circumstance, secured debt redistributes wealth from uninformed creditors (who fail to react to security) to firms. Firms would then be anxious to make secured loans, so demand for these loans would increase; thus secured creditors—primarily banks and finance companies—would share some of the gains made at the expense of the uninformed creditors.

This distributional explanation predicts that firms will issue secured debt only when substantial number of their creditors are uninformed. The prediction has some empirical support. Consider retailers in consumer markets. A retailer's creditors include not only its financers and sellers but also its customers and employees. A customer who buys from a retailer has a potential warranty claim. Further, hard goods, such as

* 10 J. Legal Studies 1 (1981).

appliances or cars, often are bought with service contracts or under the standard repair or replacement warranty. Customers who have made partial or full payment would be entitled to restitution if the goods are defective. Retailers are debtors respecting consumer-warranty claims; that is, customers have potential claims against retailers for money or services, and the retailers have a corollary potential liability. If assets are withdrawn from the pool otherwise available to satisfy the warranty claims of customers and devoted to the claims of different creditors, the purchase risks of the customers are increased; their claims against firms will be more difficult to satisfy. Purchases from "secured firms" are, consequently, less attractive than purchases from unsecured firms, so the secured firms should command lower prices. These lower prices are the product-market equivalent of the higher interest rates that unsecured creditors in financial markets charge to a firm that issues secured debt. But if retail customers are unaware of the existence of security, their demand for the goods of secured firms will be unaffected by it. These customers consequently will pay higher prices than they should pay, as measured by their own (informed) preferences. The excess will be shared by retailers and their financers.

The offensive distributional explanation seems correctly to predict that firms will issue secured debt when a substantial number of their creditors are uninformed. It apparently predicts wrongly the absence of security, however, in cases when most of a firm's creditors would be aware of security and could react to its existence. As Part II–B showed, when creditors are informed and capable, security generates no reductions in net interest rates for the firm. Thus the offensive distributional explanation predicts that those industrial firms whose sellers, buyers, and financers all seem sophisticated will rarely secure the debt they sell. In practice, however these firms often issue some secured debt. This explanation therefore is also unconvincing.

The "Defensive" Distributional Explanation

The defensive distributional explanation assumes that creditors are informed and competent. Suppose that a creditor is asked to lend unsecured to a firm that has issued no secured debt. Will it charge an interest rate reflecting that all of the firm's assets are available to satisfy creditor claims? It may not because, if this relatively low rate is charged, the firm has an incentive to issue secured debt after the initial loan is made. By so doing, it would obtain the advantage of the lower rate secured debt commands without the disadvantage of the higher rate unsecured creditors would charge in response Creditors, however, anticipating the later issuance of secured debt, will charge the interest rate for unsecured debt that would be charged if the firm were already secured. But if this is done, the firm must promptly issue secured debt; only in this way can it offset the high interest rates required by its creditors' anticipation that such debt will later be issued. Further, the two distributional explanations can be combined; firms issue secured debt to defend themselves against informed creditors who expect it and to exploit uninformed creditors who are ignorant of it.

The "defensive" distributional explanation suffers from familiar difficulties. It predicts that all firms initially will borrow secured, and will secure as much debit as they can. This is because if a firm's first creditor will charge an interest rate that reflects later security, the firm should secure the first creditor (and all others so long as it has free assets). In this way, it can receive the benefit of secured debt's lower interest rate as soon as possible. Nothing is gained an something is lost by securing the seventh rather than the first creditor, when some creditors will have to be secured in any event. Yet many firms fail to borrow according to this pattern.

Another difficulty with the explanation is that firms to some extent can prevent early unsecured creditors from charging interest rates that reflect anticipated security by using loan covenants. Common covenants prohibit firms from issuing late debt with a higher priority than early debt. These prohibitions sometimes specifically refer to purchase money and real estate mortgages. In addition, covenants sometimes expressly protect early creditors against later issuance of security by providing that the early creditors "must have their priority upgraded and be given an equal claim on the collateral with the secured debtholders." If security performs the function of forestalling initially high interest rates, it must be because in some cases it does so more cheaply than loan covenants would. Explanations of when and how this would occur are lacking.

If valid, the defensive distributional explanation is nevertheless normatively troubling. Should security generate no reductions in net interest rates but be used to prevent creditors from capturing the wealth of firms, the giving of security represents a deadweight efficiency loss. No new wealth is created by the issuance of security, yet since resources are devoted to creating it, someone is made worse off by its existence.

The Uneasy Case for the Priority of Secured Claims in Bankruptcy*
LUCIAN A. BEBCHUK and **JESSE M. FRIED**

This Article challenges the desirability of a fundamental and long-standing feature of bankruptcy law: the principle that a secured creditor is entitled to receive the entire amount of its secured claim—the portion of its bankruptcy claim that is fully backed by collateral—before any unsecured claims are paid. There is a widespread consensus among legal scholars and economists that the rule of according full priority to secured claims is desirable because it promotes economic efficiency. The analysis

* 105 YALE L. J. 857, 859–866 (1996).

we offer demonstrates that, contrary to this conventional view, the efficiency case for full priority is at best problematic. We find that according full priority to secured claims leads to distortions in the arrangements negotiated between commercial borrowers and their creditors, which in turn generate a number of inefficiencies. Our analysis indicates that these inefficiencies could be reduced or eliminated by according only partial priority to secured claims, and that a rule of partial priority therefore may well be superior to the rule of full priority from the perspective of efficiency. Accordingly, the Article offers two rules of partial priority that should be considered as possible alternatives to the rule of full priority.

In a secured transaction, the borrower gives the creditor a security interest in specified property of the borrower that, if the borrower defaults, permits the creditor to take possession of the property in partial or full satisfaction of the debt. The practice of taking a security interest in a borrower's property, which has ancient origins, continues to be widespread: Although there is no comprehensive source of information on secured commercial lending, the available data suggest that a substantial percentage of total U.S. business debt is secured. In the United States, large, publicly traded firms tend not to borrow on a secured basis. Thus, most commercial secured debt in the United States is issued by small and medium-sized companies.

Under state laws governing transactions in personal and real property, a security interest in favor of a lender becomes effective when credit is extended and certain procedural requirements are met. Unless the parties agree otherwise, the secured lender generally retains all of the baseline rights of an unsecured creditor with respect to the borrower. That is, if the borrower defaults on the terms of the loan agreement, the secured lender may seek to reduce its claim to judgment, and then instruct an agent of the court to enforce the judgment against any of the debtor's property. As a secured creditor, the lender also enjoys two additional rights: a "repossessory right" and a state-law "priority right." In the event of default, the "repossessory right" gives the lender a qualified right to take possession of the assets covered by the security interest without resorting to judicial process. The state-law "priority right" gives the lender a right to these assets that is generally superior to the rights of other claimants, including purchasers, transferees, and other creditors. The state-law "priority right" is typically established when the lender "perfects" its security interest, either by taking possession of the assets or by filing a financing statement in the appropriate public registries. The secured creditor can fully exercise both its "repossessory right" and its state-law "priority right" only outside of bankruptcy.

Our focus, however, is on the rights of the secured creditor when an insolvent debtor enters bankruptcy. Once the debtor enters bankruptcy, bankruptcy law "stays" the secured creditor from exercising its "repossessory right" to take possession of the collateral covered by the security interest. The secured creditor's state-law "priority right" in the collateral is also suspended. To compensate the secured creditor for the loss of its "priority right," bankruptcy law requires generally that, by the end of the proceeding, the creditor receive an amount equal to its secured claim. In practice, however, the compensation actually received by secured creditors is sometimes less than the value of their secured claims at the beginning of the bankruptcy process.

Even though secured creditors do not always receive the full value of their secured claims in bankruptcy, they still retain a substantial advantage over general unsecured creditors, which have a claim to only those assets that remain after secured claims and the claims of certain priority unsecured creditors are paid or provided for. The effect of this priority scheme on the allocation of bankruptcy value among creditors is significant. If, as is usually the case, the business debtor is immediately or eventually liquidated, general unsecured creditors can expect to receive only a few cents on the dollar. Even in the relatively few cases where a business debtor successfully reorganizes under Chapter 11, the mean recovery by general unsecured creditors is typically only 20 cents to 30 cents on the dollar.

The principle of according full priority to secured claims in bankruptcy is firmly established in the law. And although some commentators have questioned the fairness of permitting a debtor to encumber its assets in favor of secured creditors at the expense of unsecured creditors, the predominant view of those who have examined full priority from an economic approach is that it is desirable to respect the state-law "priority right" of secured creditors to the greatest extent possible in bankruptcy. It is this view-sometimes described as the "creditors' bargain" theory—that we challenge in this Article.

We will show that a rule according full priority to secured claims in bankruptcy tends to reduce the efficiency of the loan arrangement negotiated between a commercial borrower and a potentially secured creditor. That is, full priority tends to reduce the total value captured by the borrower, the potentially secured creditor, and all other parties affected by the arrangement, which we assume to be the borrower's other creditors.

Our analysis does suggest that the loan arrangement between a commercial borrower and a potentially secured creditor under the rule of full priority would be efficient in a hypothetical world in which the use of a security interest does not have distributional consequences for the borrower's other creditors. Assume that when a security interest is created, the amount owed to all other creditors changes in such a way as to offset the impact of the transaction on them, including the effect on them of permitting the recipient of the security interest to have a secured claim with full priority in bankruptcy. Under these circumstances, the creation of a security interest under full priority would never impose a negative externality on the other creditors, and a security interest could not, therefore, be used to divert value from these creditors. Consequently, a security interest would be chosen only if it were efficient. In this hypothetical world, efficiency would thus require giving full priority to the secured claim in the event of bankruptcy.

In the real world, however, the creation of a security interest under the rule of full priority has distributional consequences. In particular, under the rule of full priority, the creation of a security interest diverts value from creditors that do not "adjust" the size of their claims to take into account the effect of the loan transaction that creates the security interest, including the fact that any security interest given to the secured creditor subordinates their unsecured claims.

A firm will have many such "nonadjusting" creditors. The size of the claims of any tort creditors will not take into account the existence of a security interest encumbering the borrower's assets. Similarly, the size of government tax and regulatory claims will be fixed by statute without regard to the possibility that the claims may be subordinated by a secured claim in bankruptcy. There will also be nonadjusting creditors whose claims arise out of voluntary dealings with the borrower. Many creditors will have claims that are simply too small to justify the cost of taking the security interest into account when contracting with the borrower, and will thus be "rationally uninformed" about the borrower's financial structure. Finally, any contractual creditor that extends credit on fixed terms before a decision is made whether to create a particular security interest, and is therefore unable to adjust its claim to take into account the fact that the security interest is created, will be nonadjusting with respect to that security interest.

The fact that security interests may be used to transfer value from nonadjusting creditors under a full-priority rule means that security interests may be used even when they give rise to inefficiencies. As our analysis will demonstrate, the ability to use security interests to divert value from nonadjusting creditors tends to distort the borrower's choice of contractual arrangements with its creditors, giving rise to certain efficiency costs. In particular, we will show that the rule of providing full priority to secured claims may cause the use of inefficient security interests, distort the choice between the use of security interests and covenants in loan contracts, skew firms' investment and precaution decisions, and reduce the incentive of secured creditors to appropriately control their borrowers' behavior.

It should be emphasized that the analysis we offer does not assume that the two categories of voluntary nonadjusting creditors described above—rationally uninformed creditors with small claims and creditors that lend before the decision regarding the security interest is made—are "victimized" by the creation of a security interest giving another creditor a secured claim. It would not affect our conclusion if all voluntary creditors extended credit on terms that reflected perfectly the expected risk of loss arising from the presence of secured claims so that, on average, no transfer of value from these creditors occurs. Nor does our analysis depend on the existence of tort or government claims; the problems we identify would still occur in a world without involuntary creditors, albeit to a lesser degree. Our analysis relies only on the fact that, with respect to every borrower, there invariably exist nonadjusting creditors, that is, creditors that do not adjust the size of their claims against the borrower when the borrower creates a security interest in favor of another creditor. This alone is sufficient to give rise to the inefficiencies we identify.

Accordingly, we believe that full priority is unlikely to be the most efficient rule for allocating value between secured and unsecured creditors. We therefore will consider as alternatives to the rule of full priority two bankruptcy priority rules that would reduce or eliminate the inefficiencies we identify by according only partial priority to secured claims. The first partial-priority rule presented—the "adjustable priority rule"— would operate like the rule of full priority, except that the bankruptcy share of each nonadjusting creditor would be determined by treating the secured claims to which it could not adjust as unsecured claims. The effect of this rule, which would prevent a secured claim from subordinating the claims of any creditors that could not adjust to it, would be to transfer some bankruptcy value from secured creditors to nonadjusting creditors. The second partial-priority rule would treat a fixed fraction of every secured claim as an unsecured claim, rendering all secured creditors at least partially unsecured. This rule, the "fixed-fraction priority rule," is similar to a priority rule that was proposed in 1985 by the German Commission on Bankruptcy Law.

Neither of the partial-priority rules presented would be superior to the rule of full priority in all respects. Any partial-priority rule would involve certain efficiency costs and create certain enforcement challenges. However, our preliminary analysis does suggest that the efficiency costs of a partial-priority rule might be relatively modest and that such a rule could be effective if implemented. Thus, there may well be a partial-priority rule that is superior to full priority from the standpoint of efficiency.

Our analysis also considers other issues related to the adoption of a mandatory partial-priority rule. We show that, if partial priority is preferable to full priority, the adoption of such a rule should not be left to private ordering. That is, borrowers should not be given the choice to opt into or out of such a rule. We also demonstrate that a mandatory partial-priority regime would be consistent with fundamental principles of contract law. We show that partial priority would give the secured creditor the benefit of its bargain and not be unfair. We also show that since the creation of a security interest in favor of a particular creditor under full priority transfers value from nonconsenting third parties, limiting the priority accorded to secured claims would not violate conventional notions of freedom of contract.

The Use of Inefficient Security Interests

A borrower and a secured creditor may have incentives under full priority to expend resources inefficiently encumbering an asset merely to transfer bankruptcy value from nonadjusting creditors. That is, a borrower and a secured creditor may adopt a security interest that gives the two parties a larger slice of the pie at the expense of nonadjusting creditors even though the security interest at the same time reduces the size of the total pie. This is the first efficiency cost of full priority.

Returning to our hypothetical Firm and Bank, suppose that Firm borrows $1 million each from three sources: Bank, a nonadjusting creditor, and an adjusting creditor. Suppose further that there is a 5% chance that Firm will fail by the end of the year and leave $600,000 of assets to its creditors. Assume that to obtain a security interest in the $600,000 worth of assets, Bank would be required to spend $2000, and that use of the security interest would affect neither the probability of Firm's failure nor the amount of assets that would be available to Firm's creditors in the event of default. Thus, creating the security interest would be inherently inefficient because it would reduce the total value captured by all of the parties by $2000.

Consider the case in which the use of a security interest would not confer any priority on Bank's claim. In such a case, Bank and Firm would have no incentive to spend $2000 to create the security interest because Bank would receive $200,000 (1/3 of $600,000) in bankruptcy whether or not the security interest had been created. Thus, Bank and Firm would act efficiently under a rule of no priority by choosing not to adopt the security interest.

Now consider the case in which the security interest would confer full priority on Bank's claim against Firm. Under a rule of full priority, the security interest would reduce Bank's risk of loss by $20,000 and would increase the other creditors' risk of loss by $10,000 each. Since Bank would incur $2000 in contracting costs in connection with the security interest, and its risk of loss would be reduced by $20,000, it would charge Firm $18,000 less in interest while the adjusting creditor would charge Firm $10,000 more in interest. Thus, full priority will give Firm an incentive to create an inefficient security interest merely to transfer value from its nonadjusting creditors.

Distorted Choice Between Security Interests and Covenants

Full priority may also cause commercial borrowers and their sophisticated creditors to use a security interest that is less efficient than a set of covenants in order to control inefficient behavior by the borrower after the loan transaction. To illustrate, suppose that Bank and Firm will choose either a set of covenants or a security interest (but not both) to reduce Firm's ability to engage in inefficient asset dilution after the transaction. Suppose that Firm already owes $1 million to a nonadjusting creditor, is borrowing $1 million from Bank, and will borrow $1 million from an adjusting creditor. Suppose further that, if Bank is given a security interest in $1 million of assets, $1.2 million will be available for distribution to creditors in the event of default, but, if Bank uses a set of covenants designed to prevent Firm's shareholders from engaging in inefficient asset dilution, $1.5 million will be available to creditors in the event Firm fails. Finally, assume that both the set of covenants and the security interest would impose the same contracting and opportunity costs on Bank and Firm and that there is a 5% chance that Firm will fail in either case. Adoption of the set of covenants would clearly be more efficient because, in the event of bankruptcy, creditors would be $300,000 better off than if the security interest had been adopted, while shareholders would be no worse off.

If the security interest were created but did not confer priority on Bank's claim, each creditor (including Bank and the adjusting creditor) would receive its pro rata share of $1.2 million—$400,000—in the event of Firm's bankruptcy. On the other hand, if the set of covenants were adopted, Bank and the adjusting creditor would receive $500,000 each—one-third of $1.5 million—if Firm fails. As a result, Bank and the adjusting creditor would each charge Firm $5000 less interest if Firm issued the set of covenants rather than the security interest. Thus, Firm would have an incentive to issue the set of covenants rather than the security interest to Bank under a rule of no priority.

If the security interest were adopted under the rule of full priority, however, Bank would receive $1 million, and the adjusting creditor would receive $100,000 in the event of bankruptcy. Since Bank and the adjusting creditor would each receive $500,000 if the set of covenants were adopted, Bank would charge $25,000 less interest, and the adjusting creditor would charge $20,000 more if Bank were given a security interest. Since Firm would thus be able to reduce its interest expense by creating the security interest rather than the set of covenants, it would have an incentive to choose the less efficient security interest.

Distorted Investment and Precaution Decisions

We have just seen that according full priority to secured claims in bankruptcy causes borrowers and their creditors to use security interests that are not efficient, or efficient but less efficient than a set of covenants, solely to transfer value from nonadjusting creditors. We now turn to a different category of costs that arises from full priority: costs that may arise whenever a security interest is used under full priority. These priority-dependent efficiency costs make the use of any given security interest less efficient or more inefficient than it would be in the absence of priority. Thus, these costs would arise even if full priority did not affect the overall use of security interests.

The first priority-dependent efficiency cost of security interests is that their use under full priority may distort a borrower's choice of investments and level of precaution. Indeed, as this section will explain, the ability of a borrower to give a creditor a security interest that subordinates the claims of nonadjusting creditors may adversely affect the borrower's behavior even before the borrower and the secured creditor negotiate their loan contract.

Consider the case in which Firm must decide, prior to contracting with Bank, whether to take certain precautions that will make its products safer and thereby reduce the number of future tort claims against Firm. Firm knows that when Bank and Firm later negotiate their loan contract, Bank will take expected tort claims into account in setting its interest rate. Thus, Bank will charge Firm a higher interest rate to the extent it anticipates that future tort *899 claims will reduce the value of its loan by diluting Bank's share of Firm's bankruptcy assets. To the extent that Bank adjusts its interest rate to take into account future tort claims against Firm, Bank forces Firm to internalize more of the cost of its failure to take precautions. Thus, to the extent that the tort claims reduce the value of Bank's claim, Firm will have a greater incentive to take precautions prior to transacting with Bank. Under the rule of full priority, however, Firm may give Bank a security interest that more or less protects the value of Bank's loan from being diluted by tort claims. To the extent that Bank is given a security interest that insulates its claim from the effect of Firm's activities, it will not charge a higher interest rate if Firm fails to take precautions and additional tort claims against Firm are expected. And, to the extent Firm does not face the prospect of a higher interest rate if it fails to take precautions, Firm will have less incentive to invest in these precautions.

To illustrate, suppose that Firm intends to borrow $2 million from Bank, its only nontort creditor. Suppose further that there is a 5% chance that Firm will fail by the end of the year, leaving $1 million of assets available to satisfy its creditors' claims. Assume that if Firm does not take precautions, there is a 50% chance that it will face $8 million in tort claims by the end of the year, but that if Firm takes precautions, it will not face any tort claims.

If Bank does not have priority in Firm's bankruptcy assets, its expected loss is $50,000 if Firm takes precautions, and $72,500 if Firm does not. Thus, Bank will charge Firm $22,500 more in interest if Firm does not take precautions. However, if Bank is given a security interest in the $1 million of assets that will be available to satisfy creditors' claims in bankruptcy, the expected value of its bankruptcy claim will be $1 million whether or not Firm takes precautions. Thus, Firm will have less incentive to take precautions if creditors' claims can be given priority through use of a security interest.

In essence, the rule of according full priority to secured claims exacerbates the distortions created by limited liability, a problem that has recently attracted considerable academic attention. As that literature has explained, limited liability allows shareholders to avoid internalizing the full costs imposed on tort victims by limiting the victims' claims to the amount of the borrower's *900 assets in bankruptcy. This leads firms to underinvest in precautions and overinvest in risky activities that externalize harm to other parties. According full priority to secured claims allows shareholders to avoid internalizing even more of the costs in the manner we have just described.

Suboptimal Use of Covenants

The second priority-dependent efficiency cost of security interests is that their use, under full priority, may cause a secured creditor to use too few covenants. In a perfect world in which the terms of other creditors' loan agreements fully reflect the consequences to them of the arrangement between a borrower and a creditor, the two parties would have an incentive to adopt any covenant that is efficient because they would capture all of the resulting benefits. In the real world, however, nonadjusting creditors would capture part of the benefits and bear none of the costs of any set of covenants negotiated between the contracting parties. Consequently, even if the set of covenants were socially optimal because its total benefits exceeded its total costs, it would not be privately optimal for the borrower and the creditor if the benefits accruing to the contracting creditor (and any other adjusting creditors) were less than the costs to the borrower.

While this problem—that a borrower and a creditor will have an insufficient incentive to adopt efficient covenants—generally occurs whenever there are creditors whose claims do not adjust to reflect fully the agreement between the parties, the problem becomes more severe if the borrower and the creditor adopt a security interest under the rule of full priority. In such a case, the creditor's risk of loss—and therefore the benefit to the creditor of an additional set of covenants—will be substantially reduced. The creditor is thus even less likely under a rule of full priority to adopt a highly efficient covenant.

Suboptimal Enforcement Efforts

We have seen that, in the presence of nonadjusting creditors, the use of a security interest under full priority may cause inefficiencies by inducing the parties to forego the use of desirable covenants once a security interest is adopted. Now let us consider the case in which the use of a security interest under full priority has no effect on the parties' adoption of covenants. As we shall see, even in this case, in which the parties adopt covenants restricting borrower misbehavior, the use of the security interest under full priority will permit the borrower to act more inefficiently following the extension of credit.

In analyzing the effect of full priority on the use of covenants in loan arrangements, we abstracted from the level of a creditor's enforcement efforts—the activities undertaken by the creditor to ascertain whether the borrower is continuing to comply with its contractual commitments. However, as was explained in Part IV, a borrower's incentive to comply with the covenants it has issued may well depend upon the level of the creditor's enforcement efforts. That is, the less the creditor monitors the borrower's compliance with its covenants, the less likely the creditor will detect a breach, and the more likely the borrower will find the expected cost of breach to be less than the expected benefit of breach. To the extent the covenants bar the borrower from engaging in inefficient activities, the level of the creditor's enforcement efforts will therefore have efficiency implications.

Even in the absence of full priority, a creditor will engage in less than the optimal amount of enforcement activity since some of the benefit of this activity will flow to other creditors, while it (and the borrower) will bear all of the costs. But the creditor will have even less of an incentive to engage in enforcement activities to the extent that it is protected from risk of loss by a security interest giving the creditor's claim full priority in bankruptcy—just as it will have less of an incentive to adopt even highly efficient covenants. As a result, a borrower may be more likely to violate a covenant and to act inefficiently when its sophisticated creditors have security interests giving them full priority in their collateral. Thus, even if full priority does not cause a borrower and a creditor to adopt fewer covenants, it may well degrade the effectiveness of the covenants they do adopt—and lead to efficiency problems—by reducing the creditor's incentive to monitor the borrower's compliance with those covenants.

The priority-dependent efficiency costs arising from the use of a security interest are of course especially high when the secured creditor is a sophisticated lender such as a bank. A bank will typically be quite knowledgeable about a borrower to which it has extended a significant amount of credit. And, by virtue of its sophistication, resources, and leverage, the bank will be able to exert a significant amount of influence over the borrower. Indeed, a bank will frequently determine whether or not a borrower files for bankruptcy and the timing of any filing. Thus, the bank is in a unique position to control a borrower's behavior. However, to the extent that the bank is insulated by a security interest from the effects of the borrower's misbehavior, the bank will have less incentive to control the borrower's behavior.

Of course, the tendency of full priority to cause secured creditors to adopt too few covenants and to suboptimally enforce the obligations of their borrowers would not be a cause of great concern if the borrowers had unsecured creditors that were capable of similar monitoring. However, the empirical data on the financing arrangements of privately held small and medium-sized firms—the issuers of most secured debt—indicate that such firms almost always have only one institutional creditor (e.g., a bank or finance company) that is capable of general monitoring. (This pattern is also seen in bankruptcy: The vast majority of all bankruptcy cases involve a debtor with a principal secured creditor and many small (usually trade) creditors.) Thus, to the extent that one institutional creditor is insulated from risk of loss by using a security interest giving it full priority, the borrower will be free to misbehave.

NOTES

1. Evaluating the "offensive" distributional strategy. Professor Schwartz distinguishes between the two distributional motivations for secured credit. The first, or "offensive" strategy, stems for the fact that a secured debt contract subordinates the claims of creditors who are absent from the negotiations and are not required to give their consent to being subordinated. Moreover, they may fail to react to the issuance of security by raising the interest rates they charge the debtor, either because they are unaware of the perfected security interest or because they cannot revise the terms of their deal with the debtor. In this case, secured credit redistributes wealth from such uninformed creditors to debtors. The wealth gain can be shared between the debtor and the secured lender, particularly the institutional lenders who take broad security interests.

Is the offensive distributional hypothesis consistent with the evidence? The hypothesis suggests that sophisticated lenders would always be given security interests and as soon as possible. Yet, casual observation confirms that firms often borrow without security from unsecured creditors who appear well informed: for example, banks and trade creditors. *See, e.g.,* Paul M. Shupack, *Solving the Puzzle of Secured Transactions*, 41 Rutgers L. Rev. 1067 (1989). Firms may be tempted, nevertheless, to exploit other less sophisticated unsecured creditors, such as tort victims. Yet, Professor Listokin examined empirically the secured debt of businesses likely to experience tort liability (in the pharmaceutical and tobacco industries), and found that they did not have a significantly larger proportion of secured-to-unsecured debt. Yair Listokin, *Is Secured Debt Used to Redistribute Value from Tort Claimants in Bankruptcy? An Empirical Analysis*, 57 Duke L. J. 1037 (2008).

2. Evaluating the "defensive" distributional strategy. Creditors may respond to the threat of the offensive strategy by charging a higher interest rate from the outset. The "defensive" distributional hypothesis therefore predicts that a debtor will bargain for secured credit at the outset in order to neutralize the high interest rate charge by creditors who anticipate the subsequent appearance of security. Does this fare any better empirically than the offensive hypothesis. The fact that many firms have unencumbered assets raises doubts about the defensive hypothesis. *See* Alan Schwartz, *Priority Contracts and Priority in Bankruptcy*, 82 Cornell L. Rev. 1396, 1414–17 (1997). We observed in the notes to Section 6.4 that there are other reasons why a firm may wish to defer issuing secured debt, particularly to preserve the option to do so at a later time when it may be more valuable to secure. Therefore, the effect of the defensive motivation may lie at the margin and be difficult to test casually.

A borrower may also try to reassure its early creditors by agreeing to negative pledge covenants that prohibit the granting of security interests. What are the advantages and disadvantages of using covenants rather than security?

3. The effects of "nonadjusting" creditors. Professors Bebchuk and Fried argue that many unsecured creditors do not adjust: notably, private involuntary creditors, government agencies, voluntary creditors with small claims, and prior voluntary creditors who are not made aware of their debtor's security. This category of nonadjusting creditors is broader than LoPucki's "reluctant" or Schwartz' "uninformed" unsecured creditors in that it includes creditors who are not victims of the issuance of secured credit. A voluntary creditor, particularly holding a relatively small claim, may be sufficiently sophisticated to charge a "pooled" rate of interest to all it debtors, that compensates the creditor for the estimated risk of finding its debtors' assets encumbered. As with insurance premiums, the lower risk debtors subsidize the higher-risk debtors, and at least some of the lower risk debtors may therefor refuse to do so by withdrawing from the market.

To the distributional concerns of other commentators, Bebchuk and Fried add an efficiency concern: the offensive and defensive motivations for secured credit skews the decision to grant security and thereby impedes optimal financial contracting. Professor LoPucki also has an efficiency concern because involuntary creditors such as tort claimants are nonadjusting. By securing their assets to the hilt, he suggests, debtors can curtail, if not entirely eliminate, exposure to tort liability, thereby undermining the deterrence principle at the heart of tort law. In other words, if a tort has little or no cost to the debtor, the debtor has little economic incentive not to commit such a tort. *See* David W. Leebron, *Limited Liability, Tort Victims, and Creditors,* 91 Colum. L. Rev. 1565 (1991) (noting that granting security "will remove assets from potential tort claimants for the benefit of creditors"). A more general allied concern has been expressed with respect to the limited liability of shareholders: Henry Ransmann & Reinier Kraakman, *Toward Unlimited Shareholder Liability for Corporate Torts*, 100 Yale L. J. 1879 (1991) (arguing that limited liability prevents tort law from determining the appropriate allocation of costs among stakeholders in a corporation).

4. Assessing the effects of interest group influence. If the distributional explanations are accurate, why does Article 9 permit such regressive redistribution of wealth? Robert Scott suggests that financial institutions were the dominant interest group participating in the drafting process. Robert E. Scott, *The Politics of Article 9*, 80 Va. L. Rev. 1783 (1994). However, he cautions that their influence does not imply necessarily that Article 9 is socially bad:

> So long as the interests of those groups are sufficiently aligned with the public interest, interest group influence is benign. By producing bright-line rules and increasing certainty, such products can help

promote the common good. But if the private lawmaking bodies . . . are more susceptible to influence than ordinary legislatures, then it follows that their products are also more likely to result in special interest legislation. Id. at 1790.

Professor Scott's suggestion that private legislatures are more susceptible to interest group pressure than elected legislatures is contradicted by the observation of very similar rules enacted by legislatures in other countries, where private legislatures are not involved. In particular, such legislation is equally rule-based and favorable to financial institutions as Article 9. See, e.g., the Ontario Personal Property Security Act, R.S.0. 1990, c.P. 10. In Chapter 2.3, we compared the likely biases of alternative law-making institutions (legislatures, courts, regulatory agencies), and their susceptibility to interest group pressure. Based on that discussion, consider whether and how the regulation of security interests might be different if it were created instead by courts (for example, pursuant to standards in the governing legislation) or by regulation?

Can special interest legislation be entirely good, or must we accept a second-best outcome that yields some purely distributional gain to the dominant interest group? The related problem of regulatory capture has been subject to extensive analysis in politics, economics and law. How does the market in which actors compete affect the focus and intensity of their lobbying efforts. If, for example, as a result of the offensive use of security interests, secured creditors were reaping supernormal profits at the expense of unsecured creditors, would this be a competitive equilibrium? Where would the distributional gains end up? *See* Barry E. Adler, *Limits on Politics in Competitive Credit Markets,* 80 Va. L. Rev. 1879 (1994); George G. Triantis, *Private Law–Making and the Uniform Commercial Code,* The New Palgrave Dictionary of Economics and the Law Vol. 3, 117, 119–20 (1998).

5. Making policy in the absence of complete information. In light of the distributional concerns discussed in this Section, Professor Warren put forward a policy recommendation that Article 9 should set aside up to 20% of the value of any given collateral for the benefit of unsecured creditors who proceed to obtain judgment liens. Elizabeth Warren, Article 9 Set Aside for Unsecured Creditors, Memorandum to the Council of the American Law Institute April 25, 1996, as reprinted in LYNN LOPUCKI AND ELIZABETH WARREN, SECURED CREDIT: A SYSTEMS APPROACH 672–3 (2003). See also Bebchuk and Fried, supra.

In the excerpt in this section, Professor Warren raises the fundamental dilemma in regulating with the benefit of imperfect information. Despite some suggestive evidence supporting the efficiency explanations of secured credit, they have not been rigorously confirmed by empirical study. Nor do we have evidence of the economic impact of the carveout proposal. Warren argues that the wait-and-see attitude prevalent among academics is misinformed. She asserts that the reformers should not bear the burden of proof: "Article 9 is in use, the UCC revision process is upon us, and it is imperative to decide how to decide." Warren, *Making Policy* at 1376.

6. The political economy of the law-making process redux. In *The Truth About Secured Financing*, 82 Cornell L. Rev. 1436 (1997), Robert Scott suggests a different framework for resolving the efficiency debate in the absence of good data:

> Rather than concentrating energies on further refinements in the debate over secured credit, it would seems far more profitable for scholars to begin to study the institutional processes which produce the relevant legal rules. Indeed, given what we know about the private lawmaking process, it appears at best naive to continue to frame the question solely in term of whether secured claims should be granted full or only partial priority in bankruptcy. Not only the substance of the legal rules, but also the process that produces these rules should be the focus of scholarly inquiry. . . . In short we need more theory and more evidence relating not just to the optimal rules governing secured credit, but to how the private lawmaking groups that produce those laws actually function.

Scott, *The Truth About Secured Financing, supra* at 1464.

Assume that the efficiency debate is framed in terms of the relative freedom of the relevant law making groups from interest group influence. Thus conceived, which institution—the ALI and NCCUSL that are responsible for drafting and securing adoption of Article 9 or the Congress which is responsible for the Bankruptcy Code—are better able to draft legislation that is relatively free from rent seeking by special interest groups? In the case of Article 9, some scholars have argued that when the products of the private legislative efforts of the ALI and NCCUSL are the kind of admirably clear, bright-line rules so distinctively present in Article 9, this is strong evidence that a dominant interest group had influenced the process. On this view, bright-line rules are prevalent when an interest group dominates because they enable the interest group that prevails in the legislative process to preserve its victory in subsequent judicial interpretations of claims and rights. *See* Alan Schwartz & Robert E. Scott, *The Political Economy of Private Legislatures*, 143 U. Pa. L. Rev. 595, 607–10 (1995). But even if one assumes that such interest influence exists, the important question is whether the legislative process that produces Article 9 is more susceptible to interest group influence than the ordinary Congressional legislative processes that produce the Bankruptcy Code. The treatment of floating liens in Bankruptcy Code § 547(e)(3) may support the inference that interest groups use the Bankruptcy Code in order to trump Article 9 concessions to secured creditors. *See* Scott, *The Politics of Article 9,* supra at 1849.

†